The Royal Institute of British Architects
A Guide to its Archive and History

1 The first official version of the RIBA badge. It was used as a Library bookplate and emblem for Institute publications from 1835 to 1891, when it was redesigned by J. H. Metcalfe. The badge was redesigned again in 1931 by Eric Gill and in 1960 by Joan Hassall. The Council Minutes record in January 1835 that 'Mr. Willament' (presumably Thomas Willement, 1786—1871, heraldic artist) had submitted a design for the Institute's arms. In May the Council ordered an engraving of them to be made and in August it ordered the Secretary to procure a seal engraved with the arms. They are described in the 1837 by-laws as 'gules, two lions rampant guardant or, supporting a column marked with lines chevron, proper, all standing on a base of the same; a garter surrounding the whole with the inscription "Institute of British Architects, anno salutis MDCCCXXXIV"; above a mural crown proper, and beneath the motto "Usui civium decori urbium".'

The Royal Institute of British Architects
A Guide to its Archive and History

by Angela Mace
with an essay by Robert Thorne

Mansell Publishing Limited, *London and New York*

First published 1986 by Mansell Publishing Limited
(A subsidiary of The H.W. Wilson Company)
6 All Saints Street, London N1 9RL, England
950 University Avenue, Bronx, New York 10452, U.S.A.

British Library Cataloguing in Publication Data

Royal Institute of British Architects
   The Royal Institute of British Architects : a guide to its archive and history.
   1. Royal Institute of British Architects—Archives
   I. Title   II. Mace, Angela   III. Thorne, Robert
   016.72′06′041   Z5944.G72LS

   ISBN 0-7201-1773-9

Library of Congress Cataloging in Publication Data

Mace, Angela, 1934–
   The Royal Institute of British Architects.

   Includes Index.
   1. Royal Institute of British Architects—Archives. 2. Royal Institute of British Architects—History.
   I. Thorne, Robert, fl. 1978– . II. Title.
Z6611.A67M32 1985 [NA12]   016.72′06′042   85–18869
ISBN 0-7201-1773-9

Printed in Great Britain at the University Press, Cambridge

The Royal Institute of British Architects and Mansell Publishing Limited are deeply grateful to the Interbuild Fund which has made the compilation of the material and the publication of the *Guide* possible through most generous financial support.

Contents

Contents

Illustrations

Illustrations

Foreword

It is not widely known what an unusually large and interesting administrative archive the Insitute has retained since its foundation 150 years ago — not known because until Angela Mace, an archivist who works for the British Architectural Library at the RIBA, carried out this impressive work of survey, analysis, classification and description, most of it was impenetrably difficult of access.

This guide will enable people to make use of an important historical resource. It opens the door to the preparation of authentic studies on the history of the Institute and its effects on British architecture, on the development of the architectural profession, architectural education and standards of private and public professional architectural practice in Britain and abroad. It also reveals the relevance of the archive to the study of the development of town planning, private and public housing, the building industry, building legislation, the conservation and restoration of buildings, the quality and control of the built environment generally and for many other issues which will interest not only architects and architectural historians but also social and economic historians and many of those connected with the building industry. In addition, many architectural historians and biographers may not have realized that a considerable amount of biographical information on over 40,000 architects is available in the archive.

The main aim of this book is to provide a practical guide to the use of the archive. But it is also welcome because it contains in its extensive historical introductory sections much new information on the growth, organization and work of the RIBA, which many people who have no intention of using the archive will find useful.

The Royal Institute of British Architects is immensely grateful for the generosity of the Interbuild Fund, which has paid for the work to be carried out. The Fund has in recent years provided grants for many projects of value to the building

Foreword

industry generally. We owe to David Dean, then the RIBA Librarian, the suggestion that one of the first exercises to be carried out under the auspices of the Fund should be the preparation of a guide to the RIBA archive. The doubtful extent and inaccessibility of our records had been a constant source of irritation to us and to many others. But we were not then to know what an extraordinary wealth of interesting material Angela Mace's work would reveal. The added generosity of Interbuild in contributing to the cost of this publication will ensure a wider public for a remarkable and fascinating undertaking.

Patrick Harrison, RIBA Secretary

Acknowledgements

I wish to thank the trustees of the Interbuild Fund for enabling me to undertake a thorough survey of the RIBA's extensive administrative archive and compile the inventory which forms the basis of this guide and for their generous contribution to the costs of its publication. I also wish to thank the RIBA Central Services Department for its additional support of the project. I would like to record my gratitude to the British Architectural Library Trust and to my colleagues on the Library staff and elsewhere in the Institute who encouraged me in this work. I am much indebted to Robert Thorne for his important essay which provides an independent appraisal of the RIBA archive and the work of the Institute in the past.

A Concise History of the RIBA

During the fifty years before the foundation of the Institute of British Architects in 1834 several architectural societies were formed in London. This was partly due to a widespread feeling among an emerging occupational class of 'professional' architects that the Royal Academy was failing to give architecture its rightful place among the arts. Very little space was allocated for the exhibition of architectural drawings, the Academy lectures on architecture had ceased and architectural students had very limited opportunities to use the Academy library. The most noteworthy societies formed in this period were the Architects Club founded in 1791, the London Architectural Society founded in 1806 and the Architectural Society founded in 1831. The Architects Club was essentially an exclusive dining club but in its early years its members conducted some scientific experiments and discussed professional qualifications, fees and conduct. However, when they were invited by the committee of the Society of British Architects in 1834 to join the proposed new Institute of British Architects they described the purpose of their meetings as mainly social and declined to join collectively but promised their support as individuals. The London Architectural Society was a learned society whose members were obliged to read an essay and exhibit an unpublished design each year or pay a forfeit. The main aim of the Architectural Society, founded in 1831, was the formation of a library and the instruction of young architects. Early attempts by the Institute to amalgamate with the Architectural Society were unsuccessful but a union between the two organizations was achieved in 1842.

By 1834 several factors including a decline in noble patronage, the post-Napoleonic Wars building boom, the emergence of general contractors, the dishonest and incompetent practices of many persons calling themselves architects and the general lack of respect for architects and surveyors felt by government officials and the public (the new potential clients) had created an urgent need for the formation

2   Portrait of Thomas Leverton Donaldson by Charles Martin, exhibited at the Royal Academy in 1872. Donaldson was Honorary Secretary, 1834 — 1839 and 1849 — 1850, Honorary Secretary for Foreign Correspondence, 1839 — 1858, Royal Gold Medallist, 1851, and President, 1863 — 1865. At the end of the Opening General Meeting in June 1835 Lord De Grey said of Donaldson 'there is no individual who has taken more pains to forward the objects [of the Institute] than he has, by his indefatigable exertions, or has contributed with more heartfelt zeal to its benefit' and Prince Albert referred to him in 1879 as the 'father of the Institute and of the profession'. (RIBA Presidential Portraits Collection, RIBA Building, 66 Portland Place)

of a professional institute. Some impression of the state of public opinion on architects and surveyors can be gained from a letter by 'Scrutator' in the *Architectural Magazine* published in November 1833. Some of the things which aroused the strongest objections were the excessive charges made by some surveyors, the common practice by architects of measuring works or taking out quantities for a builder at the builder's request and receiving payment from him without the client's knowledge, and the practice among some architects of exacting a commission from the builder for all works done under their direction and, if this was refused, telling the builder that his services were no longer required. The remedy suggested by Scrutator was to form a society 'not for eating and drinking or backbiting their brethren but to make rules for the governance of the profession, to make a fair tariff of prices according to the variation of the market, to regulate the mode of measuring and to inquire into every abuse or infringement connected with the profession'.

Early in 1834 the Society of British Architects was formed with the explicit intention of founding a professional institute of British architects. After a disagreement with another group, the Society of Architects and Surveyors, over the question of whether or not to exclude surveyors (who at that time were mainly builders' measurers) from the new body, the Institute of British Architects was founded in the summer of 1834. Its members were to be elected by ballot and be of three classes, Fellows, Associates and Honorary Members. It was to be directed and managed by an elected Council which was subject to the control of the General Meetings. In October, Thomas Leverton Donaldson and John Goldicutt were elected the first honorary secretaries and in December the first Council meeting and the first Ordinary General Meeting were held. In January 1835 Sir Thomas Farquhar was appointed Treasurer and in March Lord De Grey, a member of the government and a Privy Councillor, was elected President.

It is clear from the statements of the founders that they had four main objectives in mind: to improve the reputation and status of architects by establishing 'uniformity and respectability of practice'; to become a learned society; to become a body representative of the architectural profession in Britain to whom individuals and the government could refer for its opinion on architectural and professional matters; to work for the cultivation and improvement of architecture and, as they put it, 'take responsibility on behalf of the public for the direction and maintenance of the national character for taste'. The Institute's motto 'Usui civium decori urbium' (rendered in the charter as 'to promote the domestic convenience of citizens and the public improvement and embellishment of towns and cities') stressed the last of these objectives but the highest priority was given by the founding members to the first, and only architects of unimpeachable character and evident respectability were encouraged to join. In 1837 this policy was rewarded, and respectability henceforward guaranteed, by the grant of a royal charter of incorporation in which the Institute is described as 'an institution for the general advancement of civil architecture and for promoting and facilitating the acquirement of the knowledge of the various arts and sciences connected therewith. . . .'.

From the outset, the objective of becoming a learned society was taken very seriously. Perhaps partly in an effort to outdo the library of the Architectural Society, founded three years earlier, the founders repeatedly exhorted the early members to build up an excellent library and museum by donating money, books, pamphlets, manuscripts, prints, drawings, models, casts of 'antique' classical details and specimens of building materials. Their efforts were so successful that the size of the library and museum forced the Institute to move to larger premises in 1845. It was also the custom from the beginning for learned papers on a great variety of artistic, archaeological, historical, scientific and technical subjects to be read at Ordinary General Meetings. These papers were usually published in *RIBA Transactions*, which later joined with *RIBA Proceedings* to become the *RIBA Journal* .

One of the first problems tackled by the Institute was the unsatisfactory state of the architectural competition system, which was completely unregulated. The Council appointed a special committee to investigate the matter in 1838 and subsequent work by both the Institute and the Architectural Association led in 1872 to the publication of *General regulations for the conduct of architectural competitions* and, eventually, to the present regulatory system. Much of the early work of the Institute was concerned with formulating rules for professional charges, practice and conduct. A report on practice concerning dilapidations and fixtures was published by the Institute in 1844 and a Professional Practice Committee was appointed in 1845. In 1862 this committee produced a guide called *Professional practice and charges of architects, being those now usually and properly made*, which was revised frequently and published in a series of editions leading eventually to the RIBA *Conditions of engagement* and the present *Architect's appointment*. The Professional Practice Committee also discussed the measurement of building works; the taking out of quantities; the employment of surveyors by architects; the conditions of building contracts, leading to the publication in 1870 of *General headings for clauses of contract, as settled between the Council of the Royal Institute of British Architects and the committee of the London Builders' Society* ; the arbitration of disputes between architects, builders and clients; the legal rights of architects; cases of unprofessional conduct by members; the regulation of architectural competitions for the design of public buildings and the conditions of engagement of architects appointed for the design and construction of public buildings.

In 1849 the Institute undertook the first of many self-appraisals. The Council was asked by the Annual General Meeting to ascertain to what extent the intentions of the founders had been carried out and to consider ways of widening the scope of the Institute's activities and increasing its usefulness. One of the main results of this review was the establishment of five standing committees: for the management of the Library; the conduct of scientific experiments; the management of the Institute's finances; for advising the members on professional practice matters and for improving the studies of the student members. At that time an intending architect nearly always obtained his training, often very incomplete and unsatisfactory, as an articled pupil of a practising architect. The Institute had opened a class of students in 1838 but had subsequently failed to offer them any very significant education. They were encouraged to 'draw from the antique' using the collection of casts in the Institute's museum, were given occasional lectures on scientific subjects, were encouraged to compete for some prizes and medals awarded in essay and design competitions and were allowed to use the library and attend Institute meetings. Dissatisfaction with the state of architectural education had been the main cause of the formation of the Architectural Association in 1847 and this body petitioned the Council of the Institute in 1855 to introduce an examination in architecture which would lead to the issue of a diploma certifying qualification to practise as an architect. After prolonged debate the Institute appointed a board of examiners in 1863 to conduct voluntary examinations, success in which was to be a qualification for candidature for election as an Associate of the Institute.

Other noteworthy achievements of the first forty years were the institution of the annual award of the Royal Gold Medal for architecture; the foundation of the Architects Benevolent Society and the Architectural Union Company; the advice given to the government on the Metropolitan Buildings Bill and the subsequent appointment of the Institute as the statutory body for the examination of intending district surveyors; the advice given to the government on the Thames embankment scheme; the advice given to the Palestine Exploration Fund and the trustees of the British Museum on various expeditions and excavations in the Eastern Mediterranean region; the move to large new premises with exhibition galleries at 9 Conduit Street in 1859 and the establishment in 1862 of a standing committee to encourage the conservation and proper restoration of historic buildings, ancient monuments and remains.

The years 1876—1889 are important in the history of the RIBA for it was during this time that the Institute significantly changed its character. The period begins with a review of the RIBA's history by its Secretary, Charles Eastlake, in which he expressed general satisfaction and pride in the achievements of the Institute. However, he also remarked that the by-laws of 1876 were almost identical with those drawn up in 1835 and that, apart from a doubling in size of the Council, the constitution was unaltered. It seems that the Institute had in essence remained a small London-based society which, though prestigious and not without influence on the government, had scarcely begun to represent the run-of-the-mill architect in the provinces. Partly reflecting this deficiency, flourishing societies of architects had been established since the foundation of the RIBA in Liverpool, Bristol, Newcastle, Nottingham, Manchester, Glasgow, Leicester, Birmingham and Leeds, some of which had combined to form the powerful Architectural Alliance. The RIBA's claim to speak for the profession was becoming increasingly unrealistic and there were also rumblings of discontent amongst a significant number of the Associates, who were dissatisfied both with their lack of a vote in the affairs of the Institute and with the lack of progress being made by the Institute towards a system of compulsory examination for architects.

In 1876 the Improvement of the Institute Special Committee recommended that the Institute should require all Associates elected after May 1882 to have passed a professional examination. It also recommended that the Institute should no longer attempt to be a teaching body, should close its class of students and should encourage the Architectural Association in its educational work. These decisions had far-reaching consequences. The RIBA was recognized by the General Conference of Architects in 1887 as the body responsible for the guidance and direction of architectural education in Britain and went on to develop a system of obligatory progressive examinations (Preliminary, Intermediate and Final). Later developments were the establishment of the (RIBA) Board of Architectural Education in 1904 and the subsequent fostering of architectural schools by a system of recognition i.e. any school in the British Empire which applied for recognition by the Board of Architectural Education (BAE), whose syllabus was approved by the BAE, whose examinations were conducted by an external examiner approved by the BAE and whose standard of attainment was guaranteed by periodical inspections by BAE Visitors, could become a 'Recognised School' and its successful students could qualify for exemption from the RIBA Intermediate Examination and, in some cases, the RIBA Final Examination.

Another important recommendation of the 1876 committee for the improvement of the Institute was that close relations should be established between the Institute and the architectural societies in the provinces. As a result, a system of formal alliances was devised whereby an alliance would be created if a resolution in its favour was passed by both the RIBA Council and the council of the society concerned. The RIBA would then undertake to pay to the Allied Society a rebate not exceeding a quarter of the subscription paid to the RIBA by a member of both bodies. These changes made it necessary for the RIBA to apply for a supplemental royal charter, which was granted in 1887. The first nine alliances were made in 1889 and by 1939 there was a national and Commonwealth network of Allied Societies, approximately half of whose members were also members of the RIBA. These societies were represented on the RIBA Council and, from 1921, were able to speak with a united voice through the medium of the Allied Societies Conference.

The main deficiency of the 1876 committee was its failure to recommend an extension of the franchise to the Associates. A consequence of this was the development of a schism in the profession. In 1884 a campaign by hundreds of RIBA Associates to be allowed to vote on the Institute's affairs was resisted by the Fellows and a direct result of this was the formation of a breakaway group called the Society of Architects. One of the main interests of the new society was to campaign for the statutory registration of architects, with the aim of eventually excluding from architectural practice all those who had not passed a professional examination. Several private parliamentary bills for this purpose were promoted between 1887 and 1906, at first by an independent committee and subsequently by the Society of Architects. These bills were opposed both by the RIBA Council and by a separate group of eminent architects and artists called the Memorialists, who included Norman Shaw and T.G. Jackson. In the opinion of the Memorialists it was the function of the RIBA to promote architecture as one of the fine arts. They thought that 'for nine buildings in ten, if not ninety-nine buildings in a hundred, no architect is or perhaps ever will be necessary' and they maintained that it was impossible to examine imagination, power of design and refinement of taste and judgement. They feared that a system of obligatory examination and registration would benefit the profession of architects rather than the art of architecture and would ultimately become a means of coercing into the Institute every practising architect in Great Britain and Ireland. They disliked the idea of a powerful professional organization, or 'trade union' as they called it, and T.G. Jackson made the plea 'let it cease to be an institute of architects and become an institute of architecture'.

By 1906, however, it was clear that the profession as a whole was in favour of registration and the RIBA Council decided to work towards this end. The Institute wanted to be appointed the statutory body responsible for registration but to accomplish this aim it was necessary to convince parliament that the RIBA represented the whole profession. To achieve this position it was necessary to absorb the Society of Architects and to draw into the RIBA a large number of the 'unattached' practising architects who belonged to neither body and could not reasonably be expected to sit the RIBA qualifying examination for election as an Associate. The device used was the creation of a class of Licentiate members, to be elected on a practice qualification without professional examination. To appease the Associates, who objected to an influx of what they regarded as 'unqualified' members, the Licentiates were not allowed to vote on Institute affairs. However, in the supplemental royal charter of 1925 the members of this by then large and successful class were declared to be full corporate voting members of the Institute. In 1927 successful opposition by the Incorporated Association of Architects and Surveyors to a bill in which it was proposed to make the RIBA the statutory registration body forced the Institute to rethink its policy and in 1931 an act was passed which established an Architects Registration Council of the United Kingdom (ARCUK) as an independent body and in 1938 the use of the title 'Architect' (with the exception of 'Naval Architect', 'Landscape Architect' and 'Golf-course Architect') was restricted to those on the ARCUK register.

To return to the 1880s, certain improvements in the organization of the Institute's work took place at the suggestion of Professor Robert Kerr, who was an active Fellow of the RIBA. He suggested that what he called the 'academical' work of the Institute, then being performed by a great number of unrelated committees, should in future be coordinated and directed by four large departmental standing committees for Art, Science, Practice and Literature. 'Art' was to deal not only with the art of architectural design and the related arts but also with archaeology and conservation; 'Science' was to be concerned with construction and the scientific problems affecting building operations; 'Practice' was to deal with the business and management side of private practice; 'Literature' was to include the direction of the Library, the sessional programmes of lectures and the conduct of the Institute's foreign relations. These departmental committees were set up in 1886 and were composed of Associates as well as Fellows. Most of their members were elected by the General Body and some were appointed by the Council. With the addition of a Finance Committee, a Board of Examiners and, later, the Board of Architectural Education, this administrative organization lasted for nearly fifty years.

During the decade before the First World War the RIBA considerably widened its horizons. In 1906 it played host to the VIIth International Congress of Architects. Ever since the early years the Institute had cultivated relations with foreign architects and architectural institutes and, during his twenty years as Honorary Secretary for Foreign Correspondence, Thomas Leverton Donaldson had developed both a widespread correspondence and a system of reciprocal hospitality offered to travelling architects and students. After the 1906 congress the Institute became more international in its outlook and from 1907—1939 the British section of the Comité Permanent International des Architectes met at the Institute, with RIBA members playing a leading role.

It was also in this period before the First World War that the Institute began to play an important part in the development of town planning. From the early years it had exerted an influence on planning schemes in London but now it began to play a national role in the field of town planning. In 1907 the Local Government Board introduced a Town Planning Bill and this prompted the RIBA to appoint a special committee, called the Development of Towns and Suburbs Committee, under the chairmanship of Aston Webb to prepare a scheme for the expansion of the suburbs of large towns in a more rational manner than under the piecemeal schemes being put forward by the Local Government Board. In 1908 the name of this committee was changed to the Town Planning Committee and it was the first of many influential RIBA standing committees on town planning policy. Other important events of this period before the First World War were the International Town Planning Conference organized by the RIBA and held at its premises in 1910 and the formation of the Town Planning Institute in 1914.

The trauma of the outbreak of war in 1914 prompted the RIBA to make a big cooperative effort on behalf of the profession. It took the initiative in setting up the Architects War Committee, which included the presidents and vice-presidents of the Society of Architects and the Architectural Association, the presidents of the Allied Societies, several 'unattached' architects and some Royal Academicians. Its main functions were to liaise with the government on the use of architects in the war effort and to alleviate the distress caused by widespread unemployment among architects due to the sudden reduction in civil building. One of its achievements was the implementation of a scheme for a series of civic surveys on which many professional people including architects were temporarily employed.

The end of the war saw another of the RIBA's periodic critical reviews of itself and of the state of the profession. In 1918 it appointed the Future of Architecture and the Architectural Profession Special Committee, which drew up a complex questionnaire for those invited to give evidence to answer. Its main concerns were how to achieve unity in the profession; how to reduce the large amount of architectural practice being done by unqualified persons; how to remedy the deficiencies in architectural education, particularly in its scientific and technical aspects; to study the nature of the increasingly problematical relationship between public and private practice and to find ways of cultivating a better relationship between architects and the general public. The most interesting evidence was given by John Murray, FRIBA, Crown Architect and Surveyor and also an architect in private practice, who argued that there was no clear line of demarcation between the design and construction of building work as practised by the architect, surveyor and engineer and that a combination of these professions was desirable. He thought that the architect's education should include a knowledge of surveying and engineering skills. This was reminiscent of Professor Kerr's warning in 1883, in his article 'English architecture thirty years hence', that the most regrettable weakness of architects then was their lack of scientific skills which they allowed engineers to monopolize. Murray recommended amalgamation with the Society of Architects and affiliation with kindred professional associations and ended his evidence with a plea for the formation of a 'Home of Architecture' which would accommodate under one roof a library, lecture theatre, exhibition galleries, committee rooms, examination halls and the administrative offices of the RIBA, the Allied Societies, the Society of Architects, the Town Planning Institute, the Society of British Sculptors, the Arts and Crafts Society, the Royal Sanitary Institute, the Concrete Institute, the British Fire Prevention Committee, the Quantity Surveyors Association and several representative societies of engineers and surveyors. Some of the consequences of this committee's work were the appointment of a Unification and Registration Committee which, with its successors, eventually achieved amalgamation with the Society of Architects in 1925 and statutory registration of architects in the 1930s; the appointment during the 1920s of committees concerned with official architecture and the needs of salaried architects; a greater interest in public relations, which led eventually to the establishment of a standing Public Relations Committee: a reappraisal of architectural education leading to the first International Congress on Architectural Education, held at the RIBA in 1924, and the remodelling of the Board of Architectural Education.

The inter-war period saw a great expansion in the Institute's membership and activities. An important new field of interest was slum clearance and new housing developments. The first of many RIBA working groups on housing was the Housing of the Working Classes after the War Special Committee appointed in 1917. This soon became a standing Housing Committee which subsequently merged with the Town Planning Committee. Its main concerns were national housing policies, campaigns for the increased employment of architects for the design of local authority housing and a revision of the RIBA fees scale so as to accomodate such housing work. The Institute was also concerned to raise housing standards and eliminate 'jerry-building' and was much exercised by the problem of the control of design by local authorities. From 1927 the RIBA worked jointly with the Council for the Preservation of Rural England and the Institute of Building to set up a system of panels of architects and others to advise local planning authorities on the aesthetic merits or faults of planning applications. In a further effort to improve the quality of design and increase public interest in architecture the Institute began in the 1920s its Architecture Bronze Medal Awards Scheme, which continued until

1965 when it was replaced by the RIBA Architecture Awards.

Unemployment amongst architects reached crisis proportions in 1931 when the RIBA, in conjunction with the Association of Architects, Surveyors and Technical Assistants and the Architects Benevolent Society, set up the Architects Unemployment Fund. The money raised was used to employ architects on survey schemes organized by the London Society and the London Survey Committee and on similar schemes in the provinces organized by the Allied Societies. It was also used to promote the work of the Architectural Graphic Records Committee, which was based at RIBA headquarters, in locating and indexing architectural drawings and employing architects to make measured drawings of important buildings for which there were no existing architectural records. This pioneering work contributed to the post-war formation of the National Buildings Record, now the National Monuments Record. The Registration Acts of the 1930s only restricted the use of the title 'Architect' and did not give architects a monopoly in the design of buildings. This fact, coupled with the severe economic depression, made it important to encourage the public and the authorities to employ architects. The RIBA tackled the problem by appointing a standing Public Relations Committee in 1933 and employing a Public Relations Secretary and an Exhibitions Officer. This committee was mainly concerned with press relations, the promotion of lectures, films, sound broadcasts and television programmes on architecture and architects, the publication of publicity pamphlets and the organization of exhibitions and conferences. It led eventually to the formation of the Public Affairs Department, the Press Office and the Clients Advisory Service.

It was during the inter-war period that the Institute first began to take seriously the interests of salaried and official architects, having been traditionally concerned almost exclusively with architects in private practice. In the 1920s, problems concerning the status and conditions of employment of salaried and official architects and their difficult relationship with architects in private practice came to a head. Many of the salaried members felt that the Institute was uninterested in their welfare and the RIBA found itself having to work hard to prevent a schism in the profession similar to the one that had occurred in 1884 with the formation of the Society of Architects. The RIBA appointed a standing Salaried Members Committee in 1928, which produced a RIBA Scale of Annual Salaries in 1930, and this was followed in 1937 by the appointment of a standing Official Architects Committee.

Other noteworthy developments during the inter-war period were the establishment of the Allied Societies Conference; the appointment of a standing Professional Conduct Committee to administer a new Code of Professional Practice; greater influence on the conditions of architectural competitions with the establishment of a system of RIBA monitoring of them as approved or unapproved; the start of a regular annual British Architects Conference, organized by the RIBA and held in a variety of provincial centres; the appointment of Edward Carter as Librarian and the reorganization and modernization of the Library; the establishment of the Executive Committee and the subsequent dissolution of the old departmental standing committees of Art, Science, Practice and Literature; the establishment of the Joint Contracts Tribunal to administer the new 1931 Form of Standard Contract and the move to the present purpose-built premises at 66 Portland Place in 1934.

The Second World War caused another unemployment crisis for architects, due to the sudden cessation of private building projects. In 1938 the RIBA had set up a National Emergency Panel and had started to compile a national register of architects to try to ensure the efficient use of architects by the government in time of war. The RIBA War Executive Committee, which ran the Institute on behalf of the Council from 1939—1945, arranged many government appointments for architects, particularly in connection with structural air-raid precautions and the repair of war-damaged buildings; influenced the terms on which architects and architectural students served in the armed forces; arranged for architectural tuition to be given and examinations to be held in German prisoner-of-war camps; secured early demobilization for architects and helped to re-establish them in practice or continue their professional education after the war. In addition, the RIBA Refugees Committee helped many foreign architects who were fleeing from Germany and Nazi-occupied countries to obtain professional employment in the United Kingdom.

During and after the war the most urgent task was to help plan the reconstruction of the country and the profession after the devastation and disruption of the war years. In 1942 the RIBA set up a Reconstruction Committee, which had both a central and a regional machinery. The provinces of the RIBA's Allied Societies were asked by the President, W.H. Ansell, to set up regional committees to devise schemes for the planning and development of their areas. The central committee was concerned with nationwide policy and research and set up working groups concerned with local and regional planning, wartime housing, building legislation, national planning, the organization of the building industry and the structure of the architectural profession. These working groups produced a series of influential reports. One of the major recommendations of this important committee was the formation of a national planning authority. The work of the Reconstruction Committee was continued by the Central Advisory Committee on National Planning, which produced the report *Plan your Greater Britain* in 1948 containing the RIBA's recommendation for a national plan.

In the post-war period there was a great increase in the salaried employment of architects in the public sector. Before the war, public bodies had put out most of their building work to private architects. After the war, building controls and the priority given to new council housing, schools, hospitals and industrial development put most building work into the hands of local authorities, regional hospital boards and the nationalized industries and many of these organizations developed their own architectural departments. By the early 1950s half the registered architects in the United Kingdom were in salaried employment. There was a considerable demand for collective bargaining for improvements in salaries and conditions of employment and in 1946 the RIBA responded to this pressure by appointing a RIBA Negotiating Officer to collect information on the salaries, conditions of employment and status of all salaried architects and to negotiate on behalf of RIBA members with their employing bodies. In the late 1950s these functions were continued by the new Professional Relations Secretary. However, the RIBA found itself unable, because of its charter and the requirement of obtaining Privy Council approval of changes in the by-laws, to engage in union activities and in 1959 it encouraged the formation of the Association of Official Architects to be a focus for trade union matters for architects in the public sector.

Another major task of the Institute after the war was to help architects to keep abreast of the rapid rate of scientific and technical change. The need to promote architectural and building research and to develop technical information services for architects had led in 1940 to the establishment, with the cooperation of the Building Research Station, of the Architectural Science Group, later the Architectural Science Board. Its main functions were to ascertain which research projects were needed and to try to get them implemented. It was reconstituted in 1951 as the RIBA Science Committee. In the 1950s the Institute set up an Economics Research Department with a Statistics Section, which carried out a detailed survey of architects' offices in 1960. Its report *The architect and his office*, published in 1962, had a considerable influence on the corporate planning of the Institute's work in the 1960s. A much wider range of technical and professional work was undertaken, much of which was hived off in the 1970s to the newly-formed commercial companies of the RIBA.

It was in the 1950s and 1960s that the Institute became fully departmentalized in its staff organization. Previously, the only truly distinct administrative departments were the Library and the Board of Architectural Education. The Secretary's Office and the General Office, headed by the Deputy Secretary, carried out much of the work subsequently done by new departments. In the 1950s the custom began of appointing assistant secretaries with specific responsibilities, for example Assistant Secretary for Practice Matters. Also in the 1950s the Technical Department was formed to provide a technical information service and the Information and Liaison Department was formed to take over responsibility for public relations, press relations, publications (including the *RIBA Journal*), relations with the Allied Societies and overseas relations. In 1962 the Institute's administration was reorganized on the model of the Civil Service, with several fully-fledged departments each headed by an Under-Secretary supported by assistant secretaries, executive officers and clerical staff. Central control and liaison between departments was provided by a newly-formed Policy Committee. The General Office was replaced by the Central Services Department, which became responsible for the internal administration of the Institute, and the Professional Services Department was established, which had a Practice Section, a Technical Section, a Building Industry Section and a Town Planning Section. This huge department dealt with matters concerning professional practice and professional conduct, practice management, legal advice to architects, the needs of salaried architects, technical standards and information, standardization of building components, industrialized building techniques, metrication, the use of computers by architects, development of the CI/SfB classification system, research and statistics, building industry relations and economics, town planning and housing, design standards for specific building types and the problem of aesthetic control by local authorities. In 1973 this department was disbanded and much of its work was continued by the recently-formed commercial company RIBA Services Ltd, a new Practice Department, an expanded Secretary's Office and a new Intelligence Unit.

It was during the 1960s that the RIBA became a regional organization rather than a central body in alliance with provincial architectural societies, thus completing a development that had begun in the 1870s. In 1963 the RIBA appointed a Membership Relations Secretary to liaise with the Allied Societies and in 1964 a working group of the Allied Societies Presidents Committee recommended the establishment of RIBA regional offices. The RIBA Council then appointed a special committee under the chairmanship of Lord Esher which, in 1965, recommended regional constituencies for Council elections and the establishment of a three-tier structure: RIBA, governed by the RIBA Council; regions, governed by regional councils; branches, governed by branch committees. All RIBA members would become members of the branch within which was their electoral address. The Constitution Committee was appointed in 1966 and its work led to the grant of a new royal charter in 1971 which formally recognised a regional structure for the RIBA. The first regional office, the Eastern Region Office, was opened in Cambridge in 1966 and by 1971 nine regional offices had been established.

Other noteworthy events of the 1960s and early 1970s were the 1961 UIA Congress, which was held at RIBA headquarters; the foundation of the Commonwealth Association of Architects; the formation of the Society of Architectural and Associated Technicians; the setting up of the commercial companies RIBA Services Ltd, National Building Specification Ltd and RIBA Publications Ltd; a remodelling of the RIBA examinations: the abandonment of the membership class system of Associates, Licentiates and Fellows; the establishment of the RIBA Research Awards Scheme and the RIBA Urban Design Diploma; the development of mid-career professional education; the publication of the *RIBA handbook of architectural practice and management* ; the establishment of the Clients Advisory Service; the formation of the British Architectural Library Trust and the subsequent further development of the Library and in particular of its collections of architectural drawings, photographs and manuscripts; the transfer of the Drawings Collection to 21 Portman Square and the opening of the Heinz Gallery for exhibitions; the evidence prepared by the RIBA for the enquiries by the Prices and Incomes Board and the Monopolies and Mergers Commission into architects' costs, fees and services and the formation of the Group of Eight to be both an effective pressure group and the main channel of communication between the government and the construction industry.

The new royal charter granted to the Institute in 1971, symbol of the beginning of a new phase in the development of the RIBA, marks the end of the period covered by this guide. In a general introduction such as this it has not been possible to do much more than indicate the great range, variety and importance of the Institute's work. However, further details and some information on more recent developments can be found in the separate introductions to each section of the guide.

Bibliography (Introductory and general)
[*See also* detailed bibliographies at end of each section of the guide]

1   'The Royal Institute of British Architects' in *Architect's, Engineer's and Building-Trades' Directory* London, Wyman & Sons, 1868 pp31—37
2   Eastlake, Charles Locke 'An historical sketch of the Institute' *RIBA Transactions* 1st Series Vol 26 1875/76 pp258—272
3   Webb, Sidney 'The organisation of the architectural profession' *Journal of the American Institute of Architects* Vol 5 1917 Jun pp269—276, Jul pp325—332 and Aug pp375—382
4   Cornford, Leslie Cope *The designers of our buildings* London, RIBA, 1921
5   Gotch, J. Alfred 'The first half-century of the RIBA' *RIBA Journal* Vol 29 1922 Jun 3 pp453—465
6   Dawber, E. Guy 'The work of the RIBA' *RIBA Journal* Vol 34 1927 Jul 16 pp580—586
7   Gotch, J. Alfred (ed) *The growth and work of the Royal Institute of British Architects. A centenary guide* London, RIBA, 1934
8   Macalister, Sir Ian 'The history and work of the RIBA' *Architectural Association Journal* Vol 50 1935 May pp425—434
9   Waterhouse, Michael 'The activities of the RIBA during the war and the place of the architect in the post-war world' *RIBA Journal* Vol 50 1943 Jul pp206—209
10   Spragg, C. D. 'The RIBA' *Architect and Engineer* (San Francisco) 1946 Feb pp28—30
11   Roberts, A. L. 'The organisation and work of the RIBA' *RIBA Journal* Vol 53 1946 Feb pp129—130
12   Pinckheard, John 'Life at Number 66' *RIBA Journal* Vol 54 1946 Dec pp90—91. Cartoon sketches of activities at RIBA headquarters.
13   'The work of the RIBA' *RIBA Journal* Vol 55 1948 Sep pp483—489 and Oct pp526—533. Several authors.
14   Bird, Eric L. 'The architectural profession' *Journal and Proceedings of the Royal Institute of Chemistry* 1949 Part 1 pp8—14
15   Bowen, Ian 'Focus on you' *Architect's Journal* Vol 119 1954 Jan 28 pp120—136
16   Kaye, Barrington *The development of the architectural profession in Britain* London, Allen & Unwin, 1960
17   Jenkins, Frank *Architect and patron. A survey of professional relations and practice in England from the sixteenth century to the present day* London, OUP, 1961
18   Jenkins, Frank 'The Victorian architectural profession' in Ferriday, Peter (ed) *Victorian architecture* London, Jonathan Cape, 1963
19   Crook, J. Mordaunt 'The pre-Victorian architect: professionalism and patronage' *Architectural History* Vol 12 1969 pp62—78
20   'Inside the RIBA' *RIBA Journal* Vol 76 1969 Oct pp409—451. Article on the work of RIBA boards, departments and companies, the Architects Benevolent Society and the Commonwealth Association of Architects.

21 Malpass, Peter 'Professionalism and the role of architects in local authority housing' *RIBA Journal* Vol 82 1975 Jun pp6—29. Based on an MA thesis, Newcastle University, 1973. Includes an historical survey of the development of professionalism in architecture.

22 Wilton-Ely, John 'The rise of the professional architect in England' in Kostoff, Spiro (ed) *The architect. Chapters in the history of the profession* New York, OUP, 1977

23 Colvin, Howard 'The architectural profession' Introduction to his *Biographical dictionary of British architects 1600—1840* London, John Murray, 1978 pp26—41

24 Kamen, Ruth 'Yellow pages. A classified directory to RIBA services, activities and resources' *RIBA Journal* Vol 85 1978 Dec pp507—530

25 Saint, Andrew 'A history of professionalism' *RIBA Journal* Vol 88 1981 Sep pp36—38

Using the RIBA Archive: a Historian's View

Robert Thorne

All professions like to imbue their expertise with a certain air of mystery, to encourage dependence on their skills by not revealing too much about their subject. Likewise professional institutions have tended to go about their business in a slightly secretive way, afraid that too much public scrutiny might inevitably harm their interests. At first glance architects would seem to have behaved as true to the professional model as doctors, lawyers and others of their kind. They have established a professional institution, encouraged specialized training, adopted certain standards of practice, and finally have obtained statutory recognition for a system of registration aimed at excluding the unqualified. Yet the professional fences which have encircled the practice of architecture are still far lower than those around many other professions. An architectural training may be long, and the knowledge acquired extensive, but that does not inhibit outsiders from suggesting the form that a design should take or from criticising the building so produced. Architecture being such a public matter the profession cannot hope to banish others from its debates even if it should want to. In fact for most of its history it has given a rather nervous welcome to such attention; after all, total neglect would be far more hurtful.

This guide is an admirable demonstration of the comparative openness with which architects have conducted their affairs. It is a great credit to the RIBA that it has preserved so many of its papers and reports and that now, properly listed and described in this book, it has made them available to anyone who wants to investigate its history. The gaps in the collection are few. As Angela Mace points out, the most galling omissions are the copies of letters written by the early Secretaries of the Institute and the papers of most of its Presidents. Had they survived these two groups of documents would have enabled us to eavesdrop on its day-by-day affairs more closely than even the best kept committee minutes allow.

Some documents which have been kept are not at present open for research, particularly the minutes and papers of the professional conduct committees dealing with delicate matters concerning members some of whom are still living. But apart from such records access to the collection is largely unrestricted and the policy regarding recent accessions is a generous one compared with other archival collections. Taken in conjunction with the published material listed in this book's bibliographies the archive leaves only a few corners of the Institute's work unmapped.

The introductions to each part of this guide describe how the structure and administration of the Institute have evolved in response to the changing circumstances of the profession. Such accounts adhere closely to the topics at hand and so tend to view the world through the Institute's eyes. The intention of this short essay is to stand that process on its head by looking at the Institute from outside. Such an alternative focus has two virtues. First it may begin to clarify the relationship between the Institute and the profession which it has represented. Only a superficial view would treat the two as synonymous, eschewing the areas of dissension which are as illuminating as those of agreement. Secondly it may help to indicate those aspects of the archive which are more rewarding than their catalogue titles suggest. Every researcher has stories to tell of discoveries made in improbable places, where documents supposedly about one subject contain revealing nuggets on another. The RIBA archive has its full share of such material waiting to be used by those who are willing to get beyond first impressions.

The limits of any archive are naturally defined by the activity which it records so it is always well to be forearmed with some understanding of what the individual or institution concerned set out to do and how influential they are thought to have been. Even a very full archive, such as the one listed here, will reveal its worth in proportion to the questions asked of it, rendering nothing when they stray outside its bounds. Much frustration can be saved by avoiding false expectations. For a professional organization such as the RIBA the obvious preliminary questions to consider concern who has belonged to it, what its declared aims have been and how it has been regarded by outsiders.

A glance through the Institute's *Transactions* for a typical mid-Victorian year, or the *Journal* for any of the early years of this century, will uncover enough familiar names to suggest that not many architects— at least not many worth their salt— have been left outside its walls. If that were truly so the history of architecture since 1834 might be written in terms of the Institute's deliberations without much reference elsewhere. But turning to other sources, especially those which have sought to list all those claiming to be architects, the impression is almost the reverse. Post Office Directories and the census returns enumerate shoals of architects whose professional lives were passed totally outside the sphere of the Institute. Using the census figures Barrington Kaye has calculated that in 1851 only 8 per cent of architects were RIBA members, rising to 15 per cent half a century later: it was not until the advent of registration in the 1930s that the Institute could claim to represent the majority of the profession.[1]

The absence of so many from the fold was partly a matter of deliberate policy, for one of the main aims in establishing the Institute had been to distinguish the practice of architecture from the business of measuring and from the building trades, both of which were connections which threatened to compromise the independent role of the architect. But without an exclusive claim to the title of architect the Institute could do nothing during the first century of its existence to stop those who chose to carry on more or less as before, and amidst such confusion the census takers and compilers of street directories could hardly be expected to draw a firm line. Amongst those that they listed were plenty who epitomized the professional ideal but behind them stood the lesser ranks of architects who mixed design work with surveying, property valuation and advice (especially on dilapidations) and arbitrations. None of these subsidiary occupations, except surveying for a builder, could be classified as wholly improper— the ranks of the Institute would have been depleted if they had— but those who depended heavily on them could hardly be counted the immediate colleagues of the best names in the field.

In studying the long period during which the boundaries of professional practice and nomenclature remained fairly nebulous it is often hard to appreciate why one architect joined the Institute and the next did not. Enough is known about architects as prominent as William Burges and William Butterfield to explain why the first overcame his prejudice that the Institute was solely a bastion of the classical revival and joined its ranks while the second consistently refused to have his name put forward; and enough can be inferred from the lives of nineteenth century architects such as those specializing in pubs, theatres and music halls to suggest why almost to a man they remained outside. But the choice of countless others, whether made on personal whim or principle or because of a reluctance to take the qualifying exams once they had been set up, cannot be summarized in a way which will hold good from top to toe of the profession. Only when those who did not join formed groups to express their alienation from the Institute's policies and attitudes can the offstage performers be properly heard. As organized outsiders their role in the Institute's development then became potentially as momentous as that of any who spoke from inside.

The earliest split in the organization of the profession was perhaps more the fault of distance than a difference of opinion. From the outset the Institute had a distinctly metropolitan bias: its headquarters were in London and its Council was composed of well-established London architects. When the profession began to get itself organized in the major provincial cities it was through local initiatives rather than in response to a metropolitan campaign. Liverpool, Bristol and Nottingham all had acquired their own organizations, and the Northern Architectural Association had been founded, before the RIBA held its first General Conference of Architects in 1871. The lesson of that and subsequent conferences, plus the setting up of the rival Society of Architects in 1884, encouraged the Institute to recognize the provincial societies through a system of alliances from 1889 onwards, but it was not until 1923 that a provincial architect— J.A. Gotch of Kettering—was elected to the Presidency. Because it has not been possible to include the records of the allied societies in this guide their influence on the Institute (especially on the issue of registration) has to be measured partly at second hand. It is no surprise to detect signs of the periphery setting the pace for reform as had happened in countless spheres throughout the nineteenth century. Those on the fringe— in the provinces or in the countries of the Empire— experienced the vulnerability of the architect's status more acutely than London architects ever did and so were far more vocal in claiming a defensive role for the Institute.

Such pressure came to a head in the early 1890s in the famous 'Profession or Art' debate, when the RIBA found itself simultaneously under attack from above and below. The Society of Architects had helped promote a Registration Bill intended to ensure (as the M.P. who introduced it wrote) 'that in future persons desirous of practising architecture should prove by examination that they know something of the scientific— not artistic— principles of their profession'.[2] The Institute dissociated itself from the Bill, largely for fear of being supplanted, but was accused by those who opposed it of having covert sympathy for the aim of licensing entry to the profession. Any qualifying exam, the critics complained, was bound to give ascendency to book-knowledge and the utilitarian aspects of architecture because artistic abilities could never be tested in the same way. In making qualification on such terms a prerequisite for practice architecture would be sunk to its lowest common denominator, bereft of its artistic ideals.

The memorial from those opposed to the Bill, sent to the RIBA in March 1891 and published in *The Times*, had seventy signatures to it— twenty-four members, twenty-two architect non-members and twenty-four artists and sculptors.[3] Richard Norman Shaw, their leader, was amongst those who had resigned their membership of the Institute because of a distaste for the tendencies which this issue had eventually highlighted. He had left back in 1869, finding that it was 'intolerably dull, and its members interested in architecture not as an art but as a more or less lucrative profession'.[4] Shaw settled his favours on the Royal Academy while other future signatories joined the Art Workers Guild, founded in 1884. The memorialists' critique of the RIBA went further than saying that it had shown 'a little accidental leaning towards Philistinism', as Robert Kerr put it.[5] Yet within their own camp they failed to offer an alternative position, at least not one around which most of the profession could usefully rally. To countenance art at the expense of the more prosaic sides of architecture, boring though they might be, was little help as a guide to everyday practice. The need to think broadly about the setting of a general standard, and an educational system to achieve it, eventually brought many of the memorialists back into the Institute. In particular John Belcher used his Presidency in 1904—6 to close the gap with the Art Workers Guild by persuading such key figures as Ernest Newton, E.S. Prior and Edwin Lutyens to become RIBA members.[6]

At the very time the memorialists were being reunited with the Institute the first tremors of a larger and more persistent schism began to be felt. One of the major threats which provincial architects claimed went unheeded was the carrying out of municipal projects— hospitals, schools, police stations and the like— by local authority engineers and surveyors. Whether or not the end results were satisfactory this habit denied architects the chance to participate in the growing number of such projects at the turn of the century. It was particularly galling to see them entrusted to a borough or county official in places where previously it had been the custom to hold a limited or open architectural competition. The RIBA response to this loss of opportunity was to send a circular to all local authorities in 1904 suggesting that they were doing themselves a disservice, not to mention storing up trouble for the future, by employing engineers and surveyors 'fettered by a lack of expert knowledge possessed by architects': they would do well to hire their own architects or, better still, commission outside practices.[7]

The RIBA circular, which sank without trace in most town halls, had more complicated implications than its drafters may have realized. Beneath the stated purpose of defending the claims of architects against the encroachments of other professions lurked the more divisive issue of whether public projects should be given to salaried local government architects or to independent practices. Some major authorities, in particular the London County Council, had got well beyond the stage of referring every project to their engineer or surveyor and had established separate architectural departments which had proved their worth in handling the ambitious schemes for which they were responsible. In 1912 the LCC had a 187-strong department supervising housing, schools, fire stations and much else besides.[8] When that year it was announced that the LCC was going to take on more staff to deal with its schools programme the RIBA was provoked into appointing an Official Architecture Committee to investigate the significance and extent of public sector architecture. The cautious conclusion it came to— that local authority work might be handled by a mixture of public and private practices— was an acknowledgement of the danger of favouring one part of the profession against another. But what sounded like an inoffensive compromise before the First World War was strained near to breaking point in the totally different world which architects confronted after 1918.

Although there was a significant public sector before the war (no exact calculation of its overall size was made) the unsung assumption amongst most architects entering the profession was that to go that way was second best to setting up in private practice. Though that attitude still endured in the 1920s the chances of following such a course became increasingly remote: instead most architects (again there were no precise figures) found themselves salaried jobs in large offices— some in private practices of the kind that had always had a fair number of assistants, some in the architectural departments of businesses such as chain stores and banks, and a substantial number in local authority and government departments. The disappointment of those in such employment that they had failed to set up on their own fuelled their resentment that the RIBA seemed increasingly blind to their existence. The Institute appeared to drag its feet in adopting a scale of recommended salaries for architectural assistants in large offices, public or private, but to leap at any chance of denigrating the achievements of the largest employers of assistants, the public sector. A Committee on Official Architecture chaired by Raymond Unwin (who ironically had gained as much as anyone from government service) reported in 1935 that local authorities were likely to stifle good architecture by favouring administrative above design abilities in their staff, and that to secure innovative work they should rely on outside architects rather than those 'cumbered about with much serving'.[9] Two years later H.S. Goodhart-Rendel turned the knife in the wound by referring in his Presidential Address to public sector departments being 'like slot-machines in which you pay your penny but cannot take your choice'.[10] Remarks and resolutions which appeared to align the RIBA with the interests of one group in the profession, essentially the heads of private practices, inevitably forced those who felt estranged to look for protection elsewhere. Amongst the alternative organizations representing the aggrieved the most vocal and long-lasting was the Association of Architects, Surveyors and Technical Assistants (AASTA).[11] This maintained the agitation for the rights of salaried assistants from the 1920s through to the years after the Second World War when the public sector was granted much higher esteem. But even then, when local authority projects in Hertfordshire, Coventry and elsewhere were being ranked with the achievements of the LCC, those who opted for that kind of work still felt that the RIBA underrated their part.

It may seem perverse to have opened this discussion of the Institute and its archive by emphasising the significance of those who for one reason or another did not become members. The reason for doing so is to stress the dark corners so that the bright areas will stand out all the better. Anyone thinking of using the archive would be mistaken in expecting to find in it material on issues or subjects which many at the time accused the Institute of neglecting, or in hoping to get a comprehensive view of matters in which it favoured a single interest. In the course of its history there have been countless moments when, depending on one's point of view, the RIBA has been in or out of step with the most progressive or interesting changes of its time. But against such fluctuations in responsiveness and outlook must be set the fact that it has had a more consistent relationship with the profession as a whole than many similar organizations in their respective spheres. For instance in engineering, the profession which architects have come into collision with most often, there were seventeen separate national institutions by 1914.[12] Such proliferation may have been a sign of vitality but it made it difficult for engineers to speak with a single voice, and on the same count it has made it hard for historians to get an overview of their profession. Because the RIBA has maintained its general authority, despite many lapses and diversions, the archival record of its membership and activities is more representative of the architectural currents of its time than any other source. So after a prolonged warning about its limitations it is now time to specify some of the most fruitful material in it.

Many people coming to use the archive will no doubt be less interested in a general problem, institutional or otherwise, than in adding to what they already know about an architect whose works have caught their eye. In such research the less prominent the architect the more helpful the archive is likely to be, for when all other sources fail there is still a good chance that if someone was a member of the RIBA— Fellow, Associate or Licentiate— some record of them will have survived, sufficient perhaps to establish the essentials of their career. Because they are so comprehensive the membership records (described more fully in Chapter 5) may be regarded as the heart of the archive. As architectural parish registers they are dependable enough to be referred to as a place of first recourse and in many instances, when no other record can be traced, as a place of last recourse as well. Yet like parish registers they cannot be relied on too far. The nomination papers for election to membership have some gaps in them and in general they grow more informative as time goes on, especially after 1872 for Associate papers and after about 1880 for Fellowship papers when the two series begin to record more about applicants' training and early careers. The extra details asked for, plus the names of the three proposers for a candidate, constitute a quite full account of an architect's progress in the world, concentrating on the years at the outset of professional life about which other documents may be silent.

The delight of discovering in whose office an architect served his articles, whom he assisted, and who come the day was prepared to nominate him to the Institute is more than just a matter of pedigree hunting. For both individual and collective biography these are the elements of experience which illuminate how architects were professionally equipped and how they entered practice. So far the nomination papers have mainly been used to identify previously unrecognized architects or to enrich the biographies of the better known. For instance Susan Beattie has relied on them to investigate the backgrounds of those who served in the LCC Architects Department before the First World War, not just for the sake of claiming reputations for those previously lost in the anonymity of local government service but so as to establish what skills they brought to their task.[13] Beyond that way of using the membership files there is the prospect of a yet wider application of their contents to demonstrate general patterns of professional change as seen not from above by those who debated what should be done but from below by those whose everyday experience was typical.

Some other parts of the archive can be classed with the membership records as primarily of biographical importance. The papers of the Refugees Committee 1936—41 are partly about the controversial problem of how many architects fleeing from Hitler's Europe could be absorbed into a profession hard up for work, but are mostly taken up by the records of individual cases including dossiers sent by individuals pleading for the RIBA to intervene on their behalf. Personal files of another, much less painful kind are those of prize essayists and the holders of studentships which are interesting as intellectual staging posts in the lives of celebrated architects (plus many not so celebrated) as they are original works of their time. Amongst them are accounts of architectural tours taken by Aston Webb, W.R Lethaby and J.J. Joass, George Wightwick's paper on Wren, Wyatt Papworth on Palladian Architecture and Ethel M. Charles (elected the first woman Associate in 1898) on 'The Development of Architectural Art from Structural Requirements and the Nature of Materials'.

Getting a prize or applying for admission are moments which spotlight the individual. Thereafter many members get lost from view either because they played no active part in the Institute or because when they did so their individual voices were submerged in the collective decisions of committees. Verbatim transcripts were kept of the discussions at the Ordinary Meetings and Annual General Meetings but seldom at committee meetings, the minutes of which record the bare bones of discussion and the decisions taken but convey very little about the tone of the occasion. It is tantalizing to get as far as knowing who was in the room and what they concluded without being privy to the full proceedings— who was impressive, who a bore, and who by sheer cussedness won the day. But for the Victorian years there is often a prelude to a meeting to be found in the letters written to the Secretary or the President urging the adoption of a particular subject or point of view. In these the opinions and reactions which subsequently get hidden by the digest given in the minutes are briefly brought into the open. Anyone interested in individual architects may find it fruitful to look for evidence of their influence on the committees which they joined, as recorded in either the minutes or the related correspondence. The higher someone rose in the Institute the more material there will be, whether accumulated through long service and office holding or concentrated at one moment of high dispute.

Yet however much may be culled from the archive about individual careers it is essentially as a record of collective endeavour that it should be seen. The mainspring of professionalism, for architects as much as any other group, has been the desire to establish a standard of expertise and practice which will be publicly recognized. From the start the Institute's commitment to that aim distinguished it from the clubs and societies which preceded it: although it too devoted gentlemanly evenings to archaeology, history and the latest projects the main theme of its development can be seen as the organization (plus occasionally the coercion) of individual architects to preserve and enhance their common status. Each section of the archive deals with a sphere of architecture in which the Institute has flexed its muscles, or the means which it has used to do so; an uneven chronicle which gradually expands to take in all the obvious aspects of architectural practice, plus many roguish items as well. Any historian whose interests reach beyond biography to the professional process as a whole, or a single part of it, will soon learn that this is where the archive comes into its own; for while particular architects may never make an appearance in it there is ultimately no general architectural problem which goes unnoticed.

Contrary to the rule that professional institutes assert their educational role early in their development the RIBA was slow to intervene in architectural training. At the time of its foundation the pupilage system was the accepted route into the profession, involving three or more years with an established architect whose office might be the perfect seedbed for a young designer or a Pecksniffian backwater where systematic instruction had never been heard of. To compensate or reinforce whatever could be picked up that way students training in London could attend an increasing array of lectures and courses with a choice between the down to earth at King's College and University College, the artistic at the Royal Academy, and co-operative self-help at the Architectural Association. If they joined the Institute as student members they could use its museum and library and sit in on its lectures. But rich though these educational pickings might be they never converged as a single qualification which outsiders could recognize as a test of attainment. While other professions followed the lead of the Civil Service in selecting their members through examination the Institute held back. Its Fellows, who themselves had been reared through pupilage and later enjoyed the income which students' fees provided, were in no hurry to set architectural education on a separate and proper footing. In support of their indifference they could point out that the voluntary exams introduced in 1863 were a failure, sometimes not held for want of candidates; and to solve their inadequacies by substituting a compulsory system, as was done in 1882, only highlighted the problem of their intended purpose and scope. The memorialists' protest of the early 1890s, directed against such exams, insisted that the analogy with what other professions were doing was demeaning to the very qualities which made architecture unique.

The Institute's shyness about education resulted in its walking into the subject backwards. First it introduced compulsory exams for Associate membership not because it was eager to have them but because something had to take the place of the earlier system: then as architecture schools rallied to the business of training candidates it awoke to the need to regulate their curricula and courses. The exciting educational developments of the 1890s — notably the expansion of the Architectural Association syllabus, the work of the LCC Technical Educational Board and the foundation of the Liverpool School in 1894 — were only indirectly RIBA inspired. Aston Webb's decision as President to set up the committee which became the Board of Architectural Education in 1904 represented a delayed recognition of what had happened: and, as Alan Powers has pointed out, its first effect was to unleash a revival of the 'Profession or Art' debate.[14] The Board's deliberations and its subsequent role as intermediary between the Institute and the architecture schools, summarized in Chapter 7, form one of the richest sequences in the archive.

Once training was completed — perhaps rounded off by a foreign tour and a year or so as an architectural assistant — a young architect going out into the world (at least before the First World War) hoped to set up on his own. Unless launched with the help of influential friends or the prospect of a regular appointment as architect to a landowner or institution the early years were inevitably precarious, but were enlivened by the excitement of entering architectural competitions. As the competition system spread after about 1820 its popularity amongst clients, especially amongst committees responsible for civic buildings, workhouses and churches, was almost outweighed by the criticisms its abuses attracted. It seemed that more often than not the rules were set aside or changed, the assessor's report was overturned, the anonymity of entries was broken, favours were shown, and finally at the end of the day the commission went to a rank outsider whose name appeared nowhere in the lists. Yet there were sufficient examples of architects catapulted to fame by a competition victory to make it hard to forgo the temptation to take a chance. Had not Harvey Lonsdale Elmes secured his reputation by winning twice over in the competitions for St. George's Hall Liverpool, and did not victory in the Manchester Assize Courts competition land Alfred Waterhouse, as he put it, 'in the thick of my business before I was really ready'?[15] The RIBA took up the matter of competitions within four years of its foundation and has hardly been rid of it since. To some it has always seemed that, whatever its benefits to individual architects, the system degrades the profession by setting one member against another, and that its fiascos undo the good publicity secured in other ways; but rather than turn its back on competitions altogether the Institute has generally chosen to try and regulate their terms and warn members about the hazards they present.

Even if competitions had been forsworn other problems of professional practice, often just as intractable, followed hard behind: as Chapter 8 shows, they recur as a constant theme, from the first meeting of the Professional Practice Committee in 1845 if not before. Those classifiable as internal squabbles might be settled without too much loss of public face, as in the case of disputes over the ownership or copyright of drawings. When John Giles won the competition for the Langham Hotel, Portland Place in 1862 he agreed to collaborate with James Murray whose designs for the interiors the judges fancied: five years later, rivalry over the design, marked by disgreement over who should keep the drawings, had to be settled not within the Institute but in the courts.[16] Similar cases between architects and builders over contracts, or with clients over fees, account for the hours spent in committee refining standard forms and conditions.

But more critical than any of these, because rooted in the circumstances which brought the Institute into existence, was the issue of the architect's disinterested service to the client. It was a measure of the importance attached to the ideal of professional independence, yet at the same time of its vulnerability, that a whiff of suspicion directed at the architect's custodial role put the Insititute on the alert. Thus when in 1877 a parson wrote to *The Times* suggesting that church architects habitually sought commissions from suppliers of every item of furniture, 'from an organ to a hassock', letters of horror at such a violation tumbled forth.[17] Almost a hundred years later, on the same grounds but much magnified, the Institute expelled John Poulsom for having financial connections with building companies.[18] That case, and others like it, comes in the 'no access' category of the archive but no such prohibition covers the papers of the committees which set the standards by which he fell.

The fact that Poulson was not only stripped of his membership but was tried and sent to prison is a reminder that architecture is no more of an island unto itself than any other profession. The law of the land stands above whatever disciplines or codes of conduct a profession imposes on its members, yet there is a still more omnipresent outside control in the form of the freedom which the client or the public has to accept or reject its services. The threat of total rejection may seem fanciful in the case of law or medicine but is far less so in the realm of building where overlapping occupations jostle for attention. Through the Institute's archive, and through the history which it embodies, runs a recurring sense of a profession mounting watch for its security and status, perhaps with more vigilance than professions which have been surer of their ground. Robert Kerr, the most persistent spokesman for his fellow architects during the Victorian period, summed up the threats to their standing in a lecture of 1863 aptly called, 'The Market Value of an Architect'. On one flank they were under challenge from 'the clever young officer of engineers, and the gentleman experienced in green-houses' — architects took great umbrage at being pushed aside in the design of the exhibition buildings of 1851 and 1862 by the gardener Joseph Paxton and the Royal Engineer Captain Fowke. On the other side they had to face 'hundreds of idle intellects' — amateurs, enthusiasts and 'any one who has an unfurnished head to let', whose intervention devalued their expertise.[19] Kerr spoke for his own time but in terms which have often since echoed through the debates and meetings of the Institute. Insert some references to the expanding powers of the planning profession and the misconceptions of contemporary critics and his words still hold true as an expression of the exposed position in which architects believe themselves to be.

William White, Secretary to the Institute at the end of the last century, voiced the fear that it had 'enveloped itself closely in the mantle of professionalism', so cutting itself off from the community at large.[20] Having at its outset chosen a non-architect President, Earl De Grey, as a demonstration of its outwardness it seemed to White to have gradually pulled up the drawbridges in resentment and suspicion of external interference. He was better placed than anyone of his time to sense this siege mentality yet perhaps, being so close to the heart of things, he exaggerated its extent. For nothing has characterized the outlook of architects so much as the ambivalence of their response to the outside world — fending it off with one hand and welcoming it with the other. Now that the routes into the Institute's archive have been so clearly signposted the subject which cries out for attention is the one raised by White's remarks. Important though it internal affairs and the lives of its members have been the level of inquiry which promises to yield most will be that which concentrates on its role as intermediary between the profession and the public it serves.

Notes

1. Barrington Kaye *The development of the architectural profession in Britain*, (1960), pp. 173—75.
2. *The Times*, 5 March 1891, p. 12.
3. *The Times*, 3 March 1891, p. 9, reprinted in R. Norman Shaw and T.G. Jackson, eds. *Architecture a profession or an art* (1892), pp. xxxiii—xxxv.
4. Reginald Blomfield, *Richard Norman Shaw* (1940), p. 21.
5. Robert Kerr, 'Architecture — a profession or an art?' *RIBA Proceedings*, vol.VII (1891), p. 301.

6. *Journal of the RIBA* 3rd series vol. XXI (1913—14), p. 56.
7. Memorial Sent to Municipal Councils, District Councils and County Councils, 17 November 1904.
8. London County Council, *Services and Staff 1911—12*, pp. 101—05.
9. *Journal of the RIBA* 3rd series vol. XLII (8 June 1935), p. 862.
10. Ibid, vol. XLV (8 November 1937). p. 9.
11. The AASTA was founded in 1919 as the Architects' and Surveyors' Assistants Professional Union. Its records are at the Modern Records Centre, University of Warwick Library.
12. R.A. Buchanan, 'Institutional proliferation in the engineering profession, 1847—1914' *Economic History Review*, 2nd ser., vol. XXXVIII (February 1985), pp. 43—45.
13. Susan Beattie, *A revolution in London housing* (1980).
14. Alan Powers, 'Architectural education and the Arts and Crafts Movement', *Architectural Education* 3 (1984), pp. 42—70; 'Edwardian architectural education: a study of three schools of architecture', *AA Files* 5 (January 1984), pp. 49—59.
15. M.B. Adams, 'Architecture from George IV to George V', *Journal of the RIBA*, 3rd ser. vol. XIX (27 July 1912), p. 644.
16. *The Builder* 23 November 1867, p. 859.
17. *The Times* 4 January 1877, p. 7; 5 January 1877, p. 10.
18. *Journal of the RIBA* 3rd ser. vol. LXXX (February 1973), pp. 63—65
19. *The Builder* 9 May 1863, pp. 331—2
20 William H. White, *The past, present and future of the architectural profession* (1885), p. 28.

Introduction to the Archive

At its headquarters at 66 Portland Place, London W1, the RIBA has retained a very large archive which forms a unique record of most of its activities since its foundation in 1834. Until recently, the archive was not very organized or developed and had therefore languished underused and relatively unappreciated by the public, the members of the Institute and its staff. A complete survey of this material was begun in September 1981 and completed in December 1983. The survey involved the identification, examination and description of all archival record series; the reconstruction of some series which had become dispersed; the location and collection of archive material which was stored in office cupboards and in many unexpected nooks and crannies; the removal from the archive of some ephemeral material unsuitable for inclusion in the permanent archive of the Institute; some study of the relationship between the various record series and some research into the history and organization of the Institute. A summary description of the scope and contents of each record series was provided and many series were also provided with box-lists of file titles but no attempt was made to compile indexes to minutebooks, correspondence or other papers. This sort of detailed work will have to await opportunities to undertake further projects. However, many individual volumes and files have their own contemporary indexes and most material relevant to any particular enquiry can now be located without undue difficulty though sometimes some assiduity is required. Unfortunately it was not possible to include the RIBA regions and the RIBA commercial companies in the survey.

The total archive occupies more than 300 metres of shelving and contains a great variety of material including the minutes, agenda papers and reports of the Council; minutes of General Meetings; minutes and reports of hundreds of committees (special investigatory committees, standing committees, departmental executive committees, central policy committees, joint committees and conferences) and their subcommittees and working groups; some of the correspondence and data files of the Secretaries, Presidents, and heads of departments and other senior staff; texts of sessional programme lectures and annual conference proceedings; official publications of the Institute; membership records; prizewinners' essays; Final Examination theses; research award reports; files on exhibitions, competitions and awards; press releases and press cuttings; title deeds and architects' drawings concerned with RIBA premises; account books; trust deeds and royal charters. Some of the most heavily-used parts of the archive are the records of past membership. These include the applications (the so-called 'Nomination Papers') of the past candidates for election as Associates, Fellows or Licentiates, which provide unique information on the full name, address, professional education and early professional experience of thousands of architects and frequently list the architectural works for which they had been responsible. Other parts of the archive which have recently aroused considerable interest among researchers are the records of the RIBA Board of Architectural Education and the records of the pioneering work done in the period just before, during and after the two world wars by the various RIBA town planning, slum clearance, housing and post-war reconstruction committees.

The hazards of several moves of premises and of war-time government exhortations to contribute to paper collections, coupled with the continual pressure exerted by lack of adequate space and suitable conditions for the accommodation of the archive, has made it quite remarkable that so much material has survived (though much of it is admittedly in very poor physical condition). Most committees' minutes have survived, the most notable omissions being some of the very early committees before 1848, the Finance Committee Minutes between 1891 and 1927, the Architectural Science Board Minutes, 1939— 1949, and the minutes of some groups of the Reconstruction Committee, 1949— 1943. Frequently, however, there are no other records of the committees (such as agenda papers, memoranda, correspondence of the committees' secretaries) besides the official minutes. In the area of correspondence there are some regrettable gaps including the out-going letters written by the nineteenth century RIBA Secretaries on behalf of the Council. Two large wooden chests survived which contained a proportion of the in-letters (labelled 'Letters to Council') and it is clear from annotations on these letters that out-letterbooks were kept, none of which has survived. Other noteworthy gaps are the correspondence of the chairmen of the RIBA Board of Architectural Education and the correspondence of most of the RIBA presidents, who have until recently regarded their correspondence as PRIBA as part of their personal papers. A great deal of correspondence obviously did not survive the move of the Institute from 9 Conduit Street to 66 Portland Place in 1934. Many parcels of correspondence were found, unopened since the move, but not nearly enough. There is also some evidence that many records went to waste-paper collections to help the war effort in the 1940s. The official membership records are fairly complete, the most unfortunate gaps being the Associates Nominations Papers between November 1842 and December 1856 inclusive and the Fellows Nomination Papers between April 1857 and

December 1865 inclusive. The surviving financial records are rather sparse, most of the old ledgers not having been retained. Although these losses are regrettable they are not in the least surprising and it is probably fair to say that the Institute has managed to preserve more material than most institutions. What remains is certainly an exceptional archive of great importance not only to researchers of architectural history and the history of the profession but also to those working in the wider fields of social and economic history.

The structure of this guide has been dictated partly by archival principles and partly by convenience. The approach is departmental but is complicated by the fact that it was only in comparatively recent times that the Institute became truly departmental in its work. Some of the same activities have been shared in the past between different committees or transferred from one department to another and back again and some departments have ceased or split, merged and split again. The chapters of this guide, therefore, are broadly thematic and occasionally the main entry for a series does not appear under the department currently dealing with that activity. However, not only is there an index to record series titles but many cross-references are provided in the text and administrative responsibilities are usually made clear either in the notes or in the introductions to each section. Most of the large chapters have been subdivided into sections which, wherever possible, reflect administrative subdivisions. Each section has it own introduction and bibliography and within each section descriptions of record series appear in chronological order by opening date. A cut-off date of 1971 was finally decided upon and any record series beginning its life after 1971 has not been included in this guide. These recent series were, however, included in the survey and many of them may be consulted by serious researchers. Information on them is available in the British Architectural Library. The appendixes consist of guides to the archives of several organizations which have, or used to have, a special relationship with the RIBA or are relevant to its history, and which have been deposited in the British Architectural Library's Manuscrpts & Archives Collection.

Conditions of use

All access to the archive is totally at the discretion of the Council of the Institute. In general, the principle of free access is in operation and restrictions are usually only applied to recent records or are imposed either to preserve the confidentiality of personal information or to prevent further damage to records which are in poor physical condition. A few series, for example those concerning arbitrations and professional conduct cases, will probably remain closed for ever, entries for them appearing in this guide merely for the sake of comprehensiveness. Users may not photograph or photocopy any document but in many instances copies can be ordered from the Archivist. The permission of the Archivist or, in some instances, of the Secretary RIBA, must be obtained before any form of publication or other reproduction of any material in the archive is undertaken. The archive is closed in

August and on bank holidays but otherwise is normally open between 10am and 5pm, Monday — Friday. Enquiries should be addressed to the Archivist, British Architectural Library, 66 Portland Place, London W1N 4AD. Tel.01—580 5533.

I
Foundation, constitution and government

Section 1 Foundation papers, charters and by-laws, constitutional committees

Early in 1834 a group of architects and surveyors formed the Society of Architects and Surveyors and another group, consisting entirely of architects, formed the Society of British Architects with the object of developing a professional institution of architects. Attempts to combine the two societies failed due to the insistence of the Society of British Architects on a clause in the regulations of the proposed institution disqualifying from membership those who measured and valued works on behalf of builders, excepting works executed from their own design or directions, and those having any interest or participation in any trade or contract connected with building. In May a specially called general meeting of architects resolved (irregularly, in the opinion of members of the Society of Architects and Surveyors who were present at the meeting) that the disqualifying clause be formally adopted. A week later several of the architect members of the Society of Architects and Surveyors received a letter informing them that they had been elected members of the Institute of British Architects. These masterly if somewhat high-handed acts proved to be the undoing of the Society of Architects and Surveyors. On 4 June 1834 the founding members of the Institute read a draft by Joseph Gwilt of the Address and Regulations, which they formally adopted on 2 July. The following week the Society of British Architects, having achieved its purpose, was wound up and the founding members of the Institute announced the names of those elected as Original Members. Further meetings of the Original Members took place that autumn at which Thomas Leverton Donaldson and John Goldicutt were elected honorary secretaries and the Council was appointed. The first Ordinary Meeting

3   The royal charter of incorporation granted to the Institute by William IV on
11 January 1837. It states that the Institue was formed 'for the general advancement
of civil architecture and for promoting and facilitating the acquirement of the
knowledge of the various arts and sciences connected therewith; it being an art
esteemed and encouraged in all enlightened nations, as tending greatly to promote
the domestic convenience of citizens, and the public improvement and embellishment
of towns and cities'. (RIBA Archive:1.1.2)

of the members and the first Council Meeting were both held on 10 December 1834.

In 1837 William IV granted the Institute a royal charter, which conferred on it the legal status and rights of a person. Supplemental charters were granted in 1887, 1909, 1925 and 1971. The charter contains the Institute's constitution and specifies the rights and obligations of its members. It contains the main principles or enabling powers, while the by-laws made under the charters set out the methods of application of the principles. The first official by-laws, replacing the original regulations of 1834, were made and ordained at the General Meeting on 1 May 1837. Since 1887 all new by-laws and amendments of existing by-laws have had to be approved by the Privy Council. The only field in which Privy Council control has proved significant has been in the exclusion of the trade union type of activities which many of the salaried members were anxious for the RIBA to undertake and the Privy Council was firm in ruling out. The disadvantages of having very detailed by-laws are avoided by having Council Regulations which cover all the detailed administration of the by-laws and can be changed by Council resolution.

The original charter, dated 11 January 1837, stipulated three classes of members, Fellows, Associates and Honorary Fellows, of whom only the Fellows could exercise a vote. A Council composed of Fellows was to direct and manage the affairs of the Institute and Annual General Meetings were to be held, at which the officers and Council members were to be elected. General Meetings could adopt, alter, add to or revoke by-laws, subject only to the laws of the realm. In August 1837 Queen Victoria consented to become the Patroness of the Institute and in May 1866 she commanded that the Institute be styled the Royal Institute of British Architects (the Institute had in practice been calling itself 'Royal' since the grant of the charter in 1837).

By 1884 it had become necessary to apply for a new charter which would recognize the wider role being played by the Institute in the field of architectural education. On 28 March 1887 Queen Victoria granted a supplemental charter which gave the RIBA power to conduct examinations, reorganized the classes of membership on the basis of examination qualification and gave the Council power to admit provincial societies into formal alliance with the RIBA.

The main purpose of the second supplemental charter, granted by Edward VII on 11 January 1909, was the introduction of the Licentiate class of membership based on a practice qualification. This paved the way for the RIBA's attempt to gather into membership, before the introduction of statutory registration of architects, those practising architects who had not and could not be expected to pass the RIBA Associateship qualifying examination. It also strengthened the Council's powers over the curriculums and examination syllabuses of architectural schools. The third supplemental charter, granted by George V on 11 March 1925, was primarily to recognize the absorption by the RIBA of the former Society of Architects and many of its provisions dealt with the assimilation of members of that society and adjusted the requirements for proceeding from one RIBA class of membership to another. RIBA Licentiates were declared to be corporate voting members, which was a large and significant extension of the franchise.

By the late 1960s the activities of the RIBA had expanded and diversified to such an extent that a new charter became an imperative need. The fourth supplemental charter was granted by Queen Elizabeth II on 6 April 1971 and revoked the previous supplemental charters and parts of the original charter. Its main purposes were to recognize the regional and branch structure which had replaced the old system of Allied Societies and to remove the restrictions on the sale or mortgaging of Institute property, so as to facilitate the setting up of commercial companies such as RIBA Services Ltd, National Building Specification Ltd or any other companies providing paid services to members and the building industry and by this means enable the Institute to retain its status as a charitable society.

1.1.1   FOUNDATION PAPERS, 1834—1848   31 items
Notes of proceedings at meetings of the Society of British Architects and at meetings of the founding members of the Institute of British Architects, Feb 1834 — Jan 1835, with drafts of the original prospectus, address and regulations, and notes on the early history of the Institute by the honorary secretaries, 1834—1848.

(Three items are bound into RIBA Pamphlets Q Series Vol.7, the rest are bound together in a volume entitled 'Miscellaneous papers connected with the foundation of the RIBA')

1.1.2   CHARTERS, 1837—1971   5 items
Original royal charter of incorporation, 11 Jan 1837, with supplemental charters of 28 Mar 1887, 11 Jan 1909, 11 Mar 1925 and 6 Apr 1971.

(Transcripts are available for consultation)

1.1.3   BY-LAWS, 1837—(1971)   1 box
Printed editions of the 1835 regulations and the subsequent by-laws of the Institute, 1837—1971, with transcripts of the charters.

1.1.4   PRIVY COUNCIL CERTIFICATES, 1889—(1981)   32 items
Privy Council certificates of approval of amendments and suspensions of RIBA by-laws and of new and revised by-laws made after grants of supplemental charters, 1889—1981.

(Copies are available for consultation)

1.1.5   CHARTER AND BY-LAWS COMMITTEE MINUTES, 1922—1924   1 vol
Signed minutes of meetings, Jul 1922 — May 1924.

Subjects : Revision of the RIBA charter and by-laws: the constitution of the Council: financial relations between the RIBA and the Allied Societies: proposed examination for the Fellowship: proposed provision for taking polls of members on important subjects: rights of the Fellows, Associates and Licentiates: statutory registration of architects: absorption of the Society of Architects.

(For minutes of earlier committees appointed to revise the charter and by-laws *see* 2.2 Special Committees Minutes Series)

1.1.6   CONSTITUTION OF THE RIBA SUBCOMMITTEE MINUTES, 1927   1 vol
Signed minutes of a meeting on 28 Feb 1927.
Subjects : Unrepresentativeness of the attendance at General Business Meetings: proposed taking of referendums on important resolutions: proposed delegation of the powers of the General Body to the Council.

1.1.7   CONSTITUTIONAL COMMITTEE MINUTES & PAPERS, 1935—1937   1 vol & 1 box
Signed minutes of meetings, Oct 1935 — Feb 1937, with memoranda, drafts of reports to Council and correspondence.
Subjects : Appointment and constitution of committees: change in status of the four departmental standing committees of Art, Literature, Practice & Science: relationship of the RIBA and its Allied Societies: the constitution of the Council: revision of RIBA by-laws.

(For minutes of an earlier Constitutional Committee *see* 2.2 Special Committees Minutes Series)

1.1.8   BY-LAWS REVISION SUBCOMMITTEE MINUTES, 1949— 1950   1 vol
Signed minutes of meetings, Jun 1949 — Sep 1950, with memoranda.
Subjects : Review of RIBA by-laws with recommendations for alterations: representation of the Association of Building Technicians (originally the Architects' and Surveyors' Assistants Professional Union and then the Association of Architects, Surveyors and Technical Assistants) on the RIBA Council.

1.1.9   CONSTITUTION OF THE COUNCIL AD HOC COMMITTEE MINUTES, 1954—1955   1 vol
Signed minutes of meetings, Nov 1954 — Feb 1955, with memoranda and report to the Council.
Subjects : Constitution of the Council: classes of RIBA membership: qualifications for the Fellowship.

1.1.10   (NEW) CONSTITUTIONAL COMMITTEE MINUTES & PAPERS, 1958—1961   1 binder & 1 box
Signed minutes of meetings, Jul 1958 — Apr 1960, with drafts of reports to the Council, 1958—1961: correspondence with other British professional institutions, Jul — Aug 1958, and copies of their charters, by-laws and regulations: signed minutes of joint meetings of the committee and the Association of Building Technicians and the presidents of UK Allied Societies, Jan 1959 and May 1960.
Subjects : Review of the constitutions of the Allied Societies in relation to the constitution of the RIBA and the Council: proposed regional grouping of the Allied Societies: finances of the Allied Societies.

1.1.11   CONSTITUTION COMMITTEE MINUTES & PAPERS, 1967   1 vol & 1 box
Signed minutes of meetings, Jan — Jul 1967, with memoranda, draft reports, papers of working groups and correspondence, 1967.
Subjects : Regionalisation of the RIBA: constitution of RIBA regions and branches: constitution of regional councils: draft supplemental charter and revised by-laws.

See also in 2.2 Special Committees Minutes Series:
Charter Committee, 1884 — 1886
Charter and By-Laws Committee, 1887 — 1888
Charter Revision Committee, 1906 — 1908
Charter and By-Laws Revision Committee, 1908 — 1910
By-Laws Revision Committee, 1911 — 1913
Constitutional Committee, 1913 — 1915
Special Meetings of the Council, 1915, 1921 — 1927, 1937
Charter Committee, 1919 — 1920
and several of the series in Chapter 3 and in Chapter 12 Section 1, in particular 12.1.1 Associates Memorial: 12.1.12 Membership Committee Minutes & Papers, 1963 — 1965: 12.1.14 Esher Committee Minutes & Papers, 1965 — 1966

Bibliography

1   *The Society of British Architects* London, 1834. Prospectus published by the Society
2   *A plain statement of facts connected with the coalition between the Society for the promotion of Architecture and Architectural Topography and the Society of British Architects* London, 1834. Published by an anonymous member of the Society of Architects and Surveyors
3   *Prospectus for the formation of a society to be called the Institution of British Architects* London, 1834. Published by the founding members of the Institute
4   *Address of the Institute of British Architects explanatory of their views and*

objects, and the regulations adopted at a meeting held on July 2nd 1834 London, IBA, 1834

5 *Institute of British Architects. Address and regulations* London, IBA, 1835

6 *Laws and regulations of the Architectural Society, 35 Lincoln's Inn Fields* London, Architectural Society, 1835

7 Taylor, W. B. Sarsfield *The origin, progress and present condition of the fine arts in Great Britain and Ireland* London, Whittaker & Co, 1841. Vol 2 pp343—352

8 *Charter and bye laws* London, RIBA, 1853. (Revised editions issued in 1868, 1874, 1877 and 1880)

9 RIBA Charter General Committee Report *RIBA Proceedings* New Series Vol 2 1886 Feb 18 pp141—160

10 *Charters and bye-laws* London, RIBA, 1905

11 *The charter, supplemental charter and revised bye laws* London, RIBA, 1910

12 Sirr, Harry 'The Architects' Club (1791) and the Architectural Society (1806)' *RIBA Journal* Vol 18 1911 Jan 7 pp183—184

13 *The charter, supplementary charters and bye-laws* London, RIBA, 1930. (Revised editions issued in 1932, 1933, 1934, 1937, 1947, 1951, 1957 & 1962)

14 'The RIBA constitution. Memorandum on the proposed revisions' *RIBA Journal* Vol 44 1937 Apr 24 pp591—592

15 Barrington Kaye 'Early architectural societies and the foundation of the RIBA' *RIBA Journal* Vol 62 1955 Oct pp497—499

16 RIBA Constitutional Committee, Interim Provisional Report *RIBA Journal* Vol 66 1958 Dec pp40—45

17 RIBA Constitutional Committee, Final Report *RIBA Journal* Vol 67 1960 Jul pp319—326

18 'Constitutional changes' *RIBA Journal* Vol 74 1967 Nov pp463—466. An account of the changes approved by the RIBA Council as the result of the work of the Charter, Membership, Esher and Constitution committees

19 RIBA Charter Steering Group 'The case for the charter and byelaws' *RIBA Journal* Vol 75 1968 Sep pp400—401

20 *The charter, supplemental charter and bye laws* London, RIBA, 1971

21 'Constitution and organisation of branches and regions of the RIBA' *RIBA Journal* Vol 79 1972 Sep pp406—407

22 Parris, John 'For crown, charter and corporation' Luder/Parris File, *Building Design* no 520 1980 Nov 7 p16

23 Parris, John 'Defending the charter' Luder/Parris File, *Building Design* no 522 1980 Nov 21 p14

Section 2 Council and General Meetings

The Council

The original regulations stated that a Council would be formed to direct and manage all the affairs of the Institute subject to the control of the General Meetings. Its members were to be elected annually by ballot at the Annual General Meeting and were to consist of six officers (a president, three vice-presidents and two secretaries) and seven ordinary members, all of whom must be Fellows. The Council was to submit to the Annual General Meetings an annual report on the state of the property and affairs of the Institute, with an audited account of the funds. It had powers to call Special General Meetings to decide on changes in the regulations or for any other stated purpose and to appoint committees to investigate specific subjects connected with the objects of the Institute. The 1837 charter confirmed the original regulations with only minor alteration and granted the Council the exclusive right to appoint and dismiss any paid officers, to prescribe their duties and determine their remuneration. The first significant revision of the by-laws took place in 1877 when the number of ordinary members of Council was increased to fifteen and it was stated that the senior vice-president should be nominated as president.

Under the by-laws of 1889 the size of the Council was more than doubled and was to include for the first time a few Associates and the presidents of the Allied Societies. It was authorized to use the Institute's funds to promote professional education and conduct examinations and was to appoint annually a Board of Examiners in Architecture. It was to have four standing departmental committees of Art, Literature, Practice & Science to advise it and it delegated the management of the Institute's establishment and the conduct of the Institute's executive business to a (paid) Secretary appointed by the Council.

The by-laws made after the absorption of the Society of Architects in 1925 again significantly enlarged the Council. It was to include Licentiates for the first time, many more Associates and representatives of Allied Societies than previously, and the chairman of the Board of Architectural Education. During the 1930s the chairmen of all the leading standing committees, the chairman of the Allied Societies Conference and the Honorary Treasurer became *ex officio* members of the Council.

In 1962 a revision of the by-laws recognized a RIBA regional organization and from then on Council has been composed of a mixture of nationally elected and regionally elected members in a ratio prescribed in the by-laws. There are now eleven regional councils and, in addition, the councils of the Royal Incorporation of Architects in Scotland and the Royal Society of Ulster Architects act as the regional councils of Scotland and Northern Ireland. These regional councils are responsible to the RIBA Council and administer funds allocated to their regions in accordance with such policy as is laid down by the RIBA Council.

The administration of Council Meetings used to be done by the Deputy Secretary and the Central Services Department and is now done by the Assistant Clerk to the Council, President's Office.

General Meetings

The 1834 regulations stated that an Annual General Meeting was to be held each May to elect the members of the Council which would direct and manage the affairs of the Institute subject to the control of the General Meetings. No alterations of the regulations were to be made except at Special General Meetings of Fellows, which could be called at any time by the Council and which the Council were obliged to call on receipt of a written requisition by eight Fellows. Only Fellows were then entitled to vote at meetings on matters concerning the Institute's affairs. Ordinary General Meetings were to be held fortnightly during the sessions but no questions relating to the regulation or management of the Institute were to be brought forward at them.

The main purpose of the Annual General Meeting was to receive and discuss the report of the Council on the state of the Institute and to elect the officers and members of the Council for the ensuing year. After the Metropolitan Building Act 1855 the AGM also elected the (Statutory) Board of Examiners for district surveyors and, from 1886—1938, a majority of the members of the four departmental committees of Art, Literature, Practice & Science.

The 1889 by-laws ordained that at least four Business Meetings, besides the Annual General Meeting, were to be held in each session. At these Business Meetings elections for Institute membership were held and any questions relating to the management and property of the Institute or any professional questions could be discussed provided that notice of any motion intended to be submitted had been given to the Secretary at least fourteen days before the meeting. Successive revisions of the by-laws increased the number required to requisition Special General Meetings and enlarged the quorums necessary at these meetings before resolutions concerning professional questions or the by-laws could be carried. The by-laws of 1889 also made certain provisions for holding polls of all corporate members on the written requisition of six Fellows but this option of holding polls did not appear in the by-laws ordained in 1910. The charter of 1925 declared that Fellows, Associates and Licentiates now had equal voting rights and the subsequent by-laws stated that the Council could, if a four-fifths majority at a Council Meeting had voted in favour of it, conduct a poll of all corporate members resident in the United Kingdom and the Irish Free State on important questions concerning the

Institute or the profession and the resolution would be carried by a simple majority of the votes polled. Further changes in the regulations for Special General Meetings and polls were made in 1930, 1962 and 1971.

The administration of General Meetings used to be done by the Deputy Secretary and the Chief Clerk and is now done by the Senior Administration Officer.

1.2.1 GENERAL MEETINGS MINUTES (Early Series), 1834—1885 7 vols
Signed minutes of Ordinary General Meetings, Special General Meetings and Annual General Meetings, May 1834 — May 1885, with annual reports of the Council to the AGM: Council's reports on essays and drawings submitted for prizes: Council's recommendations for the Royal Gold Medal: reports of special committees appointed at the instance of General Meetings: reports of the Examiners and Moderators: drafts of memorials to public figures, government offices and royalty.

Subjects : Elections of members and officers: constitution of the Institute, its charter and by-laws: Institute premises: employment of Institute staff: donations to the Library and Collections: papers read at sessional meetings: publication of Institute papers: subjects for prize essays and drawings: election of Royal Gold Medal winners: presentation of medals and prizes, including the Royal Gold Medal: appointment of special committees: annual dinners and conversaziones: portraits of RIBA presidents: architectural examinations.

(Abstracts of proceedings at General Meetings were printed in *RIBA Proceedings* from 1845 onwards. In May 1885 this series split into two separate series, the Ordinary General Meetings Minutes Series and the Annual & Special General Meetings Minutes Series)

1.2.2 COUNCIL MINUTES & PAPERS, 1834— 31 vols & 54 binders
Signed minutes of proceedings at Council Meetings from Dec 1834 onwards, and of the annual joint meetings of the Council and the Allied Societies Conference for 1945, 1947—1951 & 1957—1959. The nineteenth century minutes often include transcripts or extracts of letters received and discussed by Council. Agenda papers are filed with the minutes from 1924, including reports of RIBA boards and standing committees: reports of special committees appointed by Council: reports of the RIBA Secretary, since the cessation of the Executive Committee in 1959: reports of the Chief Executive, 1976—1979: reports and accounts of subsidiary companies: reports of the Council to the AGM: drafts of petitions, memorials and parliamentary bills: drafts of Institute charters and by-laws: drafts of Institute regulations concerning architectural competitions, professional practice and conduct, schedule of charges etc.

4   Sketch by Richard Phené Spiers of a lively Special General Meeting at the RIBA in February 1876 at which important changes in the constitution of the Institute were discussed.
1 Frederick Pepys Cockerell (Hon. Sec.)   2 John Whichcord (Vice-President)   3 Charles Eastlake (Secretary)   4 William White   5 John Pollard Seddon   6 Robert Kerr   7 Thomas Leverton Donaldson   8 Arthur Cates   9 Horace Jones   10 Henry Dawson   11 Edmund Ferrey   12 The Silent Member   13 Ewan Christian   14 Thomas Roger Smith   15 Richard Phené Spiers

Subjects : Appointment of committees: committees' reports: nomination and election of members: appointment of employees: donations received: amalgamation with other societies: relations with other institutions: arrangements for papers to be read at General Meetings and lectures given: constitution of the Institute, with alterations to charter and by-laws and internal administrative reforms: Institute finances: Institute premises: government policy and legislation concerning building: professional status, conduct and regulations: architectural education: architectural competitions: statutory registration of architects: general policy matters

(For signed minutes of the annual joint meetings of the Council and the Allied Societies Conference for 1946, 1952 and 1956 *see* 12.1.2 Allied Societies Conference Minutes Series. For correspondence addressed to the Hon. Secretaries and the Council, 1835—1907, *see* 1.2.3 Letters to Council Series)

1.2.3   LETTERS TO COUNCIL, 1835—1907   41 boxes
Letters addressed to the President, the Honorary Secretaries including the Honorary Secretary for Foreign Correspondence, the Secretary, and various Council members, 1835—1907. The authors were mainly members, including honorary and foreign corresponding members, but there are also many letters from aristocrats, politicians, central and local government officials, other institutions and societies. Most of the letters were shown to the Council and many were quoted in the Council Minutes. Types of documents enclosed with the letters include petitions and memorials, draft reports by committees and conference secretaries, drafts of deeds and various RIBA official documents, reports and notices from Allied Societies, reports on prize essays, royal approvals of awards of the Royal Gold Medal, competition conditions and contract documents connected with cases of dispute, requisitions and draft resolutions for Special General Meetings, reports of prizewinners, applications for election or examination not approved by Council, returned membership certificates of members resigning in 1896.
Subjects : Original benefactions: donations of books, drawings and manuscripts to the Library and of casts, models and specimens of building materials to the Museum (later transferred to the Royal Architectural Museum and, later still, to the Victoria and Albert Museum): apologies for absence from meetings: acceptance of honours, such as election to office, the Royal Gold Medal and various prizes and studentships offered by the Institute: notifications of resignations, retirements and deaths of members: questions of professional conduct and professional charges: the proper conduct of architectural competitions: conservation and restoration of historic buildings: national and international exhibitions: architectural

education and examinations: the Metropolitan Building Acts and other government legislation affecting architects and builders: conditions of building contracts: artistic copyright and ownership of architectural drawings: terms of appointment for architects of public buildings: employment of surveyors: registration of architects: reforms of the Institute and changes to its charter and by-laws: improvement of the Institute's premises: news from eminent foreign architects, mostly French, German or Italian.

(This series is not complete, particularly after the retirement of William White in 1897. Some letters which were read out at General Meetings were bound up in volumes of the Papers Read at General Meetings Series (q.v.). Had they not been read out at these meetings they would have been filed with Letters to Council. From annotations on many of the letters it is evident that a series of out-letter books containing the Secretaries' replies was kept. Sadly, not one of these (probably a series of at least fifty wet-copy flimsy-paper leather-bound volumes) is known to have survived. Could they have gone in a war-time waste paper collection effort? For correspondence of the RIBA Secretary from 1919 onwards *see* Chapter 4 Section 1)

PAPERS READ AT GENERAL MEETINGS, 1835—1858
see   11.4.1

1.2.4   ANNUAL REPORTS OF COUNCIL, 1836—(1984)   149 items
Printed reports of the activities of the Council, committees and staff of the Institute, with annual balance sheets of accounts, read and discussed at the Annual General Meetings in May, 1836—(1983).

1.2.5   REPORTER'S NOTES OF GENERAL MEETINGS, 1850—1858   4 vols
Manuscript record of proceedings at Ordinary, Special and Annual General Meetings, Jan 1850—Jun 1858, including accounts (often verbatim) of business discussions and discussions of papers read at Ordinary General Meetings.
Subjects : Papers read at meetings (*see* 11.4.1 Papers Read at General Meetings Series): award and presentation of the Royal Gold Medal, the RIBA Silver Medals and the Soane Medal: alterations of the RIBA by-laws.

(From these manuscripts the official accounts of meetings were prepared for publication in the *RIBA Proceedings* 1st Series, with the texts of the papers read.)

1.2.6   ORDINARY GENERAL MEETINGS MINUTES, 1885—1962   4 vols

Signed minutes of Ordinary General Meetings and Business General Meetings, Nov 1885—Mar 1962, with deeds of award of prizes and medals made annually by the Council, 1890—1962. Also included are the signed minutes of the following (which should have been entered in the Annual and Special General Meetings Minutes Series): Special General Meetings for election of Royal Gold Medal winners in Mar 1895, 1896, 1897 and 1906: Special General Meeting to amend regulations concerning election of Fellows, May 1906: Annual General Meetings in May 1907 & 1908.

Subjects : Elections of new members: record of decease, expulsion and reinstatement of members: results of elections for Council and for the four departmental standing Committees of Art, Literature, Practice & Science: discussion of reports of the four departmental committees: record of the titles and authors of papers read at General Meetings: presentation of RIBA prizes and studentships, the Royal Gold Medal, the London Architecture Bronze Medal, the Diploma of Distinction in Town Planning: record of those awarded certificates of competency to act as district surveyors or building surveyors (Vol 1): results of the RIBA Examination in Architecture (Vol 1): donations to the Institute (Vol 1): RIBA presidents' portraits: amendments to the charter and by-laws: professional practice regulations: proposals to memorialise government and other bodies: controversial public building projects.

(General Meetings ceased with the outbreak of the Second World War so there are no minutes between Jul 1940 and Oct 1946. For minutes of Ordinary General Meetings before Nov 1885 *see* 1.2.1 General Meetings Minutes (Early Series). It was resolved in Feb 1961 to keep no more minutes of General Meetings, but the proceedings at Ordinary General Meetings continued to be recorded in these volumes until Mar 1962).

1.2.7   ANNUAL AND SPECIAL GENERAL MEETINGS MINUTES, 1885—1968   2 vols
Signed minutes of proceedings at Annual General Meetings, May 1885—May 1964, and at Special General Meetings, 1885—Jun 1968.

AGM subjects : Election of members of Council and of the four departmental standing committees of Art, Literature, Practice and Science until 1888 and, subsequently, election of scrutineers to direct those elections and report results to the next Ordinary General Meeting: discussion and adoption of the annual report of the Council, the auditors and the chairmen of the departmental committees: election of the Honorary Auditors: annual appointment of the (statutory) Board of Examiners: announcement of the names of those awarded certificates of competence to act as district or building surveyors (until 1898): announcement of names of candidates nominated for election as RIBA members (until 1917).

Special General Meetings subjects : Election of Royal Gold Medal winners (until 1930): selection of subjects for RIBA medals, prizes and studentships and adjudication of the entries (until 1889): financial accounts, including sale of stock to meet extraordinary expenditure: leasing, mortgaging, buying or selling of Institute premises: amendment of the charter and by-laws: alliance with architectural societies outside the London area — the 'Allied Societies': architectural education and compulsory examinations: statutory registration of architects: amalgamation with the Society of Architects: regulations for the conduct of architectural competitions: schedules of professional charges: forms and conditions of building contracts: scheme for the unification of the profession, 1920—1922: classes and conditions of RIBA membership: qualifications for election as Fellow.

(For signed minutes of the Special General Meetings for the election of Royal Gold Medal winners in Mar 1895, 1896, 1897 and 1906, and of the Special General Meeting on election of Fellows, May 1906, and of the Annual General Meetings in May 1907 and 1908 *see* 1.2.6 Ordinary General Meetings Minutes Series, Vol 2.
No Annual General Meetings were held in the years 1940—1943.
For minutes of Annual General Meetings and Special General Meetings before May 1885 *see* 1.2.1 General Meetings Minutes (early series).
For verbatim transcripts of proceedings at Annual General Meetings and Special General Meetings from 1965—1971, and 1973 onwards *see* 1.2.8 General Meetings Transcripts Series).

1.2.8   GENERAL MEETINGS TRANSCRIPTS, 1961, 1965—1971, 1973—(1982)   3 boxes
Verbatim transcripts of proceedings at Annual General Meetings and Special General Meetings. Tapes are also available for consultation.

(Minutes of Ordinary General Meetings ceased to be kept in 1962: of Annual General Meetings, in 1964: and of Special General Meetings in 1968).

Bibliography

1   'Representation of Associates on the Council' *RIBA Journal* Vol 19 1912 Mar 9 pp346—350
2   'Report of the committee on the constitution of the Council' *RIBA Journal* Vol 62 1955 May pp279—281
3   Bradbury, Ronald 'Mistress Parliament. The RIBA Council in session' *RIBA Journal* Vol 63 1956 May pp286—288

1 *Foundation, constitution and government*

4 'Making STV work' *RIBA Journal* Vol 79 1972 Feb pp69—70. Article on the new single transferable vote system used for electing the Council

2
Early Committees and Special Committees Minutes Series

Before the establishment in 1886 of the four large departmental standing committees of Art, Science, Practice and Literature much of the Institute's work was carried out either by the honorary officers, the Secretary with his assistants and the Librarian, or by special committees appointed either by the Council or the General Body. Many of these special committees developed into standing committees. Apart from the Library and the Board of Architectural Education, the work of the RIBA was not truly departmentalized until the 1950s, most of the administrative work up till then having been performed by the Secretary, the Deputy Secretary and the staff of the General Office.

The earliest volume of minutes of committees, the Early Committees Minutes Series, begins in 1847. The earliest Institute committee concerned with other than purely internal administrative matters was appointed in 1836 to examine the Elgin Marbles to see if colour had been used in their decoration (see 9.1). The next committee of any importance was appointed in 1838 to consider the conduct of architectural competitions for public buildings. Its minutes have not survived but a draft of its report can be seen in the Public Competitions for Architectural Design Committee Papers Series (see 11.5.1). Other committees appointed by Council before 1847 included a committee on practice with regard to dilapidations and fixtures in 1842, a committee on professional charges in 1845 and a committee on the improvement of the Metropolitan Buildings Act appointed in 1845.

After the Early Committees Minutes volume comes a magnificent series of ten volumes, the Special Committees Minutes Series, containing the minutes of meetings of over 200 special committees, subcommittees of Council, some subcommittees of standing committees, some joint meetings of committees and conferences with delegates of other institutions.

2.1   EARLY COMMITTEES MINUTES, 1847—1868   1 vol
Signed minutes of meetings of twenty-four committees, Apr 1847 — Dec 1868, including the Finance Committee, 1864—1868, the Professional Practice Committee, 1866—1867, and the Conservation of Ancient

Monuments and Remains Committee, 1864—1868, which later had their own separate series. Contains the following committees, many of which were very short-lived:

Ancient Lights Committee, Jun 1865 — Dec 1866

Appointment of a Paid Secretary Committee, Jun—Aug 1866

Architects Benevolent Fund Committee, Apr 1847 — Dec 1848

Artistic Architectural Education Committee, May 1864 — Nov 1868

Artistic Copyright Committee, May 1860 — Jun 1861

Britton Memorial Committee, Feb — May 1857

Cockerell Portrait Committee, Jun 1861

Conservation of Ancient Monuments and Remains Committee, Nov 1864 — Mar 1868

Conversazione Committee, Mar 1850 — Jun 1868

Experiments and Professional Investigations Committee (Monsieur Rochas' process for hardening stone), Jan—Apr 1854

Finance Committee, Feb 1864 — Dec 1868

Lighting and Ventilation Committee (of the Institute's meeting room at 9 Conduit Street), Jun—Aug 1863

Metropolis Buildings Bill, Mar—May 1851

Metropolitan Buildings Bill 1855 Committee, May 1855

Metropolitan Improvements Committee, Jan 1864

New Premises Committee, Nov 1850 — Jul 1857

Preserving the Open Space adjoining St. Paul's Churchyard Committee, May 1854 — Jan 1858

Professional Practice Committee, Aug 1866 — Apr 1867

Proposed Purchase of the International Exhibition Buildings at South Kensington Committee, Jun 1863

Public Health Bill 1855 Committee, Mar 1855

Publication of Papers Read Subcommittee of Council, Jul 1862

Pugin Memorial Committee, May 1863—Feb 1865

Tite Portrait Committee, Jul 1868

Voluntary Architectural Examination Committee, Feb 1860 — Jun 1868

2.2 SPECIAL COMMITTEES MINUTES, 1868—1955   10 vols

Signed minutes of meetings of 223 committees, including special committees appointed by Council or the General Body, subcommittees of Council and of some standing committees, joint meetings of committees, and conferences with delegates of other institutions. Some of the committees were very short-lived while some others split off at various stages to become separate record series. The minutes often include transcripts of letters received by committees, drafts of memoranda and reports. Contains the minutes of the following committees:

Admission of Fellows Committee of Council, Feb 1884

Advisory Appointments Committee *see* War Office Advisory Appointments Committee

Advisory Council of the Architects War Committee, Mar 1917

Affairs of the Institute Committee, May—Oct 1875

Allied Societies and the RIBA Joint Committee, Oct 1917—Mar 1918

Air Raid Precautions and the Protection of Industry Conference Organising Committee, Feb 1942

Allied Societies Resolutions Committee, May 1918

Alterations to the Premises of the Institute Committee *see* Building Committee of Council

Ancient Lights Joint Committee (RIBA & Surveyors' Institution), Jul 1900—Feb 1904

Annual Dinner Committee, Jun 1897—May 1914, Feb 1922—Apr 1925

Application of Major Morant, R.E., Hon. Associate, to be admitted as a Fellow Special Committee of Council Meeting, Nov 1884

Applications for Deferment of Military Service Committee *see* Deferment of Military Service Committee

Architects' and Surveyors' Assistants Professional Union and the RIBA Joint Conference, Mar —May 1924

Architects and the Organisation of the Building Industry Subcommittee (of the War Executive Committee), Jan —Feb 1942

Architects War Committee, Aug —Oct 1914, Feb —Nov 1917

Architects War Committee (Advisory Council) *see* Advisory Council of the Architects War Committee

Architects War Committee & Executive and General Purposes Committee Joint Meetings, Apr —Jun 1917

Architects War (Executive and General Purposes) Committee *see* Executive and General Purposes Committee (of the Architects War Committee)

Architects War (Selection) Committee *see* Selection Subcommittee (of the Architects War Committee)

Architectural Alliance Subcommittee of Council, Nov 1871

Architectural Association and the RIBA Joint Meeting (on the Allied Societies conference to discuss unification in the architectural profession), Oct 1941

Architectural Education, Board of *see* Board of Architectural Education

Architectural Education Committee, Jul —Nov 1903

Architectural Examination Committee, Apr 1873—Jul 1880

Architectural Gallery at the Royal Academy Committee, Jul —Oct 1869

Art, Science, Literature, and Practice Standing Committees & the Town Planning and Housing Committee Joint Meeting (on the Royal Commission on Greater London), Feb 1922

Art and Science Standing Committees & the Town Planning and Housing Committee Joint Meeting, Feb 1922

5   Cartoon by Fred May of a RIBA Dinner held in the Florence Hall at the RIBA Building, 66 Portland Place in 1939. (British Architectural Library Drawings Collection)

Assessorships Committee (for architectural competitions), Apr 1902

Baden Competition Committee (RIBA Industrial Housing Competition sponsored by Bertram Baden, a director of Matthew Hall & Co.), Jul 1940

Barnet Competition Committee (Barnet Municipal Offices Competition), Feb 1914

Board of Architectural Education, Jun 1904—Dec 1906

Board of Architectural Education and Board of Examiners Joint Committee, Jun 1907—Feb 1909

Board of Architectural Education Appointment Subcommittee of Council, Apr 1910

Board of Examiners, May 1881—Apr 1882

Board of Examiners and Architectural Education Joint Committee *see* Board of Architectural Education and Board of Examiners Joint Committee

Board of Examiners in Architecture *see* Board of Examiners

Board of Examiners under By-Law 14 *see* Board of Examiners

Board of Professional Defence (sometimes gave grants to support architects involved in legal proceedings if it was considered to be in the interest of the profession), Feb 1904—Apr 1914

Board of Professional Defence & Competitions Committee Joint Conference, Mar 1908

Bomb-struck Buildings Committee, Oct 1917

Bridges and Traffic Committee of the Thames Bridges Conference, Oct—Nov 1925

Building after the War Conference, Jan —Mar 1918

Building Committee of Council (alterations to the Institute's premises), May—Dec 1879

Building Industries Consultative Board, Jun 1919—May 1921

Building Regulations for the United Kingdom Committee *see* General Building Regulations Committee

By-Law 9 Committee, Dec 1891—Mar 1892

By-Laws Revision Committee (became a subcommittee of the Constitutional Committee in Jul 1913), Feb 1911—Jun 1913

Central Consultative Board for Housing in the London Area, Jul 1919

Charing Cross and Victoria Embankment Approach Act (Clause 30) Committee, Feb 1877

Charing Cross Bridge Joint Committee, Mar 1916—Nov 1918

Charter and By-Laws Committee, Apr 1887—Feb 1888

Charter and By-Laws Revision Committee, Oct 1908—Dec 1910

Charter Committee, Oct 1884—Nov 1886, Aug 1919—Apr 1920

Charter Revision Committee, Jun 1906—Oct 1908

Civic Survey Conference (scheme for temporary employment of distressed architects and surveyors), Apr 1915

Civic Survey Subcommittee (of the Civic Survey Conference), Jun 1915

Classes of Membership Committee (concerning establishment of a new class of non-professional members, the Honorary Associateship), Dec 1920

Committee of the Council Special Meetings *see* Special Meetings of the Committee of the Council

Competitions Committee (concerned with particular architectural competitions and complaints about their conditions), Jan 1883—Jun 1920

Competitions Committee & Board of Professional Defence Joint Conference *see* Board of Professional Defence & Competitions Committee Joint Conference

Conditions of Contract Committee, Dec 1898—Mar 1900, Mar 1919

Conditions of Contract Revision Committee, Jun 1914—Jun 1915

Conditions of Membership Subcommittee of Council, Jun 1921

Conference (1881) General Committee, Feb —May 1881

Conference (1884) General Committee, Feb —Apr 1884

Conference (1887) Committee, Feb —Mar 1887

Congress Committee of Council *see* General Architectural Congress Committee

Constitutional Committee, Apr 1913—Feb 1915

Consultants Fees Joint Subcommittee (RIBA & the Association of Consulting Engineers), Nov 1933

Conversazione Committee, Jun 1875, May 1882

Copyright Bill Committee, Sep 1910—Jan 1911

Copyright of Architects Drawings Committee, Jan 1877

Cost of Building during and after the War Committee, Apr 1915

Council Dinner Club, Jul 1912

Council for the Preservation of Rural England & RIBA Advisory Panel for the Harrow District of Middlesex Joint Meeting, Jun 1933

Council, Practice & Science Standing Committees Joint Meeting (on Canadian timber), Mar 1918

Deferment of Military Service Committee, Aug 1941—Jul 1944

Deputation Subcommittee of the Architects War Committee (deputation to Neville Chamberlain concerning the employment of architects), Jan 1917

Deputation to the Department of Scientific and Industrial Research Committee, Jun 1924

Development of Towns and Suburbs Committee *see* Town Planning and Housing Committee

Ecclesiastical Commissioners and Parsonage Houses Committee, Oct 1912

Ecclesiastical Dilapidations Bill Committee, Jun 1869

Education of the Public Committee, Jan —Feb 1905

Establishment of a Drawing School for Architectural Students Committee, Nov 1869

Examinations Committee, Mar —Apr 1909

Examinations; By-Law 14 Committee, Jul 1879—Feb 1880

Examiners, Board of *see* Board of Examiners

Executive and General Purposes Committee (of the Architects War Committee), Sep 1914—Apr 1920

Exemption of Service Candidates Conference (exemption of war service candidates from the RIBA Final Examination), Jan 1920

Exhibition of Architecture Paris 1914 Joint Organising Committee *see* Paris Exhibition (1914) Joint Committee

Export Group for the Constructional Industries & the RIBA Joint Meeting, Apr 1946

Facilities for Young Architects to set up in Practice Ad Hoc Committee, Jan —Mar 1946

Federation Committee (to consider federation with other architectural bodies in the U.K. and the colonies), Mar —Dec 1886

Fees for Housing Work Committee, Apr 1933—Mar 1934

Fellows Committee (to consider changing the rules for the admission of Fellows), Feb 1896—Mar 1897

Fine Arts Copyright Consolidation and Amendment Bill Committee, May 1869

Fire Prevention Circular Committee, Sep 1911

Freehold Premises at 20 Hanover Square Subcommittee of Council (as possible new premises for the RIBA), May 1883

Future of Architecture Committee and Subcommittee, Jun 1918—Mar 1919

General Architectural Congress Committee, Feb —May 1900

General Building Regulations Committee, Jun —Dec 1876

General Conference of Architects Committee, Apr 1871—Jun 1878

Greater London Town Planning Joint Conference of Delegates, Jun 1913

Health Conference Committee (to arrange a conference of architects at the International Health Exhibition), May—Jun 1884

Henry Jarvis Bequest Committee *see* Jarvis Bequest Committee

Honorary Members Committee, Mar 1910, Apr 1915

Houses of National Importance Committee, Mar —Apr 1949

Housing after the War Committee *see* Housing Committee

Housing Committee, Aug 1917—Feb 1918

Housing (Fees) Committee, Dec 1923—Mar 1925

Housing for the Working Classes after the War Committee *see* Housing Committee

Housing Production Ad Hoc Committee, Feb —Mar 1945

Housing Production Conference, Jan 1945

Hulot Drawings Committee (drawings of Louis Jean Hulot and Honore Daumet for exhibition), May 1908

Improvement Committee (improvement of Ordinary Meetings and the papers read), May—Jun 1880

Improvement of the Institute Committee (concerned with reform of the constitution), Mar 1876—Feb 1877

Improvement of the RIBA Premises Committee *see* Premises Committee

Improving the Premises Committee *see* Premises Committee

Informal Conferences Committee, Dec 1916

Information for Members on RIBA Activities Ad Hoc Committee, Nov 1944—Nov 1945

Institute Dinner Committee, Jun 1869, Mar 1879

Institute of Builders & the National Federation of Building Trades Employers & the RIBA Joint Conferences, Jun 1915 & Apr 1919

Institute of Builders & the RIBA Joint Meeting (on forms of contract), Oct 1934

Institute Special Committee on Competitions *see* Competitions Committee

(VIIth) International Congress of Architects Executive Committee, May 1904—Sep 1906

International Exhibition of Architecture and the Decorative Arts Committee, Mar 1908—Jun 1909

Irish Societies Committee, Jan —May 1916

Jarvis Bequest Committee, Apr 1911—Jan 1912

Journal and Kalendar Subcommittee (of the Literature Standing Committee), Feb 1912—Jun 1915

Junior Organisation Committee, Apr 1947—May 1949

Lambeth Bridge Committee, Dec 1911—Feb 1912

Librarianship Subcommittee *see* Selection Committee for the Librarianship

Library Administration Committee, Jun 1896

Licentiates Admission Subcommittee (of the Parliamentary Bill Committee), May—Sep 1910

Licentiates and the Fellowship Committee, Oct 1912

Light and Air Committee, Feb 1882—Jun 1883

London Building Act Amendment Bill Committee, Jan 1903—May 1905

London Building Acts Committee, Apr — Nov 1920

London Master Builders Association & the RIBA Joint Meetings, Mar 1925

London Society's Prize Subcommittee, Nov 1913—Mar 1914

Manchester Meeting and Dinner Committee, Feb 1926

Materials and Construction Committee, May 1876

Methods of Improving Facilities for Young Architects to set up in Practice Ad Hoc Committee *see* Facilities for Young Architects, etc.

Metropolis Management and Building Acts Amendment Bill 1878 Committee, Feb 1878—Feb 1879

Metropolitan Board of Works By-Laws Committee, Mar 1886

Metropolitan Buildings and Management Bill Committee, Feb 1868—Jun 1874

Metropolitan Water Board Lead Services Subcommittee, Apr 1924

Ministry of Health and the RIBA Joint Meeting, Mar 1922

Ministry of Town and Country Planning Ad Hoc Committee *see* Town and Country Planning Bill Ad Hoc Committee

Municipal Officials and Architectural Work Committee, Feb 1904

Municipal Officials and Public Works Committee *see* Municipal Officials and Architectural Work, etc.

National Cottage Building Deputation (to the Board of Agriculture and Fisheries), Mar 1914

National Federation of Building Trades Employers & the RIBA Joint Conferences, Dec 1923—Feb 1925

New Addenda to By-Laws of the Metropolitan Board of Works Committee *see* Metropolitan Board of Works By-Laws Committee

New Charter Committee *see* Charter Committee

New Government Offices Competition Committee of Council Meeting, Oct 1883

Nominations for the Special Election to the Fellowship and to the Honorary Associateship Committee of Council, Dec 1921

Official Architects and the Fellowship Committee of Council, Feb 1922

Official Architecture Committee and Subcommittees, Oct 1912—Feb 1915

Organisation of Future British Architects Conferences Ad Hoc Committee, Oct 1953

Organisation of the Architects War Committee Subcommittee (of the Executive and General Purposes Committee of the Architects War Committee), Jun 1917

Overcrowding of the Architectural Profession Joint Committee (RIBA & the Association of Architects, Surveyors and Technical Assistants, formerly the Architects' and Surveyors' Assistants Professional Union), Dec 1924—Jul 1925

Paper of Instructions to Architects issued by H.M. Office of Works for the New Government Offices Competition Committee of Council *see* New Government etc.

Paris Exhibition Committee (Exposition Universelle, Paris, 1878), May 1877—Jan 1878

Paris Exhibition (1914) Joint Committee (RIBA & the Architectural Association), Jan —Feb 1914

Paris Exhibition Subcommittee (of the Finance Committee), Mar 1915

Parliamentary Bill Committee (for inclusion of Licentiates), Nov 1909—Nov. 1910

Payment of Examiners Committee (Board of Architectural Education & the Finance and House Committee), Nov 1913—Feb 1914

Permanent International Congress (British Section) Committee, Nov 1907—Jul 1908

Photographic Records Joint Subcommittee (of the Art & Literature Standing Committees), Nov 1924

Position and Privileges of Country Members Committee, Dec 1877—Feb 1878

Post War Hospital Building Committee, May 1946—Jun 1949

Prefabrication and Standardisation Subcommittee (of the War Executive Committee), Oct —Nov 1943

Premises Committee (for the improvement, decoration and repair of the Institute's premises), Jan 1878, Jul —Aug 1883, Oct 1909—Nov 1910

Presidents of Allied Societies Committee *see* Provinces of Allied Societies Committee

Private Practitioners and Official Architects Subcommittee (of the War Executive Committee), Oct 1943—Jun 1945

Privileges of Non-Metropolitan Fellows Committee of Council, Dec 1882

Prizes and Studentships Committee & Records Committee Joint Meeting, Mar 1909

Professional Advertisement Committee, Feb 1900

* Professional Conduct Subcommittee (of the Practice Standing Committee), Dec 1914—Mar 1915, Jul —Oct 1923

Professional Defence, Board of *see* Board of Professional Defence

Professional Questions Committee (questions by members concerning individual examples of professional practice, conduct and etiquette), May 1911—Jun 1914

Propaganda Joint Subcommittee (of the Deputation on Unemployment in the Building Industry), May—Jun 1932

Proposed Alteration of By-Law 31 Committee, Jun 1884

Proposed Alterations at Hyde Park Corner and the Removal of the Wellington Arch Committee of Council, Jun 1882

Proposed Annual Conference of Architects Committee, Feb —Mar 1871

Proposed Architectural Scholarship at Rome Committee, Oct 1911

Proposed Building Industries National Council Conference, Aug —Oct 1932

Proposed Central Council for the Building Industry Conference *see* Proposed Building Industries National Council Conference

Proposed School of Architecture in Italy Committee of Council, Dec 1908—May 1909

Provinces of Allied Societies Committee (concerning re-arrangement of their boundaries and their representation on the RIBA Council), Dec 1913—Mar 1914

Public Officials and Architectural Work Committee *see* Municipal Officials and Architectural Work Committee

Public Utility Society Subcommittee (to consider forming a national Public Utility Society to build low-rent houses), Oct 1932

Qualifications of Town Planners Committee, Nov 1942

Records Committee (concerned with forming a record of old buildings and with the preservation of architectural records generally), Jan 1909—Apr 1913

Reform of the Institute Special Meeting of Council, Feb 1876

Regents Park Terraces Subcommittee (of the Town and Country Planning Committee), Mar 1946

Registration Committee (1), Jul 1887—Feb 1888

Registration Committee (2), Mar 1904—Mar 1906

Registration Committee (3), Feb 1912—Mar 1913

Reinforced Concrete Joint Committee and Subcommittees, Mar —May 1906, Apr 1910—Jun 1917, Feb 1925

Rejection of Designs by Local Authorities Committee, Mar 1936

Report of the Allied Societies and the RIBA Joint Committee Committee of Council, Jul 1918

Report of the General Committee on Architectural Education Committee of Council, Jun 1869

Report of the Special Committee on Departmental Action Subcommittee of Council, Mar 1886

Review of the Architects (Registration) Acts Ad Hoc Committee, Mar 1955

RIBA and the Allied Societies Joint Committee *see* Allied Societies and the RIBA etc.

Royal Academy Exhibition Committee, Dec 1909

Royal Gold Medal Committee of Council Meeting (to report on future mode of election of Royal Gold Medallists), Nov 1882

Royal Gold Medal Committee of Council, 1883—1888, 1909, 1914—1917, 1920—1926

Rural District By-Laws Committee, Feb —Apr 1899

St. Paul's Bridge Committee (against the City of London (Bridges) Bill), Feb —Jun 1911

St. Paul's Bridge Conference (RIBA, Architecture Club, London Society & Town Planning Institute), Feb 1924—Jan 1925

St. Paul's Bridge Petition Committee *see* St. Paul's Bridge Committee

Scale of Charges Committee, May 1927—Apr 1935

Scale of Fees for Housing Schemes Committee, Aug 1919

Schedule of Charges Committee, Nov 1911—Mar 1913

Scheme for an Annual Conference of Architects at the Institute Committee *see* Proposed Annual Conference of Architects Committee

School Design and Construction Ad Hoc Committee, Mar —Dec 1945

Scientific Qualifications of Candidates for the Fellowship Committee, Nov 1933

Scrutineers Meeting (concerning voting procedure for annual elections of Council committees and departmental standing committees), Oct 1933

Secretarial Committee (to consider the appointment of a new Secretary), Feb —Apr 1897

Secretary Committee (concerning absence of Ian Macalister on active service), Dec 1918

Secretaryship Committee (to consider the appointment of a new Secretary and the position of other officials of the Institute), Nov 1907—Jan 1908

Selection Committee, Jul 1930

Selection and General Purposes Committee (selection of members of committees), Jul 1913—Jul 1915, Jul 1920

* Selection Committee for the Assistant Secretaryship, Jan 1951

* Selection Committee for the Librarianship, Oct 1930, Jun 1946, May 1948

Selection Subcommittee (of the Architects War Committee), Sep 1914—Jun 1918

Sessional Papers Committee, Oct 1873—Nov 1884, Mar 1908—Apr 1915, Mar 1920—Mar 1926

Sessional Papers and Informal Conferences Committee, Oct 1917—Oct 1918

Shortage of Skilled Labour Committee, Jan —Mar 1924

Site Committee (investigation of new site for RIBA premises), Feb 1900

Society of Architects Absorption Committee *see* Society of Architects Committee

Society of Architects and the RIBA Joint Conference, Jan 1911

Society of Architects Committee, May—Jun 1911

Special Competitions Committee (concerned with general regulations for architectural competitions), Jul 1908—Apr 1910

Special Education Committee, Mar 1886—Feb 1889

* Special Meetings of the Committee of the Council (called to discuss a variety of particular topics and individual cases), Jul 1915, Jan 1921—Mar 1927, Aug 1937

Staff Committee (concerning RIBA staff organisation and committee work), Mar —Apr 1921

Standardisation of Building Materials Subcommittee (of the War Executive Committee), Jan 1942

Stoppage of Building Committee, Jun —Nov 1920

Street Architecture Committee (proposed bronze medal award for best street façade), Dec 1920

Surveyors Institution & the RIBA Council Committee Joint Meeting, Mar 1924

Technical Institutions Committee, Jul 1898

Technical Institutions Committee & Association of Technical Institutions Conference, Oct 1898

Thames Bridges Conference (RIBA, Town Planning Institute, London Society, Society for the Protection of Ancient Buildings & the Royal Academy), Apr —Dec 1925

Timber Specification Committee, Feb 1916

Town and Country Planning Bill Ad Hoc Committee, Aug 1944

Town Planning and Housing Committee and subcommittees, Jul 1907— Nov 1920

Town Planning Committee *see* Town Planning and Housing Committee

Ulster Alliance Subcommittee of Council (concerning direct alliance of the Ulster Society of Architects with the RIBA), Nov 1908—Mar 1909

Ulster Subcommittee of Council *see* Ulster Alliance Subcommittee of Council

Unemployment in the Building Industry Conference, Mar —Jul 1932

Vauxhall Bridge Committee of Council, Feb 1899

Ventilation of the Meeting Room Committee, May 1875—Feb 1876

Voluntary Architectural Examination Committee, Nov 1869—Aug 1872

Voluntary Architectural Examiners & Moderators Meetings, Jun —Jul 1870

War Committee *see* Architects War Committee

War Memorial Subcommittee (concerning war memorial panels at 66 Portland Place), Nov 1946

War Office Advisory Appointments Committee, Oct 1940—Aug 1941

War Record Committee (for a tablet recording the names of all architects serving with H.M. forces), Jun —Jul 1915

Waterloo Bridge Conference (RIBA, Architecture Club, London Society, Society for the Protection of Ancient Buildings & Town Planning Institute), Feb —Sep 1926

Waterloo Bridge Conference Committee, May 1925—Sep 1926

Waterloo Bridge Conference Drafting Committee *see* Waterloo Bridge Conference Committee

Westminster Abbey Committee (concerning protection from war damage), Dec 1915

William Woodward Presentation Committee, Dec 1926

Working of the RIBA Scale of Charges Committee *see* Scale of Charges Committee

* Access at the discretion of the Archivist

3
Central policy and executive committees

This chapter contains committees concerned with central rather than departmental RIBA policy and with issues of great concern to the architectural profession as a whole, such as its optimum nature, its future, and the statutory registration of architects. Section 1 contains central policy-forming and executive committees concerned with the objectives of the RIBA, the optimum organization required to achieve those objectives, the administration of the Institute as a whole, and the policies it should adopt in its relations with national and local government departments and other bodies, such as related professional institutions. Section 2 contains policy-formulating and executive committees concerned with the question of the statutory registration of British architects, which was a dominating topic for more than fifty years.

Section 1 General

The Council was the main policy-formulating agency up to 1886. It was helped in the formulation of policy by many special committees appointed to consider particular topics and by some standing committees, of which the most significant were the Professional Practice Committee and the Conservation of Ancient Monuments and Remains Committee. Until 1886 the Council was a small and select body of Fellows resident in London. Subject only to the requirement of being elected to office by their fellow Fellows and to the sanction of Special General Meetings which could only be requisitioned by Fellows, they performed their function during the first thirty years of the Institute's life admirably, energetically and with great concern for the architectural profession. Increasingly, however, their policies were felt by the Associates, who formed the bulk of the membership, to be too restrictive, too 'metropolitan' (i.e. London-based) in outlook and undemocratic.

3 Central policy and executive committees

The events of 1884, the Associates Memorial and the formation of the Society of Architects, caused a significant change in the organization of the Institute's affairs. In 1886 the Council was greatly enlarged to include representatives of the Associates and of the Allied Societies (architectural societies outside the London area which had entered into formal alliance with the RIBA) and four partially elected departmental standing committees for Art, Science, Practice and Literature were established to coordinate the work of the Institute's numerous committees and to advise the Council on departmental policies. Inevitably, with the enlargement of the Council, the RIBA Secretary became an important policy-formulating figure working closely with the honorary officers in small committees of the Council.

At the outbreak of war in 1914 the Institute made an effort to form a body to speak for the entire profession. On the initiative of the RIBA a large committee was constituted which was broadly representative of the profession in the United Kingdom. It was called the Architects War Committee and included the presidents and vice-presidents of the Architectural Association and the Society of Architects, the presidents of the Allied Societies, several 'unattached' architects and some Royal Academicians. It was a very large committee which appointed a small Executive and General Purposes Committee as its policy-making and executive agent and several subcommittees (for the minutes of these committees, which met at the RIBA, see 2.2 Special Committees Minutes Series). Its main purposes were to liaise with the government on the use of architects in the war effort and to alleviate the distress caused by sudden widespread unemployment in the profession at that time (see Professional Employment Committee Minutes, Applications and Immediate Works Subcommittee Minutes and minutes of the Civic Survey committees, in Chapter 11 Section 6).

By 1925 the existing machinery for carrying on the work of the RIBA was becoming overstrained. The volume of work had increased greatly since the war and a new charter had significantly enlarged the Council, a substantial proportion of whose members now lived outside the London area. Its fortnightly meetings were becoming inconvenient and overloaded with business and it was therefore decided to meet once a month in future and to establish an Executive Committee of the Council, consisting of the President, the Honorary Secretary, the chairmen of the main standing committees and the chairman of the Allied Societies Conference. All RIBA committees except the Board of Architectural Education, were to report to the Council through the Executive Committee which had powers to deal summarily with all routine matters and all business requiring urgent attention and could appoint investigatory and policy-formulating subcommittees. The establishment of this Executive Committee and of several other important standing committees such as the Professional Conduct Committee and the Public Relations Committee which were independent of the old departmental standing committees of Art, Science, Practice and Literature set up in 1886, led to the disbanding of these old departmental committees in 1938/39.

In August 1939 the honorary officers of the Institute decided to suspend Council meetings, General Meetings and most committees' meetings and appointed a War

Executive Committee to act in all matters on behalf of the Council. In addition, in October 1940, the President appointed a small committee to make recommendations to the War Executive Committee on policy matters.

In May 1945 the War Executive Committee reverted to being the Executive Committee. It was discontinued in 1959 on the establishment of a small Policy Committee composed of the honorary officers. Its functions were then, and still are, to formulate policy, establish priorities, oversee the work of the RIBA departments and co-ordinate the work of the various committees. In 1967 the Finance and House Committee was discontinued and the Policy Committee was reconstituted as the Policy and Finance Committee.

In 1971 a state of financial crisis, caused both by the great expansion in the activities of the RIBA and a referendum of the membership which rejected Council's proposal for a large increase in subscriptions, led to the resignation of the Council and the disbanding of the Policy and Finance Committee. A new Policy Committee was established in 1972, separate from a new Finance and House Committee, and having several advisory groups covering most aspects of the Institute's work.

In the past the RIBA Secretary acted as Secretary to the Policy Committee but this function is now performed by the Assistant Clerk to the Council.

ARCHITECTS WAR COMMITTEE MINUTES, 1914—1917
(A joint committee with all the architectural societies)
see   2.2 Special Committees Minutes Series

ARCHITECTS REORGANISATION COMMITTEE MINUTES, 1917—1919
(A joint committee with all the architectural societies, which met at the Society of Architects)
see   Appendix 7. Archive of the Society of Architects

3.1.1   SELECTION AND GENERAL PURPOSES COMMITTEE MINUTES, 1921—1925   1 vol
Signed minutes of meetings, Jul 1921—Jul 1925.
Subjects : Recommendations concerning which committees to appoint and the numbers to serve on each: recommendation of names of members of boards and committees, for Council's consideration: scrutiny of the annual elections of members of Council and the four departmental standing committees.

(The work of this committee was taken over by the newly established Executive Committee in July 1925. For minutes of earlier Selection and General Purposes Committees, 1913—1915 and 1920 and of the Selection Subcommittee of the Architects War Committee, 1914—1918, *see* 2.2 Special Committees Minutes Series)

3.1.2 * EXECUTIVE COMMITTEE MINUTES, 1925—1959   1 vol &
11 binders
Signed minutes of meetings of the committee and its subcommittees and
of special meetings and joint meetings with other committees, Jul 1925—
Jun 1959. Includes transcripts of letters received, various memoranda,
and reports of most RIBA committees, including reports of the Recon-
struction Committee, 1941—1943.
Contains the minutes of the following subcommittees, special meetings
and joint meetings, listed in chronological order:
Development of the RIBA Subcommittee, Feb —Mar 1928
President, Vice-Presidents and Honorary Secretary Special Meeting, Feb
1930
Harpenden Hall Competition Subcommittee, Jun 1936
Honorary Associateship Subcommittee, Jan 1937
Hackney Baths Competition Subcommittee, Jul 1937
Executive Committee & Official Architects Committee Joint Meeting,
Dec 1937
Shrewsbury Senior School Competition Subcommittee, Apr 1939
President, Vice-Presidents & Officers of the Institute Meeting (re war-
time arrangements), Aug 1939
President's War Emergency Committee, Sep 1939
War Executive Committee, Oct 1939—Apr 1945
Honorary Officers Meeting, May 1940
War Executive Committee & Architectural Science Board Joint Meeting,
Jul 1942
War Executive Committee & Housing Committee Joint Meeting, Jan
1944
Registration Subcommittee, Mar —Apr 1946
Executive Committee, Public Relations Committee & Central Advisory
Planning Committee Joint Meeting, Oct 1948
Subjects : Consideration of the reports of other committees: consideration
of membership applications: appointment of subcommittees: nomina-
tion of members of RIBA committees: consideration of letters received:
relations with other organizations: international congresses: British
Architects Conferences: professional conduct complaints: general
RIBA policy and administration.

* Access at the discretion of the Archivist

3.1.3   NATIONAL EMERGENCY PANEL MINUTES, 1938—1939   1
vol
Signed minutes of the panel (also called the RIBA Emergency Panel)
and its committee, from Oct 1938—May 1939.

Subjects : Consultation with government departments concerning use of architects in war: enrolment of architects on a national register: training in military engineering: use of architects in ARP: temporary work for unemployed architects: planning for evacuation of towns and cities.

3.1.4   POLICY COMMITTEE OF THE WAR EXECUTIVE COM-MITTEE MINUTES, 1940—1943   1 vol
Signed minutes of meetings, Oct 1940—Aug 1943, with memoranda.
Subjects : Proposed Ministry of Works and Buildings: the 'problem' of the structural engineer: registration policy: unification of the architectural profession: post-war housing policy: the Committee for the Industrial and Scientific Provision of Housing: the Association of Building Technicians: the Building Surveyors Association: RIBA publicity: the status of the architect: reinstatement of architects after war service.

3.1.5   POLICY COMMITTEE ON DEVOLUTION AND QUALIFICA-TION FOR MEMBERSHIP MINUTES, 1956—1957   1 vol
Signed minutes of meetings, Dec 1956—Feb 1957.
Subjects : Devolution and RIBA examinations abroad: problem posed, since the Architects (Registration) Acts, by RIBA policy that the qualification for Associateship of the RIBA and the qualification for statutory registration in the U.K. should be identical: question of whether the RIBA was to become a Commonwealth society or one restricted to British subjects as members.

(For continuation *see* Overseas Examinations Panel Minutes, 1957—1959, in 7.1.4 Officers of the Board of Architectural Education Minutes Series, Binder 4)

3.1.6   POLICY COMMITTEE MINUTES & PAPERS, 1959—1967   1 vol & 4 boxes
Signed minutes of meetings, Jan 1960—Jun 1967, with agenda papers, policy memoranda, reports of Policy Committee Conferences, and correspondence file kept by the Secretary, RIBA, who acted as Secretary to the Policy Committee, 1959—1967. Also signed minutes of a meeting of chairmen of committees, 16 Jul 1962
Subjects : Organization, work and finances of the RIBA: regionalization of the RIBA: Policy Committee conferences: RIBA Bronze Medals: relations with government: public relations: architects in public offices: building industry staff study: activities of the Civic Trust.

HOUSE COMMITTEE MINUTES, 1963—1967
(A subcommittee of the Policy Committee)
see   5.3.12

MEMBERSHIP STEERING GROUP PAPERS, 1965—1966
(A group of the Policy Committee)
see   12.1.13

PATRONAGE WORKING GROUP PAPERS, 1966—1967
(A group of the Policy Committee)
see   11.6.11

3.1.7   POLICY AND FINANCE COMMITTEE MINUTES & PAPERS,
1967—1972   1 vol & 4 boxes
Signed minutes of meetings, Jul —Oct 1967, with copies of minutes,
agenda papers, policy memoranda, correspondence files kept by the
Secretary, Jul 1967—Mar 1972, and files on Policy and Finance Committee Conferences, including the signed minutes of the 1967 conference.
Subjects : Organization, work and finances of the RIBA: regionalization
of the RIBA: new charter for the RIBA: public relations: government
relations: membership relations: RIBA premises

FINANCE SUBCOMMITTEE MINUTES, 1967—1972
(A subcommittee of the Policy and Finance Committee)
see   5.2.15

HOUSE COMMITTEE MINUTES, 1967—1972
(A subcommittee of the Policy and Finance Committee)
see   5.3.12

NATIONAL BOARD FOR PRICES AND INCOMES & MON-
OPOLIES COMMISSION STEERING GROUP MINUTES &
PAPERS, 1967—1970
(A group of the Policy and Finance Committee)
see   8.2.25

PATRONAGE SUBCOMMITTEE PAPERS, 1968—1970
(A subcommittee of the Policy and Finance Committee)
see   11.6.12

CLIENTS BUREAU WORKING GROUP MINUTES & PAPERS,
1970—1972
(A group of the Policy and Finance Committee)
see   11.6.14

MONITORING GROUP PAPERS, 1971
(A group of the Policy and Finance Committee)
see   5.2.16

See also in 2.2 Special Committees Minutes Series:
Affairs of the Institute Committee, 1874—1875
Reform of the Institute Special Meeting of Council, 1876
Improvement of the Institute Committee, 1876—1877
Report of the Special Committee on Departmental Action Subcommittee of Council, 1886
Architects War Committee, 1914—1918
Executive and General Purposes Committee of the Architects War Committee, 1914—1920
Future of Architecture Committee, 1918—1919
and several of the series in Chapter 4, Sections 1 & 2

Bibliography

1   RIBA 'Report of the Council on the matters referred to their consideration by the Annual General Meeting held on the 7th May 1849' *RIBA Proceedings* 1st Series 1849/50 29 Oct 1949. A review of the position and prospects of the Institute

2   Tite, William 'Some remarks on the present condition and future prospects of architecture in England' *RIBA Transactions* 1st Series Vol 6 1855/56 pp1—10

3   Tite, William 'An address delivered at the first meeting of the Royal Institute of British Architects in the new rooms in Conduit Street' Copy bound in with *RIBA Proceedings* 1st Series 1859/60

4   RIBA 'Report of the Committee for the Improvement of the Institute, 1877' *RIBA Proceedings* 1st Series 1876/77 pp1—12

5   Kerr, Robert 'English architecture thirty years hence' *RIBA Transactions* 1st Series Vol 34 1883/84 pp218—230

6   White, William H. *The past, present and future of the architectural profession* London, Spottiswoode & Co, 1885

7   Kerr, Robert 'A suggestion for the performance of the higher work of the Institute by departmental committees' *RIBA Proceedings* New Series Vol 1 1885 Jun 11 pp218—219

8   'Report of the Special Committee on Departmental Action' *RIBA Proceedings* New Series Vol 2 1886 Feb 4 pp126—128

9   'The function of an architectural society' *RIBA Journal* Vol 25 1917 Dec pp29—40

10 Murray, John *The future of architecture and the architectural profession* London, RIBA, 1920

11 'The development of the RIBA' *RIBA Journal* Vol 36 1928 Dec 22 pp168—170

12 RIBA Council 'The RIBA and current affairs' *RIBA Journal* Vol 40 1933 Sep 9 pp804—805. A statement issued in response to the proposal for the formation of the Institute of Registered Architects

13   Carter, E. J. 'The case for a learned society' *RIBA Journal* Vol 45 1938 Jan 10 pp217—228

14   Holford, W. G. 'The next twenty years' *RIBA Journal* Vol 46 1938 Dec 19 pp165—174

15   RIBA Reconstruction Committee 'Reconstruction and the architectural profession' *RIBA Journal* Vol 49 1941 Dec pp21—23

16   'Institute affairs' *RIBA Journal* Vol 57 1950 Mar pp178—179, May pp285—286 & Jul pp351—353

17   RIBA Council 'RIBA committee structure and organisation' *RIBA Journal* Vol 67 1959 Nov pp19—23

18   'New model' *RIBA Journal* Vol 74 1967 Jul p259. Editorial leader on the new administrative organization of the RIBA

19   'Programme of work and priorities for the RIBA Boards' *RIBA Journal* Vol 75 1968 Jan pp11—12

20   Esher, Lord & Llewelyn-Davies, Lord 'The architect in 1988' *RIBA Journal* Vol 75 1968 Oct pp448—455. Paper written at the request of the PRIBA to provide the Policy & Finance Committee with a framework in which to plan the RIBA's educational and professional policies

21   Macleod, Robert 'The life and death of the profession' *RIBA Journal* Vol 78 1971 Apr pp151—153

22   MacEwen, Malcolm 'The professional dilemma' *RIBA Journal* Vol 78 1971 May pp188—193

23   Harrison, Patrick 'Inside the RIBA: Secretary Harrison talks frankly to the AJ' *Architects' Journal* Vol 153 1971 Jun 23 pp1388—1394

24   'What should we be doing?' *RIBA Journal* Vol 79 1971 Nov pp460—462. Paper for Council on RIBA priorities

25   RIBA Intelligence Unit 'Objectives in the seventies' *RIBA Journal* Vol 78 1971 Nov pp494—497. Article on the recent history of the RIBA and the need for changes in the Institute's objectives

26   Luder, Owen 'A new strategy for the RIBA' *Building* 1971 Dec 10 pp73—74

27   Gordon, Alex 'Architecture: for love or money?' *RIBA Journal* Vol 78 1971 Dec pp535—540. Presidential address concerned with the role of the RIBA

28   'RIBA cuts: staff revolt' *Architects' Journal* 2 Feb 1972 p233. Editorial leader on the 'Grey paper' submitted by a group of RIBA staff to the RIBA Policy and Finance Committee 15 Jan 1972

29   RIBA Policy & Finance Committee. 'Finance and policy' *RIBA Journal* Vol 79 1972 Mar pp95—97

30   RIBA Policy & Finance Committee 'What kind of Institute?' *RIBA Journal* Vol 79 1972 May pp179—181

31   RIBA Monitoring Group 'The structure of financial control' *RIBA Journal* Vol 79 1972 May pp182—183 & 217. Paper on financial control within the Institute and the regions, the structure of the RIBA companies and their relationship to the Institute.

32 'Renewing the RIBA' *RIBA Journal* Vol 79 1972 Jun pp225—227. Article by a group of RIBA staff

33 'Where should our work be done?' *RIBA Journal* Vol 80 1973 Jan pp13—14. Paper for Council on the future policy and structure of the RIBA

34 'How should our work be done?' *RIBA Journal* Vol 80 1973 Mar pp126—128. Paper for Council on the future policy and structure of the RIBA

35 RIBA Council 'RIBA action programme: responding to a crisis' *RIBA Journal* Vol 80 1973 May pp224—227. Statement on the objectives, organization, structure and financial management of the RIBA

36 'A two year programme' *RIBA Journal* Vol 80 1973 Aug pp389—390. A paper for Council on a new board structure for the RIBA

37 MacEwen, Malcolm *Crisis in architecture* London, RIBA Publications Ltd, 1974

38 Jones, Nicholas 'Are there better uses for the Institute's building?' *RIBA Journal* Vol 82 1975 Jan p19. Report of a discussion meeting on Malcolm MacEwen's proposal to turn the RIBA headquarters into an Architecture Centre, with a modified membership structure that would include clients, users and members of allied professions

39 'Pruning can be fruitful' *RIBA Journal* Vol 82 1975 Apr, supplement ppi—iv. Report of the senior Vice-President's group on the restructuring of the Institute, the 'Lyons Report'

40 Edmonds, Don 'RIBA restructure' *RIBA Journal* Vol 83 1976 May p167.

Section 2 Statutory registration of architects

The preoccupying policy issue of statutory registration of architects led to the appointment of many RIBA registration special committees from 1887 onwards, leading to a standing Registration Committee from 1924—1959. In 1884 a campaign by a group of Associates of the RIBA to be allowed to vote on the Institute's affairs was resisted by the Fellows and resulted in the formation of the Society of Architects. One of the main interests of that society was to campaign for the compulsory examination and registration of architects. In 1887 an independent committee, the Architects and Engineers Registration Act Committee, promoted a bill for the registration of architects, engineers and surveyors. The chief bodies representing engineers and surveyors petitioned against it and the bill was withdrawn. In 1889 and 1891 the Architects Registration Bill Committee put forward bills for the registration of architects which were strongly supported by the Society of Architects

6 Letter to the RIBA Council by Hugh Roumieu Gough, chairman of the independent Architectural Federation Committee, which later that year became the Architects & Engineers Registration Act Committee. It was one of the early moves in the very long campaign to introduce the statutory registration of British architects. In this letter, dated 25 April 1887, the committee seeks the support of the RIBA for a draft bill which proposed to constitute the RIBA the sole examining body in architecture for England. Acts for the registration of architects were not achieved until 1931 and 1938. (RIBA Archive:1.2.3   Letters to Council Series)

but opposed by the RIBA and by an independent group of prominent architects and artists known as the Memorialists, who objected to the principle of a qualifying examination for architects.

In December 1902 the Architects Registration Bill Committee was amalgamated with the Council of the Society of Architects as a joint Registration Committee, chaired by the President of the Society of Architects, and further unsuccessful attempts to pass private member's bills were made. By 1905 it was evident that the profession as a whole was in favour of registration and the RIBA Council decided in principle that the satisfactory training of architects could only be obtained by statutory powers. The aim was to ensure that no-one should have the legal right to the title 'architect' unless he had been trained to a high standard and had his qualifications tested by a competent authority. So the policy was adopted that statutory registration was to be obtained by and through the RIBA, as the only existing body which could claim to be a competent authority. This feeling was strengthened by a fear that the creation of a new statutory body would diminish the RIBA's hard-earned authority and influence and might even lead eventually to its extinction. There was no possibility of a registration act reaching the Statute Book until the great majority of British architects were agreed on the constitution of the body which would administer the act. It was in the interests of the RIBA, therefore, to increase its membership to the extent that it could convincingly claim to speak for British architects as a whole. The problem was how to do this without lowering its standards. It was obviously impracticable to expect large numbers of the 'unattached' practising architects to sit the RIBA qualifying examination but to open the Associateship to entry without examination was unacceptable.

Accordingly, in 1908 a class of Licentiate membership was created, open without examination to architects who could show evidence of their competence. The class was closed in 1913, by which time over 2000 applications had been accepted, and the RIBA then drafted a registration bill, the introduction of which to Parliament was prevented by the outbreak of war. Although an amalgamation and registration scheme had first been agreed by the councils of the RIBA and the Society of Architects in 1911, it was not until 1925 that the amalgamation was achieved, with most of the members of the Society of Architects transferring to the reopened RIBA Licentiate class.

The RIBA Registration Committee then drafted a bill, introduced to Parliament in 1927, stipulating that the RIBA was to become the statutory body. Opposition was mounted by the Incorporated Association of Architects and Surveyors and by the Faculty of Architects and Surveyors and in 1931 the RIBA Council had to decide between dropping the bill completely and recasting it. It chose the second course and in July the Architects (Registration) Act 1931 was passed, which authorized the setting up of an Architects Registration Council of the United Kingdom (ARCUK) which was to comprise representatives of all architectural bodies in the U.K. in proportion to the numbers on the register of their respective members, together with a limited number of representatives appointed by certain government departments and related professional bodies. The ARCUK Council and its boards and committees, therefore, have always contained substantial majorities of RIBA representatives. The Act also constituted a Board of Architectural Education to set up statutory examinations and lay down conditions of training for admission to the register. In the event, the system of examinations and exemptions evolved by the RIBA was ratified as the one and only method of qualifying as an architect, largely because the qualifying standards set by all other bodies were found to be inadequate.

For a limited period after the passing of the Act admission to the register was open to anyone who was practising as a principal architect or who had been in practice for a specified time as an assistant architect. Provision was made for the disciplining of registered architects found guilty of unprofessional conduct. Architects enrolled on the register were entitled to use the title 'Registered Architect' but there was nothing to stop an unregistered person from describing himself or herself as an 'Architect'. A second act was passed in 1938 which restricted the use of any description containing the word 'Architect' to those enrolled on the register (with the exception of 'Naval Architect', 'Landscape Architect' and 'Golf-course Architect'). This does not prevent unregistered and unqualified persons acting as architects under such titles as 'Architectural Consultant' or 'Architectural Surveyor'. Further attempts were made to amend the Acts but it was a political impossibility to obtain legislation ensuring that no buildings in this country would be erected without the services of an 'Architect'. This would have been regarded as monopoly legislation in favour of the profession rather than a public measure for the good of the community as a whole, and as a restriction on the liberty of the subject.

In 1969 the Architects Registration (Amendment) Act was passed, repealing Section 14 of the 1931 Act with the purpose of enabling grants to be made out of registration fees for the support and furtherance of education and research in architecture. Registration has provided only partial protection of both the public and architects and remains an important policy issue, with a significant body of opinion in favour of repeal of the present Acts.

See also Appendix 7. Archive of the Society of Architects, 1884—1926.

3.2.1   UNIFICATION AND REGISTRATION COMMITTEE MINUTES & PAPERS, 1920—1922   1 vol & 1 box
Signed minutes of meetings of the committee and its subcommittees, Jul 1920—May 1922, with memoranda and reports and a file of correspondence by [Sir] Ian Macalister, Secretary to the committee, May 1920—May 1922, including material concerning the Future of Architecture Committee going back to 1918.
Subjects : Unification of the profession: statutory registration of architects.

(This committee was first known as the Unification Committee. 'Unification' meant bringing into the RIBA the professional members of the

Society of Architects, the Architectural Association and the Allied Societies, and properly qualified architects unattached to professional societies. It was a joint committee consisting of representatives of the RIBA, the Allied Societies, the Architectural Association, the Society of Architects, the Architects' and Surveyors' Assistants Professional Union, the Official Architects Association and the Ulster Society of Architects. For minutes of earlier registration committees, 1887—1888, 1904—1906, 1912—1913; minutes of the Society of Architects Committee, 1911, and minutes of the Future of Architecture Committee *see* 2.2 Special Committees Minutes Series)

3.2.2 ASSOCIATES COMMITTEE MINUTES, 1921—1922   1 vol
Signed minutes of meetings, Jun 1921—Oct 1922, with the report of the Conditions of Membership Subcommittee (representing the councils of the RIBA and the Society of Architects).
Subjects : Unification of the profession: statutory registration of architects: terms of absorption of the Society of Architects into the RIBA.

(For minutes of the Conditions of Membership Subcommittee *see* 2.2 Special Committees Minutes Series)

3.2.3 REGISTRATION COMMITTEE (4) MINUTES, 1922—1923   1 vol
Signed minutes of meetings of the committee and its subcommittee, Jul 1922—Feb 1923, with draft registration bill and comments by the councils of the Allied Societies.
Subject : Drafting of a Registration of Architects Bill.

(For minutes of previous registration committees *see* 2.2 Special Committees Minutes Series)

3.2.4 * REGISTRATION COMMITTEE (5) MINUTES, 1924—1959   2 vols
Signed minutes of meetings of the Registration Committee, Dec 1924—Dec 1959, the Amending Act Subcommittee, 28 Nov 1935, and the Registration and Practice Committees Joint Meeting, 18 Jul 1945. Includes the report of the Review of the Architects Registration Acts Ad Hoc Committee, Oct 1958.
Subjects : Promotion of an Act for the statutory registration of architects: drafting of a registration bill: relations with the Architects Registration Council of the United Kingdom (ARCUK): amendment of the 1931 Act: nominations for ARCUK committees.

(A joint committee of representatives of the RIBA and the Society of Architects, with advisory members representing the Allied Societies and other bodies affected. In 1932, it was reconstituted by adding to it the

members of the RIBA and its Allied Societies on the Architects Registration Council. For minutes of the Review of the Architects (Registration) Acts Ad Hoc Committee, 1955 *see*   2.2 Special Committees Minutes Series. *See also*   3.2.6 Amending Act Subcommittee Papers Series)
* Access at discretion of the Secretary RIBA

3.2.5   *   REGISTRATION   POLICY   COMMITTEE   PAPERS,   1931—1933   1 box
File of correspondence and memoranda kept by [Sir] Ian Macalister, Secretary RIBA, Jul 1931—Jan 1933.
Subjects : Statutory registration of architects: the RIBA Development Scheme: policy of the RIBA with regard to the Architects Registration Council of the UK (ARCUK).

* Access at discretion of the Secretary RIBA

3.2.6   AMENDING ACT SUBCOMMITTEE PAPERS, 1931—1936   2 vols
File of data and background papers concerning the Architects (Registration) Acts and the ARCUK.
Subject : Amendment of the Architects (Registration) Acts.

(A subcommittee of the Registration Committee (5). For minutes of a meeting of this subcommittee on 28 Nov 1935 *see*   3.2.4 Registration Committee (5) Minutes Series)

3.2.7   REGISTRATION COMMITTEE (6) MINUTES, 1960—1965   1 binder
Signed minutes of meetings of the main committee, Oct 1960—Nov 1962, and of the Registration Committee Steering Group, Jul 1964—Jul 1965, with memoranda and drafts of reports.
Subject : Reform of the Architects (Registration) Acts.

(The Acts were objected to on the grounds that they gave insufficient protection to practising architects by allowing unqualified persons to use descriptions such as 'Architectural Consultant' or 'Architectural Designer', and that public companies and other organisations which had an architect on their staff could describe themselves as 'Architects'. The committee also wanted to bring the ARCUK Code of Conduct more into line with the RIBA Code of Professional Conduct.)

See also in 2.2 Special Committees Minutes Series:
Federation Committee, 1886
Registration Committee (1), 1887—1888
Registration Committee (2), 1904—1906
Parliamentary Bill Committee, 1909—1910

Society of Architects & the RIBA Joint Conference, 1911
Society of Architects Committee, 1911
Registration Committee (3), 1912—1913
Conditions of Membership Subcommittee, 1921
Review of the Architects (Registration) Acts Ad Hoc Committee, 1955
and 12.1.3 Licentiateship Committee Minutes, 1930—1956, and 3.1.2 Registration Subcommittee (of the Executive Committee), 1946

Bibliography

1 *Draft bill, The Architects and Engineers Act, 1887* [50 & 51 Vict.]
2 Cates, Arthur 'The registration question' *RIBA Proceedings*, New Series Vol 4 1887 Nov 10 pp33—35
3 Connon, John Wreghitt *The legal registration of architects* Leeds, 1888
4 *Architects' Registration Bill. Statement of the Council of the Institution of Civil Engineers against the second reading of the bill* House of Commons, 1888
5 Architects' Registration Bill 1888. *Statement of the Council of the Surveyors' Institution against the second reading of the bill* House of Commons, 1888
6 *Architects' Registration Bill 1890* [53 Vict.] [Bill 121] Eyre & Spottiswoode, 13 Feb 1890
7 *Architects' Registration Bill 1890: statement against second reading* London, RIBA, 1890
8 Report of proceedings of the RIBA Special General Meeting on registration held on 31 Mar 1890 *RIBA Proceedings* New Series Vol 6 1890 Apr 3 pp261—273
9 'Architecture — a profession or an art?' *RIBA Proceedings* New Series Vol 7 1891 May 7 pp297—303
10 Shaw, R. N. & Jackson, T. G. (eds) *Architecture: a profession or an art* London, J. Murray, 1892
11 White, William H. *The architect and his artists. An essay to assist the public in considering the question is architecture a profession or an art* London, 1892
12 *Architects' Registration Bill 1895* [58 Vict.] [Bill 132] Eyre & Spottiswoode, 19 Feb 1895
13 *Architects' Registration Bill 1898* [61 Vict.] [Bill 137] Eyre & Spottiswoode, 16 Mar 1898
14 *Architects' Registration Bill 1900* [63 Vict.] [Bill 213] Eyre & Spottiswoode, 15 May 1900
15 *Architects' Registration Bill 1903* [3 Edw. 7] [Bill 165] Eyre & Spottiswoode, 24 Apr 1903
16 Wilson, Thomas Butler *Draft bill re Architects' Registration* Gibbs, White & Strong (1904)
17 Pite, Beresford 'The registration of architects' *RIBA Journal* Vol 11 1904 Mar 5 pp221—234

18   Seth-Smith, W. H. 'The statutory training and registration of architects' *RIBA Journal* Vol 11 1904 Mar 5 pp234—239

19   *Architects (Registration) Bill 1905* [5 Edw. 7] [Bill 220] Eyre & Spottiswoode, 15 May 1905

20   *Enrolment of Architects Bill 1906* [6 Edw. 7] Markby, Stewart & Co, 1906

21   RIBA Registration Committee. Report of the committee, with discussion on its recommendations at the Special General Meeting held on 3 Apr 1906. *RIBA Journal* Vol. 13 1906 Apr 7 pp302—315

22   *VIIth International Congress of Architects. Summary of proceedings* London, RIBA, 1906. Papers and discussion on 'A statutory qualification for architects'. Included as a special supplement to *RIBA Journal* Vol 13 1906 Aug 25

23   'The Institute and the Society of Architects' *RIBA Journal* Vol 19 1912 Feb 24 pp306—320

24   RIBA Council 'Statutory registration of architects' *RIBA Journal* Vol 21 1913 Dec 6 pp80—103 & 1914 Jan 17 pp167—174

25   'Registration by charter' *RIBA Journal* Vol 21 1914 May 9 pp429—438, 515—522 and 597—605

26   'Unity of the profession' *RIBA Journal* Vol 25 1918 Jan pp49—58

27   RIBA Charter Committee 'Unification and registration' *RIBA Journal* Vol 27 1920 Apr 10 pp254—258

28   RIBA Unification Committee. 'Unification of the architectural profession' *RIBA Journal* Vol 27 1920 Aug 28 pp445—450

29   RIBA Unification and Registration Subcommittee Report *RIBA Journal* Vol 28 1921 May 28 pp428—435

30   Simpson, John W. 'The unification and registration of the architectural profession' *RIBA Journal* Vol 28 1921 Jul 30 pp497—500

31   Barnes, Major Harry 'Unification and registration' *RIBA Journal* Vol 29 1922 Jul 15 pp523—528

32   'The RIBA Council's proposals for registration and consolidation of the profession' *RIBA Journal* Vol 31 1924 Apr 26 pp393—397

33   Report of discussion at the RIBA Special General Meeting on registration on 17 Jun 1924, in *RIBA Journal* Vol 31 1924 Jun 28 pp541—551

34   Butler, C. McArthur *The Society of Architects* London, Society of Architects, 1926

35   *Architects (Registration) Bill 1927* [17 Geo. 5] Markby, Stewart & Wadesons, 1927

36   'Architects (Registration) Bill 1927' *RIBA Journal* Vol 34 1927 Apr 2 pp378—381

37   *Memorandum on the Architects Registration Bill for the information of the members of the Houses of Parliament* London, RIBA, 1927

38   *Special report of the Select Committee on the Architects (Registration) Bill together with proceedings of the committee, minutes of evidence, appendices and index* London, House of Commons, 26 Jul 1927

39   'A full report of the debate on the registration bill in the House of Commons

on 8 Apr 1927' *RIBA Journal* Vol 34 1927 Oct 15 Supplement (30pp)

40 'Architects (Registration) Bill' *RIBA Journal* Vol 35 1928 Jan 14 pp149—151

41 *Architects (Registration) Bill 1928* [18 Geo. 5] [Bill 3] HMSO, 10 Feb 1928

42 Barnes, Major Harry 'Registration of architects' *RIBA Journal* Vol 37 1930 Mar 22 pp341—349

43 *Architects (Registration) Bill 1930* [21 Geo. 5] [Bill 27] HMSO, 31 Oct 1930

44 *Architects (Registration) Act 1931* 21 & 22 Geo. 5, Ch. 33

45 Butler, C. McArthur 'The registration of architects in Gt. Britain' *RIBA Journal* Vol 38 1931 Aug 8 pp687—689, with discussion at RIBA dinner to celebrate the passing of the registration act, pp689—696

46 Architects' Registration Council of the United Kingdom *Regulations made by the Council in pursuance of Section 13 of the Architects (Registration) Act 1931 and approved by the Privy Council on October 24th 1932* London, ARCUK, (1932)

47 *Architects (Registration) Act 1934* 24 & 25 Geo. 5, Ch. 38

48 Barnes, Major Harry 'The RIBA and statutory registration of architects', in Gotch, J. A. (ed) *The growth and work of the Royal Institute of British Architects* London, RIBA, 1934

49 *Architects (Registration) Act 1938* 1 & 2 Geo. 6, Ch. 54

50 Architects' Registration Council of the United Kingdom *Regulations made by the Council in pursuance of Section 13 of the Architects (Registration) Act 1931 and approved by His Majesty's Most Honourable Privy Council on April 4th 1944* London ARCUK, (1944)

51 *Architects Registration (Amendment) Bill 1969* [Bill 72] 44/3 HMSO, 28 Jan 1969

52 Parris, John 'Tale of two registers' Luder/Parris File, *Building Design* no 521 1980 Nov 14 p19

53 Startup, H.M. 'Institutional control of architectural education and registration 1834—1960' CNAA M.Phil. thesis, 1984

4
Central secretariat

Section 1 Secretary's Office

The original regulations stated that the officers of the Institute should consist of a president, three vice-presidents and two secretaries who, with seven other Fellows, should form a council for the direction and management of the Institute's affairs. These honorary officers were to be annually elected by ballot at the Annual General Meeting. The duties of the honorary secretaries were to take the minutes of all meetings, keep records of membership and donations, superintend Institute employees, conduct the correspondence of the Institute and Council and take charge of printing and publishing the Institute's papers. The first two honorary secretaries were Thomas Leverton Donaldson and John Goldicutt. As a result of Donaldson's energy and enthusiasm in corresponding with foreign architects a third honorary secretary not envisaged in the charter was instituted, the Honorary Secretary for Foreign Correspondence, whose duties were performed by Donaldson from 1839— 1858.

Pressure of work led to the employment of Francis Dollman as Assistant Secretary, Librarian and Clerk from 1862 until 1866 when the Council decided to employ a paid full-time secretary, to be called the Assistant Secretary. His duties were to assist the honorary secretaries, to whom he was responsible, to attend the premises from 10—5 daily, to keep the accounts, to edit and illustrate Institute papers where necessary and to superintend their publication in the *Transactions*. Charles Locke Eastlake was appointed to this post in December 1866 and the number of honorary secretaries was reduced from three to two, one for foreign correspondence and one for 'home duties'. In 1869 Eastlake, who had been trained as an architect but had never practised, was elected a Fellow and in 1871 his title was changed to Secretary and he was made directly responsible to the Council instead of to the honorary secretaries, of which there would henceforward be only one (although they were paid officials, Eastlake and his successor, White, were also repeatedly-elected members of the Council). Eastlake resigned in 1878 to take up the post of Keeper of the National Gallery and applications were invited from the Fellows for the vacant post. The successful candidate was William Henry White who remained as Secretary until his death in 1896.

Under the revised by-laws of 1889, the Council was to include one honorary secretary and was to appoint a Secretary (not necessarily a Fellow or an elected member of Council, as previously) to manage the establishment and conduct the executive business of the Institute. Early in 1897 they advertised for a 'gentleman of culture and literary attainments', with facility in French and German, not necessarily an architect or a member of the RIBA but with a knowledge of architecture. The successful candidate was William John Locke, then a schoolmaster and relatively unknown novelist. At the same time the Council appointed Herbert Tayler as Assistant Secretary. On the resignation of Locke in 1907 to devote himself entirely to writing, a similar advertisement was issued and Ian Macalister (later Sir Ian) was appointed Secretary. He was a professional administrator who remained in the post for thirty-six years during which there was a great expansion in the work of the Secretary's Office and the General Office.

By 1951 it had become necessary to appoint two additional assistant secretaries and the former Assistant Secretary, William Ellis, was renamed Deputy Secretary. By 1960 the number of assistant secretaries had risen to five, each with departmental responsibilities. In 1962 the General Office and post of Deputy Secretary ceased to exist and the heads of four new departments, Central Services, Professional Services, Membership Services, and Information Services, were named under-secretaries (on the Civil Service model). In 1974 the Secretary's Office took over the function of dealing with town-planning and housing policy and affairs.

In 1976 a Chief Executive was appointed by Council to be responsible for the management of the Institute, traditionally the responsibility of the Secretary who henceforth was to concentrate on the external relationships of the RIBA. This arrangement was found to be unsatisfactory and in 1979 the Secretary reverted to his former role of chief executive officer. Since 1979 the Secretary's Office has included the Professional Conduct Office, the Legal Adviser's Office, the Research and Statistics Office, the Energy Office and the Press Office (now transferred to the Promotions Department, 1983). The President's Office is jointly organized with the Secretary's Office, of which it forms a part.

HONORARY SECRETARIES' CORRESPONDENCE, 1835—1878
see   1.2.3 Letters to Council Series

SECRETARY'S CORRESPONDENCE (EASTLAKE), 1866—1878
see   1.2.3 Letters to Council Series

7   Portrait of Sir Ian Macalister, RIBA Secretary for thirty-six years, by Harold
Knight RA, exhibited at the Royal Academy in 1936. During his time as Secretary,
due in no small part to his efforts, there was an enormous expansion in the work
of the Institute. He was very influential in finally bringing about the Architects
(Registration) Act 1931 and in achieving the removal of the Institute in 1934 from
9 Conduit Street to its new purpose-built premises at 66 Portland Place, a view of
which is shown in the picture. (In RIBA Building, 66 Portland Place)

SECRETARY'S CORRESPONDENCE (WHITE), 1878—1896
see   1.2.3 Letters to Council Series

SECRETARY'S CORRESPONDENCE (LOCKE), 1897—1907
see   1.2.3 Letters to Council Series

4.1.1   *   SECRETARY'S CORRESPONDENCE (MACALISTER), 1919—
1942   8 boxes
Correspondence files kept by [Sir] Ian MacAlister, Secretary RIBA, and
C. D. Spragg, Assistant Secretary RIBA, Oct 1919—Dec 1942
Subjects The RIBA constitution: services offered by the RIBA: finances
of the RIBA: RIBA premises: statutory registration of architects: the
RIBA Development Scheme: relations with the Allied Societies: relations
with other bodies, including the Incorporated Association of Architects
and Surveyors, the Institute of Registered Architects, and the Association
of Architects, Surveyors and Technical Assistants: the Professional Conduct Committee: building industry relations.

(This series of files is very incomplete. No correspondence for the period
1907—1918 has survived)

* Access at the discretion of the Secretary RIBA.

4.1.2   *   ILLEGAL USE OF AFFIX CASE FILES, 1924—1954   5 boxes
Correspondence files kept by the Secretary RIBA concerning cases of
wrongful use of the affix 'RIBA' or 'Chartered Architect', 1924—1954

* No access. Closed series.

4.1.3   *   SECRETARY'S   CORRESPONDENCE   (SPRAGG),   1943—
1959   23 boxes
Correspondence files kept by C.D.S. Spragg, Acting Secretary then
Secretary RIBA, and William Ellis, Deputy Secretary RIBA, Oct 1943—
Jul 1959.
Subjects : Registration of architects and relations with ARCUK: RIBA
premises: RIBA finances: RIBA committee structure: RIBA constitution
and by-laws: RIBA membership and British nationality: income and
status of architects: official architects and private work: relations with
other institutions and societies: relations with local and central government: building industry relations: control of elevations: the Council
for the Preservation of Rural England's Central Panels Committee:
conservation and preservation of historic buildings: care of churches:
Royal Gold Medal awards: RIBA Honorary Fellowships.

(For further files kept by the Deputy Secretary *see*   5.1.1 'General
Office' Papers Series)

* Access at the discretion of the Secretary, RIBA

4.1.4   NATIONAL CONSULTATIVE COUNCIL OF THE BUILDING
AND CIVIL ENGINEERING INDUSTRIES (NCC); RIBA
SECRETARY'S PAPERS, 1948—1979   9 boxes
Files kept by the Secretary RIBA, who was usually one of the RIBA
representatives on this council, containing copies of minutes of meetings,
memoranda, reports and some correspondence, Jan 1948—Sep 1979.
Subjects : Most aspects of the building industry: building methods:
building legislation: codes of practice: training: building materials:
government building programmes: employment.

4.1.5   * SECRETARY'S   CORRESPONDENCE   (RICKETTS),   1959—
1968   45 boxes
Correspondence files kept by Gordon Ricketts, Acting Secretary RIBA,
from Mar 1959, and Secretary RIBA from Aug 1959 to his death in
1968.
Subjects : The work of RIBA departments and committees: RIBA
committee structure: RIBA staff management: RIBA finances: RIBA
premises: RIBA constitution and by-laws: RIBA membership and British
nationality: relations with related institutions and societies: the Commonwealth Association of Architects: the ARCUK: the Architects Benevolent Society: the President's and Secretary's engagements and official
visits: relations with government and parliament: construction industry
relations: EPACCI: NEDC and EDC for the Building Industry ('Little
Neddy'): professional relations: architects and directorships: the 'Package
Deal': index of architectural practices: employment of architects by
central and local government.

* Access at the discretion of the Secretary RIBA.

4.1.6   * LIAISON GROUP OF PROFESSIONS: RIBA SECRETARY'S
PAPERS, 1967—1973   3 binders
Notes of proceedings at meetings, Jan 1967—Jun 1973, with agenda
papers, policy memoranda, reports, correspondence, and statements of
the group to the Monopolies Commission.
Subjects : Monopolies Commission inquiry into the rules and practices
of the professions which might be restrictive, 1967: the Industrial
Relations Bill, 1971: Value Added Tax: implications of the Common
Market on the professions.

* Access at the discretion of the Secretary RIBA

Bibliography

1   'Appointment of a paid Secretary and other paid officers of the Institute' *RIBA Proceedings* 1st Series 1865/66 18 Jun 1866

2   'Office of Secretary to the RIBA' *RIBA Proceedings* 1st Series 1870/71 7 & 14 Mar 1871

3   Gruning, Edward A. 'Memoir of the late Professor Donaldson' *RIBA Transactions* New Series Vol 2 1885/86 pp89—95

4   Papworth, Wyatt 'The late Professor Donaldson: his connection with the Institute' *RIBA Transactions* New Series Vol 2 1885/86 pp96—108

5   Graham, Alexander 'William H. White, Fellow, eighteen years Secretary of the Royal Institute of British Architects' *RIBA Journal* Vol 4 1896 Nov 5 pp11—15

6   Simpson, Sir John W. 'William John Locke, Honorary Associate, Secretary RIBA 1898—1908' *RIBA Journal* Vol 37 1930 May 24 p518

7   'The presentation to Sir Ian and Lady Macalister' *RIBA Journal* Vol 52 1944 Nov pp3—8. On the occasion of his retirement from the RIBA Secretaryship

8   'Sir Ian Macalister, MA, Hon. ARIBA' *Builder* Vol 192 1957 Jun 14 p1080. Obituary notice

9   'Presentation to Mr. C. D. Spragg, CBE' *RIBA Journal* Vol 66 1959 Aug pp342—343. On the occasion of his retirement from the RIBA Secretaryship

10 Blutman, Sandra 'The father of the profession' *RIBA Journal* Vol 74 1967 Dec pp542—544. Article on Thomas Leverton Donaldson, first Hon. Secretary of the Institute & Hon. Secretary for Foreign Correspondence

11 'Gordon Ricketts' *RIBA Journal* Vol 75 1968 Feb pp47—48. An appreciation of Gordon Ricketts, RIBA Secretary 1959—1968

12 'RIBA Secretary Harrison talks to AJ' *Architects' Journal* Vol 148 1968 Dec 18 & 25 pp1432—1434. Interview with Patrick Harrison, the new RIBA Secretary

13 'The President and the Secretary' *RIBA Journal* Vol 74 1969 Oct pp412—413. Part of a feature article 'Inside the RIBA'

14 Harrison, Rex 'Patrick Harrison, Secretary of the RIBA' *Building Design* no 121 1972 Oct 6 p6

15 'Chief Executive' *Architects' Journal* Vol 163 1976 Feb 4 pp215—216. Interview with Don Edmonds, RIBA Chief Executive

16 'Restructure of the RIBA' *RIBA Journal* Vol 83 1976 Apr p132. Article on the roles of the new Chief Executive and the Secretary RIBA

17 'Man for all seasons' *Building* Vol 243 no 7250(29) 1982 Jul 16 pp32—33. Interview with Patrick Harrison, RIBA Secretary

Section 2 President's Office

The original regulations stated that the officers should include a president and three vice-presidents who must be Fellows of the Institute. They were to be elected annually by ballot at the Annual General Meeting and no member who had filled the office of president or vice-president for two successive years would be eligible for election to the same situation until a further year had passed. The duties of the president were to take the chair at meetings and to execute the regulations of the Institute.

The charter of 1837 stated that the president could be an Honorary Fellow and that the first president was Thomas Philip, Earl De Grey. The advantages of having as president a member of the government and a Privy Councillor were so great that the Earl De Grey was annually re-elected and the by-law concerning repeated election to the office of president was waived until his death. He was instrumental in obtaining the royal charter and in persuading Queen Victoria to become the Institute's patron and to provide annually a Royal Gold Medal for architecture.

On the death of Earl De Grey the Institute paid tribute to the 'Grand Old Man' of British architecture, Charles Robert Cockerell, Royal Academician and Honorary Fellow of the Institute, by electing him president. His successor as president, Sir William Tite, an architect, Member of Parliament and member of the Metropolitan Board of Works, was a wealthy and influential figure who served two terms as president from 1861—1863 and 1867—1870. From 1863—1865, the Institute honoured one of its founding fathers, Thomas Leverton Donaldson, who had contributed so much to the early success and high international reputation of the Institute. In 1865 the Institute again elected a public figure as its president, Alexander James Beresford-Hope, Honorary Fellow, writer, patron of art, Member of Parliament and President of the Ecclesiological Society. From then on the president was always a practising architect.

The revised by-laws of 1877 stated that the senior vice-president should be nominated as president and those of 1925 stated that one of the four vice-presidents must be an architect practising outside the London area. Any corporate member or Honorary Fellow of the Institute is now eligible to serve as president and is elected by a postal ballot of the corporate membership. The normal period of office for the president is two years and his functions, in addition to being the figurehead of the Institute and, since 1885, *ex-officio* president of the Architects Benevolent

8 Portrait of John Whichcord, President 1879 — 1881, by Sir Lawrence Alma-Tadema RA, exhibited at the Royal Academy in 1882. Whichcord is shown wearing the presidential badge and chain presented to the RIBA by T. L. Donaldson in 1879. Whichcord was a believer in compulsory architectural education and, with Arthur Ashpitel, Arthur Cates, Robert Kerr and Wyatt Papworth, prepared the way for the Institute's Obligatory Examination for Associate Membership, first held in 1882. (RIBA Presidential Portraits Collection, RIBA Building, 66 Portland Place)

Society, are to represent the Institute at official and social functions, to conduct an official correspondence on behalf of the Institute and to take the chair at General Meetings, Council meetings and Policy Committee meetings. He has the right to nominate the Honorary Secretary, the Honorary Treasurer and a number of vice-presidents and to nominate members of standing committees. He also exercises considerable patronage by nominating architects for important projects (*see* Chapter 11 Section 6).

The President's Office is organized jointly with the Secretary's Office of which it forms a part. It is managed by the Assistant Clerk to the Council, who also provides liaison between the president and the other honorary officers and between the President's Office and the Secretary's Office.

(For a list of past presidents *see* the *RIBA Directory of Members* .)

PRESIDENTIAL PORTRAITS, 1850—
See   6.3

4.2.1   PRESIDENTS' ADDRESSES, 1859—
Addresses by RIBA presidents at General Meetings, including the Opening Address of the session, the Inaugural Address, and the Address to Students, printed from 1859—1878 in *RIBA Proceedings, Ist Series*, from 1879—1883 in *RIBA Transactions, Ist Series*, from 1884—1893 in *RIBA Proceedings, New Series*, and from 1894—1973 in *RIBA Journal*, 3rd Series. (Since 1975 tape-recordings of Presidents' Inaugural Addresses are available, and typescripts of most can be seen in the Sessional Programmes Record Series).

4.2.2   *   PRESIDENT'S CORRESPONDENCE, 1953—   5 boxes & 2 cabinets
Correspondence of the presidents with RIBA members, the press, heads of other professional bodies, government ministers and officials, public authority officials, academics, businessmen, etc. Also includes drafts of presidents' speeches and inaugural addresses, and lists of presidents' engagements.
Subjects : Public and social engagements: public affairs: public relations: President's Media Group: members' complaints: Institute administration and constitution: RIBA regional affairs: RIBA companies: the Library Appeal: Clients Advisory Service: architectural competition: architectural education: overseas relations: RIBA Architecture Awards: Royal Gold Medal awards, from 1975: U.K. Interprofessional Group: the Group of Eight: President's Committee for the Urban Environment: energy conservation in building: use of computers by architects.

(This correspondence does not include departmental letters requiring the president's signature, copies of which are filed in the departments concerned.

In the past, presidents have regarded their correspondence as PRIBA as part of their personal archive rather than as part of the RIBA archive. H. S. Goodhart-Rendel's and Sir Giles Gilbert Scott's correspondence as PRIBA has returned to the Institute as part of the deposits of their papers made to the RIBA Manuscripts Collection after their deaths (*see* Guide to the British Architectural Library's Manuscripts Collection, RIBA). Lord Holford's correspondence as PRIBA is with his papers deposited in the Liverpool University Archives).

* Access at the discretion of the Assistant Clerk to the Council.

PRESIDENT'S NOMINATIONS REGISTER, 1958—
see   11.6.7

4.2.3   *   PRESIDENTS OF PROFESSIONAL BODIES MEETINGS: RIBA PRESIDENT'S PAPERS, 1969—1976   1 binder
Copies of minutes of meetings, Jan 1970—Mar 1976, with agenda papers and correspondence, Dec 1969—Apr 1976.
Subjects : Proposed central professional organisation: transferability of pensions: professional conduct: reference of the professions to the Monopolies Commission: future of the professions: the professions and trade unionism: the professional employee and the Industrial Relations Act: professional competence: the Buchanan Report Standing Joint Committee.

* Access at the discretion of the Assistant Clerk to the Council

Bibliography

1   RIBA *The presidents of the Royal Institute of British Architects reproduced from original paintings in the possession of the Royal Institute* London, RIBA [c.1909] Photographic reproductions of portraits of RIBA presidents
2   'The President and the Secretary' *RIBA Journal* Vol 74 1969 Oct pp412—413. Part of a feature article 'Inside the RIBA'
3   Goulden, Gontran 'Portraits and sculpture at 66 Portland Place: past presidents of the RIBA and others' *RIBA Journal* Vol 85 1978 Dec pp531—536
4   Luder, Owen 'All power to the president: explanation of the RIBA decision process' Luder/Parris File, *Building Design* no 519 1980 Oct 31 p10
5   Macvicar, Steve 'RIBA Council regularises presidential contests' *Building* Vol 242 no 7235(14) 1982 Apr 2 p12
6   Jackson, Neil & Thomas, John 'Presidents of the RIBA' *RIBA Journal* Vol 91 1984 May pp43—66. Short biographies of all RIBA presidents, 1834—1984

Section 3 Professional Conduct Office

The original by-laws stated 'The following shall be deemed grounds for the expulsion of any Fellow or Associate viz. for having engaged since his election in the measurement, valuation or estimation of any works undertaken or proposed to be undertaken by any building artificer, except such as are proposed to be executed or have been executed under the member's own designs or directions; or for the receipt or acceptance of any pecuniary consideration or emolument from any builder or other tradesman whose works he may have been engaged to superintend; or for having any interest or participation in any trade, contract or materials supplied at any works; or for any conduct which, in the opinion of the Council, shall be derogatory to his professional character'. Every elected member had to sign a declaration form stating that he would abide by the conditions of membership (these forms are attached to the Nomination Papers *see* Chapter 5, Section 4) and instances of alleged breach of them were investigated either by specially summoned subcommittees of the Council or, from 1845—1869, by the Professional Practice Committee. The Council's disciplinary powers were either to administer an unpublished reprimand, to publish a reprimand, to suspend the member or to expel the member.

From 1862 the RIBA Practice committees published scales of professional charges to which members were expected to adhere (*see* 8.2.1 Conditions of Engagement Series) and from 1900 Council resolutions concerning professional conduct were regularly published in the *RIBA Journal*. From 1923 the Institute published in the *Kalendar* 'Suggestions governing professional conduct and practice of architects' which from 1929 was known as the Code of Professional Practice and from 1950 as the Code of Professional Conduct. In 1926 a standing Professional Conduct Committee was established which considered revisions of the code and which investigated on behalf of the Council all charges of alleged unprofessional conduct under the RIBA by-laws and breach of the RIBA Code of Professional Practice (later, the RIBA Code of Professional Conduct). It reported its findings to the Council and recommended the type of disciplinary action to be taken. Charges mainly related to members engaging in the business of an estate agent or builder, undercutting fees, supplanting other architects or advertising professional services. In 1933 there was a change of procedure in professional conduct cases. Whenever a charge was made the defendant was to be allowed an opportunity of submitting a reply before the matter was brought before the Council and all references to a case were to be by number, not name, until the charge was substantiated sufficiently to justify disciplinary action.

In 1931 the Architects (Registration) Act came into force and the Architects Registration Council of the United Kingdom (ARCUK) subsequently produced its own code of professional conduct. This code, however, had no statutory authority. The ARCUK has a statutory obligation to place on the register all persons entitled to be registered and it has no statutory right to remove an architect from the register except for criminal conviction or for 'conduct disgraceful to him in his capacity as an architect'. There is no definition in the Act of disgraceful conduct and if an architect is struck off the register he may appeal to the High Court. The RIBA, however, has the absolute discretion, granted to it by royal charter, to exclude anyone it wishes from admission to membership and to expel any member, subject to the provisions of its by-laws.

In 1968 the Institute set up the Investigation Committee to consider policy issues with regard to revisions of the RIBA Code of Professional Conduct; to investigate allegations of unprofessional conduct by members and to formulate charges for the Professional Conduct Committee to determine. If the Professional Conduct Committee's finding was guilty as charged, it would report accordingly to the Council. In July 1971 the Council delegated its disciplinary powers to the Professional Conduct Committee, which had the final decision. At the same time provision was made for an Appeals Committee to deal with appeals concerned with the severity of the decisions. In 1979 a new Professional Conduct Committee and a Code Policy Committee were set up, which between them continued the work of the disbanded Investigation Committee, and the old Professional Conduct Committee was renamed the Disciplinary Committee. A Professional Conduct Secretary was appointed, who acts as Secretary to both the Professional Conduct Committee and the Code Policy Committee.

4.3.1   *   PROFESSIONAL CONDUCT COMMITTEE MINUTES, 1926—
1978   4 vols & 6 binders
Signed minutes of meetings, Mar 1926—Nov 1978.
Subjects : Charges of alleged unprofessional conduct by members: investigation of complaints concerning the conduct of architectural competitions: regulation of competitions: code of conduct policy: revisions of the code.

* No access

4.3.2   *   DISCIPLINE CASE FILES, 1926—(1974)   58 boxes
Correspondence and documents concerning individual cases of unprofessional conduct by members.

* No access

4.3.3   REVISION OF BY-LAWS 23 & 24 SUBCOMMITTEE PAPERS,
          1964—1970   1 box
          Minutes of a meeting, 23 Oct 1964, with memoranda, a report of the
          subcommittee, 1965, and correspondence, 1964—1970.
          Subjects : Grounds for reprimand, suspension or expulsion of RIBA
          members; procedure of investigation of charges of unprofessional conduct
          by members.

          (A subcommittee of the Professional Conduct Committee, set up at the
          request of the Charter Committee)

4.3.4 * INVESTIGATION COMMITTEE MINUTES, 1968—1978   5
          binders
          Signed minutes of meetings, Aug 1968—Dec 1978, with agenda papers.
          Subjects : Investigation of allegations of unprofessional conduct by
          members: code of conduct policy: amendments to disciplinary procedures:
          revision of the code of conduct: publication of Practice Notes.

          * No access

See also in 2.2 Special Committees Minutes Series:
Professional Advertisement Committee, 1900
Professional Questions Committee, 1911—1914
and many of the series in Chapter 8, Section 1

Bibliography

1   RIBA 'Suggestions governing professional conduct and practice of architects'
    RIBA Kalendar 1923/24—1928/29
2   RIBA *Code of Professional Practice*, London, RIBA, 1929. (Revised editions
    were published in 1935, 1938, 1941, 1945 and 1946)
3   Watson, W. E. *Professional conduct and practice* London, RIBA, 1929
4   Wilson, Geoffrey C. 'RIBA Code of Professional Practice' *RIBA Journal* Vol
    43 1936 Sep 5 pp1033—1035
5   Architects' Registration Council of the United Kingdom *Code of professional
    conduct* London, ARCUK, 1946. (Revised editions were published in 1960,
    1974 and 1976)
6   RIBA *Code of professional conduct* London, RIBA, 1950. (Revised editions
    were published in 1953, 1976, 1978, Jan 1981, Jun 1981 and Jul 1982)
7   Telling, A. E. 'The professional conduct of architects' *Builder* Vol 189 1955
    Jul pp89—90, 129—130, 178—179
8   Barrington Kaye 'Professional conduct in the eighteenth and nineteenth cen-
    turies' *RIBA Journal* Vol 63 1956 Jul pp377—380
9   'The architect's place in the building industry. Some reflections on Clause 5
    of the Code of Professional Conduct' *RIBA Journal* Vol 66 1959 Sep pp376—
    378

10   Higgin, Gurth 'The architect as professional' *RIBA Journal* Vol 71 1964 Apr pp139—145

11   RIBA Professional Services Board 'What kind of code?' *RIBA Journal* Vol 77 1970 Aug pp366—369

12   Gundrey, Walter 'RIBA working groups (3), Appeals Committee' *RIBA Journal* Vol 78 1971 May pp206 & 222

13   Carter, John 'Directorships' *RIBA Journal* Vol 78 1971 Oct pp452—454

14   MacEwen, Malcolm 'Thou shalt not sneak: Poulson and the RIBA' *RIBA Journal* Vol 81 1974 Dec pp4—5

15   RIBA Council 'Code of professional conduct' *RIBA Journal* Vol 82 1975 Nov /Dec pp10—13

16   Goldstein, Barbara 'Architects as developers?' *RIBA Journal* Vol 84 1977 Nov p451

17   Pearce, David 'The architect as builder' *RIBA Journal* Vol 85 1978 Jan p3

18   Pearce, David 'The architect as director' *RIBA Journal* Vol 85 1978 Feb pp46—47

19   Parris, John 'Builders versus gentlemen' Luder/Parris File, *Building Design* no 515 1980 Oct 3 p15

20   'The new code' *RIBA Journal* Vol 87 1980 Nov pp67—69. Practice note on the new RIBA Code of Professional Conduct

21   Parris, John 'Tale of two registers' Luder/Parris File, *Building Design* no 521 1980 Nov 14 p19

Section 4 Legal Adviser's Office

In 1963 David Waterhouse was appointed Legal Adviser having worked since 1958 as the assistant secretary with responsibility for practice matters. As Assistant Secretary Practice, and as Legal Adviser, his work consisted mainly of answering members' questions concerning professional practice and conduct; giving advice in disputes between members, clients and contractors; dealing with the appointment of arbitrators and acting as the RIBA Joint Secretary of the Joint Contracts Tribunal. He was followed in 1968 by George Stringer and in 1970 by Robert Johnstone. Since the setting up of the RIBA Services Ltd's Legal Advice Service in 1970, the Legal Adviser no longer gives legal advice to members, clients and contractors. His present functions are to give legal advice to the Institute as its Solicitor; to act as Secretary to the Disciplinary Committee; to deal with the appointment of arbitrators and to act as the RIBA Joint Secretary of the Joint Contracts Tribunal.

4.4.1   * JOINT CONTRACTS TRIBUNAL: RIBA JOINT SECRETARY'S
PAPERS, 1932—1944, 1952—1971   28 boxes
Copies of minutes of meetings, memoranda and reports, 1932—1944,
1960—1971: general correspondence files, 1963—1971: papers concerning general revision of the RIBA Form of Contract, 1955—1961:
various subject files, including several subcommittees, 1952—1971.

(The tribunal was established jointly in October 1932 by the councils of
the RIBA and the National Federation of Building Trades Employers
(NFBTE) to consider suggestions for the amendment of the 1931 Form
of Contract that might arise from difficulties experienced in its use and
to consider and advise on points of interpretation. It has a RIBA Joint
Secretary and an NFBTE Joint Secretary. In the early years the Secretary
RIBA, acted as the RIBA Joint Secretary but in the early 1960s this
duty was performed by the Practice Secretary and then by the Legal
Adviser).

  * Access at the discretion of the Legal Adviser

4.4.2   * ARBITRATORS REGISTER, 1960—   1 vol
Record of individual arbitrators' work, giving name and address of
arbitrator, number of each case, with date of appointment, names of
parties, and (from 1974) whether concluded, settled before hearing, or
award issued.

  * No access

4.4.3   * LEGAL ADVISER'S PAPERS, 1963—(1970)   17 boxes
Correspondence files of David Waterhouse, 1963—1967, and George
Stringer, 1968—1970
Subjects : Queries concerning the RIBA Standard Form of Contract,
arbitration of disputes, the RIBA Code of Professional Conduct: public
and private parliamentary bills: partnerships and practices: architects'
copyright in and ownership of drawings: formation of the service companies, RIBA Services Ltd, RIBA Publications Ltd, National Building
Specification Ltd: the SfB agreement.

  * Access at the discretion of the Legal Adviser

4.4.4   * ARBITRATION CASES REGISTER, 1965—   3 vols
Chronological record of arbitration cases, giving number of case, date of
application, name of applicant, names of parties, names of three suggested

arbitrators, name of arbitrator appointed, date of appointment, and whether case concluded, settled before hearing or award issued.

* No access

See also in 2.2 Special Committees Minutes Series:
Fine Arts Copyright Consolidation and Amendment Bill Committee, 1869
Copyright of Architects Drawings Committee, 1877
Board of Professional Defence, 1904—1914
Copyright Bill Committee, 1910—1911
Professional Questions Committee, 1911—1914
and many of the series in Chapter 8, Practice, for contract law, arbitration, legislation affecting architects, professional legal advice before the appointment of a Legal Adviser.

Bibliography

1   RIBA *The architect as arbitrator* London, RIBA, 1959. (Revised edition, 1978)
2   Scott, Charles, Chairman of Working Group H of the RIBA Professional Practice Committee 'A new look at arbitration' *RIBA Journal* Vol 72 1965 May p253
3   RIBA Legal Adviser 'What is reasonable supervision?' *RIBA Journal* Vol 73 1966 Dec pp575—576
4   Stringer, George, RIBA Solicitor & RIBA Joint Sec. of the Joint Contracts Tribunal 'Amateurs or professionals?' *RIBA Journal* Vol 77 1970 Apr pp177—179. Article on the responsibilities and liabilities of the architect under the standard forms of contract.
5   Lord-Smith, Peter & Waters, Alwyn 'RIBA and the JCT: should we stay in — or get out?' *RIBA Journal* Vol 80 1973 Apr pp173—176
6   'Fairness without immunity: architects and the contract' *RIBA Journal* Vol 81 1974 Dec pp32—34. Council paper on the duties of architects appointed for the purposes of the standard form of building contract
7   Close, Howard A. *The evolution of the standard form of building contract* London, NFBTE, 1975. A republication note bringing up to date an address given at the RICS on 21 Nov 1951

See also the bibliographies of Chapter 4 Section 3 and Chapter 8 Sections 1 and 2

Section 5 Research and Statistics Office

A Statistics Section was started in 1958 as part of a new Economic Research Department. Its function was, and remains, to collect and process data on the structure and costs of the profession. This led to the establishment of the Research and Statistics Section of the Professional Services Department (*see* introduction to Chapter 8) which carried out several investigations of which the most influential was a survey of architects' offices in 1960—1962.

A boost to the development of architectural research was provided by the discussions held at the Oxford Conference on Architectural Education in 1958 (*see* introduction to Chapter 7) which led to the appointment of the Postgraduate Training and Research Committee by the RIBA Board of Architectural Education in 1962, followed by the appointment of the Research Committee by the RIBA Board of Education in 1967. The Research Committee centred its work on the Research Awards Scheme, which helps to finance architectural research work in the United Kingdom. In 1971 an Intelligence Unit was set up which included the Statistics Section. It assumed responsibility for advising on RIBA policy on town planning and housing matters and took over the Research Section which guided research policy, administered the Research Awards Scheme, oversaw the *Journal of Architectural Research and Teaching* and maintained liaison with government research councils. When the Intelligence Unit was wound up in 1976 the Statistics Section came under the Central Services Department and the Research Section became part of the Education and Practice Department. In 1979 a Research and Statistics Office was set up as part of the Secretary's Office.

4.5.1   QUARTERLY STATISTICAL BULLETIN, 1958—(1983)   3
boxes
Quarterly bulletins giving results of statistical surveys by the RIBA Statistics Section.
Subjects : Analyses of new commissions for private architects: census of private practices, 1968 and 1972: annual architectural education statistics, 1969—1972 and 1975—1976: survey of student membership, 1970: distribution by size and region of private practices, 1970: local authority design statistics, 1970—1979: survey of private practice costs and incomes trends, 1970: progress of metrication: architects' earnings, 1970, 1973: extent of job-changing, 1967—1970: women in the profession, 1957—

1971: proportion of public work put out to private practice, 1975: survey of construction of new office or factory premises, 1975: RIBA Appointments Bureau statistics, 1970—1975: architects' employment in private practice, 1976 onwards.

4.5.2   OFFICE SURVEY PAPERS, 1960—1969   1 box
File of correspondence, notes and data kept by Miss J. M. N. Milne, then Assistant Secretary Economics and Statistics, concerning the RIBA survey of the organization, staffing, quality of service provided and productivity of architects' offices, 1960, with copy of the report *The architect and his office*, Feb 1962, and the Office Survey Fund cash book recording donations to the fund, 1962—1969.
  Subjects : Fees and salaries; architectural education; office and job management; technical competence.

(The project was financed by a grant from the Leverhulme Trust and donations by RIBA members. The report was influential in determining the future policy of the Institute, being used almost as a corporate plan for the requirements of the profession and the development of the RIBA in the 1960s and early 1970s.)

POSTGRADUATE TRAINING AND RESEARCH COMMITTEE MINUTES & PAPERS, 1962—1967
see   7.1.7

4.5.3   JOURNAL OF ARCHITECTURAL RESEARCH PAPERS, 1962—1975   9 boxes
Correspondence files of the initiators and editors of the journal, Malcolm MacEwen and John Musgrove, editors of the *RIBA Journal*, and Bill Hillier and Adrian Leaman of the RIBA Intelligence Unit, between 1962 and 1975. Also, texts of articles submitted for the journal, 1969—1975.

(The *Journal of Architectural Research and Teaching* was initiated by the RIBA and partly supported by the ARCUK. It was first published in 1970 by the RIBA Research Committee. In 1974 it changed its name to the *Journal of Architectural Research* and was then published jointly by the RIBA and the American Institute of Architects.)

4.5.4   GROUP PRACTICE AND CONSORTIA RESEARCH STUDY PAPERS, 1963—1965   6 boxes
Files kept by Jeremy Mackay Lewis, appointed as a RIBA Research Fellow to carry out the study. They contain progress bulletins, correspondence, notes on meetings and visits, and drafts of the handbook *Guide to group practice and consortia* .

Subject : Ways and means of establishing and organizing group practice and consortia.

4.5.5 * RESEARCH AWARDS SCHEME PAPERS, 1965—(1972)   5 boxes
Lists of research award winners and project titles, project assessment forms, correspondence of the scheme administrators, register of payments made to award winners, 1965—(1972).
Subjects : RIBA Research Awards; Cumbernauld Research Awards; Pearce Edwards Awards.

(In 1964 the Institute amalgamated twenty-seven of its charitable trust funds (*see* 5.2.4) into three groups, the Modern Architecture and Town Planning Trust, the Historical Research Trust and the Prizes Trust. The first two are used for the payment of grants for full-time and part-time research projects in the fields of contemporary and historical architecture, building and planning).

* Access at the discretion of the Research Officer

4.5.6 RESEARCH AWARDS FINAL REPORTS, 1965—
Final reports of research award winners on completion of their projects, from 1965 onwards.

(Not all projects resulted in final reports, either because the projects were unfinished or because the RIBA was credited in a published article or other publication and this was considered sufficient acknowledgment).

4.5.7 STATISTICAL SURVEYS REPORTS, 1966—   2 boxes
Reports of surveys made by or for the RIBA Statistics Section, from 1966 onwards.
Subjects : Architects' costs and incomes, with information back to 1956: architects' employment: profitability of private practice: student surveys: women in the architectural profession: surveys of local authority architects' departments: architectural education statistics.

RESEARCH COMMITTEE MINUTES & PAPERS, 1967—1971
see   7.1.12

Bibliography

1   Hall, E. Stanley 'The RIBA Research Board. A statement of the formation and aims of the RIBA Research Board' *RIBA Journal* Vol 47 1940 May 20 pp169—171
2   RIBA Statistics Office *Quarterly statistical bulletin* London, RIBA, 1958—
3   'A survey of private architectural practice' *RIBA Journal* Vol 66 1959 Apr

pp201—203 & Jun 1959 pp273—275

4   'RIBA survey of new building work for which private architects have been appointed' *RIBA Journal* Vol 66 1959 Oct pp414—416

5   Milne, Joan, RIBA Economic Research Dept. 'A survey of the architects' departments of local authorities' *RIBA Journal* Vol 67 1960 Mar pp160—163

6   Milne, Joan 'From statistics to education' *Architects' Journal* 1961 Jan 19 pp84—85. Article on her work as head of the RIBA Economic Research Department, 1957—1961

7   RIBA Office Survey Team *The architect and his office* London, RIBA, 1962

8   'The architect and his office' *RIBA Journal* Vol 69 1962 Apr pp 126—128. Summary of the main conclusions of the RIBA Office Survey Team

9   RIBA Research Section 'New work for private architects. Results of RIBA survey' *RIBA Journal* Vol 72 1965 Jul pp340—341

10 Robson, Morrow & Co *Survey of cost and income trends* London, RIBA, 1966

11 RIBA Postgraduate Training and Research Committee 'A new RIBA policy for research in architecture' *RIBA Journal* Vol 74 1967 Feb pp50—51

12 'Report on office costs and incomes suggests a gloomy future for private practice' *RIBA Journal* Vol 78 1971 Jan pp34—35. Article on a survey conducted for the Professional Services Board by the RIBA Research and Statistics Section.

13 RIBA Statistics Office *Costs and profitability of private architectural practice* London, RIBA, 1971—

14 Musgrove, John, Chairman of the RIBA Research Committee 'R & D. How much and who pays? What kind and who does it?' *RIBA Journal* Vol 78 1971 Nov pp480—489

15 'Architects' earnings — survey shows no improvement since 1967' *RIBA Journal* Vol 78 1971 Dec pp553—556

16 Hillier, Bill & Leaman, Adrian, RIBA Intelligence Unit 'A new approach to architectural research' *RIBA Journal* Vol 79 1972 Dec pp517—521

17 'What are roles and profiles?' *RIBA Journal* Vol 81 1974 Mar p27. Article on RIBA's research study into the structure of the profession.

18 RIBA Research Steering Group 'Keeping in touch with the real problems' *RIBA Journal* Vol 81 1974 Mar pp28—29

19 RIBA Structure of the Profession Steering Group 'Looking hard at the profession at work' *RIBA Journal* Vol 81 1974 Dec pp20—21. Paper for Council on a proposed RIBA research study into the current constraints on architectural responsibility.

20 RIBA Intelligence Unit 'Architectural research: a matter for public concern' *RIBA Journal* Vol 81 1974 Dec p24

21 RIBA Statistics Section 'Size of the profession' *RIBA Journal* Vol 84 1977 Jan pp262—264

22 RIBA Statistics Office *Architects' employment and earnings* London, RIBA, 1978—

23 RIBA Research Section 'Meet the profession — at last!' *RIBA Journal* Vol 86 1979 May p188. Article on the result of the section's research study into the structure of the profession.
24 RIBA Structure of the Profession Study Steering Group *The structure of the profession* London, RIBA, 1980
25 'Research' Stephen Trombley talks to RIBA's Head of Research and Statistics Mike Kondra. *RIBA Journal* Vol 91 1984 Aug p87.

5
Central services

Section 1 General administration

Up to the mid-1950s the General Office was the administrative centre of the Institute. Until then the only truly distinct departments were the Library and the RIBA Board of Architectural Education, so the General Office dealt not only with internal administration but also some of the work later performed by the Membership and Public Affairs departments, the Press Office, the Journal Office, the Information Services and Professional Services departments, the Practice Department, the Professional Conduct Office and the Legal Adviser's Office. The General Office was under the control of the Chief Clerk, who was responsible to the Assistant Secretary, later called the Deputy Secretary (*see* introduction to Chapter 4). The Deputy Secretary was a link between the Secretary's Office and the General Office. He had direct responsibility for the administration of RIBA premises, Council elections, Council Meetings and General Meetings and serviced the constitutional committees concerned with revision of the by-laws, the Royal Gold Medal committees, the Bronze Medal committees and the Professional Conduct Committee. He also conducted a correspondence with the United Kingdom Allied Societies until 1960, and with the Overseas Allied Societies until 1964.

The staff of the General Office included the Chief Clerk (assisted by three senior clerks, a Records Clerk and several junior clerks), the Cashier (assisted by two clerks), the House Engineer and the Receptionist. The Chief Clerk supervised the clerical work of the office, made arrangements for the annual British Architects Conferences, appointed junior staff, kept staff records and was responsible for the membership records and the production of the annual *Kalendar*. He also assisted members seeking partnerships to contact members wishing to take on partners.

Frederick George Baker was appointed Chief Clerk in 1900 and served until 1946, when he was succeeded by Henry Richard Williamson who retired in 1968. The duties of the senior clerks included the administration of Institute meetings, Allied Society conferences, the Annual Dinners and Receptions, the Bronze Medal Awards, and the preparation of official notices for the *RIBA Journal*. They were also responsible for checking competition conditions against the model form, reporting any differences to the Secretary and passing one copy to the Competitions Committee Secretary and one to the Library.

The finances of the Institute were administered by the Cashier until the appointment of an accountant in 1963 (*see* introduction to Section 2). In the reorganization of 1962/63 the General Office ceased to exist and four new departments were formally recognized, Central Services, Professional Services, Membership Services, and Information Services. The Central Services Department was set up as successor to the General Office. It has an Administration and Records Office, a Finance Office, a House Office and a Personnel Office. From 1965—1975 it was also responsible for membership relations. In 1973 its name was changed to Membership Services and the Finance Office was separated from it. In 1976 its name was changed to Internal Services and it again included the Finance Office. In 1977 it reverted to the title Central Services. In 1984 the title Deputy Secretary RIBA, was revived for the head of Central Services.

[Since the work of the Personnel Office is mainly confidential, descriptions of its record series are not included in the Guide.]

5.1.1   * 'GENERAL OFFICE' PAPERS, 1896—1964   40 boxes
Files of correspondence and data kept by the Deputy Secretary, the Chief Clerk, the Senior Clerks and the Cashier, 1896—1964, including solicitors' opinions on RIBA charter and by-law interpretation, 1904—1957, and correspondence with the Allied Societies, 1940—1964.
Subjects : RIBA staff and pensions: administration of RIBA premises: RIBA finances: administration of meetings: administration of the Bronze Medal awards for architecture and the New Zealand Institute of Architects Gold Medal: RIBA by-law amendments: constitutions of new Allied Societies: administration of social events. (A very incomplete series)

* Access at the discretion of the Archivist

CHIEF CLERK'S PAPERS, 1896—1964
   see   'GENERAL OFFICE' PAPERS, 5.1.1

5.1.2   COMMITTEES ATTENDANCE BOOKS, 1925—1968   9 vols
Contain signatures of those present at meetings of RIBA committees, subcommittees, joint committees and conferences, Annual General Meetings and meetings of the Architects Benevolent Society's Council.

5.1.3   COUNCIL, EXECUTIVE COMMITTEE & COMMITTEES OF COUNCIL ATTENDANCE BOOKS, 1926—1938, 1958— (1983)   3 vols
Contain the signatures of those present at meetings of the Council, committees of Council, the Executive Committee and its subcommittees. From 1961, Council Meetings only.

DEPUTY SECRETARY'S PAPERS, 1946—1964
see   4.1.3 and 5.1.1

5.1.4   * CENTRAL SERVICES DIRECTOR'S PAPERS, 1964— (1980)   15 boxes
Correspondence files of Joan Milne, 1964—1976, and John Grigg (incomplete).
Subjects : Amendments of RIBA constitution: classes of membership: RIBA membership and British nationality: registration: regionalization: relations with Commonwealth and other foreign architects: RIBA budgets: RIBA administration and maintenance of premises: Lyons Report on RIBA policy and administration: subscriptions policy: staff pension scheme: Joint Staff Consultative Committee.

(Joan Milne was also Acting Secretary RIBA, from Jan —Aug 1968)

* Access at the discretion of the Deputy Secretary RIBA

Bibliography

1   Baker, F. G. 'Forty-eight years at the RIBA' *RIBA Journal* Vol 55 1948 Sep p502. Reminiscences of the Chief Clerk of the RIBA.
2   'Central Services Department' *RIBA Journal* Vol 74 1969 Oct pp443—448. Part of a feature article 'Inside the RIBA'.

Section 2 Finance

The original regulations stated that two auditors were to be annually appointed and that the Treasurer should be a banker in London or Westminster; no sums of money were to be paid on account of the Institute except by order of the Council; half the surplus money after the payment of expenses was to be annually invested as an accumulating fund, and the whole of the effects and property of the Institute was to be vested in three Trustees. In January 1835 Sir Thomas Farquhar accepted the appointment of Treasurer. He died the following year and was replaced by Sir W.R. Farquhar who remained in the office of Treasurer until it was abolished under the 1887 charter. Until 1864 the Council directly managed the finances of the Institute without the aid of a standing finance committee and the annual statements of income and expenditure were prepared by the honorary secretaries. A special Finance Committee was appointed in May 1843 to review the Institute's finances. Its minutes have not survived but its conclusions can be seen in the Council Minutes of December 1843. Another special Finance Committee was appointed in 1849 mainly for the purpose of drawing up guiding regulations for keeping the accounts and other financial procedures (*see* 5.2.2). A standing Finance Committee of the Council, started in 1864, passed the responsibility of administering the finances from the honorary secretaries to the chairman of the Finance Committee and the (paid) Secretary, first appointed in 1866, was made responsible for keeping the accounts.

Unfortunately, no minutes of any finance committee have survived from 1892—1926. In 1913 the Finance Committee was enlarged and became the Finance and House Committee. In 1926 Edward Henry Bevan was appointed Cashier and remained in this post until the first RIBA Accountant was appointed in 1963. The Cashier kept the cash books and the various ledgers, prepared forward estimates of income and expenditure and the statements of accounts for the Annual Report and dealt with the payroll, invoices, petty cash, tax payments, expenses and payment of rebates to the Allied Societies. He was assisted by a Stock Clerk and a Publications Clerk who accounted for the stock, sale, despatch and binding of Institute publications and stationery.

In 1965 a new independent Finance Committee was set up, from which the House Committee was separated. In 1967 the Finance Committee became a subcommittee of the Policy and Finance Committee. In 1972 a new Finance and House Committee was set up as an independent committee of Council. The present Finance Office, apart from providing supporting services to all other departments, prepares the annual budget and annual accounts and services the Finance and House Committee. The financial policy of the Institute is determined by the views of the General Body, advised by the Council, and interpreted by the President and the Honorary Treasurer (an honorary office of the Council, instituted under the by-laws of 1934).

5.2.1   CASH BOOK, 1835—1837   1 vol
         Accounts kept by Sir Thomas Farquhar, Treasurer, of cash payments and receipts, donated funds, disbursements for purchase of books, casts, etc., members' life compositions and members' subscription payments.

         ANNUAL BALANCE SHEETS, 1836—
         see   1.2.4 Annual Reports of Council Series

5.2.2 (Special) FINANCE COMMITTEE MINUTES, 1850   1 vol
Signed minutes of meetings, Mar —Dec 1850.
Subjects : Review of the Institute's finances and accounting procedures.

5.2.3 FINANCE COMMITTEE MINUTES, 1864—1892   2 vols
Transcript of minutes of meetings, Feb 1864—Dec 1868; signed minutes
of meetings, Apr 1869—Apr 1891; rough minute-book, 1879—1892.
Included are draft balance sheets of Trust Funds and Ordinary Funds
and estimates of annual income and expenditure.
Subjects : Subscriptions defaulters: bequests and legacies: rents:
investments: staff salaries and wages: expenses of social events and
conferences: costs of printing the *Transactions* etc.: costs of medals: the
Library Funds: fees paid to examiners: repairs and heating of the
premises.

(The signed minutes of this committee from Feb 1864—Dec 1868 are
in the Early Committees Minutes Series, *see* 2.1)

5.2.4 * TRUST FUNDS DEEDS, BEQUESTS & DEEDS OF COV-
ENANT, 1864—(1981)   1 box & 9 envelopes
Deeds of trust and copies of wills relating to the various RIBA prizes,
studentships and bursaries funds, 1864—1957: declarations of trust by
Architectural Union Company shareholders, 1875, 1901 and 1912: deeds
of covenant between the RIBA and its commercial companies, 1969—
1981: Building Fund covenants, 1973—1974, etc.

    * Access at the discretion of the Archivist

5.2.5 ORDINARY FUNDS JOURNAL, 1925—1959   1 vol
Journal of Ordinary Funds accounts, Jan 1925—Dec 1959.

CASHIER'S PAPERS, 1926—1963
see   5.1.1 'GENERAL OFFICE' PAPERS

5.2.6 EXPENSES LEDGERS, 1926—1952   3 vols
Record of expenses kept in three sections, General, Examinations, and
Journal.

5.2.7 FINANCE AND HOUSE COMMITTEE MINUTES, 1927—
1965   13 binders
Signed minutes of meetings of the committee and its subcommittees, May
1927—Jun 1963, with reports, policy memoranda, draft accounts and
balance sheets. Includes minutes of the following subcommittees:
Annual Dinner Subcommittee, Jan 1937—Jan 1939
Annual Dinner Committee, Dec 1946—May 1947

Annual Reception Subcommittee, Dec 1947—Feb 1951
Annual Dinner and Reception Subcommittee, Nov 1951
Dinner Subcommittee, Oct 1953
Coronation and Reception Subcommittee, Dec 1952—Feb 1953
Reception Subcommittee, Nov 1954
RIBA Finances Subcommittee, Sep —Oct 1957
House and Routine Management Subcommittee, Oct 1958—Apr 1959
Budget and Income Subcommittee, Jan —Oct 1963
House Subcommittee, Nov 1963—Mar 1965
Subjects : Defaulters: grants to the British Engineering Standards Associ-
ation and other institutions and associations: letting of the RIBA Galleries
(at 9 Conduit Street): staff salaries: RIBA mortgage and rate of interest:
RIBA Premises Fund: accounts for payment (running of premises,
repairs, costs of printing, exhibitions, general meetings, examinations,
prizes, Library Fund, travelling expenses of provincial members, etc.):
bequests: RIBA Maintenance Scholarships: grants for international
congress committees and the Franco-British Union of Architects: costs
of annual conferences: contributions to the Allied Societies: the RIBA
Journal and advertisements: the New Premises Fund (1920s and 30s):
the Institute's Appeal (1940s): the Premises Redemption Fund (Binder
7): the RIBA Staff Pension Scheme (Binder 8): the Development Fund
(Binder 12).

(These minutes are filed with the Council Minutes until Nov 1933.
Correspondence and other supporting papers from 1958 onwards are
kept in the RIBA Accountant's Office and are available for consultation
at his discretion).

5.2.8   TRUST FUNDS CASH BOOKS, 1932—1973   2 vols
Record of revenue from and expenditure of trust funds, mainly used for
the payment of student prizes, bursaries, studentships and maintenance
scholarships up to 1964 and since then mainly used for payment of
research grants.

(In 1960 the Institute had over thirty separate charitable trust funds and
in that year permission was obtained from the High Court of Justice
Chancery Division to aggregate the various capital sums for investment
purposes. In 1964, twenty-seven of the trusts were amalgamated into
three groups, the Historical Research Trust, the Modern Architecture
and Town Planning Trust and the Prizes Trust. These, with the Annie
Spink Memorial Scholarship, comprise the Institute's Education Fund.
The Institute's Library Fund comprises the Sir Banister Fletcher Library
Bequest, the W. H. Ansell Bequest and the C. McArthur Butler Bequest.
The Premises Fund includes the Henry Jarvis Bequest. Two other trust
funds are the Sawyer Bequest and the Thomas Malvern Prize).

5.2.9 NEW PREMISES FUND ACCOUNT, 1934—1939   1 vol
Record of donations received for the construction of the new RIBA
Building at 66 Portland Place, Apr 1934—Jan 1939.

5.2.10 COMPLETION OF PREMISES FUND ACCOUNT, 1939—
1950   1 vol
Record of donations and subscriptions received for the completion of the
new RIBA Building at 66 Portland Place, Jan 1939—Nov 1950.

5.2.11 TRUST FUNDS LEDGER, 1942—1952   1 vol
Record of trust funds investments, with accounts of revenue and expenditure of funds, Jan 1942—Dec 1952

5.2.12 ORDINARY FUNDS LEDGERS, 1951—1962   7 binders
Ledgers of Ordinary Funds, classified into fifty-six separate categories,
Jan 1951—Dec 1962.

5.2.13 ORDINARY FUNDS CASH BOOKS, 1957—1962   6 binders
Record of receipts and expenditures of Ordinary Funds.

5.2.14 (NEW) FINANCE COMMITTEE MINUTES, 1965—1967   2
binders
Signed minutes of meetings, Sep 1965—Jun 1967, with memoranda,
reports and draft accounts. Also minutes of a meeting of the Charter
Subcommittee, 14 Dec 1965.
Subjects : Similar to Finance Subcommittee Minutes, *see* 5.2.15

(Correspondence and other supporting papers are kept in the RIBA
Accountant's Office and are available for consultation at his discretion).

POLICY AND FINANCE COMMITTEE MINUTES & PAPERS,
1967—1972
see   Chapter 3, Section 1

5.2.15 * FINANCE SUBCOMMITTEE MINUTES, 1967—1972   5 folders
Signed minutes of meetings, Oct 1967—Mar 1972, with memoranda,
reports and draft accounts.
Subjects : Control of expenditure: departmental budgets: *RIBA Journal*
budget: regional finances: the RIBA commercial companies: membership
subscription rates: the Trust Funds: investments: annual accounts:
Library Appeal for funds: insurance: taxation: staff salaries: staff pensions: mechanisation and computerization of RIBA offices.

(A subcommittee of the Policy and Finance Committee. *See also* 3.1.7
Policy and Finance Committee Minutes & Papers).

* Access at the discretion of the RIBA Accountant.

5.2.16   MONITORING GROUP PAPERS, 1971   1 box
File kept by the Secretary to the Group, containing minutes of meetings, memoranda and reports, Aug —Oct 1971.
Subject : Administrative economies and financial control within the Institute and its regions in view of severe financial restraints.

(A working group of the Policy and Finance Committee)

Bibliography

1   RIBA 'Report of the committee appointed to investigate the financial affairs of the Institute, 1843' *RIBA Notices of Meetings* 1843/49 1843 Dec 19
2   'Members' subscription rates and rebate to the Allied Societies' *RIBA Journal* Vol 53 1946 Jun p315
3   'A statement on RIBA finances' *RIBA Journal* Vol 65 1958 Feb pp115—117
4   RIBA 'Report of the Finance and House Committee' *RIBA Journal* Vol 66 1959 Jan pp76—77
5   RIBA Finance and House Committee 'Finance of Allied Societies in the United Kingdom' *RIBA Journal* Vol 68 1961 Feb pp126—127
6   Mathews, E. D. Jefferiss, RIBA Hon. Treasurer 'RIBA Finances' *RIBA Journal* Vol 70 1963 May p174
7   Lakin, Christopher 'Finance for regions, branches and societies' *RIBA Journal* Vol 73 1966 Jan p9
8   Hollamby, Edward, RIBA Hon. Treasurer 'Must subscriptions go up?' *RIBA Journal* Vol 76 1969 Jan pp8—9
9   Foster, Robert, RIBA Hon. Treasurer 'Paying for the RIBA' *RIBA Journal* Vol 78 1971 May pp185—187
10   RIBA Policy and Finance Committee 'Finance and policy' *RIBA Journal* Vol 79 1972 Mar pp95—97
11   RIBA Monitoring Group 'The structure of financial control' *RIBA Journal* Vol 79 1972 May pp182—183 and 217. Paper on financial control within the Institute and its regions, the structure of the RIBA companies and their relationship to the Institute.
12   RIBA Finance Committee & House Subcommittee 'Moving from Portland Place' *RIBA Journal* Vol 79 1972 Jun pp228—229
13   Groves, Alan, chairman of the Membership Relations Board 'A long term strategy for RIBA subscriptions' *RIBA Journal* Vol 81 1974 Nov pp21—22
14   Luder, Owen 'An Hon. Treasurer's job' *RIBA Journal* Vol 83 1976 Oct pp409—410

Section 3 House (RIBA premises and hospitality)

From July 1834 to January 1835 the Institute held its meetings at the Thatched House Tavern in St. James's Street, which was a regular meeting house for several clubs and societies including the Dilettanti and the Royal College of Physicians. In January 1835 the Institute rented three rooms at Covent Garden Chambers, King Street, which the proprietor transformed into Evans' Coffee House and Grand Hotel the following year. Seeking more suitable accommodation the Institute, in June 1837, took rooms at No. 16 Lower Grosvenor Street, but these soon proved inadequate.

The search for better premises was continued throughout the 1840s and early 1850s. In 1857 the Architectural Union Company (AUC) was formed by members of the RIBA and the Architectural Exhibition to provide accommodation for themselves and several other societies, with adequate facilities for exhibiting architectural drawings (*see* Appendix 5). The original shareholders were almost all architects and the board of directors was chosen from those holding at least ten shares. The AUC bought No. 9 Conduit Street in 1858. The house was remodelled inside by Charles Gray and James Edmeston, 1858—1859, and several alterations were also made between 1910 and 1925 to designs by Sir Aston Webb and Arthur Keen. Several photographs of the exterior and interior of No. 9 Conduit Street can be seen in J.A. Gotch (ed.) *The growth and work of the Royal Institute of British Architects*, London, RIBA, 1934. By 1910 the RIBA occupied the whole building and, after buying up all the shares, wound up the company.

In 1930 it was decided to hold a competition for the design of a new RIBA Building at 66 Portland Place and in 1934 the present premises, built to a revised design by Grey Wornum, were completed. Grey Wornum's competition design, revised design and working plans for the RIBA Building can be seen in the RIBA Drawings Collection. Between 1956 and 1958 the building was enlarged to the designs of Playne and Lacey by the addition of two floors to No. 66 and a rebuilt No. 68. Lady Casson was appointed to design schemes for the interior decoration of No. 68 and the public rooms in No. 66. Until the end of 1962 Anthony Williams, an architect on the staff of the RIBA, acted as part-time Surveyor to the Fabric. In 1963 the President appointed Leonard Manasseh as House Architect. He was followed in October 1965 by William Apps, in February 1972 by Richard Finch and in October 1973 by Garnett Cloughley Blakemore and Associates. In 1980 John Phillips was appointed Surveyor to the Fabric, responsible for maintenance and minor works, and the position of House Architect was discontinued.

9   View of the west front of the RIBA Building, 66 Portland Place, taken in 1983. The building was designed by George Grey Wornum and built by Ashby and Horner Ltd, 1933 — 1934. Between 1956 and 1958 two floors were added to No. 66 and No. 68 was rebuilt, to the designs of Playne & Lacey. (British Architectural Library Photographs Collection)

Since the 1950s the RIBA has taken on leases of several additional premises
including No. 21 Portman Square, home of the Drawings Collection since 1972.

The present House Office deals with the management, alteration and repair of
all RIBA premises and the dispensation of hospitality, including social functions,
room bookings and catering services.

5.3.1   (EARLY) NEW PREMISES COMMITTEES PAPERS, 1847—
1854   1 box
File kept by the honorary secretaries containing rough minutes of
meetings, Nov 1850—Jul 1954: correspondence, draft memoranda and
reports, Apr 1848—Jun 1854, and including the following sketches and
drawings: Plan of the Institute's meeting room (no date): plans of
bookcases, 12 Jul 1847: copy of a plan of a proposed site for the Institute
(between Marylebone Street, Air Street and Regents Quadrant) by
James Pennethorne, Apr 1853: sketches for a RIBA building on a site
in Piccadilly by George Bailey, 1854.
Subjects : Search for new, larger premises for the Institute: possible
costs of moving.

(For signed minutes of New Premises committees, Nov 1850—Jul 1857
see 2.1 Early Committees Minutes Series)

5.3.2   TITLE DEEDS & AGREEMENTS CONCERNING RIBA PRE-
MISES, 1859—(1980)   1 box & 14 envelopes
Counterpart leases and agreements concerning use, sale, repair and
alterations to RIBA premises at No. 9 Conduit Street: No. 28 Bedford
Square: Nos. 66 and 68 Portland Place: Finsbury Mission, Moreland
Street, Clerkenwell: No. 78 Wimpole Street: No. 21 Portman Square: No.
5 Clanricarde Gardens, Tunbridge Wells: Nos. 15 and 16 Trumpington
Street, Cambridge: No. 4 St. John's Road, Tunbridge Wells.
Includes ground plans and a drawing of details of the Meeting Room at
No. 9 Conduit Street by James Edmeston and Charles Gray, 1858, and
plans for the rebuilding of No. 68 Portland Place by Wornum & Playne,
1955, and Playne & Lacey, 1957.

5.3.3   PREMISES COMMITTEES MINUTES, 1923—1930   1 vol
Signed minutes of seven successive and short-lived committees concerned
with achieving new premises for the RIBA, Dec 1923—Jun 1930.
Subjects : Proposed rebuilding of Nos. 9 and 10 Conduit Street:
proposed raising of a Centenary Building Fund: proposed alteration of the
Architectural Association's premises, to include Nos. 33—36 Bedford
Square: future of No. 28 Bedford Square (formerly the premises of the
Society of Architects): proposed new RIBA Building on a new site:
consideration of forty-seven potential sites in central London: proposed

competition for new building.

(For previous premises committees minutes *see* 2.1 Early Committees Minutes Series and 2.2 Special Committees Minutes Series)

5.3.4   ANNUAL DINNER COMMITTEE MINUTES, 1926—1936   1 vol
Signed minutes of meetings, Sep 1926—Jan 1936, with lists of guests.
Subject : Arrangements for the Annual Dinners.

(For information on conversaziones and dinners before 1926 *see* 2.1 Early Committees Minutes Series, 2.2 Special Committees Minutes Series and 5.2.3 Finance Committee Minutes Series.
For minutes of Annual Dinner & Reception subcommittees, 1937—1954, *see* 5.2.7 Finance and House Committee Minutes.
For information on Annual Dinners after 1954 *see* 5.2.7 Finance and House Committee Minutes and 5.3.12 House Subcommittee Minutes)

FINANCE AND HOUSE COMMITTEE MINUTES, 1927—1965
  see   5.2.7

5.3.5   NEW PREMISES COMMITTEE MINUTES, 1930—1931   1 vol
Signed minutes of meetings of the committee, its subcommittee and the RIBA Premises Competition Jury of Assessors, Oct 1930—Mar 1931.
Subjects : Promotion of a competition for a new RIBA Building: conditions of the competition.

(This volume is shared with the New Building Committee, which continued this committee's work)

5.3.6   HOUSE ARCHITECTS' DRAWINGS, 1931—(1982)   *c.* 300 items
Drawings for the design, construction, alteration, decoration and maintenance of the RIBA Building and No. 68 Portland Place, by Grey Wornum, Wornum & Playne, Playne & Lacey, Leonard Manasseh & Partners, Black Bayes Gibson & Apps, Garnett Cloughley Blakemore & Associates, DEGW Space Planners (Duffy Eley Giffone Worthington) and John Phillips. Include Grey Wornum's competition design, revised design and working plans for subsequent alterations, 1931—1950, and Playne & Lacey's designs for the RIBA Building extension, 1956—1959.

(Most of the drawings by Grey Wornum have been transferred to the RIBA Drawings Collection at No. 21 Portman Square and can be seen there by appointment. The rest of the drawings are in the House office

at the RIBA Building and can be seen with the permission of the House Manager.
See also   5.3.14 House Architects' Files, 1965—1979)

5.3.7   NEW BUILDING COMMITTEE MINUTES & PAPERS, 1932—1937   2 vols & 3 boxes
Signed minutes of the committee and its Portraits and Busts Subcommittee, Jun 1932—Jun 1934: copies of minutes until Dec 1935: demolition and building contract documents: correspondence of the Secretary to the Committee, Ian Macalister, with the architect, Grey Wornum, the chairman of the committee, Maurice Webb, and the Howard de Walden Estate Office: miscellaneous papers, 1932—1937, with background papers back to 1929.
Subjects : New Premises competition: site of new premises: revision of Grey Wornum's design to reduce costs: foundation stone ceremony: conditions of the lease: tendering: building contract with Ashby & Horner: appointment of consultants and clerk of works: architect's and consultants' fees: heating and ventilation: sculpture, finishings, fittings, decorations: statements of accounts: allocation of rooms: fire precautions.

5.3.8   SOCIAL COMMITTEE MINUTES, 1932—1939   2 vols
Signed minutes of meetings of the committee and its subcommittees, Mar 1932—Jul 1939.
Subjects : Arrangement of informal receptions with music, dance and drama: the Architects' Ball at Olympia in aid of the Architects Unemployment Relief Fund: activities of the RIBA Dance Club, Dramatic Society, Music Group and Camera Club.

CENTENTARY COMMITTEE MINUTES & PAPERS, 1933—1934
see   11.4.7

5.3.9   WAR MEMORIAL COMMITTEE PAPERS, 1946—1948   1 box
Correspondence of the committee, Apr 1946—Jun 1948
Subjects : Design, inscription and unveiling of the war memorial plaque at RIBA headquarters.

(For minutes of this committee *see* 2.2 Special Committees Minutes Series)

5.3.10   WORLD REFUGEE YEAR BRITISH ARCHITECTS APPEAL COMMITTEE MINUTES & PAPERS, 1959—1960   1 box

10   George Grey Wornum, the architect, and Joseph Pile, the general foreman, meeting on site during the construction of the RIBA Building, 66 Portland Place, in 1933. The unusually large voids of the interior presented several problems in the design of the steel frame. The structural engineers were R. T. James & Partners and the steelwork was done by Matthew T. Shaw Ltd. (British Architectural Library Photographs Collection)

Signed minutes of meetings, Dec 1959 — Apr 1960, with correspondence and reports of subcommittees.

Subjects : Entertainments to raise funds for the World Refugee Year U.K. Committee, including a special function at the RIBA.

5.3.11   (NEW) SOCIAL COMMITTEE MINUTES & PAPERS, 1959—1962   1 vol & 1 box
Signed minutes of meetings, Dec 1959—Jul 1962, with correspondence file of the Secretary to the committee, 1959—1960.
Subjects : Opening of a Members Club Room: organization of the 1960 Reception: RIBA Balls: scheme for the redecoration of the RIBA Building.

5.3.12   * HOUSE (SUB)COMMITTEE MINUTES, 1963—(1979)
11 binders
Minutes of meetings, from July 1963, with House Architect's reports and other agenda papers.
Subjects : Maintenance, furnishing, decoration and alteration of the Institute's premises: domestic administration including catering services, social functions and hospitality: letting of accommodation: liaison with House Architect and House Engineer: the Building Fund and the Maintenance Fund.

(For House matters, 1927—1962 *see* 5.2.7 Finance and House Committee Minutes. In 1962 the House committee became a subcommittee of the Policy Committee, in 1967 of the Policy and Finance Committee and in 1973 of the (New) Finance and House Committee. For House Committee working files, 1964—1978 *see* 5.3.13)

* Access at the discretion of the House Manager

5.3.13   * HOUSE MANAGER'S PAPERS, 1964—(1982)   25 boxes
House Committee working files, 1964—1978: correspondence with the House Architect, 1965—1982: room bookings records, 1966—1980: files on office accommodation and maintenance of premises at Nos. 66/68 Portland Place, Nos. 42—46 Weymouth Street, No. 13 Bridford Mews, No. 86 Marylebone High Street (including drawings) and No. 6 Higham Place, Newcastle-on-Tyne: and various subject files.
Subjects : Maintenance, decoration, furnishing and alteration of RIBA premises: House Committee meetings and finances: room booking service: catering services: office accommodation: the Building Fund Programme: installation of the computer.

* Access at the discretion of the House Manager

5.3.14   HOUSE ARCHITECT'S FILES, 1965—(1979)   7 boxes

Working files of William Apps, Jul 1965—Jan 1972, and of Garnett Cloughley Blakemore & Associates, 1974—1979, including correspondence with the RIBA House Manager, the quantity surveyor, structural engineer and other specialists, minutes of site meetings and architect's reports.

Subjects : Maintenance, decoration, furnishing, repair and alteration of RIBA premises.

(*See also* 5.3.6 House Architects' Drawings, 1931—(1982))

See also in 2.1 Early Committees Minutes Series:
New Premises Committee, 1850—1857
Conversazione Committee, 1850—1868
Lighting and Ventilation (of the premises) Committee, 1863
and in 2.2 Special Committees Minutes Series:
Institute Dinner Committee, 1869 & 1879
Conversazione Committee, 1875 & 1882
Ventilation of the Meeting Room Committee, 1875—1876
Premises Committee, 1878, 1883, 1909—1910
Building Committee of Council (alterations to premises), 1879
Freehold Premises at 20 Hanover Square Subcommittee of Council, 1883
Annual Dinner Committee, 1897—1925
Site Committee (seeking site for new RIBA premises), 1900
War Record Committee, 1915
War Memorial Subcommittee, 1946
and 5.1.1 'General Office' Papers Series

Bibliography

1   'The RIBA meeting room' *RIBA Journal* Vol 31 1924 Mar 22 pp312—314. Article on the reconstruction of the meeting room at No. 9 Conduit Street.

2   'New premises for the RIBA' *RIBA Journal* Vol 36 1929 Apr 13 pp438—442

3   'The New Building Competition' *RIBA Journal* Vol 39 1932 May 14 pp568—584. Article on the exhibition of competition drawings for the new RIBA Building at 66 Portland Place.

4   Wornum, Grey 'The new RIBA premises' *Builder* Vol 143 1932 Dec 9 pp971—978. Notes on his revised design for No. 66 Portland Place.

5   Atkinson, Robert 'The RIBA New Premises Competition' *RIBA Journal* Vol 40 1932 Dec 10 pp80—91

6   'The RIBA and No. 9 Conduit Street' *RIBA Journal* Vol 40 1932 Dec 10 p100

7   Wornum, Grey 'The new RIBA premises. The architect's note on the revised scheme' *RIBA Journal* Vol 40 1932 Dec 10 pp93—99

5.3   House (RIBA premises and hospitality)

8   'The laying of the foundation stone of the RIBA new building in Portland Place' *RIBA Journal* Vol 40 1933 Jul 8 pp686—688

9   'Obituaries of buildings no. 35. No. 9 Conduit Street, London' *Architect and Building News* Vol 40 1934 Nov 2. Insert between pp128—129

10   'The Royal Institute of British Architects, Portland Place' *Architect and Building News* Vol 40 1934 Nov 2 pp129—157. Article on the RIBA Building.

11   White, L. W. Thornton 'The new headquarters of the RIBA' *Builder* Vol 147 1934 Nov 2 pp752—762

12   'The RIBA new headquarters. Design of the steelwork' *Builder* Vol 147 1934 Nov 2 p769

13   'The buildings of the RIBA, 1834—1934' *RIBA Journal* Vol 42 1934 Nov 6 pp5—17

14   RIBA Premises Committee 'The New Building scheme. A short history of the work of the Premises Committee and the sites considered' *RIBA Journal* Vol 42 1934 Nov 6 pp18—20

15   'The RIBA New Building' *RIBA Journal* Vol 42 1934 Nov 6 pp22—90

16   Edwards, A. Trystan 'The RIBA Building. An appreciation of the exterior' *Architects' Journal* Vol 80 1934 Nov 8 pp669—672

17   'RIBA Building' *Architects' Journal* Vol 80 1934 Nov 8 pp673—699

18   'The opening ceremony' *RIBA Journal* Vol 42 1934 Nov 24 pp101—127. Article on the royal opening of the RIBA Building, No. 66 Portland Place.

19   Reilly, Professor C. H. 'Grey Wornum and his building' *Architectural Review* Vol 76 1934 Dec pp192—202. Article on the RIBA Building, No. 66 Portland Place, and its architect.

20   Tripe, A. C. 'The building in detail' *Architectural Review* Vol 76 1934 Dec pp203—210. Article on details of the RIBA Building, No. 66 Portland Place.

21   'The centenary banquet' *RIBA Journal* Vol 42 1934 Dec 8 pp161—166

22   'Extensions to the RIBA Building' *RIBA Journal* Vol 64 1956 Dec pp51—55

23   MacEwen, Malcolm 'RIBA working groups (2). House Subcommittee' *RIBA Journal* Vol 78 1971 Mar pp119—120

24   RIBA Finance Committee and House Subcommittee 'Moving from Portland Place' *RIBA Journal* Vol 79 1972 Jun pp228—229

25   Jones, Nicholas 'Are there better uses for the Institute's building?' *RIBA Journal* Vol 82 1975 Jan p19. Discussion of proposal to turn the RIBA Building into an Architecture Centre.

26   Richardson, Margaret 'The RIBA Building' *Architectural Design* Vol 49 No 10/11 1979 pp60—71. Special issue 'Britain in the thirties'

27   Richardson, Margaret *66 Portland Place. The London headquarters of the Royal Institute of British Architects* London, RIBA Publications Ltd, 1984

Section 4 Membership records

The original regulations stipulated three classes of members, Fellows, Associates and Honorary Members. Fellows should be architects who had been engaged as principals in the practice of civil architecture for at least seven successive years; Associates should be persons aged twenty-one and over engaged in the study or practice of civil architecture for less than seven years; Honorary Fellows should be noblemen or gentlemen unconnected with any branch of building as a trade or business, who had contributed twenty-five guineas to the Institute's funds; Honorary Members should be persons eminent for their works or scientific acquirements, not being British architects. Fellows and Associates were to pay annual subscriptions, Honorary Members were not expected to contribute to the funds and, if resident abroad, were called Honorary and Corresponding Members.

In 1838 the Institute introduced a class of Student Members which gave the right of using the Library and attending Institute lectures and meetings but did not provide any very significant element in their architectural education. In 1877 it was decided to require all candidates for Associate membership after May 1882 to have passed a professional examination (*see* introduction to Chapter 7). It was also decided that the Institute itself should not attempt to be a teaching body and the class of Student Members was discontinued.The revised by-laws of 1877 introduced a class of Honorary Associates, who should be persons engaged in the study, but not the practice, of civil architecture who could contribute to the advancement of professional knowledge and who must not be connected with any branch of building as a trade or business (such persons had, since 1855, been allowed to become Contributing Visitors).

The new charter of 1887 stated that Fellows must be architects aged thirty and over who had been a principal in architectural practice for at least seven successive years and that, from 1892, the Institute could either require candidates for direct entry to the Fellowship to pass an examination or dispense with such examination in special cases. All candidates for the Associateship must have passed an examination as directed by the Institute.

The charter of 1908 introduced the class of Licentiate members as a means of bringing into the Institute, prior to achieving an act for the statutory registration of architects, as many practising architects as possible who, while competent and in many cases experienced architects of long standing, could not be expected to submit themselves to the RIBA qualifying examination. A Licentiate should be an architect aged thirty and over who had either worked as a principal in architectural practice for at least five successive years or had been engaged for at least ten successive years in the practice or study of architecture. Licentiates did not become corporate members entitled to the vote until the absorption of the Society of Architects in 1925, most of whose members entered the RIBA as Licentiates. The charter of 1908 also stated that no-one should be admitted as a Fellow unless he was an Associate (or had passed the examination qualifying for admission to the Associateship) or a Licentiate who had passed an examination qualifying for admission to the Fellowship, or a person whom the Council had specially resolved was desirable to be elected as a Fellow.

The charter of 1925 stated that an Associate not in private practice who was or had been in a position of responsibility for the design of architectural work could be elected to the Fellowship, and so could a Licentiate in a similar position. Also, Licentiates who were over sixty years old and had been engaged as principals in the practice of architecture for at least seven successive years could be elected to the Fellowship without passing a qualifying examination. The charter of 1925 started a new non-corporate class of Subscribers, who could be persons who were not professional architects but who were interested in the Institute and in architectural matters. This class never flourished and was closed in 1929. The charter also reintroduced the non-corporate elected class of Student RIBA.

The supplemental charter of 1971 introduced a single class of Corporate Members which replaced the classes of Fellows, Associates and Licentiates. Former Fellows and Retired Fellows can be recognized in the Directory of Members as they have numbers beginning with 98, and former Licentiates and Retired Licentiates have numbers beginning with 99; former Associates and Retired Associates have numbers in the range 0—030740. Under the 1971 charter the class of Honorary and Corresponding Members was closed. Those foreign architects who were formerly eligible for this class are now eligible for nomination to the class of Honorary Fellows.

All candidates for election to RIBA membership had to submit 'Nomination Papers', application forms with recommendations and declarations, which, from the 1870s onwards, usually provide unique information on the professional education and experience of the candidate and, in the case of Fellows and Licentiates, usually include a list of architectural works for which they had been responsible.

5.4.1   MEMBERSHIP REGISTER (EARLY SERIES), 1834—1892   1 vol

Register of all members and office-bearers elected between 1834 and 1891, classified as follows: Fellows, May 1834—Mar 1892: Associates, Jan 1835—Mar 1892: Life Members, Jan 1835—Jul 1872: Honorary Fellows, May 1835—Jan 1873: Honorary Members, May 1835—Jan 1873: Honorary and Corresponding Members, May 1835—Jan 1892: Students, Jan 1839—Feb 1877: Contributing Visitors, Jan 1855—Feb

1873: Honorary Associates, Dec 1877—Jan 1892: retired, deceased or expelled members of all classes, 1834—1885: office bearers, 1834—1891: members of Council, 1834—1891.

Normally provides full name, date of election, Institute offices held, prizes won, whether or not a donor to the funds or the collections. Often includes remarks, mainly date of death, but in the case of Honorary and Corresponding Members sometimes a description of professional position, and whether or not a Royal Gold Medal winner.

(From the 1880s separate registers began to be kept for the different classes of membership.

A names card index to RIBA members, 1834—1886, was compiled by H. V. Molesworth-Roberts from this register, and is available for consultation in the Library. From 1886, names of members, with dates of election, membership numbers, and addresses are listed in the annual RIBA *Kalendar* (and, later, in the *Directory of Members*), which are available for consultation in the Library).

5.4.2   * FELLOWS   NOMINATION   PAPERS,   1834—1857,   1866— 1971   25 vols, 24 boxes & several hundred folders
Recommendations and declarations of Fellows elected from 1834 onwards, accompanied from 1880 onwards (and frequently from 1872) by some particulars of their professional education, practice, architectural and literary works. Vols 1—6 include the nomination papers of Honorary Members, Honorary Fellows, and Honorary and Corresponding Members, 1834—1882. Vol 1 includes letters from the Original Members acknowledging their election, Jun —Dec 1834, and the special declarations of the previous members of the Architectural Society who became Fellows of the Institute in 1842.

(Vol 3 covering the period Apr 1857—Dec 1865 is missing)

 * Access at the discretion of the Archivist

5.4.3   * ASSOCIATES   NOMINATION   PAPERS,   1835—1842,   1857— 1971   33 vols, 21 boxes, & several thousand folders
Recommendations and declarations of Associates elected from 1835 onwards, accompanied from 1872 onwards by particulars of their architectural education and experience. Vol 1 includes the special declarations of the previous members of the Architectural Society who became Associates of the Institute in 1842.

(Vol 2 covering the period Nov 1842—Dec 1856 is missing.
When a computerized system was introduced in 1973, noughts were prefixed to Associates' original numbers, as required, to make the number contain six digits, e.g. a former Associate whose number was 5967 became 005967).

 * Access at the discretion of the Archivist

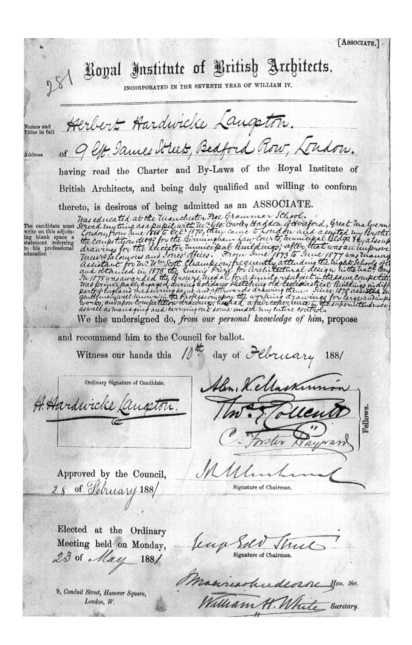

11   Part of a candidate's application to be elected an Associate of the RIBA, 1881.
The Associates Nomination Papers, from which this example is taken, give valuable
information on the professional education and early career of thousands of British
architects. The Associateship was replaced by Corporate Membership in 1971.
(RIBA Archive:5.4.3)

CANDIDATE'S SEPARATE STATEMENT. [FELLOW.]

It is required, in accordance with By-law 8, that every Candidate desirous of being admitted a Fellow of the Royal Institute of British Architects furnish the Council with information suggested in the items herebelow printed, and that each date be given clearly and precisely.

*** The particulars written below must also be inserted in a condensed form by the Candidate on his Nomination Paper.

ITEMS.	DATES.	DESCRIPTION.
I.—The manner in which he received his professional education, and the date of commencing same.	1864-6	Educated at University College London, where I obtained prizes and certificates for architecture, civil engineering, geology, mineralogy, mathematics, philology, French, German, &c
	1866	and the first Donaldson silver medal for architecture -
II.—Particulars as to his engagements, time spent in travelling, &c., before he commenced independent practice.	1866-70	Pupil of Sir Matthew Digby Wyatt -
	1869	Student Royal Academy
	1872	Passed district Surveyors Examination
	1871	Clerk of Works Burlington Fine Arts Club, Savile Row (M.D.W. arch)
	1871-2	Do. Ottoman Bank (W. Burnet, archt)
	1872	Travelled in Italy for 3 months
		(besides short visits to Paris, Vienna, Frankfort, Holland &c at various
III.—The year in which he commenced independent practice, and the locality.	1872	assisted Mr Meakin of Clements Lane E.C. for a while -
	1872	at 17 Southampton Street, Bloomsbury, London -
IV.—A list of the principal buildings in the erection, alteration, decoration, &c, of which he has been engaged since he commenced independent practice, with their respective dates.	1873	East Hill House, Wimbledon for F. B. Thomas Eq. (A)
	—4	Borough Jewish Schools, Heygate St, Walworth - (N&A)
		1 America Square. E.C. (A) 22 Oxford Street (A)
	—5	Borough Synagogue (A) 64 Charlotte St. W. (A) 32 Tottenham St. (N)
	—6	55 G. Queen St. W.C. (A) 7 Maddox St. (N) [2d old Bailey (N)
	—7	43 Ludgate Hill (N) Hambro Synagogue (A) Woodland Hedrope (A
	—8	7 Little Pulteney St. (N) Factory Wood Green (A) 71 Surrey Place (A)
	—9	Inner Chambers, Queen Victoria St. (N) 25 Catherine Street E.C. (N)
	—80	Commercial St. Model Dwellings &c (N) 7 Back Lane (A) Museum St (A
V.—A list of any literary or artistic works of which he is the author.		Villas at Westgate on Sea (N) 86 Bishops Rd (A) 8th Salem School (A)
	—81	28 & 28½ Little St Andrews St. (N) 19 Gloster pl. (A) 59 Pall Mall, W. (N)
	—82	122 G. Suffolk St. (N) Stables &c Maida Vale (N) 30 Little Queen St (N)
		Stables & another Kensington (N) 74 Park Crescent (A) 26 Ely Place (A)
		Frankly House Brook Green (A) Cambridge Road. S. (N) Villa Sitwell (A)
		27 Ely Place (A) 34 & 36 Haraway St. (N) 27 Ely Place (A)
		various articles in papers - especially a series entitled "the History of furniture & decoration from the earliest times till the rise of Greek art - illustrated -

I hereby declare that the above statement made by me this _First_ day of _March_, 18_83_, is a full and true account of my professional education and works.

Signature of Candidate _Lewis Solomon_

Address of Candidate _7 Grays Inn Square_

_____, Hon. Sec.

William H. White, Secretary.

ROYAL INSTITUTE OF BRITISH ARCHITECTS,
9. Conduit Street, Hanover Square, London, W.

12 Part of a candidate's application to be elected a Fellow of the RIBA, 1883. The Fellows Nomination Papers, from which this example is taken, and a similar series of Licentiates Nomination Papers, often give otherwise unobtainable information on the architectural works done during the first seven years or more of practice of thousands of British architects. The Licentiateship ceased in 1956 and the Fellowship in 1971. (RIBA Archive:5.4.2)

5.4.4   STUDENTS NOMINATION PAPERS, 1838—1877   1 vol
Applications to be admitted to the Student class of membership, Dec
1838—Feb 1877, giving name and address of applicant, signatures of
two Fellows, date of application, date of admission and sometimes
annotated with date of subsequent election as Associate or Fellow or
retirement from the class. From 1862 a few of them take the form of an
application for admission to the Voluntary Architectural Examination
administered by the Institute.

(After a qualifying examination for Associate membership became obligatory, students were no longer nominated by their employers for election
as Student Members but applied to take the examinations organized by
the Institute and to be enrolled as Probationer RIBA, after passing the
Preliminary Examination, and as Student RIBA, after passing the
Intermediate Examination, *see* Chapter 7, Education, Section 2, RIBA
Examinations.)

5.4.5   HONORARY ASSOCIATES NOMINATION PAPERS, 1877—
1966   3 vols
Recommendations and declarations of Honorary Associates, Dec 1877—
Jul 1966, giving full name, title, address, signature and date of election.

5.4.6   HONORARY FELLOWS & HONORARY AND CORRES-
PONDING MEMBERS NOMINATION PAPERS, 1882—
1980   2 vols
Recommendations of Honorary Fellows and Honorary and Corresponding Members, Mar 1882 onwards, giving full name, title, signature,
date of election, and occasionally grounds for recommendation.

(For nomination papers of Honorary Fellows and Honorary and Corresponding Members before Mar 1882 *see* 5.4.2 Fellows Nomination
Papers, Vols 1—6)

5.4.7   ASSOCIATES REGISTER, 1882—1971   14 vols
A register of Associates elected between Nov 1882—Jul 1971, and of
Fellows elected from the Associate class from Oct 1964—Jul 1971, giving
serial number, name, address, date of election, and remarks such as date
of election as Fellow, deceased, retired, resigned, suspended, expelled or
reinstated. On the first three folios of Vol 1 are written the names of
those who had passed the Voluntary Architectural Examination between
1863 and 1881.

(For Associates elected before Nov 1882 *see* 5.4.1 Membership Register
(Early Series). In Oct 1964 it was decided that corporate members were

to retain the same serial number throughout their membership instead of changing number when transferring from the Associateship to the Fellowship, so from 1964—1971 Fellows elected from the Associate class were not entered in the Fellows Register, but had their change of status recorded in the remarks column of this register. The last volume of this register includes the start of the register of Corporate Members, elected from Oct 1971—Apr 1973)

5.4.8   FELLOWS REGISTER, 1888—1971   4 vols
A register of Fellows elected between Nov 1888—Jul 1971, giving serial number, name, address, date of election, and remarks such as deceased, transferred to Retired Fellow, resigned, suspended, expelled or reinstated.

(For Fellows elected before Nov 1888 *see* 5.4.1 Membership Register (Early Series). In Oct 1964 it was decided that corporate members were to retain the same serial number throughout their membership instead of changing number when transferring from the Associateship to the Fellowship. For Fellows elected from the Associate class from Oct 1964—Jul 1971 *see* 5.4.7 Associates Register).

5.4.9   HONORARY ASSOCIATES REGISTER, 1889—1966   1 vol
A register of Honorary Associates, from Nov 1889—Jul 1966, giving serial number, name, address, date of election, and remarks such as deceased, resigned, ceased, made an Honorary Fellow.

(For Honorary Associates elected between Dec 1877 and 1889 *see* 5.4.1 Membership Register (Early Series))

5.4.10   LICENTIATES REGISTER, 1910—1912, 1925—1956   6 vols
A register of Licentiates elected between Jun 1910 and Jun 1912 and between Feb 1925 and Dec 1956, giving serial number, name, address, date of election, and remarks such as deceased, resigned, retired, expelled, reinstated, made a Fellow, transferred from the Society of Architects.

(The class of Licentiates was opened in Jun 1910, closed in Jun 1912, reopened in Feb 1925 and closed in Dec 1956)

5.4.11   *LICENTIATES NOMINATION PAPERS, 1910—1912, 1925—1956   27 vols, 27 boxes, & several hundred folders
Recommendations and declarations of Licentiates elected between Jun 1910 and Jun 1912 and between Feb 1925 and Dec 1956, with particulars of professional experience and statements of architectural works, except in the case of those transferring in bulk from the Society of Architects in 1925.

(Box 2 covering part of March 1925 is missing. The Licentiateship class was closed between July 1912 and Jan 1925)

* Access at the discretion of the Archivist

5.4.12   REGISTER OF MEMBERS TRANSFERRED FROM THE SOCIETY OF ARCHITECTS, 1925—1927   3 vols
Register of members of the Society of Architects who transferred to the RIBA between Feb 1925 and Apr 1927, classified as follows: Fellow SA to Fellow RIBA, Member SA to Licentiate RIBA, Licentiate SA to Student RIBA. Gives date of admission, RIBA serial number, name and address.

5.4.13   SUBSCRIBERS REGISTER, 1925—1929   1 vol
A register of members of the Subscriber class, from Jul 1925—May 1929, giving name, address, date of election, and remarks such as resigned, reinstated or ceased.

5.4.14   NON-MEMBERS INDEX, *c* .1930—1982   *c* .50,000 cards
Card index of ex-members of the RIBA (e.g. because of death, retirement, resignation or expulsion), of students who did not become Corporate Members, and of architects registered with ARCUK who were not RIBA members. This index was started *c* .1950 and extended retrospectively back to the 1930s. Cards give name, membership number, ARCUK number, reason for cessation of membership, with date.

(Now superseded by a computerized system)

5.4.15   PRACTICES INDEX, 1962—1974   *c* .7,000 cards
Cards on private architectural practices in the U.K. and N. Ireland which had a RIBA member as a principal or partner, 1962—1974. They provide date, registered name of practice, address of head office and any branch offices, names of partners and other staff. They are often annotated with date of closure or amalgamation of the practice, and change of name or status.

(Superseded by a computerized system in 1973)

5.4.16   CORPORATE MEMBERS AND STUDENT MEMBERS REGISTER, 1971—(1983)   5 vols
Register of Corporate Members, from Oct 1971, and of Student Members and Corporate Members, from May 1973, giving serial number, name, address, date of election as Student Member (where applicable), date of election as Corporate Member (where applicable), and remarks such as deceased, resigned, suspended, expelled or reinstated.

(The start of this register, Oct 1971—Jul 1973, is to be found in the last volume of the Associates Register. A second start was made in May 1973 coinciding with a new computerized registration procedure in which

Student Members and directly elected Corporate Members (i.e. not having been Student Members) form one numerical sequence).

5.4.17   * CORPORATE MEMBERS & STUDENT MEMBERS NOMINA-
TION PAPERS, 1971—(1983)   1 box & several hundred folders
Recommendations and declarations of Corporate Members and Student Members, from Oct 1971, giving full name, address, date of birth, nationality, name of architectural school, particulars of architectural education and examinations passed, date of commencement of course, date of election, and sometimes correspondence concerning membership and subscriptions.

* Access at the discretion of the Archivist

Bibliography

1   Goldring, Patrick 'Just for the record' *RIBA Journal* Vol 72 1965 May p 251. Article on the work of the RIBA Records Department.
2   'From Kalendar to Directory' *RIBA Journal* Vol 73 1966 Oct p 439

6
Library and Collections

The Institute's Library, which started as a special collection for the exclusive use of the members, has developed into the national architectural archive which is open to all and whose staff provides an information service by post and telephone. It is one of the largest and finest architectural libraries in the world and includes outstanding collections of early printed works, manuscripts, photographs, drawings, models, drawing instruments and medals. Its geographical range is worldwide and its subject range includes not only the practice, theory, design and history of architecture but also the allied arts, planning, building techniques and materials, industrial design, interior decoration and landscaping.

The original prospectus for the formation of an architects' institute in 1834 gave as two of its main objectives the formation of a library of architectural works and a museum of antiquities, models, casts and specimens of building materials. The purpose of the museum was to enable students to practise drawing 'from the antique' and to provide the means of performing experiments in building construction and materials. These aims were repeated in the Opening Address of 1835 and Charles Barry set the Library off to a good start by donating £20 for the purchase of standard works. Members were repeatedly exhorted to donate books, pamphlets, manuscripts, prints and drawings and they responded generously. Thomas Leverton Donaldson, Honorary Secretary, conducted an enthusiastic correspondence with foreign architects who were elected Honorary and Corresponding Members and, as a result, many of them donated published works, manuscripts and drawings. By 1838 the collections were extensive enough to justify the printing of a catalogue and in 1839 the Library declared its intention to collect a complete series of the editions of Vitruvius and to possess 'some autograph specimens of the talents of every distinguished architect'.

In 1842 the Library was enhanced by the addition of the library of the Architectural Society which had merged with the Institute. By 1843 the collection of drawings and prints required some attention and a special committee was appointed to arrange and classify it. The size of the Library and Museum forced the Institute to move to larger premises in 1845 and new printed catalogues were produced between 1846 and 1848. In 1850 a standing committee for the management of the Library was appointed and in 1854 the Library was thrown open to

Contributing Visitors, in addition to members and student members. The move to No. 9 Conduit Street in 1859 provided the Library for the first time with adequate premises but by the 1870s the bulky collection of casts, which consisted mainly of plaster casts of capitals, friezes, etc. of classical Greek and Roman temples, was becoming an embarrassment and in 1873 most of it was transferred to the Royal Architectural Museum (whence some of it eventually made its way to the Victoria and Albert Museum.) By 1883 the collection of photographs of architects' works was extensive enough for it to be necessary to appoint a subcommittee of the Library Management Committee to consider how best to classify the photographs and bind them into volumes.

In 1886 the Institute set up four large departmental standing committees, one of which was the Literature Standing Committee which took over responsibility for the management of the Library in 1891. In 1894 it appointed a subcommittee for the development of the Library which recommended greatly enlarging the Loan Collection. By 1910 the large collection of building stones, which included the specimens prepared for the royal commission appointed to select the stone for the Houses of Parliament, had become an embarrassment, being disarranged, space-consuming and outclassed by the collection of building stones and bricks at the Museum of Practical Geology in Jermyn Street, so it was given to the Architectural Association.

In 1930 E. J. 'Bobby' Carter, ARIBA, was appointed Librarian, and editor of the *RIBA Journal*, and set about modernizing the Library, completely reclassifying its contents and greatly expanding the UDC classification system in the classes of Building Science, Architecture and Planning. His enthusiasm for modern architecture, his wide acquaintance with British and foreign architects, his attractive personality, energy and unorthodox views all combined to make the Library an international centre for progressive architectural, building and planning studies in addition to being what it always had been, a superb historical collection. During his time the indexing of periodicals was expanded and put on a systematic footing and a regular 'Review of Periodicals' was published in the *RIBA Journal* which was the forerunner of the present *Architectural Periodicals Index* (API). In 1934 the Library moved, with the Institute, to No. 66 Portland Place.

In 1935 a subcommittee examined the RIBA collection of photographs and visited the photographs collections at the Courtauld Institute and the Victoria and Albert Museum. It reported that the collection was unindexed and difficult to use and that no proper storage was available and recommended that it should be offered to the Courtauld Institute and the V & A Museum. Most of the collection was given to the Courtauld Institute, with photographs of foreign buildings going to the V & A Museum, and subsequently much of it was transferred to the National Buildings Record, now the National Monuments Record.

The Library remained open during the war but some of its most valuable treasures were put into store at the National Library of Wales at Aberystwyth. 1944 saw the start of the Professional Literature Committee, then called the Professional Text and Reference Books Committee, to review and promote books

13   Drawing by Hanslip Fletcher of the RIBA Library at 9 Conduit Street just before its removal to the new RIBA Building at 66 Portland Place in 1934. The Institute had been at 9 Conduit Street since 1859. The building was designed in 1779 by James Wyatt and remodelled inside by Charles Gray and James Edmeston in 1858 — 1859. (British Architectural Library Drawings Collection)

likely to be of value to the profession and prepare the annual *RIBA Book List* of recommended books. After the war a new library managing committee was set up which appointed a standing Drawings Committee and one of the main features of the history of the Library in the 1950s and 1960s was the indexing and development of the Drawings Collection, leading to the appointment of a Drawings Curator in 1954 and culminating in 1971 in the removal of the Drawings Collection to larger premises at No. 21 Portman Square and the opening of the Heinz Gallery for exhibitions. In 1952 the Library had been a substantial beneficiary under the will of Sir Banister Flight Fletcher, President of the RIBA from 1929—1931 and was renamed the Sir Banister Fletcher Library.

In 1967 an administrative restructuring of the Institute resulted in the appointment of a Library Board to which the Books Committee, the Drawings Committee, and the Professional Literature Committee reported. In 1971 the RIBA ceased to have an Exhibitions Officer and the RIBA Loan Collection of Exhibition Photographs, consisting partly of photographs of buildings which had won Bronze Medal Awards (*see* Chapter 11, Section 3), was transferred to the Library where it formed the basis of a resuscitated Photographs Collection. The main event of the 1970s was the launching of the Library Appeal for funds, with the consequent change of name to the British Architectural Library and the setting up of the British Architectural Library Trust to administer the funds. This injection of resources has led to the indexing and development of the Manuscripts & Archives Collection and the Photographs Collection, the further development of the Drawings Collection and the preparation of a scholarly catalogue of the Early Works Collection, a world famous collection of some 3500 items of pre-1841 printed material on all aspects of architectural design which includes copies of fifty-seven different editions of Vitruvius published between c.1482 and 1837. The latest development in the Library is the introduction in 1985 of a comprehensive computerization scheme for cataloguing, indexing and administration.

The Drawings Collection

The collection contains over 400,000 drawings made by architects for buildings, furniture, gardens, stage sets, stained glass and many other things that sometimes fall within the architect's province. It includes preliminary sketches, design drawings, contract drawings, working drawings, perspective views, competition drawings, measured drawings, topographical drawings, prints, sketchbooks and about 100 architectural models. Most of the drawings are by British architects but there are important groups of foreign material including drawings by Palladio, a collection of eighteenth century Italian and French stage designs and a large number of drawings of buildings in India. The period covered extends from the late 15th century to the present. Most leading British architects are represented in the collection and there are some very large deposits for several Victorian and Edwardian architects. The 1920s and 1930s and the Modern Movement are well represented and there are plenty of examples of the work of every period. The collection is housed at No. 21 Portman Square and is open to everyone, by appointment with the curatorial staff, from 10am to 1pm. Comprehensive card indexes are available and a printed catalogue, *Catalogue of the Drawings Collection of the Royal Institute of British Architects* in 19 vols. edited by Jill Lever, 1969— , (*see* Bibliography).

The Manuscripts & Archives Collection

A large collection of the papers of architects, designers, builders, craftsmen, tradesmen and architectural historians and the archives of several architectural or related societies. It occupies more than 300 metres of shelving and extends from the early seventeenth century to the present. The collection relates mainly to British architecture and British architects but includes some important material from other countries, particularly France and Italy. It contains material in a variety of forms including manuscripts, typescripts, printed ephemera and microfilm and the types of document include personal correspondence, diaries, travel journals, office letter-books, job files, accounts ledgers, building contracts, estimates, specifications of works, apprenticeship indentures, minutebooks, notebooks, presscutting collections, and manuscripts of published and unpublished books, essays, theses, articles and lectures. Noteworthy features include the large Scott family archive, from Sir George Gilbert Scott to Sir Giles Gilbert Scott, and over 2,500 letters written by Sir Edwin Lutyens.

The use of the collection is open to everyone and the finding-aids available in the Library include a guide, descriptive lists and indexes.

The Photographs Collection

An extensive collection of approximately 80,000 prints (and other images) and 15,000 negatives illustrating mainly, but by no means entirely, British architecture from *c* .1850 to the present. Outstanding nineteenth century features include 200 rare photographs of American architecture, a large collection of views of Egypt and the Far East and the office collection of William Butterfield. Early twentieth century architects represented include Sir Reginald Blomfield, Lutyens, Voysey, Walton and Temple Moore. The inter-war years are the best documented for there is a special collection of 3,500 large exhibition prints covering foreign and British architecture of the period, which is supplemented by major holdings of Berthold Lubetkin & Tecton, Oliver Hill, Goodhart-Rendel, Sir Edward Maufe and Connell, Ward & Lucas. Characteristic structures of the period are also well represented, especially cinemas and the work of Harry Weedon. The collection also chronicles the work of many contemporary architects. There is a special collection of photographic portraits of architects and the Library also possesses many early photographically-illustrated books. The collection is open to all, but one day's notice is preferred. A variety of retrieval aids is available in the Library.

The Drawing Instruments Collection

This collection contains several single instruments and sets of instruments used in architectural drawing, including British and continental pieces made between 1589 and 1931. The collection can be seen at No. 21 Portman Square by appointment with the Drawings Collection curatorial staff. A descriptive list is available for consultation at the Drawings Collection and in the RIBA Library.

The Medals Collection

This collection contains over 150 medals, plaquettes and insignia presented by members since 1835. Most of the medals commemorate the opening of buildings but there are also many which are memorials of architects, several prize medals awarded by the Institute and other organizations, some exhibition prize medals and some insignia of honours. The medals were struck between *c* .1806 and 1957 and include the portrait medal of T. L. Donaldson struck in 1865 to mark his retirement from the chair of architecture at University College, London and the Royal Gold Medal awarded to Grey Wornum in 1952. Some examples can be seen of the RIBA Soane Medallion, the RIBA Pugin Studentship Medal, the RIBA Silver Medal for an Essay, the RIBA Arthur Cates Prize Medal and the Society of Architects' Travelling Studentship Medal. The collection can be seen by appointment with the Drawings Collection curatorial staff. A descriptive list is available for consultation at the Drawings Collection and in the Library.

The Coins Collection

A small collection of eighty-two coins, mainly ancient Greek and Roman, bearing architectural motifs. Presumably, the collection bequeathed by T. L. Donaldson and exhibited at the General Meeting on 14 Jan 1895. May be seen by appointment with the Librarian.

6.1   LIBRARY CATALOGUES, 1836—1938   23 vols
        Printed and manuscript catalogues of books, pamphlets, manuscripts, drawings, photographs, portraits, busts, building stones and marbles, plaster casts of architectural ornaments, models and medals in the Library and Museum, 1836—1938.

        (For descriptions of current catalogues *see* 'Guide to the British Architectural Library', duplicated typescript available from the Library.

6.2   LIBRARY MANAGEMENT COMMITTEE MINUTES, 1850—1891   2 vols
        Signed minutes of meetings, Jul 1850—Jun 1891, with rough minutes, 1850—1865 and 1879—1891.
        Subjects : Care of the books and special collections: preparation of catalogues and book lists for students: binding and repair: lists of

books purchased and books recommended for purchase: donations to the Library: annual reports of the Librarian: appointment of Library staff: insurance and valuation of stock: the Library Trust Fund.

(Originally known as the 'Committee for the superintendence of the Library and Collection', it soon became known as the 'Library Committee' and, from 1886, as the 'Library Management Committee'. In 1891 the management of the Library was transferred to the Literature Standing Committee).

6.3   PRESIDENTIAL PORTRAITS AND BUSTS COLLECTION, *c.* 1850—
Forty-nine portraits (mainly in oil) and eight busts of presidents of the Institute, most of which are on display in the public areas of the RIBA Building, No. 66 Portland Place.

(A list is available for consultation in the Library).

6.4   *   LIBRARIAN'S PAPERS, 1861—(1983)   40 boxes
Correspondence kept by the RIBA Librarian, consisting mainly of the files of E. J. 'Bobby' Carter, 1930—1946, James Palmes, 1948—1969, and David Dean, 1969—1983. Some of the correspondence is with prominent architects and town planners and covers a wide variety of topics: much of it is with donors of books and other material for the Library's collections and with contributors to the *RIBA Journal*. No pre—1931 files have survived and many of the surviving general files have been heavily weeded by past Librarians: surviving subject files are complete.
Subjects : Administration of the Library and Collections: gifts to the Library: contributions to the *RIBA Journal* : current architectural news: architectural history: preservation of architectural records: the Architectural Graphic Records Committee, 1931—1933: Library air-raid precautions, 1938—1946: Leverhulme Grant Community Centres Joint Research Committee, 1939—1944: the British Council: the Library Association: the bequest of Sir Banister Fletcher: the RIBA Technical Information Service: development of the SfB System.

* Access at the discretion of the Librarian.

6.5   LIBRARY ACCESSIONS AND STOCK REGISTERS, 1862—
23 vols
Registers recording accessions of books, pamphlets, manuscripts, drawings and photographs, with some information on provenance, purchases, sales and exchanges and some valuations of the stock, from 1862.

(Annual lists of presentations to the Library, which formed the bulk of the accessions, were published with the Annual Report of the Council from 1835—1849: from 1849—1884 they were published in *RIBA Proceedings*, 1st Series (from 1878, lists of purchases were also included): accessions lists were published in *RIBA Proceedings*, New Series from 1885—1893: in the *RIBA Journal*, from 1894—1946: in the *RIBA Library Bulletin* from 1946—1972 and, since 1972, in the *Architectural Periodicals Index* .)

6.6   LIBRARY ATTENDANCE REGISTERS, 1866—1879, 1954—1956, 1964—1971   4 vols
A very incomplete series recording visitors to the Library, Dec 1866—Jan 1879, Jun 1954—Oct 1956, Jul 1964—Apr 1971, and visitors to the Early Works Room, Feb 1964—Apr 1971.

6.7   LITERATURE STANDING COMMITTEE MINUTES, 1886—1938   4 vols & 2 binders
Signed minutes of meetings of the main committee, Jun 1886—Jun 1938, and of several subcommittees, 1908—1933, with memoranda and reports including the annual reports of the Librarian, the report of the subcommittee appointed to examine the RIBA collection of photographs, 1936, and a draft of the constitution of the Architectural Graphic Records Committee by F. H. Mansford, 1931. Included are the minutes of the following subcommittees:
Literature Subcommittee (Measured Drawings), Mar —Oct 1908
Records Committee (Measured Drawings), Nov —Dec 1908
Literature Subcommittee, Apr 1909—Mar 1921
Valuation of Books for Fire Insurance Subcommittee, Feb —Mar 1912
Burlington-Devonshire Drawings Subcommittees, Jun 1912 and Jan 1924
Belgian Architectural Records Subcommittee, Mar —Nov 1915
Library Accommodation Subcommittee, Jan 1921—Feb 1926
Lectures Subcommittee, Jan 1921—Nov 1922
By-Laws Subcommittee, Dec 1922
Library Catalogue Subcommittee, Apr 1923—Jan 1926
Officers of the Literature Standing Committee Meeting, Feb 1925
Slides and Photographs Subcommittee, Mar 1925
National Book Council Subcommittee, Mar 1927 and Jul 1929
British Architects Conference Subcommittee, Jun 1927
Library Insurance Subcommittee, Nov 1927
Travelling Libraries (Allied Societies) Subcommittee, Mar —May 1928
Museums and Galleries Subcommittee, Dec 1928
Publications Subcommittee, Jun 1929
Publication of Cheap Books on Architecture Subcommittee, Dec 1929
Public Lectures Joint Committee, Feb 1931—Nov 1933

Architectural Graphic Records Committee Subcommittee, Mar 1931

Subjects : Management of the Library (from 1891): donations to the Library: the RIBA Drawings Collection: the RIBA Photographs Collection: preservation of architectural records: Belgian architectural records, 1915: exhibitions, including the Berlin Exhibition, 1891: RIBA sessional papers: publication of the *RIBA Proceedings* , *Transactions* and *Journal* : architectural publications in general.

(The Literature Standing Committee was one of the four large 'departmental' committees set up in 1886. It gradually took over the work of the Library Management Committee, the Sessional Papers Committee, the Journal and Kalendar Committee and the Records Committee. It was superseded in 1938 by the Library Committee (*see* 6.11 Library Committees Minutes & Papers Series) and some aspects of its work, such as RIBA publications, were continued by the Public Relations Committee).

6.8   COMPETITION CONDITIONS COLLECTION, 1884
Copies of several hundred British and foreign architectural competition conditions, instructions and answers to questions, 1884 onwards, plus a Library register of competitions, 1920—1931, containing particulars of competitions for which the Library had applied for copies of the conditions and some press-cuttings of competition results.

(Between 1920 and 1967, two copies of most competition conditions were applied for, one copy was kept by the Library and one by the Competitions Committee Secretary (see Chapter 11, Section 5). The senior clerks in the General Office would check to see if conditions complied with the RIBA model regulations and report to the Competitions Committee. A list of the competitions from 1884 onwards is available for consultation in the Library.)

6.9   LIBRARY ACCOUNTS JOURNAL, 1909—1936   2 vols
Record of purchases, binding expenses and journal subscriptions, 1909—1936.

6.10   GREY BOOKS INDEX, 1920—1974   146 vols
Manuscript looseleaf index compiled between 1920 and 1974. Vol 1 is an index of buildings illustrated in the principal architectural journals, 1900—1919. Vols 2—146 comprise an index of RIBA members' work illustrated in architectural periodicals, 1920—1974 (the number of periodicals indexed increased over the years).

(Superseded by some of the current Library card catalogues (*see* British Architectural Library Guide) and the *Architectural Periodicals Index* .)

DISPLAY OF PRIZEWINNERS NAMES SUBCOMMITTEE
PAPERS, 1935—1938
(A subcommittee of the Literature Standing Committee)
see   7.4.5

6.11   LIBRARY COMMITTEES MINUTES & PAPERS, 1938—1959,
1964—1967   3 binders & 3 boxes
Signed minutes of meetings of the following committees:
Library Committee, Jul 1938—Jul 1939
Library Reconstruction Committee, Nov 1943—Mar 1945
(New) Library Committee, Jan 1946—Oct 1959
Book Purchasing Subcommittee, Jan 1946
Accessions Subcommittee, Feb 1946—Oct 1947
Drawings Subcommittee, Jul 1947—Oct 1947
Accessions (Books) Subcommittee, Nov 1947—Oct 1959
Technical Reference Library Advisory Committee, Apr —Sep 1959
Books Committee, Aug 1964—Oct 1967
Drawings Committee, Aug 1964—Sep 1967
Library Liaison Committee, Oct 1964—Jun 1967

Also administrative files kept by the Secretaries to the Committee and
RIBA Librarians, E. J. Carter, R. E. Enthoven and J. C. Palmes.
Subjects : Management of the Library and Collections: reorganization
of the Library after the war: accessions to the Library: development of
the Drawings Collection.

(The minutebook covering the period Nov 1959—Jul 1964 is missing.
For previous administration of the Library *see* 6.7 Literature Standing
Committee Minutes. In 1967, the Library Board was set up and took
over the functions of the Library Liaison Committee)

6.12   BIOGRAPHY FILES, *c* .1940—
Approximately 10,000 personal files containing biographical information
and correspondence between Library staff and enquirers relating to
British architects of any period, and including some designers, architectural critics and foreign architects.

(More of a current administrative aid than an archive, it was initially
based on biographical material collected by William Walter Begley and
donated to the Library).

6.13   PROFESSIONAL LITERATURE COMMITTEE MINUTES &
PAPERS, 1944—(1981)   4 vols, 2 binders & 4 boxes
Signed minutes of meetings, Dec 1944—(May 1981), with copies of
memoranda and reports and correspondence files kept by the Librarian,
who was Secretary to the Committee.

Subjects : Monitoring and promotion of literature needed by the profession: location of gaps in the literature: liaison with publishers and authors: assessment of manuscripts of intended publications: annual revision and publication of the *RIBA Book List* of recommended books.

(Originally called the Professional, Text and Reference Books Committee. In December 1959 it became a subcommittee of the Library Committee and was called the Text Books Subcommittee, changing its name in 1963 to the Professional Literature Committee.)

6.14   *RIBA LIBRARY BULLETIN*, 1946—1972
Quarterly publication containing RIBA Library news, the Review of Periodical Articles (selective lists of UDC classified index entries for periodical articles) and lists of accessions to the Library, 1946—1972.

(Reviews of articles in periodicals had been published in the *RIBA Journal* from 1933—1946. Annual accumulations were published as the *RIBA Annual Review of Periodicals*, from 1965—1972. The *RIBA Library Bulletin* was superseded by the *Architectural Periodical Index* in 1972.)

6.15   ARCHITECTURAL LIBRARIES CONFERENCE PAPERS, 1950—1970   3 boxes
Reports of proceedings, with administrative correspondence of the RIBA Librarian, of conferences of representatives of architectural school libraries held at the RIBA in 1950, 1953, 1956, 1959, 1962, 1966 and 1970. Includes some texts of lectures delivered.

6.16   DEPUTY LIBRARIAN'S PAPERS, 1961—1983   5 boxes
Correspondence files kept by David Dean, Deputy Librarian 1961—1968, G. James Broadis, 1968—1971, and Jan van der Wateren, 1971—1983.
Subjects : Documentation: information retrieval: CIRIA Information Liaison Group: Stanley-Morgan Report on architectural library facilities in the provinces: proposed index to finalists' theses: removal of RIBA Drawings Collection to No. 21 Portman Square: proposed development of the RIBA Manuscripts Collection.

6.17 *   DRAWINGS COLLECTION CURATORS' PAPERS, 1965— (1983)   3 filing cabinets and 5 binders
Correspondence files concerning the policy management and administration of the Drawings Collection, the exhibitions held in the Heinz Gallery and Drawings Collection publications, from 1972: with correspondence concerning provenance of drawings from 1965, and information files, mainly on individual architects and practices.

* Access at the discretion of the Drawings Collection staff

6.18   LIBRARY BOARD MINUTES, 1967—1975   2 binders
Signed minutes of the Library Board, Sep 1967—Feb 1975: the Books
Committee, Nov 1967—Aug 1969: the Drawings Committee, Nov
1967—May 1969 and joint meetings of the Library Board and its
committees, Jun 1969—Jul 1975.
Subjects : Administration of the Library: the Library Appeal: the British
Architectural Library Trust.

(In 1967 the Institute set up four departmental boards, one of which was
the Library Board, which superseded the Library Liaison Committee.
Committees of the Board were the Books Committee, the Drawings
Committee and the Professional Literature Committee.)

6.19   BOOKS AND DRAWINGS COMMITTEES MINUTES, 1969—
1975   1 binder
Signed minutes of meetings of the Books Committee and the Drawings
Committee, Aug 1969—Mar 1975.
Subjects : Routine management of the Library: book selection: recommen-
dations for book reviews: management of the Drawings Collection.

6.20   *RIBA BOOKLIST*, 1969—
Annual list of recommended books compiled by the Professional Literature Committee as a general guide to the literature for students, schools
of architecture, librarians and architects.

(Immediate predecessors of the *RIBA Booklist* were the *RIBA Basic
List of Books* and the *RIBA Technical Reference List*. Lists of books
recommended for architectural students were published in the *RIBA
Kalendar* from 1886—1930 and after that were published separately,
with occasional revisions.)

See also in 2.2 Special Committees Minutes Series:
Library Administration Committee, 1896
Records Committee, 1909—1913
Selection Committee for the Librarianship, 1930, 1946, 1948.

Bibliography

1   RIBA *Catalogue of the Library and Collection* London, RIBA, 1846
2   RIBA *Catalogue of the printed books and manuscripts in the Library of the
    Royal Institute of British Architects* London, RIBA, 1865
3   RIBA *Catalogues of the drawings, prints and photographs in the Library of
    the Royal Institute of British Architects* London, RIBA, 1871

4 RIBA *Catalogue of the medals, busts, casts, marbles and stones in the Collection of the Royal Institute of British Architects* London, RIBA, 1874

5 RIBA *The Library Catalogue. Printed books and manuscripts, 1834—1888* London, RIBA, 1889

6 Papworth, Wyatt 'The Library and Collection' *RIBA Proceedings* New Series Vol 5 1889 Feb 28 pp174—176, 233—237

7 White, William H. 'The Burlington-Devonshire collection of drawings' *RIBA Transactions* New Series Vol 8 1892 pp349—364

8 Millard, Walter, 'The Institute collections: exhibition of some past masters in architecture' *RIBA Journal* Vol 17 1910 Jun 11 pp599—605

9 Gotch, J. A. 'The Burlington-Devonshire collection of drawings' *RIBA Journal* Vol 18 1911 Mar 18 pp317—342

10 Townsend, C. Harrison 'The Royal Institute Library and some of its contents' *RIBA Journal* Vol 19 1912 Apr 27 pp429—450

11 Ricardo, Halsey 'The RIBA collection of architects' plans and designs' *RIBA Journal* Vol 23 1916 Feb 19 pp129—130

12 Dircks, Rudolf 'The Library and collections of the Royal Institute of British Architects' *RIBA Journal* Vol 28 1920 Dec 4 pp49—64 and Dec 18 pp81—89

13 Briggs, Martin S. 'Rudolph Dircks: an appreciation' *RIBA Journal* Vol 38 1930 Dec 6 pp79—81. Article on Dircks on the occasion of his retirement as RIBA Librarian and Editor.

14 Kitson, Sydney D. 'The RIBA Library', in Gotch, J. A. (ed) *The growth and work of the Royal Institute of British Architects* London, RIBA, 1934

15 RIBA *A short guide to the use of the Library* London, RIBA, 1934

16 RIBA Library *Exhibition of books and drawings from the library of the Royal Institute of British Architects February 11—March 6 1935* London, RIBA, 1935

17 Carter, Edward 'The Royal Institute of British Architects Library' *Library Association Record* Vol 2 1935 Jan pp4—15

18 Turner, Philip J. 'The library of the Royal Institute of British Architects' *Journal of the Royal Architectural Institute of Canada* Vol 13 1936 Sep pp172—175

19 RIBA *Catalogue of the Royal Institute of British Architects' Library* London, RIBA. Vol 1 *Author catalogue of books and manuscripts*, 1937; Vol 2 *Classified index and alphabetical subject index of books and manuscripts*, 1938.

20 'The future of the RIBA Library' *RIBA Journal* Vol 53 1945 Nov pp9—13. Extracts from the report of the Library Reconstruction Committee.

21 Ansell, W. H. 'Edward Carter' *RIBA Journal* Vol 53 1946 Apr p250. An appreciation on his resignation from the post of RIBA Librarian and Editor.

22 Pierce, Rowland 'The RIBA Library reorganised' *RIBA Journal* Vol 53 1946 Sep pp496—497

23 'RIBA Librarian. Mr. Roderick Eustace Enthoven' *Architects' Journal* Vol 104 1946 Dec 12 p424

24   Notice of appointment of James C. Palmes as RIBA Librarian, in *Architects' Journal* Vol 107 1948 May 13 pp429, 432

25   'A question for Portland Place' *Architects' Journal* Vol 107 1948 Jun 24 p576. Note on the appointment of the new RIBA Librarian.

26   Butler, A. S. G. 'The RIBA Drawings Collection' *RIBA Journal* Vol 64 1957 Oct pp483—489

27   RIBA *Architectural drawings from the collection of the Royal Institute of British Architects* London, RIBA, 1961

28   Girouard, Mark (ed.) 'The Smythson Collection of the Royal Institute of British Architects' *Architectural History* Vol 5 1962 pp21—184

29   Harris, John 'Some drawings in the Royal Institute of British Architects' Part 1: 16th & 17th centuries, Part 2: 18th century. *Connoisseur* 1962 Jul pp147—154 & Aug pp213—220

30   Harris, John 'Modern Movement: drawings in the RIBA Collection' *RIBA Journal* Vol 72 1965 Feb pp83—86

31   Goldring, Patrick 'Yours for the asking, the RIBA Library' *RIBA Journal* Vol 72 1965 Mar pp122—125

32   Lever, Jill (ed.) *Catalogue of the Drawings Collection of the Royal Institute of British Architects* in 19 vols, Farnborough (Hants.), Gregg International, 1969—

33   'The Library' and 'George Atkinson. John Carter interviews the chairman of the Library Board' *RIBA Journal* Vol 74 1969 Oct pp430—433 and 434. Parts of a feature article 'Inside the RIBA'.

34   Colvin, Howard 'The RIBA Drawings Collection' *RIBA Journal* Vol 77 1970 Feb p83

35   'The work of the Library' *RIBA Journal* Vol 77 1970 May p229

36   RIBA Library Board 'The work of the Library' *RIBA Journal* Vol 78 1971 May pp216—217

37   Binney, Marcus 'New home for a unique collection. The RIBA drawings at Portman Square' *Country Life* Vol 151 1972 May 11 pp1146—1147

38   'Drawings Collection opened' *RIBA Journal*, Vol 79 1972 Jun p224. Opening by the Queen of new premises for the Collection at No. 21 Portman Square.

39   'Gallery for RIBA Drawings Collection, Portman Square, London' *Architectural Review* Vol 151 1972 Jun pp365—367

40   Irvine, Alan 'Designing the Heinz Gallery' *RIBA Journal* Vol 79 1972 Jul pp288—290. Article on the conversion of No. 21 Portman Square to house the RIBA Drawings Collection.

41   'RIBA Library: progress and prospects' *RIBA Journal* Vol 80 1973 Aug pp392—393

42   'What's happening to the RIBA Drawings Collection' *Architects' Journal* Vol 160 1974 Oct 2 p783

43   'Dean of the RIBA' *Building Design* 1974 Nov 1 pp16—17. Article on David Dean, RIBA Librarian, and the RIBA Library.

44   'Now is the time to support your Library' *RIBA Journal* Vol 82 1975 Mar

pp14—17. An appeal for funds for the British Architectural Library.

45 Dean, David 'A great library in need' *Architectural Review* Vol 157 1975 Jun pp324—326

46 Dean, David 'The richest mine of instruction and ideas in our world' *Library Association Record* Vol 79 no 6 1977 Jun p315. Article on the British Architectural Library.

47 Richardson, Margaret 'The RIBA Drawings Collection, 1834—1978' *Architectural Design* Vol 48 no 5/6 1978 pp384—386

48 Lever, Jill 'Cataloguing the RIBA Drawings Collection' *Architectural Design* Vol 48 no 5/6 1978 pp395—399

49 'British Architectural Library. Books, manuscripts and services' *Transactions* (RIBA) Vol 1 no 1 1981/82 pp117—21

50 Lyall, Sutherland 'Cash and the RIBA Drawings Collection' *Building Design* no 599 1982 Jun 18 pp20—21

51 Games, Stephen 'Bobby Carter: an appreciation' *RIBA Journal* Vol 89 1982 Aug p17. Article on Edward J. Carter, RIBA Librarian & Editor from 1930—1946.

52 Dean, David 'Bobby Carter' *Architectural Review* Vol 172 no 1027 1982 Sep pp5—6. Obituary of Edward Carter, RIBA Librarian from 1930—1946.

53 Trombley, Stephen 'The Library's future' *RIBA Journal* Vol 90 1983 Sep pp27—28. Article on the British Architectural Library and its retiring director, David Dean.

54 Lever, Jill & Richardson, Margaret *Great drawings from the collection of the Royal Institute of British Architects* London, Trefoil Books Ltd, 1983. With introduction by John Harris

55 Lever, Jill *The art of the architect: treasures from the RIBA's collections* London, Trefoil for the RIBA, 1984

7
Education

Section 1 General

In the *Prospectus for the formation of a society to be called the Institution of British Architects* published by the Society of British Architects early in 1834 it was stated that candidates for election as Associates were to be examined by a committee of the Fellows in the theory and practice of architectural design and construction and in the 'usual and customary practice of business'. However, the original regulations of the Institute adopted in July 1834 merely stated that Associates must be at least twenty-one years old and have been engaged in the study or practice of civil architecture for less than seven years. In 1838 the Institute started a class of student members but the education it offered them was sporadic and piecemeal. Students were encouraged to 'draw from the antique' using the collection of casts in the Institute's museum, were given occasional lectures in chemistry, botany, geology, building materials, construction and mechanics, and were offered prizes and medals for essays and designs and a few travelling bursaries. The main advantage of student membership was that it gave access to the Institute's meetings and the use of its Library.

From 1855 architectural education came to the forefront of the Institute's discussions, since dissatisfaction with the current state of affairs was widespread particularly among the young and had been the main cause of the foundation of the Architectural Association. In those days the would-be architect nearly always obtained his training as an articled pupil of a practising architect who might, or might not, take any interest other than a pecuniary one in the arrangement. Some lectures and courses were available, particularly in London, but there was no organized system of education and no qualifying examination. In 1855 the members

14 C. R. Chorley's articles of apprenticeship, 1847, by which he bound himself to Perkin & Backhouse, architects, of Leeds for five years. In 1890 the RIBA issued an approved form of articles of pupilage, which included an undertaking by the principal to grant enough leave of absence to his pupil to enable him to attend lectures and classes and qualify for passing the examinations for Studentship and Associateship of the RIBA. The practice of pupilage began to die out in the 1920s with the increasing availability of architectural schools. (British Architectural Library Manuscripts & Archives Collection)

of the Architectural Association submitted a memorial to the Council of the Institute in which they expressed their desire for the establishment of an examination which would lead to the issue of a diploma certifying qualification to practise as an architect. This idea had a mixed reception, since many senior and successful Institute members derived a considerable income from the system of articled pupilage and had no interest in fostering alternative methods of training.

In 1863 the Institute appointed a Board of Examiners to conduct voluntary examinations, success in which was a qualification for candidature as an Associate member of the Institute. The existing system of direct election to the Associateship, based on the submission of general evidence of qualification, continued to apply. In 1877 it was decided to require all candidates for Associateship after May 1882 to pass a professional examination before their election. The class of students was discontinued and the decision was taken to encourage the Architectural Association in its educational work and that the Institute should not attempt to be a teaching body but should, through its examination system, establish standards for students and teachers of architecture. The RIBA Obligatory Examination for membership was begun in 1882. At the General Conference of Architects in 1887 it was agreed that the guidance and direction of the education of those entering the architectural profession should be undertaken by the RIBA, and during the 1890s a complete system of progressive examinations — Preliminary, Intermediate and Final — was established by the RIBA. In 1904 the RIBA Board of Architectural Education (BAE) was set up. It consisted of distinguished architects interested in education and included non-members of the RIBA. At first it had no control over the Board of Examiners, which continued to work independently and report directly to the Council. In 1910 the BAE was remodelled. It was enlarged to make it more representative of the leading schools of architecture and was given authority over the whole field of education and examination.

The development of architectural schools was fostered by the system of 'recognition', i.e. any school in the British Empire which applied for recognition, whose syllabus was approved by the BAE, whose examinations were conducted by an external examiner approved by the BAE and whose standard of attainment was guaranteed by periodical inspections and reports by Visitors from the BAE, could be placed on the list of 'recognized schools' and its successful students could qualify for exemption from the RIBA Intermediate Examination and, in some cases, the RIBA Final Examination. As early as 1902 the Liverpool School of Architecture and the Architectural Association School had been recognized for exemption from the Intermediate Examination and, by 1931, twenty-seven schools had been recognized for exemption from either the Intermediate only or both the Intermediate and Final. Of these twenty-seven schools one was in Australia, three in Canada, two in South Africa and one in India. In addition there were other schools holding courses in architecture which were recognized to the extent that the work done by the students could be submitted in lieu of the Testimony of Study drawings required for approval before a candidate could sit for the RIBA Intermediate Examination.

In 1924 an international congress on architectural education was held in London, which emphasized the desirability of full-time training in recognized schools and in the following years many more schools were set up in universities, colleges of art and technical colleges. In 1925 the RIBA Visiting Board was set up to monitor the course syllabuses, examinations, and standards of assessment of architectural schools and the Board of Architectural Education was again remodelled and enlarged. The new Board considered matters of general education policy and most of its routine work was delegated to standing committees. Its constitution was as follows:-

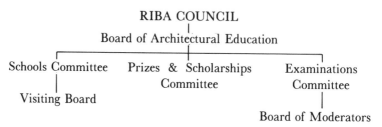

In 1931 the RIBA Devolution Scheme was instituted, under which the RIBA delegated to certain Allied Societies in South Africa, New Zealand and Australia the control of architectural education and examinations in their areas. The scheme was instituted before the Architects Registration Acts of 1931—1938 were passed. By the 1950s complications arose due to the fact that while certain dominion schools of architecture were recognized for the Associateship of the RIBA, they were not recognized by the Architects Registration Council of the United Kingdom (ARCUK) and the scheme was therefore abandoned.

In 1958 a conference on architectural education was held at Oxford which significantly affected the course of architectural education. The main recommendations of this conference were that the standard of qualification for entry into training should be raised; courses based on the RIBA external examination should be progressively abolished; courses should be in universities or institutions of a similar standard; courses should be full-time or possibly 'sandwich'; other forms of training not leading to qualification as an architect should be encouraged (e.g. as an architectural technician); post-graduate research should be encouraged. The RIBA subsequently played a major part in setting up the Society of Architectural and Associated Technicians, the body which represents the specially-trained architectural and other technicians in the construction industry. In 1960 the BAE was again reconstituted. A large Advisory Council on Architectural Education was to be elected annually by the Council and a much smaller Board of Architectural Education was to be appointed by the Council. This board became the Board of Education in 1967. The Advisory Council on Architectural Education was terminated in 1965. The Board of Education was superseded in 1975 by the Education and Practice Executive Committee, which was itself superseded in 1979 by the Education and Professional Development Committee.

Between 1964 and 1968 the whole system of RIBA examinations was reviewed and a new structure was adopted in 1970. By this time, over 90 per cent of students starting their architectural education were entering full-time or sandwich courses of degree level. The usual pattern of education for an architectural student now is five years' study in a higher academic institution and two years practical training in an architect's office. At the end of the seventh year candidates for entry to the profession are eligible to sit an examination in professional practice and practical experience which they must pass before admission to membership of the RIBA and registration. Architects may obtain an additional qualification if they take a further year of full-time study on an urban design course recognised by the RIBA for the award of the RIBA Urban Design Diploma. Full qualification as a town planner is regulated by the Royal Town Planning Institute but there is no statutory registration of town planners and no restriction on the use of that title.

7.1.1 * BOARD OF ARCHITECTURAL EDUCATION MINUTES, 1907—1967   5 vols & 11 binders
Signed minutes of the Board of Architectural Education (BAE), Feb 1907 — Jul 1967, with minutes of the Officers of the Board, Sep 1925—Dec 1933, and of the Proposed Conference on the Content of a Course in Architecture Subcommittee, Jul —Nov 1960. Included in the minutes are policy papers, memoranda, reports of committees, RIBA Visiting Board reports, applications by architectural schools to become 'recognized', with copies of their syllabuses, annual statistics for examinations in architectural schools, and copies of letters received by the Board.
Subjects : Appointment of Committees of the BAE and consideration of their reports; recognition of architectural schools and approval of their syllabuses (Vols 1—4): consideration of the reports of the Visitors and, later, of the RIBA Visiting Board (Vols 1—5, Binders 1—3): setting up the RIBA Visiting Board (Vol 3): reconstitution of the BAE, in 1910 (Vol 1), in 1925 (Vols 3, 4), in 1960 (Binder 6): the RIBA progressive examinations and exemptions: recommendation of Probationers for election as Students RIBA: consideration of applications to sit the Special Final Examination (Vols 1—4): the Special War Examination (1st World War) and exemptions (Vols 2, 3): results of examinations held in Germany for prisoners of war (2nd World War) (Binder 3): examination of Licentiates wishing to qualify for election as Fellows: architectural education and examinations in the British dominions and colonies: appointment and payment of RIBA examiners (Vols 1—4): revision of the RIBA Articles of Pupilage (Vols 1, 4): recommendations to Council on the award of RIBA prizes, studentships, scholarships and bursaries, and appointment of RIBA

The Castle . West Caistor
near Yarmouth -

built of brick with stone dressings

Corbel of Brick

H. Walker
1867.

15   Part of a Pugin Student's report. The Pugin Travelling Studentship commemorated A. W. N. Pugin and its holder had to undertake a study tour of medieval
buildings in Britain or Ireland and subsequently submit a report illustrated with
sketches and measured drawings. Henry Walker included this sketch of the ruins
of West Caister Castle in the report of his tour of Norfolk in 1867. (RIBA
Archive:7.4.1)

prize juries: proposed architectural ateliers similar to those in France connected with the Ecole des Beaux Arts (Vol 1): the International Congress on Architectural Education, 1924 (Vol 4): architectural education in relation to town planning and the inception of the RIBA Diploma in Town Planning (Vols 3, 4): parliamentary bills for registration of architects (Vol 5, Binder 1): schemes for practical experience as a compulsory part of architectural training (Binders 3—4, 7—8): the Oxford Conference on Architectural Education, 1958 (Binders 5, 6): sandwich courses in architecture (Binder 7): postgraduate training in architecture (Binder 7): training of architectural technicians (Binders 7, 8): diversification in architectural education (Binder 8): management training for architects (Binders 7, 8): training in the building industry (Binder 8): activities of the British Architectural Students Association (Binder 8): the 8th congress of the International Union of Architects, on architectural education, 1965, Paris (Binder 8): postgraduate training and research: training in conservation and restoration: management education: review of RIBA examinations (Binders 9—11).

For continuation *see* 7.1.11 Board of Education Minutes & Papers, 1967—1975.

* Access at the discretion of the Archivist

7.1.2   BOARD OF ARCHITECTURAL EDUCATION COMMITTEES MINUTES, 1910—1962   5 vols & 4 binders
From 1910—1925 this series contains the signed minutes of all the standing and special committees and subcommittees of the BAE, except the Examiners committees which were kept in a separate series. From 1926 onwards it does not include the minutes of the Schools Committee, the Prizes and Scholarships Committee, the Examinations Committee, and the Officers of the BAE meetings, which each have a separate series. The chief standing committees included in this series were the Board of Moderators (later, the Moderators Committee), the Visiting Board, the Maintenance Scholarships Committee, the Archibald Dawnay Scholarships Jury and the Teachers Committee (later, the Schools Committee).

Included in the minutes are policy papers, memoranda, Visiting Board reports, RIBA examination question papers (1926—1932), and transcripts of letters received by committees. Contains the minutes of the following committees:
Aerodrome Competition Jury, May—Jun 1928
Aerodrome Competition Subcommittee (of the Schools Committee), Oct—Nov 1927
Aerodrome Subcommittee *see* Aerodrome Competition Subcommittee

Alfred Bossom Research Fellowship Jury, Jun 1949

Alfred Bossom Travelling Studentship Joint Committee, May 1929

Alfred Bossom Travelling Studentship Jury, Oct 1923—Dec 1926

American Travelling Studentship Subcommittee, Feb 1923

Applications for Admission to the Examination for the RIBA Diploma in Town Planning Special Committee, Mar 1934

Archibald Dawnay Scholarships Jury, Oct 1923—Oct 1950

Architectural Association and RIBA Joint Committee on the Henry Saxon Snell Prize *see* Henry Saxon Snell Prize Joint Committee

Architectural Association Jarvis Scholarship Committee, Jul 1915

Architectural Education Ad Hoc Committee, Jan —Apr 1951

Architectural Education Congress Committee *see* International Congress on Architectural Education Committee

Architectural Education Joint Committee, Apr 1952—Sep 1954

Architectural Education Special Committee, Jul 1939—Apr 1945

Architecture in Public and Secondary Schools Special Committee, Mar —May 1930

Arthur Cates Prize Subcommittee, Mar 1926

Australian Medallion Subcommittee, Nov 1927

Australian Students in London Informal Meeting, Dec 1929

Award of the RIBA Distinction in Town Planning Committee *see* RIBA Distinction in Town Planning Committee

Board of Architectural Education and the Council Joint Subcommittee (to consider the 2nd report of the Architectural Education Joint Committee, 1954), Mar —May 1955

Board of Architectural Education and the Examiners Joint Committee, Apr 1914

Board of Architectural Education and the Training of Technicians Committee Joint Meeting, Apr 1962

Board of Moderators (later the Moderators Committee), Nov 1925—Dec 1944

Board of Moderators and the Examiners for the Intermediate, Final and Special Final Examinations Joint Meeting, Mar 1934

Charter and By-laws Subcommittee, Nov 1922

Committee of Moderators *see* Moderators Committee

Conference on Prizes *see* Prizes Conference

Congress Executive Committee *see* International Congress on Architectural Education Committee

Congress Exhibition Subcommittee (of the International Congress on Architectural Education Committee), Jul 1923—Jun 1924

Congress Finance Subcommittee (of the International Congress on Architectural Education Committee), Mar 1924—May 1925

Congress Papers Subcommittee (of the International Congress on Architectural Education Committee), Dec 1923—Jun 1925

Congress Publicity Subcommittee (of the International Congress on Architectural Education Committee), Nov 1923

Design of Traffic Roundabouts Special Committee, Mar —May 1936

Distribution of Schools of Architecture Special Committee, Apr 1927

Distribution of Schools of Architecture Subcommittee, Dec 1926

Examinations Committee, Dec 1910—Jun 1911, Jul 1913—Nov 1925

Examinations Committee (Interim), Oct —Dec 1925

Examinations in India Committee, Apr 1917—Nov 1920

Examinations Special Subcommittee, May—Oct 1925

Examiners appointed by the Council to conduct the examination of Licentiates desirous of becoming Fellows *see* Fellowship Examination for Licentiates Examiners

Exemptions Committee, Oct 1913, Sep 1920—Jul 1922

* Fellowship Examination for Licentiates Examiners, May 1912—Nov 1920

Future Constitution of the Board of Architectural Education Subcommittee, Jan —Apr 1920

Garage Competition Jury, Jun 1928

Grissell Prize Subcommittee, Feb —Mar 1921

Henry Jarvis Bequest Committee *see* Jarvis Bequest Committee

Henry Saxon Snell Prize Joint Committee (Architectural Association & RIBA), Jan —Jun 1927

Henry Saxon Snell Prize Jury, Feb 1928

Herbert Baker Scholarship Committee, Mar 1912—Oct 1920

Home Counties Area Committee for the RIBA Maintenance Scholarships, Jun 1926—Sep 1927

Home Counties Province Subcommittee (of the Maintenance Scholarships Committee), Jul 1930—Jul 1931

Interim Examinations Committee *see* Examinations Committee (Interim)

Interim Prizes and Scholarships Committee *see* Prizes and Scholarships Committee (Interim)

Interim Schools Committee *see* Schools Committee (Interim)

International Congress on Architectural Education Committee, Jul 1922—Jul 1924

Jarvis Bequest Committee, Oct 1912

Landscape Architecture Ad Hoc Committee, May 1945—Feb 1946

Licentiate Examiners *see* Fellowship Examination for Licentiates Examiners

London County Council Scholarships in Architecture Subcommittee, Jun 1926

London Members of the Architectural Education Special Committee Informal Meeting, May 1941

* Maintenance Scholarships Committee, Mar 1926—Jul 1962

Methods of Interesting Boys and Girls in Schools of Architecture and Kindred Subjects Subcommittee, Mar 1928

Moderators, Board of *see* Board of Moderators

Moderators Committee (previously, the Board of Moderators), Feb 1945—Jan 1954

Moderators Committee and the Examiners for the Intermediate, Final and Special Final Examinations Joint Meeting, Apr 1946

Moderators Committee and the Final Examiners Joint Meetings, Mar 1947—Nov 1949

Need for a Second Category Subcommittee *see* Second Category Subcommittee

Officers of the Board of Architectural Education and the Visiting Board Joint Meeting, Nov 1927

Owen Jones Studentship Jury, Jul 1926—Sep 1929

Oxford Conference on Architectural Education Committee, Jul 1958—May 1959

Payment of Examiners Committee, May 1911—May 1914

Practical Experience Ad Hoc Committee, Feb —Apr 1948

Preliminary Examination Committee, Jun 1914

Prizes and Scholarships Committee (Interim), Oct —Nov 1925

Prizes and Studentships Juries General Meeting, Feb 1923

Prizes and Studentships Subcommittee, Jan —Feb 1913

Prizes Conference, Oct 1924—Feb 1925

Prizes Conference Committee, Oct 1924

Prizes for Public and Secondary Schools Jury, Dec 1929—Dec 1930

Prizes Improvement Committee, Jan —Feb 1922

Prizes Special Subcommittee, Mar 1925

Probationers Registration Committee, Oct 1922—Jun 1928

Probationership Special Committee, Nov 1928—Jan 1929

Problems in Design and Testimonies of Study Examiners, Mar 1912—Mar 1926

Publication of the work of Rome Scholars in Architecture and RIBA Henry Jarvis Students Subcommittee, Jun 1929—Jul 1931

Recognised Schools Medal Subcommittee, Apr —May 1922

Reports Subcommittee (of the Prizes and Scholarships Committee), Sep 1949

Revision of Syllabus Committee, Feb —Apr 1913

RIBA Diploma in Town Planning Examiners, Mar 1924, Jul 1927—Mar 1930

RIBA Distinction in Town Planning Ad Hoc Committee, Oct —Nov 1953

RIBA Distinction in Town Planning Committee, Nov 1947—Jan 1962

16 One of a set of Arthur Ebden Johnson's Soane Medallion prize drawings, 1843. The subject set for the competition that year was to design a princely palace as described by Lord Bacon in his 'Essay of Building'. The Soane prize commemorated Sir John Soane, a major benefactor of the Institute, and included a bursary to be used in travel abroad for the purpose of architectural study. (British Architectural Library Drawings Collection)

RIBA Town Planning Examination Subcommittee, Dec 1923—Feb 1924

Schools Committee (Interim), Oct —Dec 1925

Schools Committee & Prizes and Scholarships Committee Joint Meetings, Dec 1933—May 1934

Schools Special Subcommittee, Nov 1925

Second Category Subcommittee of the Oxford Conference on Architectural Education (to consider the need for a second category of membership, eg. architectural assistants), Oct 1958—Mar 1959

Soane Medallion Jury, May 1927

Special Examination Subcommittee (to consider a scheme for a new Special Examination), Apr 1926

Special War Exemption Candidates Subcommittee, Mar 1920

Standard of General Education Required for the Probationership of the RIBA Special Committee *see* Probationership Special Committee

Study of the Scientific Aspect of Building for Students of Architecture Subcommittee, Feb 1930

Teachers Committee, Jan 1921—Jun 1925

Teachers Committee & Prizes and Studentships Juries Special Meeting, Feb 1924

Teachers Informal Conference, Sep 1925

Technical Institutions Subcommittee, Jan 1925—Mar 1926

Technicians and Technologists Subcommittee, Jan—Feb 1960

Testimonies of Study Committee *see* Problems in Design & Testimonies of Study Examiners

Testimonies of Study Examiners & Examinations Committee Joint Meetings, Oct—Dec 1948

Testimonies of Study Examiners Meetings, Mar 1949, Jul 1953

Thesis Examiners, Nov 1912—May 1913

Tite Prize Jury, May 1926—Apr 1928

Town Planning Education Subcommittee, May 1945—Feb 1946

Town Planning Examination Subcommittee *see* RIBA Town Planning Examination Subcommittee

Town Planning Examiners *see* RIBA Diploma in Town Planning Examiners

Training and Organisation of a Second Category Subcommittee *see* Second Category Subcommittee, etc.

Training of Architects in Town Planning Committee, Dec 1942—Jan 1944

Training of Technicians Committee, Dec 1959—Feb 1962

Training of Technicians and Technologists and Classes of Membership Committee *see* Training of Technicians Committee

Victory Scholarship Jury, May 1926—Apr 1928

Victory Scholarship Medal Subcommittee, Apr —Jun 1926

* Visiting Board, Nov 1925—Oct 1938, Dec 1951—Feb 1962

* Access at the discretion of the Archivist

7.1.3 * SCHOOLS COMMITTEE MINUTES, 1926—1973   1 vol & 4
binders
Signed minutes of the Schools Committee, Jan 1926—Feb 1973, the
Short Courses for Staffs of Schools of Architecture Subcommittee,
Oct 1957—Feb 1959, and the Exhibition at the Building Centre
Subcommittee, 14 Nov 1960, with copies of memoranda, reports, and
correspondence received.
Subjects : Reports of subcommittees and the Visiting Board:
applications for exemption from RIBA examinations: annual statistics
concerning students in 'Recognised' schools: examinations recognised
for RIBA Probationership: registration of Probationers: exhibitions of
designs by students exempted from the RIBA Intermediate and Final
exams: lists of books recommended to students: official publications for
students: personnel of juries for the RIBA prizes, studentships and
scholarships: the formation of new schools of architecture: libraries of
schools of architecture: education of architectural students in building
construction: teaching the ethics of architectural practice: informal
conferences of teachers: salaries of architectural teachers: postgraduate
architectural studies and research: practical training of architects:
industrialized building: Robbins Report on higher education: review
of the RIBA examinations: management training for architects: mid-
career courses: technicians and architectural education: Cambridge
Conference, 1970.

(This committee took over the work of the Teachers Committee, for
minutes of which *see* 7.1.2 Board of Architectural Education Committees
Minutes Series. Between Jan 1939 and Apr 1944 the business of the
Schools Committee was dealt with by the officers of the BAE *see* 7.1.4
Officers of the Board of Architectural Education Minutes Series)

* Access at the discretion of the Archivist

7.1.4 * OFFICERS OF THE BOARD OF ARCHITECTURAL EDUCA-
TION MINUTES, 1934—1960   4 binders
Signed minutes of meetings of the Board's officers, Feb 1934—Apr
1960, and of the Overseas Examinations Panel, Sep 1957—Jan 1959,
and the Conference Organising Committee of the Oxford Conference
on Architectural Education, Mar 1957—Mar 1959. Also included are
policy memoranda, drafts of annual reports to the Council, reports of
the Visiting Board, reports of subcommittees and related committees,
and booklists for students.

Subjects : The general business of the BAE, especially during the war years, 1939—1944, when most of the BAE committees were suspended: annual estimates of the expenditure of the Board: recognition of schools for exemption from the Testimonies of Study for the RIBA Intermediate Exam: special exemption from the RIBA Intermediate Exam: annual exhibitions of designs by students exempted from the RIBA Intermediate and Final Exams: competitions between students of British 'Recognised' schools and students of the Ecole Nationale des Beaux-Arts, Paris: administration of RIBA maintenance scholarships, studentships and bursaries: adjudication of RIBA prizes and medals for students: devolution scheme for the Royal Australian Institute of Architects, the South African Institute of Architects and the New Zealand Institute of Architects: annual exhibitions at the RIBA of architects' working drawings (Binder 1): lectures on architecture to public and secondary schools (Binder 1): architectural training in art schools and technical institutions (Binder 1): the RIBA statutory examination for district surveyors (Binder 1): consideration of reports of the RIBA Visiting Board (from 1940): salaries of architectural teachers (Binder 2): consideration of the report of the Special Committee on Architectural Education, 1945 (Binder 3): proposed professorial chairs in architectural science (Binder 3): consideration of the MARS Group and Architectural Students Association's interim report on architectural education, 1948 (Binder 3): higher education in technology (Binder 3): practical training for architectural students (Binder 3): examination in professional practice (Binders 3 & 4): the Oxford Conference on Architectural Education, 1958 (Binder 4): the University Grants Committee's study of the role of the universities in architectural education (Binder 4).

(This committee acted as the policy committee of the Board. For the minutes of this committee from 1925—1933 *see* 7.1.1 Board of Architectural Education Minutes Series)

* Access at the discretion of the Archivist.

7.1.5   EDUCATION SECRETARY'S PAPERS, 1960—1975   10 boxes
Correspondence files kept by Elizabeth Layton, Under Secretary for Education, and by Michael Darke and Michael Shoul, Assistant Secretaries.
Subjects : Architectural education in general and the administration of the RIBA Education Department: the External Architectural Students Association: correspondence with Listed Schools: setting up of new departments and schools of architecture in universities and polytechnics: educational forums, seminars and conferences.

(W. J. Locke, Secretary RIBA, acted as Secretary to the Board of

Architectural Education from 1904—1905, and Herbert G. Tayler, Assistant Secretary RIBA, from 1906—1920. Everard James Haynes was appointed full-time Secretary to the BAE in 1921 and continued in that post until 1964. Unfortunately, the papers of these Secretaries to the BAE have not survived.)

7.1.6   *   VISITING BOARD PAPERS, 1961—(1976)   5 binders & 1 box
Copies of minutes of meetings, 26 Jan 1961 & 20 Oct 1964, with memoranda on Visiting Board procedures. Visiting Board reports on schools of architecture in the U.K. and Commonwealth, 1963—1976.

(For minutes of meetings of the Visiting Board, with copies of their reports, 1925—1938 & 1951—1962 *see* 7.1.2 Board of Architectural Education Committees Minutes Series, Vols 4—5 & Binders 1—4. For copies of Visiting Board reports to the Council, 1926—1938 *see* 7.1.3 Schools Committee Minutes Series)

    * Access at the discretion of the Secretary to the Visiting Board

7.1.7   POSTGRADUATE TRAINING AND RESEARCH COM-
MITTEE MINUTES & PAPERS, 1962—1967   1 box
Minutes of meetings, Dec 1963—Jul 1967, with memoranda, reports, lists of RIBA Research Awards winners, and correspondence from Mar 1962.
Subjects : RIBA policy on architectural research: sources of research finance: development of specialised studies in the schools of architecture: diversification in architectural education: RIBA Research Awards scheme: visits by the committee to schools of architecture: proposed Journal of Architectural Research and Teaching.

(A committee of the Board of Architectural Education. Its work was continued by the Research Committee *see* 7.1.12)

7.1.8   JOINT SUBCOMMITTEE OF THE BOARD OF ARCHITEC-
TURAL EDUCATION & SCHOOLS COMMITTEE PAPERS, 1963—1964   1 box
Minutes of meetings, with correspondence and memoranda, Nov 1963—Oct 1964.
Subjects : Relationship between the Board of Architectural Education and schools of architecture: responsibility for practical training: value of the RIBA Visiting Board: relationship with ARCUK: Part III of the Examination in Architecture.

7.1.9   REVIEW OF THE PRACTICAL TRAINING SCHEME SUB-
COMMITTEE PAPERS, 1964—1966   1 box

Minutes of meetings, correspondence and memoranda of the committee and the working group on the Log Book, Nov 1964—Aug 1966.
Subject : Review of the log book used in the scheme of practical training for architectural students introduced in 1963.

7.1.10　RIBA/SAAT JOINT EDUCATION COMMITTEE PAPERS, 1965—1975　5 boxes
Files kept by the RIBA representative, Chris Territt, RIBA Assistant Secretary, Education, including copies of minutes, memoranda, reports, and correspondence, 1965—1975, and papers of the RIBA/SAAT Professional Services Working Group, Nov 1970—Mar 1971.
Subjects : Education of architectural technicians: relationship between architect and technician.

MEMBERSHIP WORKING GROUP PAPERS, 1967
(A working group of the Board of Architectural Education) *see* 12.1.16

7.1.11　*BOARD OF EDUCATION MINUTES & PAPERS, 1967—1975　7 binders
Signed minutes of meetings, Sep 1967—May 1975, with policy papers, memoranda and reports, Jan 1969—May 1975.
Subjects : Visiting Board programmes and reports: mid-career courses: liaison with BASA and EASA: architectural research: the Urban Design Diploma: practical training: new courses at universities and polytechnics: examinations: relations between architects and technicians: training in conservation of buildings.

(This board superseded the Board of Architectural Education)

* Access at the discretion of the Archivist

7.1.12　RESEARCH COMMITTEE MINUTES & PAPERS, 1967—1971　2 binders & 6 boxes
Minutes of meetings, Oct 1967—Jul 1971, with memoranda, reports, correspondence, and files on visits to architectural schools by members of the committee.
Subjects : Funding and development of architectural research: RIBA Research Awards: Cumbernauld Research Awards: the *Journal of Architectural Research and Teaching* : education for research: RIBA research visits to architectural schools: research and development in the design and construction of buildings.

(A committee of the Board of Education. It continued the work of the Postgraduate Training and Research Committee *see* 7.1.7)

7.1.13　CONTINUING EDUCATION WORKING GROUP PAPERS, 1968—1970　1 box
Copies of proceedings at meetings, Mar —Dec 1968, with correspondence, discussion papers, lists of courses, reports of the group, 1968—1970.
Subject : Establishment and development of mid-career courses for architects.

(A group of the Board of Education. It was originally called the Mid-Career Courses Working Group)

7.1.14　RIBA URBAN DESIGN DIPLOMA WORKING GROUP PAPERS, 1969—1970　1 box
Notes of meetings, Jul 1969—Jul 1970, with memoranda and final report.
Subjects : Education for environmental planning: setting up a diploma for RIBA recognised courses in urban design for corporate members of the RIBA.

(A working group of the Board of Education)

7.1.15　COURSES AND FORUMS SUBCOMMITTEE PAPERS, 1970—1972　1 box
Copies of minutes of meetings, with correspondence, memoranda and reports, 1970 — Oct 1972.
Subject : Arrangement of courses and forums for teachers in architectural schools.

(A subcommittee of the Schools Committee)

7.1.16　PRACTICAL TRAINING WORKING GROUP PAPERS, 1970—1975　1 box
Minutes of meetings, Nov 1970—Dec 1975, with memoranda, reports and specimen of the Practical Training Log Book.
Subjects : Revised scheme for practical training of graduate architectural students preparing for Part 3 Examination in Professional Practice: scheme for practical training in urban design.

(A working group of the Board of Education)

See also in 2.2 Special Committees Minutes Series:
Report of the General Committee on Architectural Education Committee, 1869
Establishment of a Drawing School for Architectural Students Committee, 1869
Special Education Committee, 1886—1889
Architectural Education Committee, 1903
Board of Architectural Education, 1904—1906

Board of Architectural Education & Board of Examiners Joint Committee, 1907—1909
Proposed School of Architecture in Italy Committee, 1908—1909
Board of Architectural Education Appointment Subcommittee of Council, 1910
and 3.1.5 Policy Committee on Devolution and Qualification for Membership Minutes, 1956—1957

Bibliography

1   Sandeman, R. 'Remarks on the proper education of an architectural pupil'. Essay read before the London Architectural Society, 1846. BAL Manuscripts & Archives Collection, RIBA

2   Knowles, J. T. *On architectural education. A prize essay of the Royal Institute of British Architects* London, Thomas Bosworth, 1853

3   Papworth, John W. 'An abridgement of M. Lance's essay entitled "On a diploma in architecture" with remarks and suggestions' *RIBA Transactions* 1st Series Vol 6 1855/56 pp23—31

4   'A diploma in architecture' *RIBA Transactions* 1st Series Vol 6 1855/56 pp37—47

5   Gray, Charles 'The Institute and the Architectural Association' *Builder* Vol 14 1856 Jul 12 pp385—386

6   Scott, G. G., RA *Thoughts and suggestions on the artistic education of architects* London, [1864]

7   RIBA 'Report of the general committee on the subject of the establishment of a School of Architectural Decoration' *RIBA Proceedings* 1st Series 1863/64 1864 Aug

8   'A discussion on the report of the Artistic Architectural Education Committee' *RIBA Transactions* 1st series 1864/65 pp15—24

9   Ruskin, John 'An enquiry into some of the conditions at present affecting the study of architecture in our schools' *RIBA Proceedings* 1st Series 1864/65 pp139—156

10 RIBA 'Report of the general committee on the subject of the establishment of a school of art accessorial to architecture, Nov. 1864' *RIBA Proceedings* 1st Series 1868/69 1869 Jan 22

11 'The origins of the A.A.' *Builder* Vol 39 1880 Dec 18 p736, Dec 25 p769, Dec 11 p703. Letters to the editor by R. Phené Spiers, J. K. Collings and Robert Kerr.

12 'What is the best system of professional education for architectural students and how can the work of the [Architectural] Association be rendered more efficient' *RIBA Proceedings* New Series Vol 1 1885 Jan 8 pp77—88

13 Webb, Aston 'Pupilage' *Builder* Vol 51 1886 Nov 13 p692—694

14 Cates, Arthur (ed) *Papers on education read at the General Conference of Architects May 1887* reprinted from *Builder* 1887 May 7

15 Architectural Association 'Report of a special committee appointed to enquire into the educational methods of the Architectural Association' *AA Notes* Vol 4 1889/90 pp123—136
16 Smith, T. R. 'On the technical education of architects' *Builder* Vol 59 1890 Oct 4 pp265—268 & Oct 11 pp285—286
17 Slater, John *A note on architectural education* Spottiswoode and Co, 1891
18 Baggallay, Frank T. 'The new educational scheme at the Architectural Association (London)' *RIBA Proceedings* New Series Vol 7 1891 Jun 11 pp340—348
19 'The educational scheme of the Architectural Association (London)' *RIBA Proceedings* New Series Vol 7 1891 Jul 23 pp379—388
20 Cates, Arthur 'Education in the provincial centres' *RIBA Proceedings* New Series Vol 8 1891 Dec 3 pp79—83
21 Shaw, R. N. & Jackson, T. G. (eds) *Architecture: a profession or an art* London, T. Murray, 1892
22 Seth-Smith, W. Howard 'The statutory training and registration of architects' *RIBA Journal* Vol 11 1904 Mar 5 pp234—239
23 Blomfield, Reginald 'On architectural education' *RIBA Journal* Vol 12 1905 Feb 25 pp237—245
24 Goulburn Lovell, R. 'The Society of Architects' scheme for ateliers' *Architects' and Builders' Journal* Vol 37 1913 Jan 8 p35
25 Blomfield, Reginald 'Architectural training: the atelier' *RIBA Journal* Vol 20 1913 May 10 p493
26 'The First Atelier of Architecture' in *Who's Who in Architecture* London, Technical Journals Ltd, 1914
27 Budden, Lionel B. 'Architectural education and the new charter' *Architects' and Builders' Journal* Vol 39 1914 Jan 28 pp56—57
28 'The education of the architect' *RIBA Journal* Vol 24 1917 Mar pp105—115, May pp153—166 & Sep pp252—262. Discussions at Informal Conferences of the RIBA.
29 Waterhouse, Paul 'The future of architectural education' *RIBA Journal* Vol 27 1920 Feb 21 pp165—172
30 RIBA *The First International Congress on Architectural Education, July 28—August 2, 1924. Proceedings* London, RIBA, 1925
31 'Reconstitution of the Board of Architectural Education' *RIBA Journal* Vol 33 1925 Nov 21 pp56—57
32 RIBA *Suggested outline course of study for the guidance of architects who accept pupils in districts where professional school education is not available* London, RIBA, 1926
33 RIBA *Report of the committee on the distribution of schools of architecture* London, RIBA, 1927
34 Webb, Maurice E. 'The progress of architectural education' *RIBA Journal* Vol 34 1927 Jul 16 pp587—590
35 Fletcher, Henry Martineau 'Architectural education' in Gotch, J. A. (ed)

The growth and work of the Royal Institute of British Architects London, RIBA, 1934

36 White, L. W. Thornton 'Architectural training to-day in England and abroad' *RIBA Journal* Vol 41 1934 Jan 27 pp299—302

37 Ansell, W. H. 'Architectural education' *RIBA Journal* Vol 43 1936 Apr 4 pp565—574

38 RIBA 'The place of science in architectural education' *RIBA Journal* Vol 48 1941 Jun pp133—143. First report of the Education Committee of the Architectural Science Group of the RIBA Research Board.

39 'RIBA assistance for prisoners of war' *RIBA News* First Issue 1944 Apr. Special supplement to the *RIBA Journal* published for the information of members serving in the armed forces. Gives details of the scheme for provision of books and holding of RIBA examinations in a number of prisoner of war camps in Germany.

40 Budden, Lionel B. 'The future of architectural education' *RIBA Journal* Vol 52 1945 Jul pp249—256

41 RIBA *Report of the Special Committee on Architectural Education* London, RIBA, 1946

42 RIBA 'The teaching of construction' *RIBA Journal* Vol 55 1948 Aug pp464—468. Second report of the Architectural Science Board.

43 RIBA Board of Architectural Education 'Architectural education: numbers under training' *RIBA Journal* Vol 56 1949 Jan pp131—132. Statement on the interim report of the Mars Group and Architectural Students Association Joint Committee on Architectural Education.

44 RIBA 'Report of the Architectural Education Joint Committee on the Training and Qualification for Associate Membership of the Royal Institute of British Architects' *RIBA Journal* Vol 62 1955 Feb pp156—164. Known as the McMorran Report.

45 RIBA 'Report of the committee on the Oxford Architectural Education Conference 1958' *RIBA Journal* Vol 67 1959 Nov pp4—13

46 'Reconstitution of the Board of Architectural Education' *RIBA Journal* Vol 67 1960 Apr p214

47 'Postgraduate training' *RIBA Journal* Vol 69 1962 Mar pp118—121

48 Layton, Elizabeth *The practical training of architects* London, RIBA 1962

49 Layton, Elizabeth 'Practical training in action' *RIBA Journal* Vol 70 1963 Nov pp430—431

50 Darke, Michael *Diversification. A report to the Board of Architectural Education* London, RIBA, 1964. Report by a working group of the RIBA Board of Architectural Education.

51 Harper, Denis 'Some notes on the education of the architect and his technical assistant' *RIBA Journal* Vol 71 1964 Oct pp441—442

52 RIBA Management Advisory Group 'Pre-Associate management training' *RIBA Journal* Vol 71 1964 Jan pp27—28

53 RIBA *The future pattern of architectural education* London, RIBA, 1965

54 Goldring, Patrick 'Architects in the pipe-line' *RIBA Journal* Vol 72 1965 Jul pp358—360. Article on the work of the RIBA Board of Architectural Education and its Visiting Board.

55 RIBA 'RIBA educational policy. Standard of architectural education' *RIBA Journal* Vol 74 1967 Jan pp6—9

56 RIBA Board of Education 'Report of the RIBA Visiting Board, 1963—1968' *RIBA Journal* Vol 75 1968 May pp204—209

57 RIBA Board of Education 'Degree level: criteria for recognition' *RIBA Journal* Vol 75 1968 May pp209—210

58 Esher, Lord & Llewelyn-Davies, Lord 'The architect in 1988' *RIBA Journal* Vol 75 1968 Oct pp448—455. Paper written at request of PRIBA to provide the Policy and Finance Committee with a framework within which to plan the RIBA's educational and professional policies.

59 *Education for research* London, RIBA & Bartlett School of Architecture, 1969

60 *Integrated and inter-related courses for the disciplines serving the building industry* London, RIBA, IOB, ISE & RICS, 1969

61 RIBA & TPI 'RIBA Urban Design Diploma' *RIBA Journal* Vol 76 1969 Feb p53

62 'The Department of Architectural Education' and 'Alex Gordon. John Carter interviews the chairman of the Board of Architectural Education' *RIBA Journal* Vol 74 1969 Oct pp424—427 & 428—429. Parts of a feature article 'Inside the RIBA'.

63 Gordon, Alex 'Continuing education: joint body needed' *RIBA Journal* Vol 77 1970 Jan p430

64 'Urban design diploma for architects' *RIBA Journal* Vol 77 1970 Jun p273

65 Keevil, Philip & Woolley, Tom 'Stay in or drop out? Two views of student involvement with the RIBA' *RIBA Journal* Vol 77 1970 Oct pp473—474

66 RIBA Board of Education 'Strategies for education in the 1970s' *RIBA Journal* Vol 78 1971 Mar pp123—125

67 *Schools of architecture recognised by the RIBA* London, RIBA Publications Ltd, 1971—   .

68 Quantrill, Malcolm, RIBA Continuing Education Working Group 'Watering horses in midstream' *RIBA Journal* Vol 79 1972 Jun pp247—249

69 RIBA Practical Training Group 'Progress in practical training' *RIBA Journal* Vol 79 1972 Nov p484

70 'School report' *RIBA Journal* Vol 86 1979 Aug pp356—357. Article on the RIBA Visiting Board.

71 RIBA Continuing Professional Development Working Group *Continuing professional development* London, RIBA, 1979

72 Cunningham, Allen 'The case for continuing education' *RIBA Journal* Vol 87 1980 Jan pp45—46

73 Markham, Geoff 'The Institute's role in education' *RIBA Journal* Vol 87 1980 Apr p18

74 Powers, Alan A. R. 'Architectural Education in Britain 1880—1914' Ph.D. thesis, Cambridge University. Submitted 1982
75 Gibbs Kennet, Peter 'Education in ferment' *RIBA Journal* Vol 90 1983 Jan pp35—37
76 Tarn, Prof. J. N. 'The education debate' *RIBA Journal* Vol 90 1983 Sep pp47—50
77 Startup, H.M. 'Institutional control of architectural education and registration: 1834—1960' CNAA M.Phil. thesis, 1984

Section 2 RIBA examinations in architecture

7.2.1   EXAMINATIONS QUESTION PAPERS, 1863—(1983)   4 boxes & 4 vols
Question papers set for the twelve Voluntary Architectural Examinations held between 1863 & 1881: papers set for the Preliminary Examination, 1898—1927: the Intermediate Examination, 1921—1924, 1928—1944, 1947—1962, 1964—1968: the Final and Special Final Examinations, 1898—1945, 1948—1949, 1960—1968: the Examination in Town Planning, 1925—1931: the Professional Practice Examination, 1951—1962: the Examination in Architecture, Parts 1 & 2 & G Papers (Professional practice), 1971 onwards.

7.2.2   VOLUNTARY ARCHITECTURAL EXAMINATION LECTURES, 1865   1 vol
Manuscripts of ten lectures delivered at the Institute for the benefit of candidates for the Voluntary Architectural Examination by Sydney Smirke, Sir Matthew Digby Wyatt, William Burges, Edward I'Anson, Francis Cranmer Penrose and others.
Subjects : Architectural history, professional practice, building materials, drawing, mechanics, geology and physics.

(The first voluntary examination was held in 1863 and the last in 1880. It was never very popular since it was difficult to pass and conferred no particular status or advantage on the successful candidate. For minutes of the (Voluntary) Architectural Examinations Committee *see* 2.1 Early Committees Minutes Series & 2.2 Special Committees Minutes Series.)

7.2.3   BOARD OF EXAMINERS MINUTES, 1882—1910   4 vols
Signed minutes of meetings of the Board of Examiners for the RIBA
examinations, Jun 1882 — Jul 1910, with reports of subcommittees,
memoranda, question papers, transcripts of letters received, tables of
marks gained by candidates (up to 1902), and lists of people qualifying
for registration as Probationer RIBA and Student RIBA and for
election as Associate RIBA.

Subjects : Examinations in London, the provinces and abroad: special
colonial examinations: selection of moderators and consideration of
their reports, with results of examinations: the General Conference
1887, which discussed architectural education and examination: introduction of three-tier system — Preliminary, Intermediate and Final:
introduction of the exemption system and 'Recognised' schools.

(First known as the Board of Examiners under By-Law 14 and then
as the Board of Examiners in Architecture, so as to distinguish them
from the (Statutory) Board of Examiners for certificates of competency
to act as a district surveyor. It was set up in 1881 to administer the
Obligatory Examination, which developed into a complete system of
compulsory examinations for qualification for election as an Associate
member of the RIBA. For minutes of the Board of Examiners, May
1881—Apr 1882 *see* 2.2 Special Committees Minutes Series. In 1910,
the responsibility for conducting the examinations passed to the Board
of Architectural Education. For continuation *see* 7.2.10 Examiners
Committees Minutes Series *and* 7.1.2 Board of Architectural Education
Committees Minutes Series.)

7.2.4   QUALIFYING EXAMINATION: REGISTER OF CANDI-
DATES, 1882—1918   2 vols
Register of candidates for the Final or Special Examination in
Architecture, Mar 1882 — Jun 1918, (originally called the Obligatory
Examination), the passing of which, under By-law 14 (1877), had
become the qualification for election as ARIBA. Gives full names and
addresses, date and place of examinations and whether passed, relegated,
etc.

7.2.5   QUALIFYING EXAMINATION: CANDIDATES' APPLICA-
TIONS, 1882—1907   14 vols
Candidates application forms for the Obligatory and later the Final
Examination in Architecture qualifying for Associate membership,
with recommendations of the Board of Examiners, Feb 1882 — May
1907. From 1895, Special Examination application forms from those
who had been exempted from the 3-tier examination, on adequate
evidence of experience or other qualifications, are included.

7.2.6   PROBATIONERS REGISTER, 1889—1960   10 vols
A register of RIBA Probationers, i.e. architectural students who had
passed or been exempted from the RIBA Preliminary Examination or
held an equivalent qualification and were studying for the Intermediate
Examination, from Nov 1889—May 1960. Gives name, address,
number, age, whether exempted from the Preliminary Examination,
date of examination, name of school, college or university, date
of admission as a Probationer, marginal 'S' indicating subsequent
qualification as a Student RIBA (by passing the Intermediate Examination). Vols 1 and 2 also give place of examination and name of
principal or firm.

7.2.7   STUDENTS REGISTER, 1890—1960   6 vols
A register of Students RIBA, i.e. architectural students who had passed
or been exempted from the RIBA Intermediate Examination, from
Nov 1890—May 1960. Gives name, address, number, age, whether
exempted from the Intermediate Examination, date of examination,
name of architectural school, date of admission as a Student RIBA

(For members of the Student class from 1838—1877 *see* 5.4.1
Membership Register (Early Series) *and* 5.4.4 Students Nomination
Papers Series.)

7.2.8   PRELIMINARY EXAMINATION: CANDIDATES APPLICA-
TIONS, 1895—1909   10 vols
Application forms of candidates for the RIBA Preliminary Examination,
Oct 1895 — Apr 1909, giving information on work experience and
education. Where appropriate, a candidate was exempted from the
examination if experience and education were considered adequate.

7.2.9   INTERMEDIATE EXAMINATION: CANDIDATES APPLICA-
TIONS, 1895—1909   5 vols
Application forms of candidates for the RIBA Intermediate Examination, Oct 1895 — Apr 1909, giving information on their education
and professional experience and listing the Testimonies of Study
submitted. On the basis of the application forms some candidates were
relegated.

7.2.10   * EXAMINERS COMMITTEES MINUTES, 1913—1977   3 vols
Signed minutes of the following committees:
Examiners (Intermediate, Final & Special Examinations), Oct 1913—
     Oct 1925
Fellowship Examiners, Feb 1926—Nov 1967

Problems in Design & Testimonies of Study Examiners, Apr 1926—Jul 1934

RIBA Diploma in Town Planning Examiners, Jun 1924—Jun 1927

RIBA Examiners for the Examination for Candidates for the Office of Building Surveyor under Local Authorities, Apr 1966—May 1977

Special Examination in Professional Practice Examiners, Oct 1923

Testimonies of Study Examiners, Jul 1951

Thesis Examiners, Nov 1914—May 1949 (no examination 1941—1948)

Visiting Board Special Meeting, Apr 1935

Also included are RIBA Examination question papers, 1915—1925: RIBA Town Planning Diploma examination questions and results, 1924—1930: titles of Final Examination theses with results, from 1923—1949: subjects and results for Testimonies of Study: names of candidates for transfer from the Licentiateship class to the Fellowship class, with design subjects set for examination and names of those successful.

Subjects : Setting the questions for RIBA examinations: methods of conducting the examinations: reporting examination results to the BAE: duties of Moderators.

(See also 7.1.2 Board of Architectural Education Committees Minutes Series, for minutes of examiners)

* Access at the discretion of the Examinations Officer

7.2.11   EXAMINATIONS COMMITTEE MINUTES, 1926—1958   1 vol & 2 binders

Signed minutes of the Examination Committee, Jan 1926—Oct 1958, the Examinations Syllabus Drafting Subcommittee, Apr—Jun 1956, and joint meetings of the Examiners Committee & the Co-ordinating Examiners for the RIBA Examination, Dec 1956—May 1957, with memoranda and reports of subcommittees, and annual statistics of numbers of students.

Subjects : General administration of the RIBA examinations and general direction of the work of the various bodies of examiners and the Board of Moderators: qualifications required for registration as a Probationer RIBA: lists of names approved for registration as Probationers: exemptions from the RIBA Intermediate and Final examinations: annual statistics of students who sat for school examinations exempting from the RIBA Intermediate and Final examinations: numbers of people passing, failing, etc. the RIBA Intermediate, Final and Special Final examinations, the Fellowship Examination for Licentiates and the Special Examination in Professional Practice for students at Recognised Schools: applications to take the Special Final Examination: remuneration of examiners (vol 1): unification of the profession (vol 1): RIBA examinations in the colonies and dominions, particularly in India (vol 1): setting up the RIBA Diploma in Town Planning (vol 1).

(Set up in 1910 as one of the committees of the remodelled Board of Architectural Education. For minutes of this committee, 1910—1925 *see* 7.1.2 Board of Architectural Education Committees Minutes Series. Between Aug 1939 and Oct 1944 the business of the Examinations Committee was dealt with by the officers of the BAE *see* 7.1.4 Officers of the Board of Architectural Education Minutes Series.)

7.2.12   * EXTERNAL EXAMINERS REPORTS: INTERMEDIATE AND FINAL EXEMPTIONS, 1926—1935, 1949—1966   1 vol & 7 binders
Reports by external examiners from schools of architecture recognized by the RIBA, containing lists of names of students who had satisfied the requirements for exemption from either the Intermediate or the Final Examination in Architecture. The lists are signed and dated by the external examiners and sometimes also by the principals of the schools or by other members of their teaching staffs.

* Access at the discretion of the Examinations Officer

7.2.13   * EXAMINATIONS RESULTS REGISTER, 1927—1952   2 vols
Register recording the results of all examinations conducted by the RIBA between May 1927 and May 1948 (and Professional Practice Examination results up to Mar 1952).

For each examination held the register gives a list of names of candidates examined: a list of names of passed candidates: a list of names of relegated candidates, with the numbers of sections to be retaken: and the percentage total of passes. Included in Vol 2 are the results of the Intermediate, Final and Special Examinations held in prisoner-of-war camps in German-occupied territory in 1943 and 1944, at Oflags 5A, 7B, 9A, 79, Stalags 48, 20A, 344, 357, 383, Stalag Luft 3 & 6, and Ilag 7.

The following examinations are included in the register:
Intermediate Examination, May 1927—May 1948
Final Examination, Jul 1927—Apr 1948
Special Final Examination, Jul 1927—Apr 1948
Professional Practice Examination, Jul 1927—Mar 1952
Special Examination in Design (to enable former members of the Society of Architects to become Associates of the RIBA), Jul 1927—Jul 1938 & Jul 1947

RIBA Diploma in Town Planning Examination, Jul 1927—Jun 1931
(from 1932 the examinations for town planning diplomas were
conducted by the Joint Town Planning Examination Board,
composed of representatives of the TPI, the ICE, the RICS and
the RIBA)

Statutory Examination for District Surveyors, Oct 1927—May 1932

Statutory Examination for Building Surveyors, Oct 1927—May 1932

Licentiate to Fellowship Examination, Nov 1929—Apr 1932

(For information on examination results before 1927 *see also* 7.2.3 Board
of Examiners Minutes, 7.2.10 Examiners Committees Minutes, 1.2.6
Ordinary General Meetings Minutes and 1.2.7 Annual and Special
General Meetings Minutes.)

* Access at the discretion of the Examinations Officer

7.2.14   * FINAL TESTIMONIES OF STUDY RESULTS REGISTER,
1927—1952   2 vols

Register recording the names of RIBA Students with the dates and
numbers of designs submitted by them for the Final Examination and
the marks gained, May 1927 — Sep 1952. Occasionally a note was
made of the type of buildings designed, the architectural school
attended, and remarks such as 'Fail', 'Pass' or 'Resubmit'.

* Access at the discretion of the Examinations Officer

7.2.15   THESES FOR THE RIBA FINAL EXAMINATION, 1928—
1962   *c.* 300 vols

Theses written for the RIBA Final Examination and deposited in the
RIBA Library. They are arranged under subject headings according
to the UDC classification system.

Subjects : History of architecture: studies of building types: architectural
decoration and ornaments: architectural details: town planning: housing:
building materials: methods of construction: drainage, lighting, heating,
ventilation, etc. of buildings: acoustics: air-raid precautions: studies of
individual architects and their work.

(For minutes of meetings of the Thesis Examiners, 1912—1913 *see*
7.1.2 Board of Architectural Education Committees Minutes Series
and for 1914—1949, 7.2.10 Examiners Committees Minutes Series.
A list of the theses is available in the Library)

7.2.16   * PROFESSIONAL   PRACTICE   EXAMINATION   RESULTS
FROM   RECOGNISED   SCHOOLS,   1930—1964   1 vol & 4
binders

Reports from schools of architecture recognised by the RIBA, containing lists of names of students who had taken the Professional Practice Examination and indicating those who had passed and those who had failed.

*Access at the discretion of the Examinations Officer

7.2.17   *INTERMEDIATE   TESTIMONIES   OF   STUDY   RESULTS REGISTER, 1931—1953   2 vols
A register recording the names of Probationers with the dates and numbers of designs submitted by them for the Intermediate Examination, May 1931 — Feb 1952, with marks gained and examiners' remarks.

*Access at the discretion of the Examinations Officer

7.2.18   *INTERMEDIATE   EXAMINATION   RESULTS   REGISTER, 1948—1954   1 vol
Register recording the results of Intermediate Examinations held between Nov 1948 and Nov 1954 (plus record of the numbers examined up to 1980). For each examination held the register gives the number of candidates examined: number of candidates passed or relegated: percentage total of passes: lists of names of passed and relegated candidates, with numbers of sections to be retaken.

(For results of this examination, 1927—1948 *see* 7.2.13 Examinations Results Register)

*Access at the discretion of the Examinations Officer

7.2.19   *FINAL   EXAMINATION   RESULTS   REGISTER,   1948— 1956   1 vol
Register recording the results of the Final Examinations held from Jul 1948—Jun 1956 (plus record of the numbers examined up to 1980). For each examination held the register gives the number of candidates examined: numbers of candidates passed or relegated: percentage total of passes: lists of names of passed and relegated candidates, with numbers of sections to be retaken.

(For results of this examination, 1927—1948 *see* 7.2.13 Examinations Results Register)

*Access at the discretion of the Examinations Officer

7.2.20   *SPECIAL   FINAL   EXAMINATION   RESULTS   REGISTER, 1948—1954   1 vol
A register recording the results of Special Final Examinations held between Jul 1948 and Dec 1954 (plus record of the numbers examined

up to 1973). For each examination held the register gives the number of candidates: numbers of candidates passed or relegated: percentage total of passes: lists of names of passed and relegated candidates, with the numbers of sections to be retaken.

(For results of this examination, 1927—1948 *see* 7.2.13 Examinations Results Register. This examination ceased in Jun 1973)

* Access at the discretion of the Examinations Officer

7.2.21 * PROFESSIONAL   PRACTICE   EXAMINATION   RESULTS REGISTER, 1952—1957   1 vol
A register recording the results of Professional Practice Examinations held between Nov 1952 and Apr 1957 (plus record of the numbers examined up to 1980). For each examination held the register gives the number of candidates examined: numbers passed or relegated: percentage total of passes: lists of names of passed and relegated candidates: details of the Final or Special Final examination previously passed.

(For results of this examination, 1927—1952 *see* 7.2.13 Examinations Results Register.)

* Access at the discretion of the Examinations Officer

7.2.22 REVIEW OF RIBA EXAMINATIONS STEERING COM-MITTEE PAPERS, 1965—1967   2 boxes
Signed minutes of the committee from Jul 1965—Jun 1967, with interim and final reports, and correspondence files kept by Michael Darke and Elizabeth Layton, Assistant Secretaries (Education).
Subject : Review of RIBA external examinations and syllabus.

(After this committee had reported, the Council proposed reform of the examinations: an end to the Testimonies of Study system: a gradual dismantling of part-time courses: a gradual raising of standards to degree level: a limitation on the number of times a student might sit the examinations.)

7.2.23 RIBA EXAMINATION IN ARCHITECTURE IMPLEMENTA-TION COMMITTEE PAPERS, 1968—1969   2 boxes
Signed minutes of the committee from Dec 1968—Jul 1969, with files of correspondence, data, reports and drafts of Guidance Notes and examination papers.
Subject : Implementation of the proposals of the Review of RIBA Examination Steering Committee.

7.2.24   * APPEALS COMMITTEE PAPERS, 1969—(1983)   1 binder

Applications to retake the Final Examination for the fifth and final time.

* No access

7.2.25   * SPECIAL ENTRY COMMITTEE PAPERS, 1971—1977   5
binders
Minutes of meetings, and applications for special entry to the RIBA Examination in Architecture

* No access

See also 2.1 Early Committees Minutes Series and 2.2 Special Committees Minutes Series for the (Voluntary) Architectural Examination Committee, 1860—1880, and the early minutes of the Board of Examiners
and 7.1.2 Board of Architectural Education Committees Minutes Series for the Examinations Committee, 1910—1925, the Board of Moderators, 1925—1944; the Moderators Committee, 1945—1954, and for several series of examiners' minutes.

Bibliography

1   Papworth, John W. 'An abridgement of M. Lance's essay entitled "On a diploma in architecture" with remarks and suggestions' *RIBA Transactions* 1st Series Vol 6 1855/56 pp23—31
2   'A diploma in architecture' *RIBA Transactions* 1st Series Vol 6 1855/56 pp37—47
3   RIBA 'Regulations and course of examination, with forms of declaration and recommendation, for the Voluntary Architectural Examination' and 'Voluntary Architectural Examination (open to all British subjects). Sketch of form of examination papers'. *RIBA Transactions* 1st Series 1861/62 1862 May
4   Ashpitel, Arthur 'On the voluntary architectural examinations' *RIBA Proceedings* 1st Series 1862/63 pp1—15
5   RIBA 'Report of the Revising Examiners 1866' *RIBA Transactions* 1865/66, 12 Feb 1866. Report on the Voluntary Architectural Examination.
6   Kerr, Robert 'Suggestions on the Architectural Voluntary Examination of the Institute' *RIBA Transactions* 1st Series Vol 20 1869/70 pp209—221
7   Smith, T. Roger 'On the voluntary examinations of the Institute', in *General Conference of Architects 1871. Report of proceedings* London, RIBA, 1871
8   RIBA *The Examination in Architecture* London, RIBA, [1885]
9   Adams, Cole A. 'Architectural education and the Examination in Architecture' *Builder* Vol 48 1885 Jan 10 pp65—66
10   'The examination in architecture. Professor Kerr's question' *RIBA Proceedings* New Series Vol 2 1886 Feb 18 pp132—138

11 Cates, Arthur 'The future of the examination' *RIBA Proceedings* New Series Vol 5 1889 Mar 28 pp214—216. Relates to the RIBA Obligatory Examination.

12 'The education report' *RIBA Proceedings* New Series Vol 5 1889 May 9 pp263—276. Report of discussion on the scheme for progressive examinations.

13 Cates, Arthur 'Examination in architecture, in the past, present and the future' *RIBA Proceedings* New Series Vol 6 1890 Jan 23 pp147—152

14 RIBA 'Architecture — a profession or an art?' *RIBA Proceedings* New Series Vol 7 1891 May 7 pp297—303. Report of discussion on a memorial to the Council petitioning against a compulsory qualifying examination for architects.

15 Blomfield, Reginald 'The Institute examination and architecture', in Shaw, R. N. & Jackson, T. G. (eds) *Architecture: a profession or an art* London, J. Murray, 1892

16 Waterhouse, Alfred 'Progressive examination' *RIBA Journal* Vol 1 1893 Nov pp20—23

17 'The examinations for admission to candidature: an historical note' *RIBA Journal* Vol 2 1895 Jan 3 pp137—141

18 Blomfield, Reginald 'A note on recent changes in the RIBA examinations' *RIBA Journal* Vol 18 1911 Oct 21 pp767—770

19 Waterhouse, Paul 'The Institute examinations' *RIBA Journal* Vol 28 1920 Nov 20 pp35—36

20 RIBA *Membership of the RIBA. Particulars of qualifications* London, RIBA, 1923. (Frequently revised editions issued, 1926—1955)

21 'RIBA assistance for prisoners of war' *RIBA News* First Issue 1944 Apr. Special supplement to the *RIBA Journal* published for the information of members serving in the armed forces. Gives details of the scheme for provision of architectural books and holding of RIBA examinations in a number of prisoner of war camps in Germany.

22 RIBA Examiners 'RIBA Final Examination theses' *RIBA Journal* Vol 61 1954 Feb p157. Guidance notes for students.

23 RIBA Board of Architectural Education 'RIBA Testimonies of Study. Notes for the guidance of students preparing Intermediate and Final Testimonies of Study' *RIBA Journal* Vol 61 1954 Mar pp181—189

24 Allen, W. A. & Jones, Prof. Douglas 'RIBA exams out of date: reform a high priority' *RIBA Journal* Vol 72 1965 Jun pp281—282

25 RIBA Board of Architectural Education 'New look for the RIBA examinations' *RIBA Journal* Vol 74 1967 May pp187—190

26 RIBA Board of Education 'New structure for RIBA examinations' *RIBA Journal* Vol 75 1968 Aug pp336—337

27 RIBA *The Examination in Architecture. Guidance notes and regulations* London, RIBA Publications Ltd, 1972

Section 3 Statutory examinations for building surveyors

Under Clause 33 of the Metropolitan Building Act 1855 the RIBA was appointed the statutory examining body for those who wished to practise as district surveyors in London and the Institute was empowered to grant certificates of competency to deserving candidates. Candidates were required to take a written, graphic and oral examination in building materials and construction. A Board of Examiners was elected at each Annual General Meeting and the certificates were signed and sealed at a subsequent meeting of the Council. In 1886 another examination was introduced for those wishing to practise as building surveyors under local acts of parliament. From 1900 one examination was held for both London district surveyors and local authority building surveyors. The examination was never popular, with few suitable candidates entering and high failure rates. The last RIBA examination for building surveyors was held in 1984. Lists of names of successful candidates were published in the *RIBA Kalendar* from 1856 to 1936.

7.3.1   *   RIBA EXAMINERS FOR THE EXAMINATION FOR CANDI-
DATES FOR THE OFFICE OF BUILDING SURVEYOR
UNDER LOCAL AUTHORITIES MINUTES, 1855— 1965,
1977—1984   4 vols
Signed minutes of meetings, Dec 1855 — May 1984. The minutes
include lists of candidates' names, sometimes with address, age and
occupation; copies of examination papers; record of passes and failures;
copies of correspondence.

(For minutes of meetings from 1966—1977 *see* 7.2.10 Examiners
Committees Minutes Series)

* Access at the discretion of the Examinations Officer

7.3.2   RIBA EXAMINATION FOR CANDIDATES FOR THE OFFICE
OF BUILDING SURVEYOR UNDER LOCAL AUTHORITIES:
RECOMMENDATIONS   FOR   CERTIFICATES,   1856—
1905   3 vols
Recommendations for the award of certificates of competency, Jan
1856 — Oct 1905, with names index to each volume. Give name and

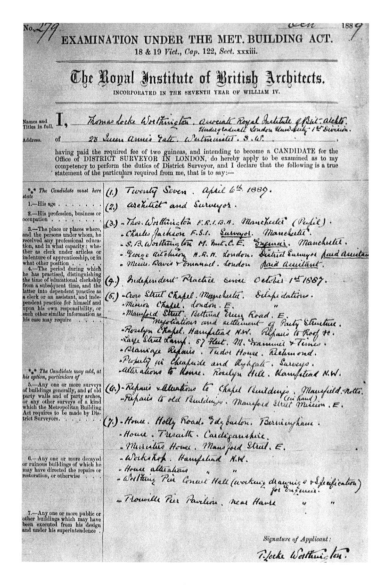

17 An example of a candidate's application to be examined by the RIBA for competency to perform the duties of a district surveyor in London, 1889, giving details of age, professional education and practice and particulars of any survey, repair or restoration work performed by him and buildings designed by him or erected under his supervision. In 1855 the RIBA was appointed the statutory body for examining those who wished to practise as district surveyors in London and, from 1886, as building surveyors appointed under local acts of parliament. The last of these examinations was held in 1984. (RIBA Archive: 7.3.2)

date of birth of candidates and, from 1878, particulars of their professional education and experience.

Bibliography

RIBA 'Statutory examinations. Examination for candidates for the office of district surveyor under the Metropolitan Building Act 1855' with 'Examination for candidates for the office of building surveyor under local authorities' and 'Particulars applicable to both examinations' *RIBA Kalendar* 1886/87. Revised annually.

Section 4 RIBA prizes, studentships and scholarships

The first annual prize offered by the Institute was the Silver Medal for an Essay, first presented in 1836 to George Godwin for an essay on the properties of concrete which was published in the first volume of the *Transactions*. This was followed in 1838 by the Soane Medallion which commemorated Sir John Soane, one of the original benefactors of the Institute, and was awarded in most years for the best set of architectural design drawings on a given subject. A sum of money was given with the Soane Medallion which was to be used in travel abroad for the purpose of architectural study. In 1855 the Silver Medal for Measured Drawings was started and in 1865 the Pugin Studentship for the study of medieval architecture in Great Britain and Ireland. This commemorated A. W. N. Pugin and its recipient had to undertake a tour of several weeks' duration and subsequently submit a report illustrated with sketches and measured drawings. In 1871 the Reverend Francis Ashpitel gave ten shares in the Architectural Union Company to found a prize for the best performance in the Voluntary Architectural Examination. This turned into an annual prize for the candidate who most distinguished himself in the RIBA Final Examination. Sir William Tite, twice President of the RIBA, died in 1873 having bequeathed £1,000 for the foundation of the Tite Prize for the study of Italian renaissance architecture and in 1874 Thomas Grissell bequeathed £250 for the foundation of the Grissell Gold Medal for the best set of drawings illustrating the construction of a building of architectural merit.

From the 1880s onwards the study of contemporary architecture was encouraged by several substantial bequests, including the Godwin Bursary founded in 1882 for the study of modern architecture abroad and the Alfred Bossom Medals and Fellowships founded in 1925 for the study of commercial architecture in the USA.

In 1913 the Rome Scholarship in Architecture, tenable for three years at the British School at Rome, was founded by the Commissioners of the 1851 Exhibition and in the same year the RIBA Henry Jarvis Travelling Studentship, tenable for two years at the British School at Rome, was started. In 1928 the RIBA undertook to guarantee the sum necessary for the Rome Scholarship and the Henry Jarvis Travelling Studentship was discontinued. The study of Greek and hellenistic architecture was fostered by the Henry L. Florence Bursary and the Athens Bursary for periods of study based at the British School at Athens, both instituted in the 1930s.

As a result of a conference held in 1924 to discuss the prizes and scholarships given in the profession as a whole, many of the prizes were reorganized and their conditions adapted to bring them more into line with the current educational system. At this conference the need for more maintenance scholarships, particularly for students in the provinces, was highlighted and the RIBA subsequently set up its Maintenance Scholarships Committee to develop and administer a comprehensive scheme.

By 1960 the Institute had over thirty separate charitable trust funds used for the payment of student prizes, bursaries, studentships and scholarships and, in 1964, most of these trusts were amalgamated into the Historical Research Trust and the Modern Architecture and Town Planning Trust which have since been used for the payment of research grants.

(*See RIBA Directory of Members*, 1965, for lists of RIBA prizewinners and holders of RIBA studentships, scholarships and bursaries, 1836—1964)

7.4.1   PRIZES AND SCHOLARSHIPS: ESSAYS AND REPORTS, 1839—1963   267 vols

Essays and reports by winners of the Athens Bursary, the Banister Fletcher Essay Silver Medal, the Alfred Bossom Gold Medal, the Alfred Bossom Research Fellowship, the Arthur Cates Prize, the Archibald Dawnay Scholarship, the Silver Medal for an Essay, the Henry Florence Bursary, the Godwin Bursary, the Hunt Bursary, the Silver Medal for Measured Drawings, the Neale Bursary, the Owen Jones Travelling Studentship, the Prentice Bequest, the Pugin Studentship, the Saxon Snell Prize, the Rose Shipman Studentship, the Soane Medallion, the Tite Prize and the Victory Scholarship.

Subjects include:- Classical Greek and Roman architecture: Italian renaissance architecture: contemporary American architecture: German, French and Spanish architecture: town planning and housing: architectural theory, principles and aesthetics: medieval buildings in

Britain: architectural decorations, ornaments and use of colour: biography and works of individual architects: architecture of specific periods: specific building types, especially churches: contemporary design and constructions of hospitals: conservation of ancient monuments and historic buildings.

(Many prize essays and drawings were not retained by the Institute but were returned to the authors. Some early prize essays which were read at General Meetings of the Institute are to be found bound up in 11.4.1 Papers Read at General Meetings Series. A list of prize essays and reports is available for consultation in the Library)

TRUST FUNDS DEEDS, BEQUESTS & DEEDS OF COVENANT, 1864—
see 5.2.4

7.4.2   PRIZES AND STUDENTSHIPS COMMITTEES MINUTES, 1869—1910   2 vols
Signed minutes of the following committees:
Pugin Travelling Studentship Committee, Feb 1869—Jan 1883
Medals and Prizes Committee, Feb 1869—Dec 1889
Mr. Peek's Prizes Committee, Feb —Mar 1872
Godwin Bursary Committee, 1883
Travelling Studentships Special Committee, Jan 1886
Studentships, Medals and Prizes Committee, Jan 1890—Jan 1892
Prizes and Studentships Committee, Feb 1892—Dec 1910

Subjects : Award and administration of RIBA prizes, studentships, scholarships and bursaries: annual exhibitions of students' drawings.

(The work of the Prizes and Studentships Committee was taken over by the Board of Architectural Education in 1910 *see* 7.1.1 Board of Architectural Education Minutes Series between 1910 and 1925. For information on prizes, medals and studentships before 1869 *see* 1.2.2 Council Minutes Series.)

DEEDS OF AWARD OF PRIZES AND MEDALS, 1890—1962
see 1.2.6 Ordinary General Meetings Minutes Series

7.4.3   PRIZES AND SCHOLARSHIPS COMMITTEE MINUTES, 1926—1958   1 vol & 1 binder
Signed minutes of meetings, Jan 1926 — Oct 1958, with memoranda, reports and copies of letters received.
Subjects : Arrangements for prize competitions: appointment of prize juries: consideration of the reports of the various juries and

18   Some RIBA prize and studentship medals. From top left: the RIBA Board of
Architectural Education Silver Medal (diameter 89 mm), awarded annually to a
student of an architectural school recognized for exemption from the RIBA Final
Examination, 1922—1957; the Soane Medallion (diameter 82 mm), awarded
annually for a set of design drawings on a given subject, 1838—1964; the RIBA
Rome Scholarship Medal (diameter 75 mm) — a scholarship tenable for three
years at the British School at Rome — awarded annually 1913—1963; the Godwin
Bursary Medal (diameter 56 mm), awarded annually for the study of modern
architecture abroad, 1882—1964; the Institute Silver Medal (diameter 57 mm),
awarded annually for an essay, 1836—1864, and for a set of measured drawings
of a historic building, 1855—1963; the Pugin Travelling Studentship Medal
(diameter 56 mm), awarded annually for the study of medieval architecture in
Great Britain and Ireland, 1865—1962. (British Architectural Library Medals
Collection)

subcommittees for the award of prizes and scholarships: consideration of the reports of the Maintenance Scholarships Committee: administration of the Maintenance Scholarships Fund: approval of prize-winners' study programmes: exhibitions of prize drawings at the RIBA: annual tours of the RIBA prize drawings to the Allied Societies: the RIBA Travelling Card and the regulations governing the measurement of public buildings and monuments in Europe: scholarships available at 'Recognised' schools of architecture: RIBA prizes and studentships overseas: architectural prizes and scholarships offered by other institutions.

7.4.4   PRIZEWINNERS REGISTER, 1926—1965   2 vols
A register of names of prizewinners with dates and record of payments made to them (usually in instalments), beginning and end dates of tours and dates when reports were submitted and considered. It was sometimes noted whether reports were retained by the prizewinners or deposited in the Library.

7.4.5   DISPLAY OF PRIZEWINNERS NAMES SUBCOMMITTEE PAPERS, 1935—1938   1 box
Correspondence by the Librarian, who was Secretary of the committee, concerning an unexecuted scheme to inscribe RIBA prizewinners names on the walls of the new HQ building.

(A subcommittee of the Literature Standing Committee.)

See also 2.1 Early Committees Minutes Series & 2.2 Special Committees Minutes Series
   and 7.1.2 Board of Architectural Education Committees Minutes Series, for the Maintenance Scholarships Committee, 1926—1962, and for many committees concerned with individual prizes, studentships, scholarships and bursaries.

Bibliography

1   RIBA *Regulations for the administration of the funds of the Pugin Travelling Studentship* London, RIBA, 1865
2   'Sir William Tite's legacy. Scheme for the application of the income' *RIBA Notices of Meetings* 1874/75 30 Nov 1874
3   RIBA *Studentships and prizes* London, RIBA, 1896 (Frequent revised editions issued up to 1912)
4   RIBA *Prizes and studentships* London, RIBA, 1913 (Frequent revised editions issued up to 1961)

5   RIBA *Prizes and scholarships* London, RIBA, 1961 (Revised editions in 1962 & 1963)
6   'The new scheme for RIBA scholarships and prizes' *RIBA Journal* Vol 70 1963 Dec pp506—507

8
Practice

As Thomas Roger Smith said in 1880 'To be trusted and trustworthy is the first necessity of professional life'. The low esteem in which British architects were held by the government and the public in the years following the Napoleonic Wars was one of the major concerns of the early members. This loss of confidence in architects was mainly due to their frequent lack of independence from the building trade and their common lack of competence. Because of this, much of the early work of the Institute was concerned with establishing standards for architectural practice, generally-accepted rules regarding conditions of engagement, professional conduct and etiquette and model procedures for the regulation of architectural competitions.

In this chapter are gathered together not only the records of the successive standing Practice committees and the Practice Department but also the papers of several committees which, though independent of the Practice committees, were concerned with the conditions of practice of official and salaried architects; the papers of several joint committees concerned with consultation between builders, quantity surveyors and the RIBA, whose RIBA representatives were responsible to the Practice committees; and the papers of several committees on building legislation, an area of work which now comes under the wing of the Practice Department but was previously the concern not only of the Practice Standing Committee but also of the Science Standing Committee and several independent committees.

The earliest standing committee of the Institute was the Professional Practice Committee set up in 1845. In 1862 this committee produced a guide called *Professional practice and charges of architects, being those now usually and properly made*. This was frequently revised and published in a series of editions leading directly to the current *Architect's Appointment*. This committee also discussed the measurement of building works, the conditions of building contracts, the arbitration of disputes between architects, contractors and clients, the legal rights of architects, the conduct of architectural competitions for the design of public buildings, and cases of unprofessional conduct by members. In 1886 the Institute set up four large departmental standing committees, one of which was the Practice Standing Committee. This committee's function was to rationalize and co-ordinate the work of numerous smaller committees concerned with the nature of architectural practice, to advise the Council on practice matters and to formulate departmental policy. It continued the work of the old Professional Practice Committee, broadening it to include dealing with building legislation, architects' indemnity insurance and relations with other professional organizations and trade associations in the building industry. An important part of its work, before the formation of the Joint Contracts Tribunal (JCT) in 1931, concerned the standardization of building contracts, a process which had started with the 1870 edition of clauses agreed with the London Builders' Society and progressed through the RIBA standard forms of 1882, 1909 and 1920 to the 1931 Standard Form of Contract agreed with the National Federation of Building Trades Employers (NFBTE), and the arbitration of disputes under these contracts. Another important part of its work was the production in 1923 of 'Suggestions governing professional conduct and practice of architects' which in 1929 developed into the RIBA Code of Professional Practice, since 1950 called the RIBA Code of Professional Conduct (*see* the introduction to Chapter 4, Section 3).

In the 1920s problems concerning the status and conditions of employment of architects in salaried and official positions and their relationship with architects in private practice came to a head. A statement by the Association of Architects, Surveyors and Technical Assistants that the salaried members felt that the Institute was uninterested in their welfare and in their branch of the profession prompted the RIBA Council to appoint a standing Salaried Members Committee in 1928. This was followed in 1937 by the appointment of a standing Official Architects Committee to represent senior official architects, i.e. heads of departments. In 1947 these committees were merged and became the Salaried and Official Architects Committee and the RIBA appointed a Negotiating Officer to deal with salaries and conditions of service of RIBA members employed in public and private offices. In the late 1950s these functions were continued by the Professional Relations Secretary and the Professional Relations Committee. They are now performed by the Salaried Architects Group and the Salaried Members' Officer.

In 1938 the four departmental standing committees for Art, Literature, Science and Practice were discontinued and a new Practice Committee took over from the old Practice Standing Committee. In the late 1950s a Practice Secretary was appointed and he and his staff were responsible for a wide range of activities, some of which were subsequently taken over and developed by the Professional Relations Secretary, the Legal Adviser, the Professional Conduct Secretary, the Professional Services Board, RIBA Services Ltd, the Salaried Architects Group, the Intelligence Unit and the RIBA Secretary and his assistants.

In 1962 a new Professional Practice Committee was set up as part of a new Professional Services Department which had a Practice Section, including a Management Advisory Service, a Technical Section, a Building Industry Section and a Town Planning Section. In 1967 the Institute set up four departmental boards, one of which was the Professional Services Board which took over the work of the Professional Practice Committee. In 1973 the Professional Services Board and Department were discontinued and their work was carried on by a new Practice

Board and Department, the recently formed commercial company RIBA Services Ltd and the Secretary's Office. In 1975 the departmental boards were discontinued and the Education Department was combined with the Practice Department, under the control of the Education and Practice Executive Committee. In 1979 the departments were separated and a new Practice Committee was instituted, which has among its subcommittees the Fees Committee, the Building Control Committee, the Contracts Committee, the Standards Committee and the Code Policy Committee.

Section 1 General

8.1.1   PROFESSIONAL PRACTICE COMMITTEE MINUTES, 1845—
1885   2 vols
Unsigned minutes (copied from non-extant originals), Jun 1845—Jul 1866: unsigned minutes (copied from Early Committees Minutes series), Aug 1866—Apr 1867: unsigned minutes (copied from non-extant originals), Apr 1867—Jun 1868: signed minutes, Nov 1868—Dec 1885, with rough minutebook, 1879—1885.
Subjects : Remuneration of architects in private practice: terms of appointment of architects employed by the Office of Works on public buildings, including E. M. Barry's fees for work on the New Palace of Westminster: measurement of building works: relations between architect and tradesman and between architect and builder: conditions of building contracts: competition conditions: ownership of architects' drawings: professional advertisement: arbitration of some individual cases of dispute over charges.

8.1.2   PRACTICE STANDING COMMITTEE MINUTES & PAPERS, 1886—1938   6 vols, 3 binders & 4 boxes
Signed minutes of meetings, with memoranda and reports, Jun 1886—Jun 1938, and general correspondence of the Hon. Secretary of the Committee, mainly concerned with the 1931 Form of Contract, Mar 1924—Feb 1932. Includes the minutes of the following subcommittees, joint meetings and conferences:
Ancient Lights Subcommittee, Jan 1923
Appointments with Building Materials Manufacturers Subcommittee, Apr —May 1934

Professional Practice Committee.

At a meeting of the Committee held on Wednesday, 5th June 1867.

Present.

James Fergusson, Fellow, in the Chair.

Messrs Barry C.M. Messrs Hayward C.F.

" Nelson C.C.

Seddon I.P. Hon. Sec.

Eastlake C.L. Assist. Sec.

The minutes of the last meeting of the Committee held on the 27th May 1867 were read & confirmed.

Copies of Professor Donaldson's "Draft Suggestions for a Report to the Council" and "Rough Memoranda on Professional Practice" were produced in the form of printed proof sheets and were duly considered in their bearing on the question before the Committee re the remuneration of the Architect to the New Palace at Westminster, when after some discussion it was

Resolved that this Committee having carefully considered the Draft Suggestions &c drawn up by Professor Donaldson determines to postpone their further deliberation on the subject referred to until Professor Donaldson (now absent from England) can be present. Meanwhile they beg to recommend to the Council that a Deputation consisting of the President, (Mr Tite M.P.) Mr Beresford Hope M.P. ex-President Professor Donaldson P.P. Hon. Sec. H.C. Mr C. Langton M.P. Fellow & the Hon. Sec. for Home Duties should wait on Lord John Manners, First Commissioner of Works for the purpose of requesting him to reconsider the case of Mr E. Barry in reference to the question recently submitted to the Office of Works.

It was also

Resolved that Mr Langton's name be added to the list of the Professional Practice Committee.

Wm Tite
President.

19   Minutes of a meeting of the Professional Practice Committee, 5 June 1867, at which E. M. Barry's dispute with the Office of Works over his fees for work on the Houses of Parliament was discussed. The committee recommended that a deputation including the President, [Sir] William Tite M.P., A. J. Beresford Hope, M.P. (ex-President) and Professor Donaldson (Past President) be sent to Lord John Manners, First Commissioner of Works, to request his reconsideration of the case. (RIBA Archive:8.1.1)

Architects and Quantity Surveyors Joint Committee, May 1932—Dec 1935

Architects Fees for Speculative Housing Work Conference, Dec 1922—Feb 1923

Architects Fees in Law Cases Subcommittee, May—Nov 1937

Architects Indemnity Insurance Subcommittee, Mar —May 1936

Architectural Work carried out by Auctioneers and Estate Agents, Concrete Engineers, etc. Subcommittee, Dec 1936

Auctioneers and Estate Agents Institute of the United Kingdom & Practice Standing Committee Joint Meeting, Nov 1932

Charges and Contracts Subcommittee, Nov 1925

Code of Professional Conduct and Practice Subcommittee, Nov 1922—Jan 1923

Code of Professional Practice Clause 5 Subcommittee, Jan —May 1935

Competitions Committee & Practice Standing Committee Joint Meetings, Jun 1920, Jan —Mar 1931

Copyright in Literary and Artistic Works Joint Subcommittee, Jan 1935

Country Members Subcommittee, Feb —Jun 1923

Current Problems in Architectural Professional Practice Subcommittee, Nov 1933

Design of Small Houses Subcommittee & National Federation of House Builders Joint Meeting, Feb 1932

Draft Form of Agreement between a Local Authority and a Firm of Architects Subcommittee, Jul —Dec 1936

Elected Members of the Practice Standing Committee, Jul 1925—Jul 1937

Fees for Reinforced Concrete Work Subcommittee, Jan 1925

Fees of Specialists and Consultants Subcommittee, Jul 1929

Law of Ancient Lights Subcommittee, Oct 1924—Jul 1928

Law of Ancient Lights and Easements Joint Committee, Mar —Apr 1932

Law of Ancient Lights Subcommittee & Surveyors Institution Joint Meetings, Nov 1925—Feb 1926

L.C.C. Drainage By-Laws Joint Committee, Jan 1927

Local Government Act 1933 Section 266 Subcommittee, Jan 1935

Members Engaged in Occupations other than Architect and Surveyor Subcommittee, Nov 1923—Dec 1924

Metropolitan Water Board Regulations Subcommittee, Mar 1923

Minimum Wage for Architectural Assistants Subcommittee, Dec 1924—Jan 1925

National Federation of Building Trades Employers & Practice Standing Committee Joint Meetings, Jan 1929—Feb 1930

New Form of Specification Subcommittee, Jun 1928

Officers of the Practice & Science Standing Committees Meeting, Dec 1925
Officials and Private Practice Subcommittee, Oct 1924—Apr 1927
Parliamentary Subcommittee, Jan 1925—Apr 1926
Payment of Fees on Account Subcommittee, Nov 1937
Professional Advertising Subcommittee, Apr 1924—May 1926
Professional Conduct Subcommittee, Apr 1925
Professional Defence Union Subcommittee, Oct 1925—Mar 1927
Professional Defence Union Subcommittee & Insurance Committee of the Architects Benevolent Society Joint Meeting, Mar 1926
Professional Fees in Claims under Fire Insurance Policies Joint Subcommittee, Nov 1933
Publicity and Advertising Subcommittee, Jan 1933
Schedule of Daywork Charges Subcommittee, Jan 1934

Subjects occurring regularly include : Revisions of RIBA standard conditions of contract: tendering procedures: professional charges: use of nominal affixes: professional advertising: 'ancient lights' and easements: cases of unprofessional conduct: professional etiquette: illicit commissions: amendment of Metropolitan Building Acts and LCC by-laws: competition conditions: arbitration of disputes: architectural copyright: fees for dilapidations: fees for government-subsidized housing schemes: quantity surveyors' fees: architects' indemnity insurance.

Particular topics include : Articles of pupilage (Vol 1): the London Streets and Buildings Bill 1894 (Vol 2): the London Government Bill 1899 (Vol 2): the Royal Commission on Greater London 1922 (Vol 4): measurement of works (Vol 3 & Binder 1): status of architects serving with the armed forces (Vol 4): fees for housing schemes (Vol 4): deputation of the Architects' and Surveyors' Assistants Professional Union concerning minimum wages (Vol 5): a national schedule of daywork charges (Binder 2): proposed formation of an Architectural Defence Union (for the legal defence of architects) (Vol 4): architects' indemnity and conditions of insurance (Vol 6): architectural practice in India (Vol 3): status of architects working in the East (Vol 4): the Burma Society of Architects and conditions of practice in Rangoon (Vol 6): remuneration of architects working in China (Binder 1): position of architects in government employment in Malaya (the Straits Settlement, the Federated Malay States and the unfederated Malay States) (Binder 1)

8.1.3   PRACTICE COMMITTEE MINUTES & PAPERS, 1938—1962   4 binders & 10 boxes
Signed minutes of meetings of the committee and several of its subcommittees, with memoranda and reports, Jul 1938—May 1962. Also meetings

files and various subject files kept by A. E. Parrish and Charles Woodward, Secretaries to the Committee, 1950—1962.

This series includes the minutes of the following subcommittees and joint meetings:

Arbitrators Fees Subcommittee, Jan 1939

Architects and Quantity Surveyors Joint Committee, Jan 1939—Oct 1947

ARCUK Professional Purposes Committee, RIBA Practice Committee & RIBA Public Relations Committee Joint Meeting, May 1955

Code of Professional Conduct Subcommittee, Dec 1953—Jan 1954

Co-opted Members & Practice Committee Joint Meeting, Apr 1944

Employment of Nominated Contractors Subcommittee, Jan —Feb 1957

Fees for Mass-produced Houses Joint Committee, Nov 1945—Jan 1946

Fees for Town Planning Work Joint Subcommittee, Sep 1945

Fees in connection with Fire Insurance Claims Subcommittee, Jun 1945

Housing Committee & Practice Committee Joint Meetings, Mar —Apr 1944

Housing Committee, Ministry of Health & Practice Committee Joint Meeting, Mar 1944

Officers of the Practice Committee, Oct 1939—Jun 1943

Registration Committee & Practice Committee Joint Meeting, Jul 1945

Revision of RIBA Code of Professional Conduct Subcommittee, Apr — Dec 1961

Scale of Annual Salaries for Architects Joint Subcommittee, Apr —May 1945

Scale of Fees for Private Enterprise Builders' Work Subcommittee, Oct 1944

Scale of Fees for Speculative Builders' Work Subcommittee *see* Scale of Fees for Private Enterprise Builders' Work Subcommittee

Scale of Professional Charges Subcommittee, Apr 1951—Apr 1953

War Damage Commission Scale of Fees Joint Committee, Oct 1944— May 1945

Subjects and documents included are similar to those in the Practice Standing Committee Minutes, with the addition of: Fees for assessment, repair or rebuilding of war-damaged buildings: fees for town planning schemes: fees for War Department housing: building work requiring a licence: ARCUK Code of Professional Conduct: design of specialist work.

8.1.4   EMPLOYMENT OF SALARIED ARCHITECTS ON THE STAFFS OF BUILDING CONTRACTORS JOINT SUBCOMMITTEE PAPERS, 1955—1958   1 box

Correspondence files of the Secretary to the committee, Dec 1955 — Jul 1958.

Subject : Investigation into the extent of the employment of architects on the staff of building contractors and the possible repercussions on the interests of the profession and the building owners.

(A joint subcommittee of the Practice Committee and the Salaried and Official Architects Committee)

8.1.5   PRACTICE SECRETARY'S PAPERS, 1958—(1967)   24 boxes
Correspondence files kept by David Waterhouse, Assistant Secretary Practice, and his administrative assistant, M. H. Waring, consisting mostly of correspondence answering members' queries on practice matters, 1958—1962. From 1962—1967, the files are those of the Assistant Secretaries in the Practice Section of the Professional Services Department.

Subjects : Scales of fees: tendering procedures: forms of contract: overseas work: formation of limited liability companies by architects: disputes and arbitration: architects in local government: the Farm Improvements Scheme: the Inspection of Churches Measure: the Council for the Care of Churches.

(Before David Waterhouse was appointed Assistant Secretary with special responsibility for practice matters in 1958, the Secretary RIBA dealt with practice correspondence, aided by the Deputy Secretary RIBA and the Hon. Secretary and Secretary of the Practice Committee *see* 8.1.3 Practice Committee Minutes & Papers Series)

8.1.6   CLAUSES 6 & 10 OF THE CODE OF PROFESSIONAL CON-
DUCT SUBCOMMITTEE PAPERS, 1958—1959   1 box
Correspondence, memoranda and reports, Jan 1958 — Jan 1959.
Subjects : Use by architects of the Board of Trade Export Services Branch to obtain work overseas: consideration of revision of Clauses 6 & 10 of the RIBA Code of Professional Conduct.

(A subcommittee of the Practice Committee. Clause 6 concerned advertising and Clause 10 concerned supplanting or competing with other architects by means of a reduction of fees or other inducements.)

8.1.7   REVISION OF THE RIBA CODE OF PROFESSIONAL CON-
DUCT SUBCOMMITTEE PAPERS, 1961—1962   1 box
Correspondence and memoranda, Feb 1961 — Feb 1962
Subjects : Revision of the Code: architects as directors of building companies: salaried employment of architects on the staffs of building companies: salaried employment of architects by public authorities: architects as directors of building materials companies: publication of architects' works.

(For minutes of this subcommittee *see* 8.1.3 Practice Committee Minutes)

8.1.8 (NEW) PROFESSIONAL PRACTICE COMMITTEE MINUTES
& PAPERS, 1962—1967   5 binders & 1 box
Signed minutes of meetings, Sep 1962 — Jul 1967, with memoranda,
reports and correspondence of the Secretary to the committee.
Subjects : Similar to the Practice Committee Minutes (*see* 8.1.3) plus
management training for architects: group practice and consortia research
project: preparation of a handbook on architectural practice and management: follow-up to the *Architect and his office* survey: working methods
of the design team: revision of the RIBA Conditions of Engagement and
Scale of Fees: the 'package deal'.

(This committee took over the functions of the Practice Committee, the
Professional Relations Committee and the Management Committee. Its
work was continued by the Professional Services Board and some of its
working groups.)

8.1.9 MANAGEMENT HANDBOOK WORKING GROUP PAPERS,
1964—1967   1 box
Minutes of meetings, Jan 1964 — Apr 1967, with some correspondence
and memoranda.
Subject : Supervision of the preparation and revision of the RIBA
Handbook of architectural practice and management.

(A working group of the (New) Professional Practice Committee)

8.1.10 OVERSEAS WORKING GROUP MINUTES, 1967   1 binder
Signed minutes of meetings, Jul—Nov 1967, with memoranda and
reports.
Subjects : Competition with foreign architects: costs of working overseas:
government subsidy for architects exporting their services: foreign architects' fees: codes of professional conduct.

(Originally set up in 1963 as 'Working Group J' by the (New) Professional Practice Committee of the Professional Services Department to
promote the work of British architects abroad and to review problems
arising from working overseas. The group became dormant in 1965 and
was reconstituted in April 1967, with the addition of members of the
Overseas Relations Committee.
For copies of minutes of meetings of Working Group J from 1963 *see*
12.2.6 Overseas Relations Secretary's Papers, Box 19)

8.1.11 PROFESSIONAL SERVICES BOARD MINUTES & PAPERS,
1967—1973   6 binders & 1 box
Signed minutes of meetings, Oct 1967—May 1973, with agenda papers,
memoranda and reports (with gap between Apr 1970 and Sep 1971);
and correspondence of the Secretary to the Board, Feb 1967—Jun 1969.

Subjects : Practice matters, including arbitration advice, management advice, contract advice, professional conduct: Joint Contracts Tribunal: standards and codes of performance: British Standards for building materials: technical advice and information: liaison with other architectural bodies and building industry organizations: National Joint Consultative Committee: building industry research, development and economics: building control and legislation: town planning and housing matters: Jury for Distinction in Town Planning: administration and policy of the Professional Services Board.

(In 1967 four departmental boards were set up, one of which was the Professional Services Board. Its job was to direct the policy and coordinate the efforts of the Professional Services Department set up in 1962, which had a Practice Section, a Technical Section, a Building Industry Section and a Town Planning Section. Its work was continued and developed by the new Practice Board, the Secretary's Office and the new commercial company RIBA Services Ltd.)

8.1.12   PROFESSIONAL SERVICES BOARD HONORARY OFFICERS PAPERS, 1967—1968   2 binders
Minutes of meetings, Oct 1967 — Aug 1968, with memoranda and reports.
Subjects : Policy matters concerning the work of the Professional Services Department.

(The work of this group was continued by the Professional Services Board Steering Group)

8.1.13   FUTURE SHAPE OF PRACTICE WORKING GROUP PAPERS, 1967—1969   1 binder
Record of proceedings at meetings, memoranda and reports, Nov 1967 — May 1969, kept by Richard Gardner, Secretary to the Group.
Subjects : Objectives of the profession and nature of its future development: forms of practice: size and numbers of practices: commercial relationship between architects and building owners: constraints on commercial initiative: workflow: relationships between practices, the public, the RIBA: quality of services provided by architectural offices: training and skills required: development of the Research and Statistics Department.

(A working group of the Professional Services Board)

8.1.14   PROFESSIONAL SERVICES ADVISORY PANEL PAPERS, 1967—1968   1 box
A folder of administrative correspondence kept by David Keate, Practice Under-Secretary, Nov 1967 — May 1968.

(A large panel of architects and others, set up by the Professional Services Board, to which practice queries from RIBA members could be referred.)

8.1.15   PROFESSIONAL SERVICES BOARD STEERING GROUP PAPERS, 1968—1973   4 binders
Minutes of meetings, Sep 1968 — Feb 1973, with memoranda and reports.
Subjects: Policy matters concerning the work of the Professional Services Department.

8.1.16   PRACTICE AND MANAGEMENT WORKING GROUP PAPERS, 1968—1972   1 box
Copies of minutes of meetings, Sep 1968 — Jan 1972, with memoranda and correspondence kept by Charles Crichton, Management Advisory Officer.
Subject : Practice and management courses for architects.

(A working group of the Professional Services Board. The RIBA Office Survey, 1962, recommended that the Institute should set up a management advisory service for architects and W. A. Watson was appointed Management Advisory Officer in 1962. In 1967 a management advisory service, which was intended to be financially self-supporting after an initial period of subsidy from the Investment Fund, was set up to provide courses and consultancy and to produce standard forms for office and project management. In 1968 Charles Crichton became Assistant Secretary responsible for management. The service proved to be a financial loss and Crichton resigned in Jan 1972. Walter Dixon took over until Jul 1972 when the service was terminated.)

INVESTIGATION COMMITTEE MINUTES, 1968—1978
see 4.3.4

See also in 2.2 Special Committees Minutes Series:
Professional Questions Committee, 1911-1914
Professional Conduct Subcommittee (of the Practice Standing Committee), 1914—1915, 1923
Facilities for Young Architects to set up in Practice Ad Hoc Committee, 1946
and in Chapter 4, Section 5, Research & Statistics Office:
Office Survey Papers, 1960—1969
Group Practice and Consortia Research Study Papers, 1963—1965

Bibliography

1   Scrutator 'On the present state of the professions of architect and surveyor, and of the building trade in England' *Architectural Magazine* Vol 1 1834 pp12—16

2   RIBA *Report of the Select Committee on Dilapidations* London, John Weale, 1844 (Reprinted 1869)

3   Smith, T. Roger 'On professional esprit de corps' *RIBA Transactions* 1st Series Vol 23 1872/73 pp19—35

3a Smith, T. Roger 'The practice of an architect' *British Quarterly Review* no 142 1880 pp420—441. (An offprint of this article can be seen in the RIBA Library pamphlet series, Vol 97)

4   RIBA *Dilapidations. A handbook prepared by the Practice Standing Committee of the Royal Institute of British Architects and issued by the authority of the Council* London, RIBA, 1903 (Revised edition, 1919)

5   RIBA 'Report of the Royal Institute committee on copyright' *RIBA Journal* Vol 18 1911 May 6 pp458—463 & Vol 19 1912 Feb 10 pp249—254

6   White, Henry & Greenop, Edward 'The newer responsibilities of architects' *RIBA Journal* Vol 19 1912 Jan 13 pp157—172

7   Clarke, Max 'Professional practice and conduct' *RIBA Journal* Vol 21 1914 Apr 25 pp381—390

8   RIBA 'Co-operation among architects and specialization' *RIBA Journal* Vol 25 1918 Feb pp73—81

9   'Professional problems of the moment' *RIBA Journal* Vol 26 1919 Mar pp110—116

10 Watson, W. E. *Professional conduct and practice* London, RIBA, 1929

11 Woodward, Charles 'Professional practice', in Gotch, J. A. (ed) *The growth and work of the Royal Institute of British Architects* London, RIBA, 1934

12 Woodward, Charles 'Notes on present-day practice and procedure'. Typescript in RIBA Library. RIBA, Dec 1948

13 RIBA Committee on the Present and Future of Private Architectural Practice 'The RIBA questionnaire' *RIBA Journal* Vol 56 1949 Mar p201

14 RIBA *Report of the committee to consider the present and future of private architectural practice* London, RIBA, 1950

15 *Responsibility of the job architect* London, RIBA, 1961

16 RIBA Office Survey Team *The architect and his office* London, RIBA, 1962

17 Eddy, J. P. 'Professional responsibility' *RIBA Journal* Vol 69 1962 Jan pp7—13

18 'RIBA Professional Services Department Conference' *RIBA Journal* Vol 69 1962 Dec p446

19 'Outline of the work of the RIBA Professional Services Department' *RIBA Journal* Vol 70 1963 Jun pp243—246

20 Gibson, Donald, E. E. 'Handbook of architectural practice and management' *RIBA Journal* Vol 70 1963 Nov pp386—387

21 RIBA Management Advisory Group 'Pre-Associate management training' *RIBA Journal* Vol 71 1964 Jan pp27—28

22 Rowe, Geoffrey 'The future shape of private practice' *RIBA Journal* Vol 71 1964 Apr pp157—164

23 Higgin, Gurth 'The architect as professional' *RIBA Journal* Vol 71 1964 Apr pp139—145

24 'Technicians in architects' offices' *RIBA Journal* Vol 71 1964 Jul pp310—312

25 'RIBA backs new organisation for technicians' *RIBA Journal* Vol 72 1965 Jan p6

26 RIBA *Handbook of architectural practice and management* London, RIBA, 1965 (Revised editions in 1967, 1973, 1980)

27 RIBA 'Effectiveness in practice' *RIBA Journal* Vol 73 1966 May pp222—225. Report of a conference on the RIBA management handbook.

28 RIBA *Management accounting for architects* London, RIBA, 1968 (Revised edition, 1972)

29 Gardner, Richard 'The future of the small private practice' *RIBA Journal* Vol 75 1968 Oct pp475—476

30 RIBA *Architect's job book* London, RIBA Publications Ltd, 1969 (Revised editions in 1973, 1977, 1983)

31 RIBA 'The case for professionalism' *RIBA Journal* Vol 76 1969 Feb pp57—61. RIBA's reply to the Monopolies Commission's question about the purpose of its professional practices and their effect on clients and the public.

32 'The Professional Services Department' and 'Andrew Derbyshire. John Carter interviews the chairman of the Professional Services Board' *RIBA Journal* Vol 74 1969 Oct pp416—420 & 421—422. Parts of a feature article 'Inside the RIBA'.

33 Kretchmer, William 'The new technicians' *RIBA Journal* Vol 76 1969 Nov pp487—490. Article on the origin, structure and policy of the Society of Architectural & Associated Technicians (SAAT).

34 Crichton, Charles 'Management: what the RIBA is doing' *RIBA Journal* Vol 77 1970 Jan p32

35 'The work of the Professional Services Department' *RIBA Journal* Vol 77 1970 Mar p133

36 GB Monopolies Commission *A report on the general effect on the public interest of certain restrictive practices so far as they prevail in relation to the supply of professional services* London, HMSO, 1970

37 'The report of the Monopolies Commission on "restrictive practices" in the professions' RIBA Journal Vol 77 1970 Dec pp557—559

38 MacEwen, Malcolm 'RIBA working groups (1) Standard Forms' *RIBA Journal* Vol 78 1971 Jan p36. Article on the Professional Services Board's Standard Forms Working Group.

39 'The Monopolies Commission: the RIBA replies' *RIBA Journal* Vol 78 1971 Jun pp240—242 & 256

40 Gardner, Richard 'Competence and sanctions: a dialogue' *RIBA Journal* Vol 78 1971 Jul pp295—296

41 RIBA Professional Services Board 'Limitation of liability' *RIBA Journal* Vol 79 1972 Feb pp88 & 90

42   RIBA *Group practice and consortia* London, RIBA Publications Ltd, 1973
43   'Monopolies Commission — your questions answered' *RIBA Journal* Vol 80 1973 Jul pp336—338
44   Jefferson, Bryan 'Should the Institute monitor competence' *RIBA Journal* Vol 81 1974 Dec pp10—12
45   RIBA Professional Competence Group *Competence* London, RIBA, 1975
46   MacEwen, Malcolm 'What can be done about incompetence?' *Architects' Journal* 1975 Nov 19 pp1063—1084
47   Harrison, Patrick 'Monopolies and Mergers Commission: public interest hearing' *RIBA Journal* Vol 83 1976 Oct p408
48   GB Monopolies and Mergers Commission *Architects' services: a report on the supply of architects' services with reference to scale fees* London, HMSO, 1977
49   Harrison, Patrick 'Monopolies. A situation report' *RIBA Journal* Vol 85 1978 Jan pp34—35
50   Harrison, Patrick 'Monopolies. A critique of the report of the Monopolies and Mergers Commission on architects' services' *RIBA Journal* Vol 85 1978 May p163

Section 2 Conditions of engagement, fees, specification, tendering, contracts, relations with builders and quantity surveyors.

8.2.1   CONDITIONS OF ENGAGEMENT, 1862—   .   1 box
Copies of RIBA approved conditions of engagement from the *Professional practice and charges of architects*, 1862, to the current *Architect's appointment*, including all revised editions and also special scales of fees for housing work.

8.2.2   PROFESSIONAL CHARGES COMMITTEE PAPERS, 1872   1 vol
Printed proof of revised Schedule of Charges, with manuscript comments of several architects, clause by clause, and covering letter to the RIBA by J. Douglass Mathews, Acting Secretary to the committee.

(A committee of the General Conference of Architects, 1871)

8.2.3   SCALE OF CHARGES SUBCOMMITTEE MINUTES, 1915— 1919   1 vol

Signed minutes of meetings Oct 1915 — Jun 1919.
Subject : Revision of the RIBA Schedule of Charges.

(A subcommittee of the Practice Standing Committee)

8.2.4   CONDITIONS OF CONTRACT CONFERENCE AND COM-
MITTEES MINUTES AND PAPERS, 1915—1928   1 vol & 2
boxes
Signed minutes of the conference and its committees, Jul 1915—Nov
1928, with correspondence and other documents relating to the new form
of contract, Jun 1922—Jun 1928.
Includes the minutes of the following committees:
Conditions of Contract Committee, Jul 1915—Nov 1928
Conditions of Contract Conference Subcommittee, Jan —Jun 1922
Professional Members of the Conditions of Contract Conference, Oct
1922—Jan 1927
Professional Members of the Conditions of Contract Drafting Committee,
Dec 1925—Nov 1927
RIBA Members of the Conditions of Contract Conference, Jul —Aug
1927
RIBA Members of the Conditions of Contract Joint Drafting Committee,
Sep 1927
Conditions of Contract Joint Drafting Committee, Dec 1927

8.2.5   CHARGES AND CONTRACTS SUBCOMMITTEE MINUTES,
1921—1929   2 vols
Signed minutes of meetings, Jan 1921 — Jan 1929, including the
conference with the Surveyors Institution on 18 Feb 1926.
Subjects : Enquiries and cases of dispute over professional charges
and conditions of contract: negotiations with fire insurance companies
concerning their forms: Queen Anne's Bounty and architects' fees:
insurance of architects' fees: conditions of engagement of architects: the
Copyright Act (1911) and architectural copyright: proposed Professional
Defence Union (scheme abandoned in 1914 and taken up again in 1921):
housing scheme fees: fees of specialists and consultants: fees for abandoned
work: cubing of buildings.

8.2.6   HOUSING   (FEES)   SUBCOMMITTEE   MINUTES,   1921—
1922   1 vol
Signed minutes of meetings, Jan 1921 — Jan 1922.
Subjects : Architects' fees for local authority housing schemes: fees
for abandoned housing schemes: Ministry of Health General Housing
Memoranda: cases of undercutting of fees.

(A subcommittee of the Practice Standing Committee)

8.2.7 FEES FOR ABANDONED HOUSING SCHEMES AD HOC COM-
MITTEE MINUTES, 1921   1 vol
Signed minutes of meetings, Jul — Oct 1921.
Subjects : Ministry of Health General Housing Memoranda on payment
of architects for work done on abandoned housing schemes.

8.2.8 ARCHITECTS AND BUILDERS CONSULTATION BOARD
MINUTES, 1925—1929   1 vol
Signed minutes of meetings, Mar 1925 — May 1929.
Subjects : Wages slips on tenders: building by-laws: the RIBA Form of
Contract: standard method of measurement: specialization and its effect
on craftsmanship: industrial relations between employers and operatives:
cost of building: awards to workmen.

(Set up in March 1925 by the RIBA and the National Federation of
Building Trades Employers to secure consultation and co-operation
between building industry employers, workmen, architects and surveyors
and to make united representations to government and other bodies.)

8.2.9 ARCHITECTS AND OPERATIVES CONSULTATION BOARD
MINUTES, 1926—1933   1 vol
Signed minutes of meetings, Jun 1926 — Mar 1933.
Subjects : Apprenticeship: preservation of craftsmanship: organisation
and cost of building: training of building industry craftsmen.

(Set up in 1926 at the instigation of the National Federation of Building
Trade Operatives to discuss problems of mutual interest)

8.2.10 SPECIFICATIONS CONFERENCE MINUTES, 1929—1932   1
vol
Signed minutes of meetings, Apr 1929 — Mar 1932.
Subject : Revision of forms of specification of materials and workmanship.

8.2.11 STANDARD FORMS OF CONTRACT, 1931— .   3 boxes
Standard forms of contract, with revisions and Practice Notes, issued
under the sanction of the RIBA, the National Federation of Building
Trades Employers, the Institute of Building, the Royal Institution
of Chartered Surveyors and the Joint Contracts Tribunal, including
agreements (with schedule of conditions) with private building owners
from 1931, with local authorities (with and without quantities) from
1939, and contracts for repair of war-damaged property, 1946—1956.

JOINT CONTRACTS TRIBUNAL: RIBA JOINT SECRETARY'S
PAPERS, 1932—1944, 1952—1971
see 4.4.1

8.2.12   FEES FOR HOUSING WORK COMMITTEE PAPERS, 1933   1
box
File of correspondence, memoranda and copies of minutes of meetings,
kept by [Sir] Ian Macalister, Secretary, RIBA and Secretary to the
committee, Mar — Jul 1933.
Subjects : Amendment of the RIBA scales of fees for housing work.

8.2.13   ARCHITECTS AND BUILDERS JOINT CONSULTATIVE
COMMITTEE MINUTES, 1944—1953   1 vol
Signed minutes of meetings, Jun 1944 — Oct 1953.
Subjects : Prefabrication: placing and management of building contracts:
government building programme: future of the Building Industries
National Council: tendering and bills of quantities.

(Consisted of representatives of the RIBA and the National Federation
of Building Trades Employers)

8.2.14   BUILDING INDUSTRIES NATIONAL COUNCIL: RIBA REP-
RESENTATIVES COMMITTEE MINUTES, 1944   1 vol
Minutes of a meeting on 14 Mar 1944.
Subject : Policy and constitution of the BINC.

NATIONAL CONSULTATIVE COUNCIL OF THE BUILDING
AND CIVIL ENGINEERING INDUSTRIES (NCC): RIBA
SECRETARY'S PAPERS, 1948—1979
see 4.1.4

8.2.15   LONDON ARCHITECTS AND BUILDERS JOINT COM-
MITTEE MINUTES, 1948—1953   1 vol
Signed minutes of meetings, Nov 1948 — Nov 1953.
Subjects : Fees for war damage repairs: the RIBA Form of Contract:
tendering procedure: cost of building works: building licences: bills of
quantities: contractual procedure.

(Consisted of representatives of the RIBA and the London Master
Builders Association)

8.2.16   BUILDING INDUSTRY WORKING PARTY & ANGLO-
AMERICAN PRODUCTIVITY TEAM COMMITTEE MIN-
UTES & PAPERS, 1950—1951   1 vol
Signed minutes of meetings, Jul—Nov 1950, and report of the committee,
13 Jun 1951.
Subjects : Practical training of architects: pre-planning of projects:
collaboration between architects and builders in preparing plans: the
building materials industry: American plumbing practice: simplification

of building by-laws: use of programme charts in building operations: value of work which might be tendered for without quantities.

8.2.17   ARCHITECTS AND QUANTITY SURVEYORS JOINT COM-
MITTEE MINUTES, 1950—1953   1 vol
Signed minutes of meetings, Apr 1950 — Nov 1953.
Subjects : Tendering procedures: building licences: costs of labour and materials: quantity surveyors' fees: National Schedule of Daywork Charges: purchase tax: Anglo-American Productivity Council: architects' fees: RIBA Standard Form of Contract: employment of quantity surveyors by local authorities: bills of quantities: the London Builders Conference.

(A joint committee of representatives of the RIBA and the Royal Institution of Chartered Surveyors, first appointed in 1932.
For minutes of this committee from 1932—1935 *see* 8.1.3 Practice Committee Minutes Series, Binders 1 & 2)

8.2.18   TENDERING PROCEDURE JOINT COMMITTEE MINUTES
AND PAPERS, 1952—1954   2 vols & 1 box
Signed minutes of meetings with memoranda and reports, Mar 1953—Mar 1954, with volume of specimen documents and correspondence, Dec 1952—Jun 1953.
Subjects : Tendering procedures: types of contract: method of selection of builder: the practice of different categories of building owner: selection of specialist sub-contractors: costs of building materials and components.

(A joint committee of representatives of the RIBA, the Royal Institution of Chartered Surveyors and the National Federation of Building Trades Employers)

8.2.19   LONDON ARCHITECTS, QUANTITY SURVEYORS AND
BUILDERS JOINT COMMITTEE MINUTES, 1955—1957   1 vol
Signed minutes of meetings, Feb 1955 — Mar 1957.
Subjects: Regional committees: local authorities and planning in advance: tendering procedures: contractual procedures: bills of quantities: labour situation in the London area: War Damage Commission tendering procedure.

(A joint committee of representatives of the RIBA, the Royal Institution of Chartered Surveyors and the London Master Builders Association.)

8.2.20   EMPLOYMENT OF NOMINATED CONTRACTORS SUBCOM-
MITTEE PAPERS, 1956—1957   1 box
Correspondence, memoranda and reports, Nov 1956 — Apr 1957.

Subject : Contractual arrangements in cases of employment of nominated contractors.

(For minutes of this subcommittee *see* 8.1.3 Practice Committee Minutes Series)

8.2.21   DESIGN OF SPECIALIST WORK AD HOC COMMITTEE MIN-
UTES & PAPERS, 1957—1960   1 vol
Signed minutes of meetings, Jul 1957—Jun 1958, with memoranda, reports and correspondence, May 1957—Mar 1960.
Subjects : Architects' responsibilities when employing consultants, specialist sub-contractors and staff engineers: design costs for structural, heating and electrical services: meetings with the Association of Consulting Engineers: the fee structure.

8.2.22   * NATIONAL JOINT CONSULTATIVE COMMITTEE OF ARCHITECTS, QUANTITY SURVEYORS AND BUILDERS (NJCC): RIBA REPRESENTATIVE'S PAPERS, 1959—1964, 1969—1974   6 boxes
Correspondence, memoranda, reports, copies of minutes of meetings, Jan 1959 — Dec 1964, Mar 1969 — Jan 1970 & Jun 1971 — Aug 1974.
Subjects : Code of tendering procedure: joint training schemes: forms of contract: building industry economics: government building programmes: employment of architects: long-term planning: codes of practice: bills of quantities.

(A joint committee of representatives of the RIBA, the Royal Institution of Chartered Surveyors and the National Federation of Building Trades Employers)

* Access at the discretion of the Practice Director.

8.2.23   NEGOTIATED CONTRACTS SYMPOSIUM ORGANISING SUBCOMMITTEE PAPERS, 1966   1 box
Copies of speeches delivered, with correspondence, Aug — Dec 1966.
Subject : Organization of the Negotiated Contracts Symposium held in Nov 1966.

(A joint subcommittee of the (New) Professional Practice Committee, the Building Industry Committee and the Joint Contracts Tribunal.)

8.2.24   1967 COMMITTEE MINUTES & PAPERS, 1967   1 binder & 1 box
Signed minutes of meetings, Mar —Nov 1967, with agenda papers, memoranda, reports, background papers and correspondence.

Subjects : Reference of the architectural profession to the Prices and Incomes Board and the Monopolies Commission: a proposed building industry staff study on the role of the architect in the building industry.

8.2.25   *NATIONAL BOARD FOR PRICES AND INCOMES AND MON-OPOLIES COMMISSION STEERING GROUP MINUTES & PAPERS, 1967—1970   5 binders
Files kept by the Practice Director containing minutes of meetings, Sep 1967—Jun 1969, with policy papers, memoranda, reports, 1967—1970, and background papers, including correspondence between the RIBA and Mrs. J. Toohey, Chairman of the Committee on Professional Fees for Construction Works, MoPBW, 1965—1966.
Subject : Reference of architects' costs and fees to the National Board for Prices and Incomes.

(A steering group of the Policy and Finance Committee)

* Access at discretion of the Practice Director

8.2.26   CONDITIONS OF ENGAGEMENT WORKING GROUP PAPERS, 1968—1970   1 binder
Minutes of meetings with memoranda, Jun 1968 — Jun 1970.
Subject : Revision of the RIBA Conditions of Engagement.

(A working group of the Professional Services Board.)

8.2.27   NJCC ENGINEERING ADVISORY GROUP MINUTES, 1971   1 binder
Signed minutes of meetings, Jan — Nov 1971, with memoranda.
Subjects : Structural and services engineering work: project management: contract documentation and tendering procedures: post-contract situation: nomination of sub-contractors: design responsibilities.

See also Several of the committees in 2.2 Special Committees Minutes Series *and* Several subcommittees in 8.1.2 Practice Standing Committee Minutes & Papers Series and 8.1.3 Practice Committee Minutes & Papers Series

Bibliography

1   Barry, Charles 'New palace at Westminster 1857. Architect's remuneration. Protest of the architect against the decision formed by the Lords Commissioners of Her Majesty's Treasury in respect of his claims and enforced on the plea of an alleged bargain between him and the government of 1839' *RIBA Proceedings* 1st Series 1856/57 27 Apr 1857
2   RIBA *Professional practice and charges of architects* London, RIBA, 1862
3   RIBA 'Report of the Committee of Professional Practice appointed by the

Council of the Royal Institute of British Architects to consider as to remuneration paid by the Commissioners of Works and Public Buildings to the architects employed by them' *RIBA Proceedings* 1st Series 1866/67 Jul 1867

4   'The case of Mr. E. M. Barry R.A. and the Office of Works' *RIBA Proceedings* First Series 1869/70 10 May 1870

5   'Office of Her Majesty's Works and Public Buildings. Memorandum of the terms of appointment of architects for public buildings' *RIBA Notices of Meetings* 1870/71 25 Feb 1871

6   RIBA 'General headings for clauses of contract, as settled between the Council of the Royal Institute of British Architects and the committee of the London Builders' Society' *RIBA Proceedings* 1st Series 1870/71 23 Dec 1870

7   Hebb, John 'On taking out quantities and measuring works' in *General Conference of Architects 1871. Report of proceedings* London, RIBA, 1871

8   Report of the Conference Committee on the Employment of Surveyors, in *General Conference of Architects 1872. Report of proceedings* London, RIBA, 1872

9   RIBA *A schedule of rules for professional practice and charges of architects* London, published under the sanction of the RIBA and confirmed at the General Conference of Architects, 1872

10   Fletcher, Banister 'On arbitrations' *RIBA Proceedings* First Series 1872/73 pp69—80

11   Young, Sidney 'The relative responsibilities of architect and surveyor in relation to quantities' in *General Conference of Architects 1878. Report of proceedings* London, RIBA, 1878

12   RIBA *Heads of conditions for builders' contracts. Sanctioned by the Royal Institute of British Architects* London, RIBA, 1882

13   Cates, Arthur 'The duties, obligations and mutual relations of architect, client and contractor, with reference to English and foreign practice' *RIBA Transactions* 1st Series Vol 34 1883/84 pp175—189

14   Kerr, Robert 'Observations on the architect's functions in relation to building contracts' *RIBA Transactions* New Series Vol 3 1887 pp128—140

15   RIBA *The professional practice as to the charges of architects* London, RIBA, 1898

16   RIBA *Form of agreement and schedule of conditions for building contracts* London, RIBA, 1909

17   RIBA *Scale of professional charges* London, RIBA, 1919
(Revised editions issued in 1933, 1935, 1937, 1938, 1939, 1945, 1946, 1947 & 1948)

18   RIBA *Model form of agreement and schedule of conditions of building contract* London, RIBA, 1920

19   RIBA Report of a conference on the formation of an advisory council for the building industry, in *RIBA Journal* Vol 38 1931 Jan 10 pp145—150

20   Rimmer, E. J. & Hoare, Michael *The standard form of building contract. Being a critical annotation of the new form of building contract issued in 1931*

under the sanction of the RIBA & the NFBTE, and a guide to its use London, the National Builder, 1931

21   RIBA *Architects' fees for private enterprise and municipal housing work* London, RIBA, 1932

22   'The proposed Building Industries National Council. An historical survey' *RIBA Journal* Vol 39 1932 Oct 10 pp847—848

23   RIBA *Scale of architects' charges for local authorities' and public societies' housing work* London, RIBA, 1933

24   RIBA *Scale of architects' fees for speculative builders' work for a minimum of ten houses* London, RIBA, 1933

25   Davies, T. R. Dingad *The standard form of building sub-contract. Annotation of the new form of sub-contract recommended by the RIBA for use in conjunction with the RIBA 1931 form of main contract* London, Federated Employers' Press Ltd [1937]

26   Smith, Walker & Close, Howard *The standard form of building contract* London, RIBA & NFBTE, 1939 (Revised editions published in 1953—1963, 1971)

27   RIBA *Scale of architects' fees for state-aided housing schemes* London, RIBA, 1944

28   RIBA *Scale of architects' fees for state-aided multi-storey flats* London, RIBA, 1944

29   Bennett, T. P. 'The architect and organisation of post-war building' *RIBA Journal* Vol 52 1945 Jan pp63—73

30   *Report of the Joint Committee on Tendering Procedure* London, published by the committee, 1954

31   RIBA *Conditions of engagement and scale of professional charges* London, RIBA, Jun 1954 (Revised editions issued in Dec 1954, 1957, 1958, 1960 & 1962)

32   RIBA Practice Committee 'RIBA conditions of engagement and scale of professional charges' *RIBA Journal* Vol 67 1959 Dec pp49—51. Recommendations concerning revision.

33   Keating, Donald *RIBA forms of contract* London, Sweet & Maxwell Ltd, 1959

34   RIBA Secretariat 'Comparison of professional incomes' *RIBA Journal* Vol 67 1960 Apr pp195—200

35   RIBA *Application of the RIBA Scale of Professional Charges to repetitive housing work* London, RIBA, 1 May 1962 (First issued on 1 Jun 1961)

36   Millard, R. E. 'The new RIBA form of contract' *RIBA Journal* Vol 70 1963 Feb pp47—53

37   RIBA Professional Practice Committee 'New approaches to design tendering and construction' *RIBA Journal* Vol 70 1963 Aug pp322—331

38   RIBA Professional Practice Committee 'Proposed new fee scale' *RIBA Journal* Vol 72 1965 Jun pp273—274

39   NJCC *A code of procedure for selective tendering* London, NJCC, 1965. Distributed by the RIBA (Revised edition issued in 1972)

40   RIBA *Conditions of engagement* London, RIBA, 1966 (Revised editions issued in Jan 1967, Jul 1967, Nov 1967, Apr 1968, Nov 1968, Jul 1971, Nov 1971, Dec 1972, 1973, 1974, 1975, 1976, 1977 & 1979)

41   'The new conditions of engagement' *RIBA Journal* Vol 73 1966 Sep p396

42   RIBA Board of Architectural Education 'The architect in the future building team' *RIBA Journal* Vol 74 1967 Feb pp49—50

43   GB. National Board for Prices and Incomes *Architects costs and fees* Cmnd 3653, HMSO, 1968

44   'Architects' costs and fees' *RIBA Journal*, Vol 75 1968 Apr 4 pp153—168. RIBA evidence to the Prices and Incomes Board.

45   Carter, John 'National Building Specification: the background to the RIBA decision' *RIBA Journal* Vol 76 1969 May pp197—198

46   'National Building Specification to go ahead' *RIBA Journal* Vol 76 1969 Aug pp314—316

47   Allott, Tony 'Specification: how NBS will help' *RIBA Journal* Vol 76 1969 Nov pp478—480

48   'Revised conditions of engagement' *RIBA Journal* Vol 77 1970 Mar pp123—130

49   Stringer, George 'Amateurs or professionals?' *RIBA Journal* Vol 77 1970 Apr pp177—179. Concerns the responsibilities and liabilities of the architect under the standard forms of contract.

50   Musgrove, John 'Professional collaboration and the plan of work' *RIBA Journal* Vol 77 1970 Nov pp512—513. Article on the RIBA Plan of Work.

51   RIBA *A guide to contract administration for architects* London, RIBA Publications Ltd, 1971

52   'Fairness without immunity: architects and the contract' *RIBA Journal* Vol 81 1974 Dec pp32—34

53   Close, Howard A. *The evolution of the standard form of building contract* London, NFBTE, 1975. A republication note bringing up to date an address given at the RICS on 21 Nov 1951.

54   *Fourth International Conference on Architectural Registration 1976. Report* 'The role of the architect as a leader of the building team' ARCUK & NCARB, [1976]

55   RIBA *The case for mandatory minimum fees* London, RIBA, 1976. A statement by the RIBA to the Monopolies and Mergers Commission.

56   GB. Monopolies and Mergers Commission *Architects' services: a report on the supply of architects' services with reference to the scale fees* London, HMSO, 1977

57   RIBA *Architect's appointment* London, RIBA, 1982

Section 3 Official architecture, salaried architects, relations between private and salaried architects

8.3.1   MUNICIPAL OFFICIALS AND ARCHITECTURAL WORK COMMITTEE PAPERS, 1904   2 boxes
Files kept by W. J. Locke, Secretary RIBA, Feb — Dec 1904, containing correspondence, replies to a RIBA questionnaire, and copies of a memorial sent to local authorities.
Subjects : Undesirability of architectural work being undertaken by borough engineers and surveyors: important public buildings to be designed by independent architects rather than official architects.

(For minutes of this committee, Feb 1904, *see* 2.2 Special Committees Minutes Series)

8.3.2   OFFICE OF WORKS COMMITTEE MINUTES, 1921   1 vol
Signed minutes of meetings, Jan — Jun 1921.
Subjects : The expanding architectural activities of the Office of Works: cases of breach of the RIBA Code of Professional Practice in the Office of Works: drafting of articles for the *Daily Telegraph* campaigning against the Office of Works: proposed deputation to the First Commissioner of Works to urge the restriction of the Office of Works to the function of maintaining state and public buildings rather than designing and erecting new ones.

8.3.3   OFFICIAL ARCHITECTURE COMMITTEES MINUTES, 1926—1935   1 vol
Signed minutes of meetings of the Official Architecture Committee, Jun 1926—Oct 1929, the Official Architecture Subcommittee of the Executive Committee, Feb —Mar 1932, and the Official Architecture Special Committee, Mar 1934—Feb 1935.
Subjects : Aspects of the employment of architects on official buildings: the relationship between official architects and private architects: whether an official architect should undertake private work: desirability of holding public competitions for important public buildings: growing encroachment of the Office of Works and other public bodies on work which had

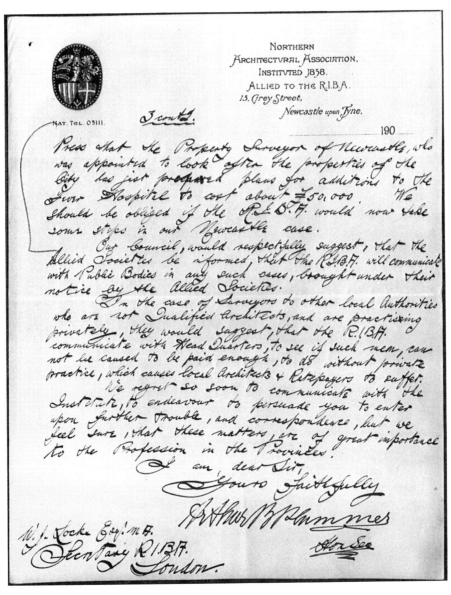

NORTHERN
ARCHITECTURAL ASSOCIATION,
INSTITUTED 1858.
ALLIED TO THE R.I.B.A.
13. Grey Street,
Newcastle upon Tyne.

NAT. TEL. 03111.   3 contd.

190___

Press that the Property Surveyor of Newcastle, who was appointed to look after the properties of the City has just prepared plans for additions to the Fever Hospital to cost about £50,000. We should be obliged if the R.I.B.A. would now take some steps in our Newcastle case.

Our Council, would respectfully suggest, that the Allied Societies be informed, that the R.I.B.A. will communicate with Public Bodies in any such cases, brought under their notice by the Allied Societies.

In the case of Surveyors to other local Authorities who are not Qualified Architects, and are practising privately, they would suggest, that the R.I.B.A. communicate with Head Quarters, to see if such men, can not be caused to be paid enough, to do without private practice, which causes local Architects & Ratepayers to suffer.

We regret so soon to communicate with the Institute, to endeavour to persuade you to enter upon further trouble, and correspondence, but we feel sure, that these matters, are of great importance to the Profession in the Provinces.

I am, dear Sir,
Yours faithfully,

Arthur B Plummer

W. J. Locke Esq. M.A.
Secretary R.I.B.A.
London.

Hon Sec

20   Part of a letter by Arthur Plummer, Hon. Sec. of the Northern Architectural Association to W. H. Locke, RIBA Secretary, dated 17 November 1903, urging the RIBA to take action over the increasing amount of architectural work being performed by local authority officials who were not architects. Strong feelings on this topic were then widespread amongst architects so the RIBA set up a special committee which made extensive investigations into current practice in Britain and abroad and subsequently memorialized many local authorities. (RIBA Archive:8.3.1)

previously been entrusted to architects in private practice.

(*See also* 8.3.5 (New) Official Architecture Committee Minutes, 1930)

8.3.4   SALARIED MEMBERS COMMITTEE MINUTES & PAPERS,
          1928—1947   3 vols, 1 binder & 1 box
          Signed minutes of the committee, May 1928—Jun 1947, with minutes
          of the Middlesex Subcommittee, Mar — May 1938, and the Scale of
          Annual Salaries for Architects Joint Subcommittee, May 1945. Also a
          file of correspondence, memorandanda and reports, kept by the Hon.
          Secretary to the committee, Feb 1930—Dec 1931.
          Subjects : Most aspects of the employment of salaried architects,
          particularly their relatively low salary scales, the lack of recognition
          of their work and their relationship to private practitioners: salaried
          architectural appointments abroad (Vol 1): public officials and private
          work: status of architects employed in Borough Engineers' and Borough
          Surveyors' departments (Vol 1): official architects in India (Vol 2):
          revision of recommended scale of salaries for salaried members (Vol 3
          & Binder 1)

          (Membership of the committee was half official architects and half private
          architects. In 1930 the Council, on the recommendation of this committee,
          approved a scale of annual salaries which was revised in 1937 and again
          in 1945. In 1937 the committee was reconstituted and its chairman or
          other representative given a seat on the Council. Its work was continued
          by the Official and Salaried Architects Committee)

8.3.5   (NEW) OFFICIAL ARCHITECTURE COMMITTEE MINUTES,
          1930   1 vol
          Signed minutes of meetings, Mar — Oct 1930.
          Subjects : Proposed government enquiry into the design and execution
          of new state buildings: letter to the Prime Minister.

          (Its work was continued by the Official Architecture Subcommittee of
          the Executive Committee *see* 8.3.3 Official Architecture Committees
          Minutes Series)

8.3.6   OFFICIAL ARCHITECTS COMMITTEE MINUTES, 1937—
          1947   3 vols
          Signed minutes of meetings, Jul 1937 — Jun 1947, with memoranda
          and reports
          Subjects : Terms and conditions of employment of official architects:
          architectural work being performed by official engineers and surveyors
          rather than architects: AASTA charter for architectural assistants in
          public offices (Vol 1): alleged conspiracy between certain public offices to
          restrict the movement of architectural assistants (Vol 1): local government

control of building: proposed County Architects Association: status of official architects compared with official engineers and surveyors: scale of annual salaries of official architects (Vol 2).

(Members consisted of senior official architects only, i.e. heads of departments. Its work was continued by the Salaried and Official Architects Committee)

8.3.7   OFFICIAL ARCHITECTS COMMITTEE AND EXECUTIVE COMMITTEE JOINT COMMITTEE MINUTES & PAPERS, 1937—1938   1 vol & 1 box

Signed minutes of meetings, Dec 1937 — Mar 1938, with correspondence, memoranda, and list of local authorities in England, Wales and Scotland employing official architects to be in charge of their architectural work.

Subjects : Building work of local authorities: pattern of employment by local authorities of architects, engineers and surveyors.

8.3.8   JOINT NEGOTIATING COMMITTEE ON SALARIES MINUTES, 1945—1947   1 vol

Signed minutes of meetings, Oct 1945 — Jun 1947.

Subjects : Architects' salary scales and conditions of service: negotiation of national scales: liaison with the Institution of Professional Civil Servants, the Association of Building Technicians and the RIBA Allied Societies: discussions with the National Whitley Council: appointment of a RIBA Negotiating Officer.

(A joint committee of representatives of the RIBA, the Institution of Professional Civil Servants and the Association of Building Technicians. Its work was continued by the Salaried and Official Architects Committee.)

8.3.9   NEGOTIATING OFFICER'S PAPERS, 1946—1957   2 boxes

Correspondence files of David Benton, appointed RIBA Negotiating Officer in 1946, who was also in charge of the Appointments Department and whose title changed to Assistant Secretary in 1951, Aug 1946 — Feb 1957.

Subjects : Salaries and conditions of service of RIBA members employed in public and private offices in Britain and the Commonwealth.

(His work was continued by the Professional Relations Secretary)

8.3.10   SALARIED AND OFFICIAL ARCHITECTS COMMITTEE MINUTES, 1947—1959   2 binders

Signed minutes of meetings of the committee, Jul 1947 — Jun 1959, with memoranda and reports, and signed minutes of the following subcommittees and joint meetings:

Salaried and Official Architects Committee & Practice Committee Joint Meetings, Oct—Nov 1947

Policy Subcommittee, May 1950—Jan 1951

Representation of Salaried Architects Subcommittee, Jul 1952—Feb 1955

Memorandum on the Appointment of Architects as Chief Officers to Local Authorities Subcommittee, Apr—Jun 1954

Liaison Panel, Jan—May 1956

Liaison Panel & Association of Building Technicians Joint Meeting, Mar 1956

Liaison Panel & L.C.C. Staff Association Joint Meeting, Mar 1956

Appointment of Architects as Chief Officers to Local Authorities Subcommittee, Dec 1957—Dec 1958

Subjects : Negotiations with the National Joint Council for Local Authorities and NALGO on architects' salary scales: wholetime official architects and private work: revision of the RIBA Scale of Annual Salaries: negotiations with the National Coal Board re salary structure of its Architects Department: revision of the RIBA Code of Professional Conduct: restrictions on changes of employment: qualifications for architectural posts in the Civil Service: salaries of Scottish official architects: scheme of minimum conditions of service for salaried assistants in private offices: appointment of architects as Chief Officers to local authorities: representation of official architects in salary negotiations.

(A merger between the Salaried Members Committee and the Official Architects Committee. Its work was continued by the Professional Relations Committee.)

8.3.11   PRESENT AND FUTURE OF PRIVATE ARCHITECTURAL PRACTICE COMMITTEE MINUTES, 1948—1950   1 vol

Signed minutes of meetings, Dec 1948 — May 1950, with printed report.

Subjects : Under-employment of private architects: questionnaire on employment of architects: relationship between official and private architects: facilities available to young architects wishing to set up in private practice.

(A committee consisting of four official architects and four architects in private practice)

8.3.12   FUTURE OF PRIVATE ARCHITECTURAL PRACTICE COMMITTEE MINUTES, 1950—1951   1 vol

Signed minutes of meetings, Oct 1950 — Jan 1951.

Subject : Methods of implementing the recommendations in the report of the Present and Future of Private Architectural Practice Committee.

8.3.13   PRIVATE ARCHITECTURAL PRACTICE BY UNQUALIFIED
PERSONS AD HOC COMMITTEE MINUTES, 1953   1 vol
Signed minutes of meetings, Mar — May 1953, with memoranda and
reports.
Subject : Methods of counteracting infringement on private architectural
practice by unqualified people: consultation with the County Architects
Society and the City and Borough Architects Society.

8.3.14   REPRESENTATION OF MEMBERS IN SALARIED EMPLOY-
MENT & REVIEW OF THE STRUCTURE OF THE PRO-
FESSION AD HOC COMMITTEE MINUTES & PAPERS, 1955—
1959   1 vol & 2 boxes
Signed minutes of meetings, Jul 1955 — Jun 1959, with memoranda,
reports, correspondence and press-cuttings.
Subjects : Negotiating machinery for architects' salaries: collection of
information on the structure of the profession, the amount and cost of
building work executed and the number of architects engaged on it:
appointment of a RIBA Secretary for Professional Relations: survey of
responsibilities and salaries of senior architects in local government:
survey of architects' incomes: status of women in the profession.

(This committee continued the work of the Representation of Salaried
Architects Subcommittee of the Salaried and Official Architects Com-
mittee Minutes Series (*see* 8.3.10). Its work was continued by the
Professional Relations Committee.)

EMPLOYMENT OF SALARIED ARCHITECTS ON THE
STAFFS OF BUILDING CONTRACTORS JOINT SUBCOM-
MITTEE PAPERS, 1955—1958
(A joint subcommittee of the Practice Committee & the Salaried and
Official Architects Committee)
see 8.1.4

8.3.15   PROFESSIONAL RELATIONS SECRETARY'S PAPERS, 1957—
1959   4 boxes
Correspondence files kept by Gordon Ricketts, Professional Relations
Secretary, Jan 1957—Nov 1959
Subjects : Status and remuneration of private, salaried and official
architects: role of the architect in planning: the 'package deal': architects
as company directors: the RIBA committee structure.

(When Ricketts was appointed Secretary of the RIBA in 1959 the
Council set up the Professional Relations Committee)

8.3.16   PROFESSIONAL   RELATIONS   COMMITTEE   MINUTES,
1959—1962   1 binder

Signed minutes of meetings, Dec 1959 — Jun 1962, with reports.
Subjects : Campaign for appointment of architects as Chief Officers to local authorities: the RIBA Appointments Department: architects' incomes: survey of architects' office organization, staffing and costs: the Architects in Industry Group.

(This committee superseded the Salaried and Official Architects Committee and the Representation of Members in Salaried Employment Committee. It published the report *The architect and his office* in 1962. Its work was continued by the (New) Professional Practice Committee.)

OFFICE SURVEY PAPERS, 1960—1969   1 box
See 4.5.2

8.3.17   SALARIES WORKING GROUP PAPERS, 1962—1965   1 box
Correspondence, memoranda, copies of minutes of meetings, Dec 1962 — Nov 1965.
Subjects : Architects' grading and salary structure in local government: conditions of service in private architects' offices: architects' pensions.

(A working group of the (New) Professional Practice Committee)

8.3.18   PUBLIC PRACTICE WORKING GROUP PAPERS, 1970— 1972   3 boxes
Minutes of meetings, Sep 1970 — Nov 1971, with memoranda and correspondence.
Subject : Position and responsibilities of the architect in local government after local government reorganisation in 1971.

(A working group of the Professional Services Board)

See also 2.2 in Special Committees Minutes Series:
Municipal Officials and Architectural Work Committee, 1904
Official Architecture Committee and subcommittees, 1912—1915
Official Architects and the Fellowship Committee of Council, 1922
Architects' and Surveyors' Assistants Professional Union & the RIBA Joint Conference, 1924
Private Practitioners and Official Architects Subcommittee of the War Executive Committee, 1943—1945
and in 8.1.2 Practice Standing Committee Minutes & Papers Series:
Minimum Wage for Architectural Assistants Subcommittee, 1924—1925
Officials and Private Practice Subcommittee, 1924—1927.

Bibliography

1   RIBA Report of the committee on municipal officials and architectural work,

with a memorial by the RIBA to local authority councils in Gt. Britain & Ireland, *RIBA Journal* Vol 12 1904 Dec 10 pp104—116

2   'The execution of important government and municipal architectural work by salaried officials' in *VIIth International Congress of Architects. Summary of proceedings.* Published as special supplement to *RIBA Journal* Vol 13 1906 Aug 25

3   RIBA 'Extracts from the report of the Official Architecture Committee (1915)' *RIBA Journal* Vol 28 1921 Jun 11 pp461—462

4   RIBA Special Committee on Official Architecture 'Salaried and privately-practising architects' *RIBA Journal* Vol 42 1935 Jun 8 pp860—862

5   Association of Architects, Surveyors and Technical Assistants *A charter for architectural assistants employed in public offices* London, AASTA, 1938

6   Curtis, W. T. 'The Official Architects Committee' *RIBA Journal* Vol 45 1938 Aug 15 p926

7   Aslin, C. H. 'The work, duties and responsibilities of the official architect' *RIBA Journal* Vol 46 1939 Jul 17 pp866—871

8   Illingworth, William 'The architect's part in municipal affairs' *RIBA Journal* Vol 50 1942 Dec pp30—31

9   'Appointment of the RIBA Negotiating Officer' *RIBA Journal* Vol 53 1946 Aug p461

10   'Salary scales for architects in municipal service' *Contract Journal* 1949 Oct 26 p1367

11   'Representation of members and students in salaried employment. Analysis of replies to [RIBA] questionnaire' *RIBA Journal* Vol 61 1954 May pp256—257

12   Howitt, Leonard C. *The architect in local government service* London, Public Works and Municipal Services Congress, City and Borough Architects Society & RIBA, 1954

13   Spragg, C. D. 'Negotiations on salaried employment' *RIBA Journal* Vol 62 1955 Jan p119

14   RIBA Representation of Members in Salaried Employment and Review of the Structure of the Profession Committee 'Salaried employment and structure of the profession' *RIBA Journal* Vol 63 1956 Jan pp97—99

15   RIBA Salaried and Official Architects Committee. Report on the representation of salaried architects, *RIBA Journal* Vol 63 1956 Jan pp99—106

16   RIBA 'Memorandum on the appointment of architects as Chief Officers to local authorities' 1955. Typescript in RIBA Library

17   RIBA Representation of Members in Salaried Employment and Review of the Structure of the Profession Ad Hoc Committee. Statement by the chairman, *RIBA Journal* Vol 64 1957 Apr pp225—226

18   RIBA Representation of Members in Salaried Employment and Review of the Structure of the Profession Ad Hoc Committee 'Two papers from the Ad Hoc Committee 1. Some thoughts on professional status. 2. Future prospects in the building industry' *RIBA Journal* Vol 65 1958 Jan pp90—-95

19   RIBA 'Report of the Joint Sub-committee of the Practice & Salaried and Official Architects' Committees appointed to inquire into the employment of architects on the salaried staffs of building contractors' *RIBA Journal* Vol 65 1958 Aug pp348—350

20   RIBA Evidence by the RIBA to the Royal Commission on Local Government in Greater London, *RIBA Journal* Vol 65 1958 Sep pp381—382

21   Layton, Elizabeth *Building by local authorities* London, Allen & Unwin, 1961

22   RIBA 'Report of the Royal Commission on Local Government in Greater London' *RIBA Journal* Vol 68 1961 Mar pp168—171. Statement by the RIBA.

23   Evidence submitted by the RIBA to the Royal Commission on Local Government, *RIBA Journal* Vol 73 1966 Dec pp540—542

24   Floyd, Michael 'Architects [public and private] unite' *RIBA Journal* Vol 73 1966 Dec pp577—578

25   Summary of RIBA evidence to the Fulton Committee on the home civil service, *RIBA Journal* Vol 74 1967 Feb p73

26   'Architects' offices in local government' *RIBA Journal* Vol 74 1967 Aug pp303—304

27   *Report of the Royal Commission on Local Government in England* London, HMSO, 1968. Written evidence of professional organisations, including the RIBA.

28   Fardell, Geoffrey 'Partnership or combat?' *RIBA Journal* Vol 76 1969 Feb pp68—69. Article by the chairman of the RIBA Patronage Working Group on relations between public and private architects.

29   County Architects Society/City and Borough Architects Society (CAS/CABAS) *The relationship between the official and the private architect* London, RIBA Publications Ltd, 1970

30   RIBA 'Local government reorganisation: the RIBA's views' *RIBA Journal* Vol 78 1971 Jun pp257—258

31   RIBA Intelligence Unit 'Salaried architects and the RIBA' *RIBA Journal* Vol 78 1971 May pp213—215

32   Keate, David, Convenor of the RIBA Salaried Architects Working Group 'Industrial relations — the debate goes on' *RIBA Journal* Vol 28 1971 Dec pp565—569

33   'Working group urges RIBA to fulfill its responsibilities to salaried architects' *RIBA Journal* Vol 79 1972 May p184. Summary of a report by the RIBA Salaried Architects Working Group.

34   Rawling, Ian 'Salaried architects want their own code' *RIBA Journal* Vol 79 1972 Dec pp505—506

35   Stanley, Tom 'RIBA and salary negotiation' *RIBA Journal* Vol 80 1973 May p212

36   RIBA Salaried Architects Working Group 'Draft code of employment' *RIBA Journal* Vol 80 1973 Aug p390

37   RIBA North West Region *The architect in his office* London, RIBA, 1974

38 McCarthy, Maurice & Rawling, Ian 'The architects' code of employment' *RIBA Journal* Vol 81 1974 May pp18—19

39 Malpass, Peter 'Professionalism and the role of architects in local authority housing' *RIBA Journal* Vol 82 1975 Jun pp6—29. Based on M.A. thesis, Newcastle Univ., 1973

40 RIBA *The role of the architectural profession in the work of public authorities* London, RIBA, 1981

41 RIBA President's Task Force on Public Offices *Architectural practice in local authorities* London, RIBA, 1982

Section 4 Building legislation

8.4.1   LIGHT AND AIR COMMITTEE PAPERS, 1881—1883   1 vol
Printed reports of the committee: reports of relevant law cases: memoranda by members: discussions at General Meetings.
Subject : The law of light and air as it affected buildings.

(For minutes of this committee *see* 2.2 Special Committees Minutes Series)

8.4.2   LONDON BUILDING ACT AMENDMENT BILL COMMITTEE PAPERS, 1903—1905   1 box
Copies of the London Building Acts (Amendment) Bills, 1903—1905: criticisms and suggestions by the RIBA and the District Surveyors Association (DSA): petitions against the bill by the RIBA, the DSA and the Corporation of London: amendments to the bill by the RIBA Practice Standing Committee.

(For minutes of this committee *see* 2.2 Special Committees Minutes Series)

8.4.3   LONDON BUILDING ACTS COMMITTEE MINUTES & PAPERS, 1921—1935   2 vols & 3 boxes
Signed minutes of the committee and its subcommittees and of the Advisory Council of the Building Industry and its subcommittees, 1921—1935, with correspondence, memoranda and reports, 1922—1930. Contains minutes of the following committees and conferences:
Administrative and Legal Subcommittee, Feb —Jun 1932

Advisory Council of the Building Industry, May 1931
Conference on the Revision of Building Regulations Joint Subcommittee,
    Jul —Sep 1930
Conference on the Revision of the London Building Acts, Jul 1930
Finance and Secretariat Subcommittee of the Advisory Council, Jan 1931
Grading of Buildings and Building Materials Subcommittee, May—Sep
    1934
Grading of Buildings and Means of Escape in case of Fire Subcommittee,
    Feb —Jun 1932
London Building Acts Committee, Jan 1921—Jul 1935
London Building Acts Committee & Town Planning Committees Joint
    Meeting, Oct 1932
Organising Committee of the Advisory Council, Jan —Apr 1931
Provisional Committee of the Proposed Advisory Council, Oct —Dec
    1930
Streets, Public Health and Sanitation Subcommittee, Feb —May 1932

Subjects : Reform of the London Building Acts: deputations to the LCC
and the Corporation of London by the RIBA, 1921: height of buildings
and their cubical contents: fire prevention and escape: dangerous and
unhealthy buildings: steel-frame and reinforced concrete construction:
deputation to the Minister of Health, 1930: public health and sanitation:
formation of streets.

(For minutes of the London Building Acts Committee, 1920 *see* 2.2
Special Committees Minutes Series)

8.4.4   BUILDING CODE JOINT COMMITTEE MINUTES, 1922   1
         vol
         Signed minutes of meetings, Jan — Sep 1972.
         Subject : Proposed establishment of a new building code by statutory
         enactment.

         (A joint committee of the Practice Standing Committee and the Science
         Standing Committee)

8.4.5   BY-LAWS AND BUILDING REGULATIONS COMMITTEE
         MINUTES, 1959   1 vol
         Signed minutes of meetings, Jan — Jun 1959.
         Subject's : Review of the English Model Building By-Laws: desirability
         of a uniform building code administered centrally.

8.4.6   BUILDING CONTROL PANEL PAPERS, 1962—1972——4 boxes
         Minutes of meetings, Jul 1965—Mar 1972: memoranda and reports,
         1962—1970: correspondence, 1962—1967.

Subjects : Rationalization of building regulations: design constraints: fire prevention.

(A panel of the Technical Information Committee and then of the Technical Committee)

8.4.7 * JOINT COMMITTEE ON BUILDING LEGISLATION PAPERS, 1965— . 1 box & 1 filing cabinet
Correspondence, memoranda and reports, Sep 1965 onwards, kept by Sylvia Locke, Secretary to the committee, 1965—1968, and John Veal, present Secretary to the committee.
Subjects : Consolidation, amendment, administration and enforcement of building regulations.

* Access at the discretion of the Secretary to the Committee

See also Several committees in 2.1 Early Committees Minutes Series & 2.2 Special Committees Minutes Series *and* Some subcommittees of 9.3 Science Standing Committee, 9.8 Science Committee, 9.10 Architectural Science Board, 9.11 (New) Science Committee and 8.1.2 Practice Standing Committee.

Bibliography

1   RIBA *Amendments proposed by the Council to the Metropolitan Buildings Bill 1851* London, RIBA, 1851. Copy of bill interleaved with manuscript amendments, in RIBA Library.

2   Gibbons, David & Hesketh, R. *The Metropolitan Building Act, 18th & 19th Victoria, Cap. 122* London, John Weale, 1855

3   RIBA *Public Health Bill 1855 Petition against the bill* London, RIBA, 1855. Copy bound into *RIBA Notices of Meetings* 1854/56

4   Kerr, Robert 'Remarks on the evidence of architects concerning the obstruction of ancient lights and the practice of proof by measurement: with reference to recent cases in the courts of equity' *RIBA Proceedings* 1st Series, 1865/66 pp149—158

5   Donaldson, T. L. 'On the practice of architects and the law of the land in respect to easements of light and air' *RIBA Proceedings* 1st Series, 1865/66 pp169—191

6   RIBA 'Metropolitan Buildings and Management Bill. Report of the committee' *RIBA Proceedings* 1st Series 1868/69 1 Feb 1869

7   RIBA 'Report on the Metropolitan Buildings and Management Bill' *RIBA Proceedings* 1st Series 1873/74 20 Mar 1874

8   Webb, C. Locock 'On the law of easements' *RIBA Proceedings* 1st Series, 1877/78 pp88—112

9   Mathews, J. Douglass 'The model bye-laws as a basis of a General Building Act', in *General Conference of Architects 1878. Report of proceedings* London,

RIBA, 1878

10   RIBA *Suggestions for a draft bill for the codification and amendment of the Metropolitan Building Acts* London, RIBA, 1891

11   RIBA *The London Building Act 1894, with the original and amended bills and papers relating thereto* London, RIBA, 1894

12   Brown, G. Baldwin 'Urban legislation in the interests of amenity at home and abroad' *RIBA Journal* Vol 12 1904 Dec 10 pp69—78

13   Ridge, Lacy W. & Gibson, James S. 'Architecture and building regulations' RIBA Journal Vol 12 1904 Dec 24 pp117—131

14   RIBA *Petition of the Royal Institute of British Architects against the London County Council (General Powers) (No. 2) Bill* London, RIBA [1914]

15   Final report of the London Building Acts Committee, *RIBA Journal* Vol 31 1924 Jun 7 pp515—519

16   *Report of conference representing the Royal Institute of British Architects, the Surveyors' Institution, the London Master Builders' Association and the London House Builders' Association re amendments to the London Building Acts* London, Apr 1925

17   RIBA *Reports of the London Building Acts Committee of the Royal Institute of British Architects* London, RIBA, 1926

18   RIBA Reconstruction Committee 'The rationalisation of building legislation' *RIBA Journal* Vol 49 1942 Feb p58 & Vol 50 1943 Apr pp139—140

19   RIBA Building Control Panel of the Technical Standards Committee 'The consolidation of building regulations under one statutory instrument' *RIBA Journal* Vol 71 1964 Jul pp321—322

20   Mitchell, Thomas *Towards a National Building Act* London, Public Works and Municipal Services Congress, Nov 1966

21   Mitchell, Thomas, chairman of the Joint Committee on Building Legislation and the RIBA Building Control Panel 'The case for a National Building Act' *RIBA Journal* Vol 74 1967 Mar pp116—118

22   RIBA 'Architects and the Building Bill' Report of a seminar at the RIBA, Jan 1973. Typescript in RIBA Library.

9
Science and technology

Gathered together in this chapter are the records of various committees and groups concerned with scientific research, development of new techniques and products, provision of technical information and other technical services, standardization of building materials, components and performance codes, and building industry economics. This work was co-ordinated from 1886—1938 by the Science Standing Committee, in the 1940s by the Architectural Science Board, in the 1950s by the (New) Science Committee and in the 1960s by the Professional Services Department and Board. From the 1970s onwards this work has been continued by RIBA Services Ltd, by the Standards Committee and the Practice Department, and by the RIBA Economics Adviser and Head of Research, Energy & Statistics.

In the original prospectus for an Institution of British Architects, published by the Society of British Architects early in 1834, one of the stated aims was 'to provide the means of performing experiments upon the nature and properties of materials and upon their constructive arrangement' and this aim was confirmed in the Opening Address of the Institute in June 1835. No doubt the founding members were influenced by the scientific investigations earlier undertaken by the Fire Prevention Committee of the Architects Club (see Appendix 1).

In 1835 the Institute elected the scientist Michael Faraday an Honorary Member and invited him in 1836 to sit on two investigatory committees, one to study a new system of warming and ventilating buildings and one to discover whether or not the ancient Greeks had used colours to decorate the Elgin Marbles.

By 1836 the Institute had amassed a large collection of specimens of building stones and had instituted a series of lectures on scientific subjects related to building construction. In 1841 the Council noted with approval the act to abolish the use of climbing boys to sweep chimneys and exhorted architects to turn their attention to designing flues which would facilitate mechanical sweeping. The Council also drew the attention of the members to the introduction of iron in modern construction and set this topic as a subject for the Prize Essay the following year. Many of the papers read by members at the General Meetings in the early years were on scientific and technical subjects and throughout the 1850s there was a standing Experiments and Professional Investigations Committee. In 1854 it investigated a new chemical process claiming to prevent damage to calcareous stones by atmospheric pollution. In 1863 a special committee was appointed to make experiments on artificial stone and during the 1870s there was a standing Materials and Construction Committee, which in 1876 made a study of the use of concrete in building construction, paying particular attention to its fire-resisting properties.

In 1886 the Science Standing Committee was appointed as one of four large departmental committees and, until its dissolution in 1938, it encouraged the scientific testing of building materials, monitored new processes, materials and methods of construction, monitored building legislation and was also concerned with fire prevention techniques, sanitation, heating and ventilation. In 1906 the RIBA set up the Reinforced Concrete Joint Committee and this influential group of architects, scientists, civil and military engineers, district surveyors and builders continued to meet until 1932.

In 1939 the President of the RIBA, Edwin Stanley Hall, approached the director of the Building Research Station with the aim of establishing closer collaboration between the two organizations. As a result of his initiative the Architectural Science Group was set up and in 1940 a special committee of the RIBA put forward a scheme for a RIBA Research Commission. The full scheme was not implemented but a RIBA Research Board was appointed which included the Architectural Science Group, whose members consisted of architects, engineers, scientists and sociologists. In 1942 the group changed its name and status and became the Architectural Science Board (*see* 3.1.2 Executive Committee Minutes Series, Binder 3, for a draft of its constitution). Its function was not to carry out research but to survey the field to ascertain which research projects and educational reforms were required and use its influence to get them executed. The Architectural Science Board was reconstituted as the (New) Science Committee of the RIBA in 1951.

In June 1959 a joint report of the (New) Science Committee and the Provision of Professional Text and Reference Books Committee (later called the Professional Literature Committee) recommended setting up a co-ordinated Technical Information Service. A Technical Department was established with a Technical Information Committee, a Technical Standards Committee and a Management Committee, and a Technical Information Officer was appointed. This led to the creation in 1962 of the Professional Services Department which was responsible for a wide range of activities and had the following standing committees: Technical Information, Technical Standards, Building Industry, Housing & Town Planning and Professional Practice. In 1964 the Technical Information Committee and the Technical Standards Committee were merged into a single Technical Committee and in 1967 the Professional Services Board was appointed which oversaw activities concerned with professional practice, professional conduct, practice management, the needs of the salaried architect, legal advice, technical standards and information, building industry relations and economics, research and statistics, design standards for specific building types, building legislation and aesthetic control by local authorities.

In 1969 two commercial companies, RIBA Services Ltd and National Building Specification Ltd, were set up which took away a lot of the work of the Professional

Services Department. In 1973 the Professional Services Board was wound up and a Practice Board appointed which took responsibility for the work of the Building Industry Group, the Conditions of Engagement Group, the Legislation Group, the Standards of Competence Group, the Salaried Architects Working Group and the Investigation Committee. The Professional Conduct Committee became directly responsible to Council.

9.1   ELGIN MARBLES COMMITTEE PAPERS, 1836—1837   35ff
      & 1 notebook
Report of the committee, with correspondence and a record of proceedings at meetings, Dec 1836 — Jul 1837.
Subject : Scientific investigation into the use of colour in the decoration of the Elgin Marbles.

(The chairman of the committee was W. R. Hamilton and its members included the scientist, Michael Faraday, and the sculptor, Robert Westmacott)

9.2   XANTHIAN MARBLES COMMITTEE PAPERS, 1843   4pp
Report of the committee, Jan 1843.
Subjects : Investigation into the condition of the sculptured figures and fragments of marble brought from Xanthus, an ancient city in Lycia, to the British Museum by the British government: possible use of colour in their decoration.

(The members of the Elgin Marbles Committee were re-appointed to examine and report on this recent discovery)

9.3   SCIENCE STANDING COMMITTEE MINUTES, 1886—
1938   3 vols & 4 binders
Signed minutes of the committee, Jun 1886—Jun 1938, and its subcommittees, Dec 1925—Apr 1938, with some memoranda, reports and draft specifications of building materials by the BESA and the BSI.
Includes the signed minutes of the following subcommittees, joint meetings and conferences, listed in chronological order:
Officers of the Practice and Science Standing Committees, Dec 1925
LCC Drainage By-laws Joint Committee, Apr—May 1926, Oct 1932
Damp Houses Subcommittee, Jan 1927—Feb 1929
Dampness in Dwellings Subcommittee *see* Damp Houses Subcommittee
Rheumatic Heart Disease in Children Subcommittee *see* Damp Houses
    Subcommittee
Building Science Laboratories Subcommittee, Feb 1927
Model Schedule of Requirements for a Building Laboratory at a School
    of Architecture Subcommittee *see* Building Science Laboratories Sub-
    committee

Economies in Building Practice Subcommittee, Feb 1927

Application of Science to Building Construction Subcommittee, May 1927

Elected Members of the Science Standing Committee, Jun 1927—Jul 1937

Smoke Abatement Subcommittee, Nov 1927—May 1928

Standard Sizes of Bricks Subcommittee, Nov 1927—Jul 1928

Institute of Builders & Science Standing Committee Joint Meeting, Feb 1928

Stonework at the Houses of Parliament Subcommittee, Mar 1928

Practice & Science Standing Committees Joint Subcommittee, Nov 1928

Timber Specifications Conference Meetings, Dec 1928—Jul 1929

Forest Products Research Laboratory, Building Research Station & Science Standing Committee Joint Meeting, 1928 *see* Timber Specifications Conference Meetings

Prevention of Fire Joint Subcommittee, Jan—Feb 1929

Plumbing Sub-committee, Apr 1929—Oct 1930

Telephone Development Association Meeting, Oct 1929

Orientation of Buildings Subcommittee, Dec 1930—Apr 1931

Review of Scientific Books for the RIBA Journal Subcommittee, Jan 1931

Standardisation of Units of Design Joint Subcommittee, Mar—May 1933

Model Building By-laws Joint Subcommittee, Mar—Apr 1938

Subjects : Scientific testing of building materials: standardization of building materials, including British Standards specifications: research into methods of construction, including steel-frame and reinforced concrete: 'ancient lights' legislation and building legislation generally: methods of preservation and repair of building materials: sanitation and hygiene in housing: dampness in buildings, dry rot, etc.: lighting, heating, ventilation, plumbing: acoustic properties of buildings: mass production of housing: fire-prevention: smoke abatement: work of the Department of Industrial Research and the Building Research Station.

(This committee took over the work of the Light and Air Committee *see* 2.2 Special Committees Minutes Series. In 1938 it was replaced by the Science Committee, which was entirely appointed by Council instead of partly elected as had been the case with the Science Standing Committee)

9.4   BUILDING STONES PHOTOGRAPHS ALBUM, 1911   1 vol
Album of enlarged (× 30) photographs of sections of building stones in the Museum of Practical Geology, Jermyn Street. Arranged by the Science Standing Committee and provided with brief descriptions and an introductory essay on the study of building stones written by Alan E.

Munby, Hon. Secretary to the Science Standing Committee, March 1911.

9.5 DAMP HOUSES SUBCOMMITTEE REPORT, 1929   4pp
Printed report of the subcommittee, Mar 1929.
Subject : Causes and prevention of dampness in domestic buildings.

(For minutes of this committee, Jan 1927—Feb 1929, *see* 9.3 Science Standing Committee Minutes Series)

9.6 SMOKE   ABATEMENT   SUBCOMMITTEE   REPORT
1929   5pp
Printed report of the subcommittee, 1929.
Subjects : Means of reducing atmospheric pollution by smoke and acid-laden fumes: advice for architects on building design for smoke abatement: effect of sulphur acids on building stones.

(For minutes of this committee, Nov 1927—May 1928 *see* 9.3 Science Standing Committee Minutes Series)

9.7 RESEARCH AND INFORMATION SERVICE IN THE BUILDING INDUSTRY COMMITTEE MINUTES & PAPERS, 1934—1939   2 vols & 3 boxes
Signed minutes of the main committee and the subcommittee, Feb 1935—Mar 1936, with reports and memoranda: also correspondence of E. J. Carter, Secretary to the committee, much of it with the Building Industries National Council, 1934—1939.
Subjects : Proposed establishment of an independent, representative and authoritative organization to provide information and co-ordinate research in the building industry: survey of existing services and organizations; insurance on building commodities.

(Sometimes known as the 'Research and Information Committee' or the 'Research and Information Service Committee'. Set up by the PRIBA, Sir Giles Gilbert Scott, in association with the Building Research Station and the Building Centre. Its work was handed over to a special committee of the Building Industries National Council in Oct 1936.)

9.8 SCIENCE COMMITTEE MINUTES, 1938—1939   1 vol
Signed minutes of the Science Committee, Jul 1938—Jul 1939, and of the New LCC Building By-Laws Joint Committee, Oct 1938—Mar 1939, and the Model By-Laws Joint Subcommittee, Feb 1939, with memoranda and British Standard draft specifications.
Subjects : Building regulations: standardization of building materials: building methods and research: status of District Surveyors.

9.9   AIR RAID PRECAUTIONS COMMITTEE MINUTES, 1938—
1939   1 vol
Signed minutes of meetings, Dec 1938—Jul 1939.
Subjects : Technical problems of structural precautions against bomb
attacks on buildings: methods of constructing air-raid shelters.

(Included representatives of the Institution of Civil Engineers, the Office
of Works, the Home Office, the Building Research Station and the
AASTA.)

9.10   ARCHITECTURAL SCIENCE BOARD MINUTES, 1950   1 vol
Signed minutes of meetings of the Board, Jan —Nov 1950, and of the
following subcommittees and study groups:
General Purposes Committee, Jan —Nov 1950
Lectures Committee, Jan —Nov 1950
Legislation Subcommittee, Feb —Nov 1950
Standard Specifications Committee, Feb —Jul 1950
Standard Specifications Committee Coordinating Committee, Feb —Nov
    1950
RIBA Members of the Architectural Science Board, Jun 1950
Study Group No. 1, Building Needs, Jan —Jun 1950
Study Group No. 2, Technical, Feb —Oct 1950
Study Group No. 3, Dimensional Standardisation, Oct 1950
Study Group No. 4, Building Economics, Feb 1950

Subjects : Building techniques: education of architects in building technique developments: lectures on scientific subjects: representation of the
architect's point of view on bodies dealing with British Standards for
building materials and codes of performance: building costs: work of the
Building Research Station: revision of the London Building Acts and by-
laws.

(This volume is labelled 'Minute Book 7'. Unfortunately, minute books
1—6 are missing. The work of this board was continued by the (New)
Science Committee. For copies of minutes of meetings, reports and
other papers of the Architectural Science Group and its successor, the
Architectural Science Board, from Nov 1939—Aug 1943 *see* British
Architectural Library Manuscripts & Archives Collection, Godfrey
Samuel Papers.)

9.11   (NEW) SCIENCE COMMITTEE MINUTES, 1951—1959   2
vols & 2 binders
Signed minutes of meetings of the main committee, Jul 1951—Jul 1959,
with memoranda, draft BSI specifications and signed minutes of the
following subcommittees:
British Standards Coordinating Committee, Oct 1951—Jun 1953

Technical Subcommittee, Jan 1953
Research Subcommittee, Nov 1954—Oct 1958
Industry Liaison Subcommittee, Apr 1956—Jul 1959
Lectures Subcommittee, Oct 1957—Jun 1958
Information Subcommittee, Oct 1958—Jun 1959

Subjects : Building techniques: education of architects in building technique developments: the role of science in architectural education: lectures on scientific subjects: building materials: British Standards: government programmes for building research: building research fellowships for architects: Rose Shipman Studentships: building industry liaison: economy in the use of building materials: heating and ventilation of farm buildings for livestock: factory buildings: standardization of building components: effect of modern synthetic detergents on sewage disposal systems: plumbing and sanitary fittings: clean air and smoke abatement: building legislation.

(This committee replaced the Architectural Science Board. The Lectures Subcommittee was defunct between 1951 and 1953, when responsibility for lectures on scientific matters was transferred to the Lectures Subcommittee of the Public Relations Committee. When the Council terminated the Hospitals Committee in 1956, it placed responsibility for studies of particular building types in the hands of the (New) Science Committee.)

9.12   BRITISH STANDARDS COORDINATING COMMITTEE PAPERS, 1951—1957   2 boxes
Correspondence, memoranda and copies of minutes of some meetings, 1951—1959.
Subjects : British Standards affecting the work of architects: coordination of the work of RIBA representatives on British Standards Institution technical committees.

(This committee continued the work of the Standard Specifications Committee of the Architectural Science Board. Its work was continued by the Codes and Standards Committee.
For minutes of this committee, Oct 1951—Jun 1953 *see* 9.11 (New) Science Committee Minutes Series.)

9.13   COST RESEARCH COMMITTEE PAPERS, 1956—1959   2 boxes
Copies of minutes of meetings, Nov 1956 — Jul 1959, with memoranda, reports, evidence on cost control methods and correspondence with the RICS Cost Research Panel, with copies of their minutes, 1956—1959.
Subject : Control of building costs.

9.14   CODES AND STANDARDS COMMITTEE MINUTES &
PAPERS, 1957—1959   1 vol, 1 binder & 1 box
Signed minutes of meetings, Jan 1958—May 1959, with correspondence,
memoranda, drafts of standards and copies of BSI News pamphlets,
1957—1959.
Subjects : Draft British Standards for building materials and codes of
practice: RIBA representation on BSI committees.

(This committee continued the work of the British Standards Coordinating Committee. Its work was continued by the British Standards
panels of the Technical Standards Committee and later the Technical
Committee.)

9.15   TECHNICAL   INFORMATION   FOR   THE   BUILDING
INDUSTRY JOINT COMMITTEE: RIBA REPRESENTATIVE'S
PAPERS, 1959—1965   1 box
Copies of minutes, Apr 1961—Apr 1965, with memoranda, reports and
correspondence, 1959—1965.
Subjects : Provision of technical information for the building industry:
guide to the preparation of trade literature for the building industry:
application of the SfB System to communications within the building
industry.

(A joint committee of representatives of the RIBA, the RICS and the
NFBTE.)

9.16   TECHNICAL   INFORMATION   COMMITTEE   MINUTES,
1959—1964   1 binder
Signed minutes of meetings, Oct 1959—May 1964, with notes on
meetings of the Honorary Officers of the committee, Nov 1961—Oct
1963.
Subjects : Provision of a technical information service for architects and
the building industry: refresher courses on technical subjects: production
of an SfB/UDC Building Filing Manual: proposed Documentation Unit:
specification clauses: publication of standard forms for architects.

(The work of this committee was continued by the Technical Committee.)

9.17   TECHNICAL   STANDARDS   COMMITTEE   MINUTES   &
PAPERS, 1959—1964   1 binder & 1 box
Signed minutes of meetings, Dec 1959—Oct 1963, with memoranda and
reports: minutes of meetings of the Honorary Officers of the committee,
Nov 1960—Oct 1963: correspondence, Dec 1959—Mar 1964.
Subjects : Standardization of building materials, components and codes
of practice: dimensional coordination in components: building industry

liaison: building legislation.

(The work of this committee was continued by the Technical Committee.)

9.18   TECHNICAL SECTION FILES, 1959—1970   55 boxes
Correspondence files kept by the Technical Information Officer and, from 1962, the Assistant Secretaries of the Professional Services Department, including general correspondence files, 1964—1970: files concerned with the Technical Information Service, 1959—1968: files concerned with the production of Technical Aids and the Technology Primers, 1965—1970: files concerned with technical conferences, exhibitions, seminars, lectures and courses, 1960—1970: files relating to the SfB System, 1961—1968, British Standards committees, 1960—1969, change to metric, 1960—1970, modular coordination 1960—1966, use of computers, 1964—1969, etc.
Subjects : Design of specific building types, including hospitals, farm buildings and factories: building materials and components: British and International Standards: building techniques: technical education of architects: change to metric dimensions: computer-aided design: Ronan Point disaster: information systems: office libraries: the SfB filing system.

9.19   STANDARDISATION PANEL MINUTES & PAPERS, 1961—1964   1 box
Minutes of meetings, Nov 1962 — Dec 1963, with memoranda, reports and correspondence, 1961—1964.
Subjects : A RIBA handbook on modular coordination: the RIBA industrialized building research project.

(A panel of the Technical Standards Committee. Its work was continued by the Standardisation Working Party of the Technical Committee.)

BUILDING CONTROL PANEL PAPERS, 1962—1972
(A panel of the Technical Information Committee and then of the Technical Committee) *see* 8.4.6

9.20   INDUSTRY LIAISON PANEL MINUTES & PAPERS, 1962—1966   1 box
Minutes of meetings, Dec 1962—Oct 1965, with correspondence and reports of working groups, 1962—1966.
Subjects : Liaison with manufacturers of building materials and components: built-in furniture: plastics development and research: standard metal windows: fire precautions.

(A panel of the Technical Standards Committee and then of the Technical Committee.)

9.21   RATIONALISATION OF TRADITIONAL BUILDING PANEL
        MINUTES & PAPERS, 1962—1963   1 box
        Minutes of meetings, Dec 1962—Sep 1963, with reports, memoranda
        and correspondence.
        Subject : Rationalization of the traditional techniques, methods and
        materials of building.

        (A panel of the Technical Standards Committee.)

9.22   INDUSTRIALISATION OF BUILDING PANEL PAPERS, 1962—
        1965   1 box
        Correspondence, memoranda and reports, Nov 1962—May 1965.
        Subjects : Industrialized building and modular coordination: the RIBA
        industrialized building research project.

        (A panel of the Technical Standards Committee.)

9.23   COLOUR PANEL PAPERS, 1962—1969   1 box
        Correspondence and memoranda, Sep 1962—Oct 1969.
        Subjects : Standards for colour in building and decorative paints: colour
        in the environment.

        (A panel of the Technical Standards Committee and then of the Technical
        Committee.)

9.24   BUILDING INDUSTRY COMMITTEE MINUTES & PAPERS,
        1962—1967
        Signed minutes of meetings, Aug 1962—Jul 1967, with agenda papers,
        reports and correspondence.
        Subjects : Relations with various government and building industry
        consultative committees, including NEDC, EPACCI, NJCC, NCC,
        CICC: future constitution of the NJCC: long-term programming of
        public building works: structure and economy of the building industry:
        proposed Building Research and Information Association: relations
        between public and private architectural practice.

9.25   BUILDING INDUSTRY SECTION FILES, 1962—1969   7 boxes
        Correspondence files of the Under Secretary, Professional Services,
        concerning government and building industry consultative committees
        and liaison organizations, 1962—1969.
        Subjects : Work of NEDC, EDC for the Building Industry (Little
        Neddy), EPACCI, FASS, CASEC, HVCA, CICC, etc.: government
        building programmes: London Building Productivity Committee:
        Banwell Committee: Phelps-Brown Committee.

9.26   BUILDING INDUSTRY COMMUNICATIONS RESEARCH
        PROJECT PAPERS, 1963—1969   2 boxes
        Files kept by Alwyn Lewis, RIBA Under Secretary for Professional
        Services and Secretary to the project, including signed minutes of the
        trustees, Jul 1963—Apr 1964, and correspondence with the trustees,
        1963—1968: signed minutes of the Communications Research Com-
        mittee, Nov 1963—May 1966, with correspondence: signed minutes of
        the Steering Committee, Dec 1963—Jun 1965, with correspondence: also
        accounts, 1964—1969, and research team correspondence and reports.
        Subject : Methods of achieving better communications in the building
        industry.

        (The project was set up at a conference on communications in the
        building industry called by the NJCC in 1963. The Communications
        Research Committee represented all sections of the industry. The project
        was carried out by a combined team of sociologists and operational
        research workers from the Tavistock Institute of Human Relations. A
        report was produced entitled 'Interdependence and uncertainty'.)

9.27   DOCUMENTATION PANEL MINUTES & PAPERS, 1963—
        1964   1 box
        Minutes of meetings, Nov 1963—May 1964, with memoranda and
        reports.
        Subjects : Proposed Professional Services Documentation Unit.

        (A panel of the Technical Information Committee.)

9.28   SPECIFICATIONS PANEL MINUTES & PAPERS, 1963—
        1964   1 box
        Memoranda, reports and correspondence, 1963—1964.
        Subjects : Proposed preparation of a coded standard National Specifica-
        tion: application of computers to production of bills of quantities.

        (A panel of the Technical Information Committee)

9.29   SfB PANEL MINUTES & PAPERS, 1963—1969   4 boxes
        Minutes of meetings, Nov 1963 — Mar 1969, with memoranda and
        reports and some correspondence.
        Subjects : Administration, development and promotion of the SfB/UDC
        classification system.

        (A panel of the Technical Information Committee and then of the
        Technical Committee. Its work was continued by the SfB Working
        Group of the Professional Services Board.
            SfB stands for Samarbetskommitten för Byggnadsfrager, a standard
        arrangement for specification clauses, product information and cost

indices, designed in Sweden in 1947. In the late 1950s the CIB (International Council for Building Research Studies and Documentation) set up an SfB Bureau to develop the system and licence national bodies to administer, develop and promote it. The RIBA Technical Information Service was an associate member of CIB licensed to sponsor the system in the U.K. It published the *SfB/UDC Building Filing Manual* in 1961 and, after several years of development and revision, followed this in 1968 with the *CI/SfB Construction Indexing Manual* .)

9.30   SfB BUILDING COMMUNICATIONS COMMITTEE: RIBA REPRESENTATIVE'S PAPERS, 1964—1967   2 boxes
Copies of minutes of meetings of the committee and its working groups, with reports and correspondence, 1964—1967.
  Subjects : The application of the SfB system to communication of technical information in the building industry: the work of B. Bindslev in Copenhagen on the application of the SfB system to contract documentation.

(This was a subcommittee of the Technical Information for the Building Industry Joint Committee of the RIBA, RICS & NFBTE. It had three main working groups, one on drawings, one on bills of quantities, and one on product control and costs.)

9.31   TECHNICAL COMMITTEE MINUTES & PAPERS, 1964—1967   1 binder & 3 boxes
Signed minutes of meetings, Aug 1964—May 1967, with minutes of meetings of the Honorary Officers of the committee, Oct 1964—Jun 1967 and memoranda, reports and correspondence.
  Subjects : Same as in Technical Information Committee Minutes & Papers and in Technical Standards Committee Minutes & Papers.

(This committee took over the work of the Technical Information Committee and the Technical Standards Committee. Its work was continued by the Professional Services Board, RIBA Services Ltd and National Building Specification Ltd)

9.32   BRITISH STANDARDS PANEL MINUTES & PAPERS, 1964—1967   1 box
Minutes of meetings, Mar 1964—Jun 1967, with memoranda, reports and correspondence.
  Subjects : The work of RIBA representatives on the many BSI committees concerned with standards relating to the building industry.

(A panel of the Technical Committee. Its work was continued by the Metric Change, British Standards, Standardisation Steering Group of the Professional Services Board.)

9.33   SfB STEERING COMMITTEE MINUTES & PAPERS, 1965   1
box
Minutes of meetings, Feb —Mar 1965, with memoranda and reports.
Subject : Revision of the SfB Manual.
(A panel of the Technical Committee. Its work was continued by the
SfB Working Group of the Professional Services Board.)

9.34   SfB INTERNATIONAL MEETINGS: UK REPRESENTATIVE'S
PAPERS, 1965—1978   12 boxes
Copies of minutes of international meetings of the SfB Development
Group, with agenda papers, memoranda and reports.
Subjects : Development and promotion of the SfB system.

9.35   TECHNICAL   AIDS   PANEL   MINUTES   &   PAPERS,   1965—
1968   2 boxes
Minutes of meetings, Nov 1965—May 1967, with memoranda and
reports: also correspondence, Apr 1965—Jan 1968.
Subjects: Preparation of a Technical Aids series of articles for publication
in the *RIBA Journal* (i.e. educational articles for architects containing
information on new technology.)
(A panel of the Technical Committee. *See also* 9.18 Technical Section
Files.)

9.36   STANDARDISATION   WORKING   PARTY   PAPERS,   1965—
1967   2 boxes
Correspondence, memoranda and reports, Mar 1965—Oct 1967.
Subjects : Theory and application of dimensional coordination in
industrialized building: development of standard ranges of building
components: conversion from Imperial to metric dimensions.
(A working group of the Technical Committee, it continued the work of
the Standardisation Panel of the Technical Standards Committee. Its
work was continued by the Metric Change, British Standards, Standardisation Steering Group of the Professional Services Board.)

9.37   COMPUTER WORKING GROUP PAPERS, 1966—1968   1 box
Correspondence, Jan 1966—May 1968.
Subject : Computer applications of interest to architects.
(A working group first of the Technical Committee and then of the
Professional Services Board. Its work was continued by the Computer
Services section of RIBA Services Ltd)

9.38   METRIC CHANGE PANEL MINUTES & PAPERS, 1967   1
box

Minutes of meetings, May—Sep 1967, with memoranda, reports and correspondence.

Subject : Change from Imperial to metric dimensions in the construction industry.

(A panel of the Technical Committee. Its work was continued by the Metric Change, British Standards, Standardisation Steering Group of the Professional Services Board.)

9.39   PROFESSIONAL SERVICES BOARD MINUTES & PAPERS, 1967—1973   6 binders & 1 box
Signed minutes of meetings, Oct 1967—May 1973, with agenda papers, memoranda and reports (with gap between Apr 1970—Sep 1971), and correspondence of the Secretary to the Board, Feb 1967—Jun 1969.

Subjects : Practice matters, including arbitration advice, management advice, contract advice, professional conduct: Joint Contracts Tribunal: standards and codes of performance: British Standards technical advice and information: liaison with other architectural bodies and building industry organization: National Joint Consultative Committee: building industry research, development and economics: building control and legislation: town planning and housing matters: Jury for Distinction in Town Planning: administration and policy of the Professional Services Board.

(In 1967 four departmental boards were set up, one of which was the Professional Services Board. Its job was to direct the policy and coordinate the efforts of the Professional Services Department set up in 1962, which had a Technical Section, a Building Industry Section, a Practice Section and a Town Planning Section. Its work was continued and developed by a new Practice Board, the Secretary's Office and the new commercial company, RIBA Services Ltd.)

9.40 * ARCHITECTS CENTRAL TECHNICAL SERVICE (ACTS) WORKING GROUP PAPERS, 1967—1970   13 binders
Background papers, back to 1963: reports of feasibility study, 1968: minutes of meetings, agenda papers and reports of the group, 1968—1969: correspondence, 1967—1970: reports of Professional Services Board Conferences, 1967—1969.

Subjects : Setting up technical information and advisory services for architects, on a commercial basis: origin and development of RIBA Services Ltd and National Building Specification Ltd, 1969—1970.

(A working group of the Professional Services Board. In June 1959 the (New) Science Committee and the Professional Text and Reference Books Committee (later called the Professional Literature Committee) jointly recommended to Council the formation of a self-supporting

Technical Information Service. Council then appointed the Technical Information Committee to develop such a service, which was set up in 1960 and received a subsidy from the Council for its first three years. In 1963 there was an abortive proposal to set up a Professional Services Documentation Unit. This was followed, in Jun 1966, by a proposal to set up a service company to deal on a commercial basis with architects' technical information needs. This project was discussed at the Professional Services Board Conference in Sep 1967 and a feasibility study was initiated to investigate which services might be offered and to make proposals for the formation and administration of an organization to provide them. A market survey was conducted by questionnaire in 1968. The response was enthusiastic and an ACTS Working Group was formed, which resulted in the setting up of RIBA Services Ltd and National Building Specification Ltd in 1969.)

* Access at the discretion of RIBA Services Ltd

9.41   METRIC CHANGE, BRITISH STANDARDS, STANDARD-
        ISATION STEERING GROUP MINUTES & PAPERS, 1967—
        1969   1 box
        Minutes of meetings, Dec 1967—Feb 1969, with memoranda, reports and correspondence.
        Subjects : Conversion from the Imperial to the metric system in the construction industry: development of standard ranges of building components: work of RIBA representatives on BSI committees concerned with standards relating to the building industry.

        (A group of the Professional Services Board, it continued the work of the Metric Change Panel, the British Standards Panel, and the Standardisation Working Party. Much of its work was continued by the British Standards Advisory Group, the Metric Advisory Group and the Product Development Panel.)

9.42 * RIBA SERVICES WORKING GROUP PAPERS, 1968—1969   1 box
        Notes of meetings, with memoranda and reports, Nov 1968—Jan 1969, and draft articles of association of RIBA Services Ltd.
        Subjects : Setting up the companies, RIBA Services Ltd and National Building Specification Ltd.

        (RIBA Services Ltd was set up in 1969 to carry out on a commercial basis many of the advisory activities previously performed by the Professional Services Department. In Nov 1968 the Economic Development Council for Building approved in principle the appointment of the RIBA as executive sponsors for the preparation of the National Building Specification. In Feb 1969 the RIBA Council agreed to the formation of RIBA

Services Ltd, National Building Specification Ltd and RIBA Publications Ltd.)

* Access at the discretion of RIBA Services Ltd

9.43   SfB WORKING GROUP MINUTES & PAPERS, 1968—1969   2 boxes
Minutes of meetings, Dec 1968—May 1969, with memoranda, reports and drafts of sections of the SfB Manual.
Subject : Revision of the SfB Manual.

(A working group of the Professional Services Board, it continued the work of the SfB Steering Committee of the Technical Committee. In 1969 it was decided that the SfB system should be less closely associated with the RIBA and as a result the SfB Agency UK was formed.)

9.44   SfB COMMITTEE OF THE PROFESSIONAL SERVICES BOARD MINUTES & PAPERS, 1969   1 box
Minutes of meeting on 29 May 1969, with reports of meeting with the NCC Working Party on Data-Coordination and the International Building Classification Committee.
Subject : Development of CI/SfB classification system.

(The work of this committee was continued by the SfB Committee of the SfB Agency UK.)

9.45   BRITISH STANDARDS ADVISORY GROUP MINUTES & PAPERS, 1969   1 box
Minutes of meetings, Feb —Dec 1969, with memoranda, reports and correspondence of the Functional Products Groups.
Subject : Work of RIBA representatives on BSI committees concerned with standards relating to the building industry.

(An advisory group of the Professional Services Board, it continued the British Standards work of the Metric Change, British Standards, Standardisation Steering Group. Its work was continued by the Performance Standards Panel.)

9.46   TECHNICAL COORDINATION GROUP MINUTES & PAPERS, 1969—1971   1 box
Minutes of meetings, Apr 1969—Feb 1971, with memoranda and reports.
Subject : Coordination of RIBA technical policy and activities.

(A group of the Professional Services Board. It continued some of the work of the Technical Committee.)

9.47   METRIC ADVISORY GROUP MINUTES & PAPERS, 1969—1970   1 box

Minutes of meetings, Jan —Dec 1970, with correspondence, Jun —Dec 1969.

Subject : Conversion from the Imperial to the metric system in the construction industry.

(An advisory group of the Professional Services Board. It continued some of the work of the Metric Change, British Standards, Standardisation Steering Group.)

9.48 DESIGN METHODS PANEL MINUTES & PAPERS, 1969—1971   1 box
Minutes of meetings, Dec 1969—Mar 1971, with memoranda and reports.
Subject : Development of design methodology.

(A panel of the Professional Services Board)

9.49 TECHNICAL ADVISORY PANEL MINUTES & PAPERS, 1970—1971   1 box
Minutes of meetings, Oct 1970—Oct 1971, with memoranda and reports.
Subject : Monitoring of important technical developments in the construction industry.

(A panel of the Professional Services Board. It continued some of the work of the Technical Committee.)

9.50 PERFORMANCE STANDARDS PANEL MINUTES & PAPERS, 1970—1971   1 box
Minutes of meetings, Mar 1970—Sep 1971, with memoranda and reports.
Subjects : Building component and product performance specifications: codes of practice specifying the environment of building components and products: revision of British Standards relating to construction industry: use of performance requirements in the efficient practice of architecture.

(A panel of the Professional Services Board. It continued the work of the British Standards Advisory Group. Its work was continued by the Standards Committee.)

9.51 PRODUCT DEVELOPMENT PANEL MINUTES, 1970—1971   1 box
Minutes of meetings, Feb 1970—May 1971
Subjects : Promotion and evaluation of well-designed building materials, components and systems: publication of Technology Primers.

(A panel of the Professional Services Board. It continued some of the work of the Metric Change, British Standards, Standardisation Steering Group.)

9.52   DATA COORDINATION PANEL MINUTES & PAPERS, 1970—
1971   1 box
Minutes of meetings, Dec 1970—Jul 1971, with memoranda.
Subjects : Management of information: data coordination systems: need for cooperation between various systems and organizations.

(A panel of the Professional Services Board.)

See also in 2.1 Early Committees Minutes Series:
Experiments and Professional Investigations Committee, 1854
and in 2.2 Special Committees Minutes Series:
Materials and Construction Committee, 1876
Technical Institutions Committee, 1898
Reinforced Concrete Joint Committee, 1906—1917
Timber Specification Committee, 1916
Deputation to the Department of Scientific and Industrial Research Committee, 1924
Scientific Qualifications of Candidates for the Fellowship Committee, 1933
Standardisation of Building Materials Subcommittee, 1942
Air Raid Precautions and the Protection of Industry Conference Organising Committee, 1942
Prefabrication and Standardisation Subcommittee, 1943

Bibliography

1   RIBA 'Report of the committee appointed by the Council of the Royal Institute of British Architects, 2nd March 1863, for the purposes of making experiments on artificial stone' *RIBA Proceedings* 1st Series 1863/64 pp159—168
2   Hansard, Octavius 'Some observations upon experiments on artificial stone, etc., upon reading the report of the committee thereon' *RIBA Proceedings* 1st Series 1863/64 pp169—181
3   Street, William & Clarke, Max *Brickwork tests: reports and statistics* London, RIBA, 1896. Report on the first series of experiments conducted by the RIBA Science Standing Committee.
4   Street, William & Clarke, Max *Brickwork tests. Report on the second series of experiments* London, RIBA, 1897
5   RIBA *Report on brickwork tests conducted by a subcommittee of the Science Standing Committee of the Royal Institute of British Architects* London, RIBA, 1905
6   'Steel and reinforced concrete construction' Papers and discussion in *VIIth International Congress of Architects. Summary of proceedings* Published as

special supplement to the *RIBA Journal* Vol 13 1906 Aug 25

7 Joint Committee on Reinforced Concrete. Report *RIBA Journal* Vol 14 1907 Jun 15 pp513—541

8 Dibdin, W. J. *The composition and strength of mortars* London, RIBA, 1911. Report on the results of an experimental investigation conducted for the RIBA Science Standing Committee.

9 *Joint Committee on Reinforced Concrete. Second report* London, RIBA, 1911

10 RIBA & Geological Survey and Museum 'Draft report on building stone tests,' 1913. Typescript in RIBA Library.

11 'RIBA standard sizes of bricks' *RIBA Kalendar* 1925/26

12 RIBA *Report on damp houses* London, RIBA, 1929. Prepared by a subcommittee of the RIBA Science Standing Committee.

13 RIBA *Report on smoke abatement* London, RIBA, 1929. Prepared by a subcommittee of the RIBA Science Standing Committee.

14 RIBA *Report on damage to plumbing work caused by frost* London, RIBA, 1930

15 RIBA Joint Committee on the Orientation of Buildings *The orientation of buildings* London, RIBA, 1933

16 RIBA Science Standing Committee *The requirements of science buildings* London, RIBA, 1933

17 RIBA *Report of the special committee appointed by the Royal Institute of British Architects to prepare a report and submit evidence if required to the Departmental Committee on the Cost of Hospitals and other Public Buildings* London, RIBA, Jan 1934

18 'The cost of hospitals' *RIBA Journal* Vol 41 1934 May 19 pp700—702. Summary of a report by a RIBA special committee.

19 RIBA Air Raid Precautions Committee 'Structural air raid precautions' *RIBA Journal* Vol 46 1939 May 8 pp661—671 & May 22 pp730—732

20 Hall, E. Stanley 'The RIBA Research Board. A statement of the formation and aims of the RIBA Research Board' *RIBA Journal* Vol 47 1940 May 20 pp169—171

21 Education Committee of the Architectural Science Group 'The place of science in architectural education' *RIBA Journal* Vol 48 1941 Jun pp133—143

22 'The Architectural Science Board lectures' *RIBA Journal* Vol 50 1942 Nov p12

23 Hartland, M. Thomas 'The influence of new developments in construction on architectural design' *RIBA Journal* Vol 51 1944 Mar pp114—118

24 Bernal, J. D. 'Science in architecture' *RIBA Journal* Vol 55 1946 Mar pp155—158

25 Architectural Science Group 'Sociology and architecture' *RIBA Journal* Vol 53 1946 Aug pp386—396 & 443—447

26 RIBA Architectural Science Board 'The teaching of construction' *RIBA Journal* Vol 55 1948 Aug pp464—468

27 Harrison, D. Dex (ed.) *Building science* London, George Allen & Unwin,

1948. Papers prepared for the RIBA Architectural Science Board.

28   RIBA Architectural Science Board 'Dimensional standardisation' *RIBA Journal* Vol 58 1951 Apr pp230—234

29   Mills, E. D., Cutbush, P. & Weston, G. 'British Standards and the architect' *RIBA Journal* Vol 59 1952 May pp252—259

30   'A note on the work of the [RIBA] Cost Research Committee' *RIBA Journal*, Vol 64 1957 May p281

31   Report of the RIBA Cost Research Committee, in *RIBA Journal* Vol 65 1958 Feb pp122—123

32   'Inquiry into the building timetable' *RIBA Journal* Vol 65 1958 Aug pp350—352. Report of an inquiry carried out by the RIBA for the Ministry of Works.

33   RIBA Cost Research Committee 'Cost control at the design stage' *RIBA Journal* Vol 65 1958 Sep pp365—375

34   *Practical fire protection* London, RIBA & Fire Protection Association, 1960

35   RIBA Technical Information Service *RIBA Hospitals Course Handbook* London, RIBA, 1960

36   Goldring, Maurice 'RIBA Technical Information Service' *RIBA Journal* Vol 68 1961 Jan pp85—86

37   RIBA *SfB/UDC building filing manual* London, RIBA, 1961

38   RIBA Technical Standards Committee 'The problem of noise. Evidence to the Wilson Committee' *RIBA Journal* Vol 69 1962 Jun pp210—213

39   'RIBA Professional Services Department Conference' *RIBA Journal* Vol 69 1962 Dec p446

40   RIBA Technical Information Service *RIBA Housing Conference Report* London, RIBA, 1962

41   RIBA Technical Information Service *Materials handling in relation to the design of factories and warehouses* London, RIBA, 1963

42   Goldsmith, Selwyn *Designing for the disabled* London, RIBA Technical Information Service, 1963 (Revised edition issued in 1967)

43   RIBA *The industrialisation of building* London, RIBA, 1963

44   RIBA Technical Section 'Report on the work of Bjœrn Bindslev in applying the SfB-system to communications within the building industry' *RIBA Journal* Vol 71 1964 Sep pp400—403

45   RIBA *The co-ordination of dimensions for building* London, RIBA, 1965

46   *The industrialisation of building* London, RIBA, 1965

47   RIBA Standardisation Working Party 'Will it fit?' *RIBA Journal* Vol 73 1966 Mar pp128—131 & Apr pp183—184

48   Green, J. R. B. 'Guide to SfB Building Filing Manual' *RIBA Journal* Vol 73 1966 May pp208—213

49   Carter, John 'The RIBA, computers and CBC' *RIBA Journal* Vol 73 1966 Oct pp481—482

50   *Industrialised housing and the architect* London, RIBA & National Building Agency, 1967

51   *Towards computer-aided building design* London, RIBA, 1968

52 Anthony Williams and Burles 'The metric change' *RIBA Journal* Vol 75 1968 Mar pp113—132

53 Mills, Jack & McCann, Wilfred *The organisation of information in the construction industry.* SfB Agency UK Development Paper No 3, London, RIBA, 1968

54 CI/SfB *Construction indexing manual* London, RIBA, 1968

55 RIBA SfB Panel 'SfB revised: the CI/SfB manual *RIBA Journal* Vol 75 1968 Aug pp384—387

56 Anthony Williams and Burles *The architect and the change to metric* London, RIBA Publications Ltd, 1969

57 RIBA Metric Advisory Group 'The change-over in the office. A guidance note by the RIBA Metric Advisory Group' *RIBA Journal* Vol 76 1969 Feb pp77—78

58 Ray-Jones, Alan 'A common language for building' *RIBA Journal* Vol 76 1969 May pp187—188. Article on the CI/SfB classification system.

59 RIBA SfB Working Group 'CI/SfB for project information' *RIBA Journal* Vol 76 1969 Aug pp347—352

60 'The Professional Services Department' and 'Andrew Derbyshire. John Carter interviews the chairman of the Professional Services Board' *RIBA Journal* Vol 74 1969 Oct pp416—420 & 421—422. Parts of a feature article 'Inside the RIBA'.

61 'National Building Specification and RIBA Services' *RIBA Journal* Vol 74 1969 Oct p423. Part of a feature article 'Inside the RIBA'.

62 'The work of the Professional Services Department' *RIBA Journal* Vol 77 1970 Mar p133

63 Goodman, David 'RIBA Standards Committee' *RIBA Journal* Vol 83 1976 Apr p130

10
Environment and design

Gathered together in this chapter are the records of various committees and groups concerned with town and country planning, metropolitan improvement schemes (London), housing developments and slum clearance, preservation and restoration of buildings, architectural aesthetics and the arts in general, design control and standards of design of specific building types. Some of this work was coordinated from 1886—1939 by the Art Standing Committee which took over and greatly expanded the work of the Conservation of Ancient Monuments and Remains Committee, 1864—1886, and from 1907 by various standing committees on housing, town planning and design.

A concern for the quality of the built environment was shown from the very beginning and was well-expressed by T. L. Donaldson in the Institute's motto 'Usui civium decori urbium'. The first annual report of the Council in 1836 drew attention to the fact that 'the style of architecture is not in all cases so pure as could have been desired' and in 1847 the Council submitted a report to Lord Morpeth, First Commissioner of Works, stating that the effect of the colossal equestrian statue of the Duke of Wellington placed on the entrance to Green Park from Piccadilly was 'most objectionable'.

In 1854 a new street development had cleared a space near St. Paul's Cathedral which opened up a view of its south front and the Institute appointed a committee to campaign for the area to remain as an open space. This was followed in 1864 by the appointment of the Metropolitan Improvements Committee set up to examine the whole question of street communication in London and to draw up a petition to Parliament. In 1877 the Metropolitan Board of Works consulted the Institute over the design of the street frontage elevations of new buildings in Northumberland Avenue and the Institute urged that the design of the constituent blocks should be harmonious and designed as parts of an overall scheme. By 1914, in its petition against the L.C.C. (General Powers) (No. 2) Bill, the Institute claimed as part of its responsibility and public duty 'the function of tendering advice to the Government and the (London County) Council on all legislation, bye-laws and regulations pertaining to architecture and building generally' and pointed out that it had been consulted over the Metropolitan Building Act 1855, the Metropolis Managementand Building Acts Amendment Act 1878, the London Building Acts 1894—1908 and the L.C.C. (General Powers) Act 1909 and that its advice had led to many alterations being made to proposals which subsequently became law.

A concern for the preservation and correct restoration of ancient and historic buildings was also shown by the early members. Several of the prizes in the early years were offered for schemes for the restoration of historic buildings in Britain and many of the papers read at General Meetings in the early years were concerned with recent archaeological discoveries in the eastern Mediterranean region and the Middle East. In 1841 an application was made to the Secretary of State for Foreign Affairs, on behalf of the architects of England, to obtain the sculptures from Halicarnassus for the British Museum. In 1845 the Council regretted that the ancient monuments in Westminster Abbey were falling into ruin and noted that the French government was undertaking a restoration scheme for historic monuments. In 1852 the Institute sent a memorial to the Queen, calling her attention to the dilapidated condition of the royal tombs in the Abbey and asking for a royal enquiry. In 1855 the desire to promote the measurement, with technical notes, of historic buildings in Britain led to the setting up of an annual prize medal for measured drawings. In 1862 Sir George Gilbert Scott read a paper at the Institute 'On the conservation of ancient architectural monuments and remains' and subsequently the Institute established a standing Conservation of Ancient Monuments and Remains Committee in 1864. Its main concern was the injury being done to historic buildings (referred to as 'ancient monuments') by ill-judged restoration and in 1865 it published two guide sheets, *Conservation of ancient monuments: general advice to promoters of restorations* and *Hints to workmen engaged on the repairs and restoration of ancient buildings*. It was also concerned about the widespread demolition of historic buildings, campaigned to save several of them and encouraged the collection of measured drawings and other architectural records of them.

In 1886 the Art Standing Committee was established as one of four large departmental standing committees. It immediately took over the work of the Conservation of Ancient Monuments and Remains Committee and also concerned itself with London improvement schemes, such as new streets and new bridges over the Thames, and with the quality of design of contemporary buildings. By the time of its dissolution in 1938 many of its functions had been taken over by other organizations, such as the Society for the Protection of Ancient Buildings and the Central Panels Committee (a joint body sponsored by the Council for the Preservation of Rural England, the RIBA and others) and by other RIBA committees such as the Public Relations Committee and the town planning and housing committees, which had started in 1907 with the appointment of the Development of Towns and Suburbs Committee. Its chairman was Sir Aston Webb and its immediate task was to prepare a scheme for the expansion of the suburbs of large towns on a rational plan, in connection with the Local Government Board bills then in course of preparation. In 1908 this committee changed its name to the Town Planning Committee and in 1920 became the Town Planning and Housing Committee. Aston Webb served as its chairman until 1922 and important figures who played an active part on this committee during the 1920s and 1930s included Professor S. D. Adshead, Professor Patrick Abercrombie and Sir Raymond Unwin.

During the war, a Reconstruction Committee was set up which had several regional branches. This committee produced a series of influential reports between 1941 and 1943. Its work was continued from 1943—1945 by the Central Advisory Committee on National Planning which in 1948 published a report *Plan your Greater Britain*, containing the RIBA's recommendations for a national plan.

In 1962 the work of several separate RIBA committees concerned with housing, town and country planning and design of specific building types came together under the (New) Town Planning Committee and the Town Planning Section of the new Professional Services Department. In 1971 responsibility for this work passed partly to the Intelligence Unit and partly to the Public Affairs Department. In 1975 responsibility for the Institute's work in the field of housing and town planning passed to the Secretary's office and is controlled by two groups of the Policy Committee, the Housing Advisory Group and the Town Planning Advisory Group.

10.1   SOULAGES   COLLECTION   COMMITTEE   REPORT, 1857   23ff
Draft report of the committee appointed to examine the Soulages Collection of majolica ware, Venetian glass, sculptures and other art objects then on display at Marlborough House with a view to memorializing the government to purchase it for the nation.

10.2   CONSERVATION   OF   ANCIENT   MONUMENTS   AND REMAINS COMMITTEE MINUTES, 1864—1886   2 vols
Copies of minutes of meetings, Nov 1864—Mar 1868, and signed minutes of meetings, Mar 1868—Feb 1886, with rough minute book, Jun 1879—Feb 1886.
Subjects : Injury done to many historic buildings by restoration: cases of particular restorations, mostly churches: protection of historic buildings from demolition: threat to some City churches posed by the Union of Benefices Bill, 1876: work of the Palestine Exploration Fund: the ruins at Baalbek: the archaeological excavations at Ephesus: desirability of collecting architectural drawings of historic buildings and restored churches.

(The signed minutes of this committee, Nov 1864—Mar 1868 are in the Early Committees Minutes Series. For information on conservation matters before 1864 *see* 1.2.2 Council Minutes Series. The work of this committee was taken over by the Art Standing Committee.)

10.3   NORTHUMBERLAND AVENUE PAPERS, 1877   1 box

Notes of proceedings at a meeting of the Works and General Purposes Committee of the Metropolitan Board of Works on 11 Jun 1877 at which a deputation from the RIBA Council discussed the question of the principles of architectural design which should be adopted for the blocks of buildings to be erected in Northumberland Avenue, London.

(*See also* Minutes of the Charing Cross and Victoria Embankment Approach Act (Clause 10) Committee, 23 Feb 1877, in 2.2 Special Committees Minutes Series, Vol 1)

10.4   ART STANDING COMMITTEE MINUTES & PAPERS, 1886—
1939   3 vols, 1 binder, 2 boxes
Signed minutes of meetings of the committee, Jun 1886—Jul 1939, and its subcommittees, Feb 1921—Jun 1939, with appended reports and memoranda. Includes correspondence files of the committee's secretary, 1934—1937.

Includes signed minutes of the following subcommittees and conferences:
Exhibition of Architecture Subcommittee, Feb —Mar 1921
Preservation of Whitgift Hospital, Croydon, Joint Conference, Nov 1922—Mar 1923
Exhibition of Architecture and Complementary Arts Subcommittee, Apr —Nov 1923
Craftsmanship Subcommittee, Nov 1924
City Churches Exhibition Subcommittee, Mar —Apr 1925
Elected Members of the Art Standing Committee, Jul 1925—Jul 1937
Garden Drawings Exhibition Subcommittee, Jan —Feb 1926
Photographic Record of RIBA Exhibitions Subcommittee, May 1927
Exhibition of Black and White and Colour Work by Members Subcommittee, Apr —Jun 1928
International Exhibition of Modern Commercial Architecture Subcommittee, Apr 1928—Apr 1929
Exhibition Subcommittee, Oct 1929—Jun 1939
Exhibition Subcommittee, Aerodromes Subcommittee & Organisers of the Permanent Collection General Meeting, Jun 1936
Organising Section of the Exhibition Subcommittee, Oct 1936—Jun 1939
House Exhibition Section of the Exhibition Subcommittee, Jun 1937—Apr 1938
Health and Sport Exhibition Section of the Exhibition Subcommittee, Aug —Sep 1937
Permanent Collection Section of the Exhibition Subcommittee, Nov 1937—Dec 1938
Road Architecture Exhibition Section of the Exhibition Subcommittee, Jul —Oct 1938

Amenities (Country) Subcommittee, Oct 1938—Jan 1939

Amenities (London and Urban) Subcommittee, Oct 1938—Mar 1939

Special Purposes Subcommittee, Oct —Dec 1938

Subjects : Preservation of historic buildings threatened with demolition: conservation of historic buildings: alteration and restoration of historic buildings, particularly churches: quality of design of contemporary buildings: London improvement schemes, such as new streets and new Thames bridges: amendments to London Building Acts: suburban building bylaws: control of elevations: the London Architecture Bronze Medal awards: advisory art committees: rural amenities: RIBA architectural exhibitions: RIBA Honorary Corresponding Members. Particular topics discussed include the restoration of St. Albans Abbey (Vol 1): reform of the Royal Academy of Arts (Vol 1): the Paris Exposition Universelle, 1889 (Vol 1): the Arts and Crafts Exhibition, London, 1890 (Vol 1): plans for the improvement of Piccadilly Circus (Vol 1): the new Admiralty buildings, Whitehall (Vol 1): the Holborn to Strand improvement scheme (Vol 1): the new Vauxhall Bridge and the deputation to the Bridges Committee of the London County Council (Vols 1 & 2): Broadcasting House, Portland Place (Vol 3): the RIBA Centenary Exhibition, 1934 (Binder 1).

(The Art Standing Committee was set up in April 1886 as a result of the report of the Special Committee for Departmental Action *See* 2.2 Special Committees Minutes series, Vol 2. It immediately took over the work of the Conservation of Ancient Monuments and Remains Committee. By 1938 the main functions of the Art Standing Committee had been gradually usurped by other committees and organizations. The Art Standing Committee was reorganized in July 1938 and became the Art Committee with four subcommittees, Amenities (London and Urban), Amenities (Country), Special Purposes, and Exhibitions. Much of its work was continued by the Public Relations Committee.)

10.5 TOWN PLANNING, HOUSING AND SLUM CLEARANCE COMMITTEE MINUTES & PAPERS, 1921—1939   3 vols, 1 binder & 1 box

Signed minutes of the main town planning committee, Aug 1921 — Jul 1939, variously called the Town Planning and Housing Committee, 1921—1922, the Town Planning Committee, 1922—1924, the Town Planning and Housing Committee, 1924—1936, and the Town Planning, Housing and Slum Clearance Committee, 1936—1939, with reports and memoranda. Also included are the minutes of the following subcommittees:

Arterial Roads Subcommittee, Jan —May 1923

Control of Elevations Joint Committee, Nov 1929—Jul 1930

Control of Petrol Filling Stations Subcommittee, Oct 1928

Housing (Financial Provisions) Bill Subcommittee, Jan 1933

Planning of London Subcommittee, Nov 1936—Apr 1939

Preservation of Historic or Architecturally Interesting Buildings, Villages, etc. Subcommittee, Feb 1937—May 1938

Rural England and Statutory Control and Development Subcommittee, Nov 1926—Jan 1927

Slum Clearance, Replanning of Blighted Areas and Housing Standards Subcommittee, Nov 1936—Mar 1939

Teaching of Regional and Town Planning Subcommittee, May 1930

Subjects : Government housing programmes: the Royal Commission on Greater London (Vol 1): local authority town planning schemes (Vol 1 & Binder 1): arterial roads and by-passes (Vols 1 & 2): Thames bridges and riverside development (Vol 1): the London Traffic Bill 1924 (Vol 1): zoning of built-up areas in London (Vols 1 & 2): Charing Cross and Strand improvement scheme (Vol 1): London squares and open spaces (Vol 1): statutory control of development in rural England (Vol 1): control of the design of petrol filling stations (Vol 1): control of elevations (Vol 1): teaching of regional planning (Vol 1): the Town & Country Planning Act 1932 (Vol 1): slum clearance (Vol 2): the Restriction of Ribbon Development Act 1935 (Vol 2): preservation of historic buildings (Vol 2): housing standards (Vols 2 & 3, Binder 1): control of design by local authorities (Vol 3): survey of cottages (Vol 3): planning of London (Vols 2 & 3, Binder 1): the Highway Development Survey (Greater London) 1937 (Vol 3 & Binder 1).

(The first RIBA committee specifically concerned with town planning was the Development of Towns and Suburbs Committee appointed in July 1907 *see* 2.2 Special Committees Minutes series, Vol 4). This became the Town Planning Committee on January 1908, which became the Town Planning and Housing Committee in Nov 1920 *see* 2.2 Special Committees Minutes series, Vols 4—9. In 1922, with the appointment of a separate Housing Committee, it reverted to being the Town Planning Committee. In 1924 it again became the Town Planning and Housing Committee and remained so until 1936 when it absorbed the Slum Clearance Committee and became the Town Planning, Housing and Slum Clearance Committee. It was wound up at the outbreak of war in 1939. Its work was continued after the war by the (New) Housing Committee and the Town and Country Planning Committee, which became the Town and Country Planning and Housing Committee in 1949.)

10.6   NATIONAL HOUSING POLICY JOINT COMMITTEE MINUTES, 1921   1 vol

Signed minutes of meetings, Apr — Dec 1921.
Subject : Promotion of a national housing policy based on personal home
ownership with help from the state.

(Included representatives of the RIBA, the Surveyors Institution, the
Public Utility Societies Committee, building societies and the government.)

10.7   HOUSING COMMITTEE MINUTES, 1922—1924   1 vol
Signed minutes of meetings, Nov 1922—May 1924, with memoranda
and reports.
Subjects : National housing policy: employment of architects for design
of local authority housing: proposed amendment of the Housing Bill
1923: revision of the scale of fees for housing work.

(The first RIBA housing committee was the Housing of the Working
Classes after the War Special Committee appointed in Aug 1917 which
became the Housing Committee in Oct 1917 and met until Feb 1918 *see*
2.2 Special Committees Minutes Series. In 1924 this committee merged
with the Town Planning Committee and became the Town Planning
and Housing Committee.)

TOWN PLANNING COMMITTEE MINUTES, 1922—1924
see 10.5

10.8   ROYAL COMMISSION ON GREATER LONDON COMMITTEE
MINUTES, 1922   1 vol
Signed minutes of two meetings, Apr —May 1922, with report and
summary of RIBA evidence.
Subjects : Evidence by the RIBA to the Royal Commission on Greater
London: desirability of a planning authority: planning of roads, railways,
housing developments and open spaces: desirability of simplifying and
coordinating the building acts and by-laws.

TOWN PLANNING AND HOUSING COMMITTEE MINUTES,
1924—1936
see 10.5

10.9   THAMES   BRIDGES   CONFERENCE   MINUTES,   1926—
1932   1 vol
Signed minutes of the Thames Bridges Conference and its committee,
Dec 1926—Feb 1932.
Subjects : Report of the Royal Commission on Cross-River Traffic in
London: proposed bridge at Charing Cross: preservation of Waterloo
Bridge: the St. Paul's Bridge.

(Included representatives of the RIBA, the Town Planning Institute, the London Society, the Society for the Protection of Ancient Buildings, the Royal Academy, the Architecture Club, the Engineers' Group and the Architectural Association. *See also* in 2.2 Special Committees Minutes Series: St. Paul's Bridge Committee, 1911: Charing Cross Bridge Joint Committee, 1916—1918: St. Paul's Bridge Conference, 1924—1925: and the Waterloo Bridge Conference and Committee, 1925—1926.)

10.10   PANEL SYSTEM AS APPLIED TO ARCHITECTURAL AMENI-
TIES COMMITTEE MINUTES, 1929—1930   1 vol
Signed minutes of meetings, Mar 1929—Jul 1930.
Subject : Scheme to create local panels of qualified architects in a series of zones covering the United Kingdom, who, working on co-partnership principles, would provide small house designs for speculative builders and others.

10.11   CONTROL OF ELEVATIONS JOINT COMMITTEE PAPERS,
1929—1933   1 box
Memoranda, reports and correspondence, Nov 1929—Sep 1933.
Subjects : Best means of ensuring that elevations and siting of new buildings were in harmony with their surroundings and that alterations to existing buildings of interest were efficiently controlled.

(A joint committee of the RIBA and the CPRE. For minutes of this committee, 1929—1930 *see* 10.5 Town Planning, Housing and Slum Clearance Committee Minutes.)

10.12   OLD KING'S HOUSE JAMAICA COMMITTEE MINUTES,
1929—1932   1 vol
Signed minutes of meetings, Jul 1929—May 1932.
Subject : Campaign for the repair and preservation of Old King's House, Spanish Town, Jamaica, damaged by fire in 1925.

10.13   AERODROMES COMMITTEE PAPERS, 1931   3 items
First interim report of the committee, *Town Planning & Aviation*, Mar 1931: paper by Major R. H. S. Mealing *The procedure for the establishment and maintenance of aerodromes*, Jun 1931: 'Notes on visits to some continental aerodromes' (in Netherlands, Germany, Switzerland & France) by John Dower, Secretary to the Committee, Jul —Aug 1931.
Subjects : Siting, layout and architectural design of civil aerodromes.

(This committee included representatives of the Air Ministry, the Ministry of Health, Imperial Airways, the Council for the Preservation of Rural England and aircraft manufacturers in addition to members of the

RIBA. An Aerodromes Exhibition was held at the RIBA in 1932. For further reports *see RIBA Journal* 1932 p470, 1933 p490 and 1934 p627.)

10.14   WATERLOO BRIDGE MEMORIAL PAPERS, 1932   2 boxes
Correspondence, signed statements of protest, copy of petition sent to the Prime Minister, Mar 1932, with background data going back to 1925.
Subject : Destruction of Waterloo Bridge.

(*See also* in 2.2 Special Committees Minutes Series, Waterloo Bridge Conference and Committee, 1925—1926.)

10.15   SLUM CLEARANCE COMMITTEE MINUTES & PAPERS, 1932—1934   1 vol & 1 box
Signed minutes of meetings, Jan 1932—Jun 1934, with memoranda and reports plus background material going back to 1914.
Subjects : Formulation of a national slum clearance and replanning scheme: liaison with organizations concerned with provision of housing for the poor: the Town and Country Planning Act 1932: preparation of plans of slum areas in London: proposed replanning of Bermondsey: the Housing Act 1930 and Improvement Areas.

(Sometimes called the Slum Clearance and Replanning Committee. It merged with the Town Planning and Housing Committee in Jul 1936.)

10.16   CENTRAL COMMITTEE FOR THE ARCHITECTURAL ADVISORY PANELS MINUTES & PAPERS, 1933—1978   4 binders & 2 boxes
Signed minutes of meetings, copies of annual reports, 1960—1976, and some correspondence of the Secretary to the committee, 1965 and 1970—1975. Also minutes of the Panels Subcommittee, Oct —Nov 1933: the Executive Committee, 1934—1937: the Panel Conveners Meetings, 1934—1935: the Housing Publication Subcommittee, 1954—1956, and the Central Panels Subcommittee, 1949—1971.
Subjects : Comprehensive scheme to provide panels of architects and others to advise local planning authorities on the aesthetic merits or faults of planning applications: role of the RIBA Allied Societies in the scheme: the Housing (Rural Workers) Act: deputation to government ministers: Schuster Committee Report: the Town and Country Planning Act 1947: control of elevations: panel reports: General Development Order 1950: relationship with the Royal Fine Art Commission: conservation and repair of old buildings: architectural award schemes: use of suitable building materials: standard of house design: layout of open spaces: preparation of plans by staff of local authorities: siting and design of farm buildings: industrialized building.

(A joint body sponsored by the RIBA and the Council for the Preservation of Rural England and, later, including the Institute of Building and representatives of 14 other bodies. It was originally called the Central Panels Committee and changed its name in 1961. Early members of this committee included Sir Percy Hurd, Professor Patrick Abercrombie, Professor S. D. Adshead and Sir George Pepler.)

10.17   RECONSTRUCTION   COMMITTEE   MINUTES,   1941—1943   1 vol

Signed minutes of the Reconstruction Committee and its General Purposes Committee, Jun 1941—Jan 1943.

Subjects : Planning for national reconstruction after the war: the 'Rebuilding Britain Exhibition' at the National Gallery.

(Allied societies were asked to appoint a regional reconstruction committee in each civil defence region. The Reconstruction Committee appointed several working groups, as follows: Policy, Professional Status and Qualifications, Planning and Amenities, Housing, Building Legislation, Building Technique and Public Relations. For reports of the Reconstruction Committee *see RIBA Journal* and 3.1.2 Executive Committee Minutes Series, Binders 4 & 5.

The work of this committee was continued by the Central Advisory Committee on National Planning, 1943—1945.)

10.18   RECONSTRUCTION   COMMITTEE   PUBLIC   RELATIONS GROUP MINUTES, 1941—1943   1 vol

Signed minutes of the Publicity Subcommittee, which became the Public Relations Group, Jun 1941—Jan 1943.

Subjects : Promotion of public interest in RIBA views on reconstruction and in the architectural profession generally: press and government relations; arrangements for lectures: publicity for exhibitions.

10.19   BUSINESS   BUILDINGS   COMMITTEE   MINUTES,   1942—1944   1 vol

Signed minutes of the main committee, Apr 1942—Feb 1944, and of the Warehouses Subcommittee, Apr 1943, and the Factories Subcommittee, Apr 1943.

Subjects : Research into the planning, design, standardization and equipment of office buildings, shops, stores, warehouses and factories.

(One of the study committees set up under the umbrella of the Ministry of Works' Directorate of Post-War Building. It reported in the first instance to the Policy Committee on Design, whose chairman was Sir Giles Gilbert Scott. For further papers *see* British Architectural Library Manuscripts & Archives Collection, Sir Giles Gilbert Scott Papers.)

10.20   ARCHITECTURAL USE OF BUILDING MATERIALS COM-
MITTEE MINUTES, 1942—1944   1 vol
Signed minutes of meetings of the committee and its subcommittee, Apr
1942—Feb 1944, with copy of final report, Jul 1944.
Subjects : The aesthetics, economics and practice of the architectural
use of various building materials.

(One of the study committees set up under the umbrella of the Ministry
of Works' Directorate of Post-War Building. Its chairman was [Sir]
Edward Maufe, and it reported in the first instance to the Policy
Committee on Design, whose chairman was Sir Giles Gilbert Scott. For
further papers *see* British Architectural Library Manuscripts & Archives
Collection, Sir Edward Maufe Papers and Sir Giles Gilbert Scott Papers.

10.21   (NEW) HOUSING COMMITTEE MINUTES, 1943—1949   1
vol
Signed minutes of meetings, Jun 1943—Jun 1949, with reports and
memoranda.
Subjects : Agricultural workers' cottages: temporary or 'limited life'
housing: prefabrication and standardization: proposed Exhibition of
Domestic Architecture: scale of fees for housing schemes: the American
Housing in War and Peace Exhibition, 1944: government and local
authority housing programmes: RIBA Conference on Housing Layout,
1948.

(This committee continued the work of the Housing Group of the
Reconstruction Committee. In July 1949 it merged with the Town and
Country Planning Committee.)

10.22   CENTRAL ADVISORY COMMITTEE ON NATIONAL PLAN-
NING MINUTES & PAPERS, 1943—1945 & 1948   1 vol & 1
box
Signed minutes of meetings, Aug 1943—Dec 1945, with memoranda and
copy of printed report, *Plan your Greater Britain*, 1948.
Subjects : Development of planning on a national scale: formation of
planning committees by the Allied Societies and appointment of liaison
officers: preparation of area maps and planning schemes: preparation of
a RIBA 'Master plan for Britain'.

(This committee continued the work of the Reconstruction Committee.
In 1945 its work was taken over by the Planning Subcommittee of the
Town and Country Planning Committee.)

TOWN AND COUNTRY PLANNING COMMITTEE MINUTES,
1944—1949
see 10.23

21   Part of the RIBA National Plan, 1948, which was a comprehensive proposal including studies of population, public utility services, industry and agriculture, recreational areas and transport by road, rail and water. (RIBA Archive:10.22   Central Advisory Committee on National Planning Minutes & Papers)

10.23 TOWN AND COUNTRY PLANNING AND HOUSING COM-
MITTEE MINUTES & PAPERS, 1944—1959   2 vols, 2 binders
& 1 box

Signed minutes of meetings of the Town and Country Planning Committee, Dec 1944—Jun 1949, and the Town and Country Planning and
Housing Committee, Jul 1949—Jun 1959, with policy memoranda,
reports and a file of correspondence and memoranda concerning evidence
given by the RIBA to the Royal Commission on Local Government in
Greater London, 1958—1959. Includes signed minutes of the following
subcommittees:

Education Subcommittee, Jan 1945
Housing Subcommittee, Nov 1950—Oct 1951
Legislation Subcommittee, Jan —May 1945
New Towns Subcommittee, Jan 1946
Planning Subcommittee, Jan 1945—Nov 1951
Town Planning Exhibition for Sweden Subcommittee, Nov 1945—Feb
   1946

Subjects : The National Plan (Vols 1 & 2): the County of London Plan
(Vols 1 & 2): control of elevations and design: control of land use: town
and country planning legislation: the Requisitioned Land and War
Works Bill (Vol 1): the War Damage Act (Vol 1): distribution of industry
and development areas (Vol 1): the advisory panel system: new towns
(Vols 1 & 2): control of outdoor advertisements and design of electrical
signs: the architect as town planner (Vol 2 & Binder 1): the RIBA
Distinction in Town Planning (Vol 2 & Binder 1): the City of
Westminster Plan (Binder 1): road design and layout (Binder 1): design
of street furniture (Binder 1): the LCC Development Plan (Binder 1):
social needs and housing (Binder 1): housing costs, subsidies and standards (Binder 1): layout of housing estates (Binder 1): 'non-traditional'
houses (Binder 1): architects' fees for state-aided housing schemes and
for small private houses (Binder 1): improvement of speculative housing
design (Binder 1): motorways (Binder 2): planning of villages (Binder
2): private garages (Binder 2): Royal Commission on Local Government
in Greater London (Box 1).

(This committee continued the work of the pre-war Town Planning,
Housing and Slum Clearance Committee. The Town and Country
Planning Committee was appointed in 1944 and absorbed the (New)
Housing Committee in 1949. This committee was superseded by the
Design and Planning Committee in 1959.)

10.24 SCHOOL DESIGN AND CONSTRUCTION COMMITTEE MIN-
UTES & PAPERS, 1946—1953   2 vols & 1 box

Signed minutes of meetings, Jan 1946—Nov 1953, with memoranda and reports, correspondence and Ministry of Education Building Bulletins.
Subjects : Ministry of Works prefabricated hutting for schools: standard plans for schools: post-war school planning and construction: school building regulations and procedures: design of school furniture: proposed survey of school building.

(For minutes of the School Design and Construction Ad Hoc Committee, Mar —Dec 1945, *see* 2.2 Special Committees Minutes Series, Vol 10)

10.25   HOUSES OF NATIONAL IMPORTANCE COMMITTEE PAPERS, 1949   1 box
Correspondence of the committee, Jan —Jun 1949.
Subjects : Proposed arrangements by government for the preservation, maintenance and use of houses of outstanding historic or architectural interest.

(Appointed to prepare evidence for submission to the Gowers Committee on houses of national importance. For minutes of this committee *see* 2.2 Special Committees Minutes Series, Vol 10)

10.26   HOSPITALS COMMITTEE MINUTES, 1949—1956   1 vol
Signed minutes of the Hospitals Committee, Oct 1949—Nov 1956, and of its General Purposes Subcommittee, Nov 1949—Oct 1951.
Subjects : Draft standard form of agreement between regional hospital boards and private architects: compilation of a register of hospital architects: survey of current research into hospital planning and construction: tendering procedures: relationship between architect and consulting engineer: training of architects in hospital design.

(All the regional hospital boards were represented on this committee. *See also* Post-war Hospital Building Committee, 1946—1949, in 2.2 Special Committees Minutes Series.)

10.27   SMALL HOUSE DESIGNS SCHEME PAPERS, 1955—1962   1 box
Memoranda, reports and copies of minutes of meetings of the scheme's executive committee, Jun 1955—Oct 1956, with progress reports on sales of designs from 1959—1962.
Subjects : Creation and launching of a scheme to provide low cost approved standard designs by chartered architects for small houses: results of RIBA/Ideal Home competition for small house designs, 1958.

10.28   ARCHITECTURAL CONTROL UNDER THE TOWN AND COUNTRY PLANNING ACT 1947 SPECIAL COMMITTEE PAPERS, 1956—1958   1 box

Memoranda, reports, and copies of minutes of meetings, 1956—1958.
Subjects : Extent and manner of the control by statutory planning powers of the design and external appearance of buildings: role of the architect in town and country planning: joint meetings with other professional bodies concerned: methods of control in Denmark, France, Germany, Holland, Sweden and Switzerland: questionnaire sent to County Architects.

(This committee consisted of representatives of the Town and Country Planning and Housing Committee, the Public Relations Committee and the Salaried and Official Architects Committee.)

10.29   DESIGN AND PLANNING COMMITTEE MINUTES & PAPERS, 1959—1962   1 binder & 4 boxes
Signed minutes of the committee, with meetings files and correspondence, Oct 1959—Jun 1962.
Subjects : Major planning issues affecting architects: application of the Town and Country Planning Acts and associated legislation: standards of design of specific building types: central area redevelopment and urban renewal: high buildings: the RIBA Bronze Medal Awards.

(This committee superseded the Town and Country Planning and Housing Committee and was superseded by the Town Planning Committee of the Professional Services Board.)

10.30   EDUCATION IN TOWN PLANNING SUBCOMMITTEE PAPERS, 1959—1962   1 box
Folder of correspondence, copies of reports and memos.
Subjects : General policy of the training of architect-planners: survey of the extent of instruction in town and country planning given in schools of architecture: role of the architect in planning.

(A subcommittee of the Design and Planning Committee.)

10.31   TOWN PLANNING COMMITTEE MINUTES & PAPERS, 1962—1966   1 binder & 2 boxes
Signed minutes of meetings, with memoranda, and correspondence, Nov 1962—Jun 1966.
Subjects : As in Design and Planning Committee Minutes & Papers *see* 10.29

(One of the committees of the newly set up Professional Services Department. Its work was continued by the (New) Town Planning and Housing Committee.)

10.32   TOWN PLANNING SECTION FILES, 1962—1971   11 boxes

Correspondence and data files of the Assistant Secretaries in the Town Planning section of the Professional Services Department, 1962—1971.
Subjects : Role and training of the architect in town planning: urban renewal and central area redevelopment: housing standards: housing layouts: housing subsidies: traffic and road planning: control of elevations: architects' fees for town planning work: Town and Country Planning Act 1968: the Roskill Commission on the siting of the third London airport.

10.33   BUCHANAN REPORT STANDING JOINT COMMITTEE PAPERS, 1963—1965   1 box
Memoranda, reports, correspondence and copies of minutes of meetings, Dec 1963 — Nov 1965.
Subjects : Implications of Prof. Colin Buchanan's report 'Traffic in Towns': discussion of possible research and courses of action to be pursued: the Piccadilly Circus problem.

(A joint committee of representatives of the RIBA, the ICE, the RICS and the TPI.)

10.34   GOSS REPORT STEERING COMMITTEE PAPERS, 1963—1965   2 boxes
Minutes of meetings, Apr 1963 — Jul 1965, with memoranda, reports and correspondence, 1963—1965.
Subjects : Contribution of architects to town planning: training of architects in town planning: visits to schools of architecture and planning, government ministries, central and local government offices and private consultants by Anthony Goss, specially appointed RIBA Research Fellow.

(A subcommittee of the Town Planning Committee.)

10.35   GOSS IMPLEMENTATION COMMITTEE PAPERS, 1964—1967   1 box
Minutes of meetings, Jun —Sep 1965, with memoranda and correspondence, Dec 1964—May 1967.
Subject : Implementation of the Goss Report on architects' contribution to and training for town planning.

(A joint subcommittee of the Town Planning Committee and the Board of Architectural Education.)

10.36   (NEW) TOWN PLANNING AND HOUSING COMMITTEE MINUTES, 1966—1967   1 binder
Signed minutes of meetings, Oct 1966—Jun 1967.

Subjects : As in previous town planning committees, with more stress on housing matters.

10.37   TOWN PLANNING GROUP PAPERS, 1966—1967   1 box
Minutes of meetings, with memoranda, Oct 1966—May 1967.
Subjects : Town planning matters affecting architects.

(A working group of the (New) Town Planning and Housing Committee)

10.38   HOUSING GROUP PAPERS, 1966—1967   1 box
Minutes of meetings, with memoranda, Aug 1966—Jun 1967.
Subjects : Housing matters affecting architects.

(A working group of the (New) Town Planning and Housing Committee)

10.39   COMMERCIAL   DEVELOPMENT   WORKING   GROUP
PAPERS, 1967   1 box
Minutes of meetings, with memoranda, Apr —Jun 1967.
Subject : Planning and architectural quality of commercial development schemes.

(A working group of the (New) Town Planning and Housing Committee)

10.40   PLANNING   PROCEDURES   WORKING   GROUP   PAPERS,
1966—1969   1 box
Correspondence, memoranda and notes of meetings, Aug 1966—Feb 1969.
Subjects : Development plans: planning application procedures: compulsory purchase orders: planning appeal machinery: Town and Country Planning Act 1968: local and district plans; control of advertisements: public participation in planning.

(Started as a working group of the (New) Town Planning and Housing Committee. In 1968 it became a joint RIBA/TPI group. Its work was continued by the Development Control Working Group.)

10.41   HOUSING WORKING GROUP PAPERS, 1967—1971   3 boxes
Correspondence, memoranda, reports, copies of minutes of meetings, 1967—1971.
Subjects : Liaison with the National House Builders Registration Council: MOHLG Cost Yardstick: fees for housing work: comments on the White Paper 'Fair deal for housing': housing conferences: housing associations and societies: design constraints: government housing policy: housing legislation: metric house shells.

(A working group of the Professional Services Board)

10.42   DEVELOPMENT CONTROL WORKING GROUP PAPERS, 1969—1974   2 boxes
Minutes of meetings, Oct 1969—Jun 1971, with copies of reports, memoranda and correspondence, Oct 1969—Mar 1974.
Subjects : Improvement of the existing development control system: discussion of the White Paper 'Local government in England': planning application procedures.

(A joint RIBA/TPI working group. It continued the work of the Planning Procedures Working Group.)

See also in 2.1 Early Committees Series:
Preserving the Open Space adjoining St. Paul's Churchyard Committee, May 1854—Jan 1858
Proposed Purchase of the International Exhibition Buildings at South Kensington Committee, Jun 1863
Metropolitan Improvements Committee, Jan 1864
and in 2.2 Special Committees Minutes Series:
Charing Cross & Victoria Embankment Approach Act (Clause 30) Committee, Feb 1877
Proposed Alterations at Hyde Park Corner and Removal of the Wellington Arch Committee of Council, Jun 1882
Vauxhall Bridge Committee of Council, Feb 1899
Development of Towns and Suburbs Committee, Jul —Dec 1907
Town Planning Committee, Jan 1908—Oct 1920
Records Committee, Jan 1909—Apr 1913
St. Paul's Bridge Committee, Feb —Jun 1911
Lambeth Bridge Committee, Dec 1911—Feb 1912
Westminster Abbey Committee, Dec 1915
Charing Cross Bridge Joint Committee, Mar 1916—Nov 1918
Housing of the Working Classes after the War Committee, Aug —Oct 1917
Housing Committee, Oct 1917—Feb 1918
St. Paul's Bridge Conference, Feb 1924—Jan 1925
Thames Bridges Conference, Apr —Dec 1925
Waterloo Bridge Conference Committee, May 1925—Sep 1926
Bridges and Traffic Committee of the Thames Bridges Conference, Oct —Nov 1925
Waterloo Bridge Conference, Feb —Sep 1926
Public Utility Society Subcommittee, Oct 1932
Rejection of Designs by Local Authorities Committee, Mar 1936
Qualifications of Town Planners Committee, Nov 1942
Town and Country Planning Bill Ad Hoc Committee, Aug 1944
School Design and Construction Ad Hoc Committee, Mar —Dec 1945
Regents Park Terraces Subcommittee, Mar 1946
Post-War Hospital Building Committee, May 1946—Jun 1949

Houses of National Importance Committee, Mar —Apr 1949
and 12.1.4 Women Members Committee Papers, 1931—1942: 11.1.5
Public Relations Committee Minutes, 1933—1967: 11.1.18 Public Affairs Director's Papers, 1967—1975: 11.1.22 Public Affairs Board Minutes & Papers, 1971—1975

Bibliography

1   Donaldson, T. L. 'On the present condition of the royal tombs in Westminster Abbey around the shrine of Edward the Confessor,' and 'Inspection of the royal tombs and other antiquities in Westminster Abbey' *RIBA Proceedings* 1st Series 1851/52 23 Feb, 8 and 15 Mar 1852
2   'Report of the committee appointed by the Council of the Royal Institute of British Architects to examine the Soulages Collection' *RIBA Proceedings* 1st Series 1856/57, 9 Feb 1857 pp81—86
3   RIBA 'Report of the proceedings of the Council in attempting to ensure the safety of certain churches, towers and steeples in the City of London which were considered endangered by the future operations of the Act for the Union of Benefices' *RIBA Proceedings* 1st Series, 1859/60, Aug 1960
4   Scott, George Gilbert, R.A. 'On the conservation of ancient architectural monuments and remains' *RIBA Transactions* 1st Series Vol 12 1861/62 pp65—84
5   RIBA 'Report of the Council on the International Exhibition Building at South Kensington with a view to petitioning Parliament as to its proposed purchase for the nation' *RIBA Proceedings* 1st Series 1862/63, 29 Jun 1863
6   'To the Honorable the House of Commons in Parliament assembled, the humble petition of the Institute of British Architects' *RIBA Notices of Meetings* 1863/64, Feb 1864. Concerns metropolitan improvements (London).
7   RIBA *Conservation of ancient monuments and remains. General advice to promoters of the restoration of ancient buildings. Hints to workmen engaged on the repairs and restoration of ancient buildings* London, RIBA 1865 (Revised edition in 1888)
8   RIBA 'To the chairman, Sir John Thwaites, and other members of the Metropolitan Board of Works' *RIBA Proceedings* 1st Series 1869/70, 20 Nov 1869. Memorial concerning preservation of the open space by the Mansion House as a result of the new street from Blackfriars Bridge to the Mansion House.
9   Stevenson, J. J. 'Architectural restoration: its principles and practice' *RIBA Transactions* 1st Series, Vol 27 1876/77 pp219—235
10 Woodward, William 'London as it is and as it might be' *RIBA Transactions* New Series Vol 2 1885 Nov 16 pp13—65

11   Stevenson, J. J. 'On laying-out streets for convenience of traffic and architectural effect' *RIBA Transactions* New Series, Vol 5 1889 pp89—104

12   Street, William C. 'Some problems of town development' *RIBA Transactions* New Series, Vol 9 1892 pp469—480

13   'The planning and laying-out of streets and open spaces' and 'The responsibilities of a government in the conservation of national monuments'. Papers and discussion in *VIIth International Congress of Architects. Summary of proceedings.* Published by the RIBA as a special supplement to *RIBA Journal* Vol 13 1906 Aug 25

14   RIBA Town Planning Committee 'Town planning: Papers collected by the RIBA Town Planning Committee, I—XXI' *RIBA Journal* Vols 16, 17 and 18, 1908—1911

15   Album of press-cuttings on the Town Planning Conference at the RIBA in Oct 1910. RIBA Library.

16   RIBA *Town Planning Conference, London, 10—15 October 1910. Transactions* London, RIBA, 1911

17   RIBA Town Planning Committee *Suggestions to promoters of town planning schemes* London, RIBA, 1911

18   Unwin, Raymond 'The Town Planning Institute' *RIBA Journal* Vol 21 1913 Dec 6 p79

19   Lanchester, H. V. 'The civic development survey as a war measure' *RIBA Journal* Vol 22 1915 Jan 9 pp107—110

20   RIBA Town Planning Committee 'Architects and town development' *RIBA Journal* Vol 23 1915 Nov 20 pp17—23

21   Niven, David Barclay 'The London Society's work in connection with the London Development Plan' *RIBA Journal* Vol 23 1915 Dec 18 pp57—59

22   Townsend, C. Harrison 'The civic survey' *RIBA Journal* Vol 23, 1916 Apr 1 pp177—180

23   'The control of street architecture' *RIBA Journal* Vol 24 1917 Jun pp177—185

24   RIBA *Housing of the working classes in England and Wales. Cottage designs awarded premiums in the competitions conducted by the Royal Institute of British Architects with the concurrence of the Local Government Board,* London, RIBA, 1918

25   'National housing and national life' *RIBA Journal* Vol 25 1918 Jun pp169—178

26   RIBA *General advice to promoters and others regarding the conservation and repair of ancient buildings* London, RIBA, 1926

27   Abercrombie, Patrick *The preservation of rural England* London, Hodder & Stoughton, 1926

28   Longden, R. T. *Some proposals in reference to the panel system as applied to the architectural amenities of the country* London, Oct 1930

29   RIBA Aerodromes Committee *Town planning and aviation. First (Interim) Report of the Aerodromes Committee* London, RIBA, 1931

30   'Report of the CPRE and RIBA Joint Committee on the Control of Elevations' *RIBA Journal* Vol 39 1931 Nov 7 pp13—16

31   RIBA, CPRE & IOB *The elevation and siting of buildings*. Report of a joint committee. London, 1933

32   RIBA *Report of the Slum Clearance Committee* London, RIBA, 1934

33   Jack, G. H. 'The working of the advisory panels system' *RIBA Journal* Vol 44 1937 Mar 20 pp483—492

34   RIBA Planning of London Subcommittee of the Town Planning, Housing and Slum Clearance Committee 'Sir Charles Bressey's London Plan' *RIBA Journal* Vol 45 1938 Oct 17 pp1016—1018. Report on the Highway Development Survey (Greater London).

35   'The Reconstruction Committee's programme' *RIBA Journal* Vol 48 1941 Jun pp144—145

36   RIBA Reconstruction Committee Planning and Amenities Group 'A national planning authority is essential' *RIBA Journal* Vol 48 1941 Sep pp187—188

37   RIBA Reconstruction Committee Housing Group 'Wartime housing' *RIBA Journal* Vol 48 1941 Sep pp188—190

38   RIBA Reconstruction Committee 'Legislation affecting town and country planning' *RIBA Journal* Vol 49 1942 Feb pp59—62

39   'Anniversary meeting of the Reconstruction Committee' *RIBA Journal* Vol 49 1942 Mar pp77—78. Review of the work of the committee.

40   RIBA Reconstruction Committee 'First general statement of conclusions' *RIBA Journal* Vol 49 1942 Aug pp165—171

41   'Evidence submitted by the RIBA to the Sub-committee on Design of Dwellings of the Central Housing Advisory Committee of the Ministry of Health' *RIBA Journal* Vol 49 1942 Oct pp207—213

42   'The RIBA exhibition "Rebuilding Britain"' *RIBA Journal* Vol 50 1943 Feb pp75—84

43   RIBA London Regional Reconstruction Committee *Greater London. Towards a master plan* 2nd Interim Report, London, RIBA, 1943

44   'House construction of a definite limited life' *RIBA Journal* Vol 50 1943 Oct pp282—283. RIBA memorandum prepared for a subcommittee of the Central Housing Advisory Committee.

45   Ansell, W. H. 'Architecture and civic planning' *RIBA Journal* Vol 50 1943 Dec pp27—29

46   Lanchester, H. V. 'Regional planning and development' *RIBA Journal* Vol 50 1943 Dec pp263—265

47   Kenyon, A. W. 'National planning. The work of the RIBA Central Advisory Committee' *RIBA Journal* Vol 52 1944 Dec pp33—39

48   RIBA Special Committee on Housing Production 'Housing production' *RIBA Journal* Vol 52 1945 Apr pp167—170

49   RIBA Housing Committee 'The conversion of single family houses into flats' *RIBA Journal* Vol 52 1945 Apr pp170—171. Memorandum to a

subcommittee of the Central Housing Advisory Committee.

50 RIBA School Design and Construction Committee. Report *RIBA Journal* Vol 52 1945 Aug pp292—294

51 RIBA Reconstruction Committee 'Town and country planning' *RIBA Journal* Vol 52 1945 Aug pp295—299

52 RIBA School Design and Construction Committee 'Ministry of Works standard hutting for schools' *RIBA Journal* Vol 53 1946 Feb pp131—133

53 RIBA School Design and Construction Committee *School planning and construction* London, RIBA, 1947

54 RIBA Central Advisory Committee on National Planning *Plan your Greater Britain* London, RIBA, 1948

55 *Industrial architecture* London, RIBA, 1949

56 'Qualification of planners' *RIBA Journal* Vol 58 1950 Dec pp62—64. Memorandum of RIBA evidence to the Schuster Committee.

57 *High flats. Report of a symposium held on 15 Feb 1955* London, RIBA, 1955

58 *Office buildings*, London, RIBA, 1956

59 *Family life in high density housing with particular reference to the design of space about buildings. Report of a symposium held on 24 May 1957* London, RIBA, 1957

60 *Design pays. The private enterprise house and its setting* London, RIBA, 1958

61 *Design of teaching laboratories in universities and colleges of advanced technology* London, RIBA, 1958

62 *The living town* London, RIBA, 1959

63 *Methods of tendering for the redevelopment of central areas* London, RIBA & RICS, 1962

64 RIBA Town Planning Committee 'The architect and town planning' *RIBA Journal* Vol 70 1963 Jun pp243—246

65 *Partnership for central area development in the smaller town* London, RIBA, 1964

66 'Frustrations and poor rewards' *RIBA Journal* Vol 71 1964 May pp182—183. Report of an RIBA inquiry into hospital projects.

67 'The Buchanan Report on traffic in towns. A statement of RIBA views' *RIBA Journal* Vol 71 1964 May pp184—186

68 Goss, Anthony, RIBA Research Fellow *The architect and town planning* London, RIBA, 1965. Known as the Goss Report.

69 RIBA Steering Committee for the Goss Report 'An RIBA policy for planning' *RIBA Journal* Vol 72 1965 May pp223—230

70 RIBA & Institute of Physics and the Physical Society *The design of physics buildings* London, RIBA Publications Ltd, 1969

71 GB. House of Commons Estimates Committee Sub-committee B. *Housing subsidies. Minutes of evidence, Monday, 21st April 1969* Evidence by the RIBA & the Institution of Structural Engineers. London, HMSO, 1969

72 'Housing subsidies: the RIBA's evidence to the Estimates Committee' *RIBA Journal* Vol 76 1969 Jun pp224—225

73   'Third London Airport: the RIBA's evidence to the Roskill Commission' *RIBA Journal* Vol 76 1969 Oct pp405—406

74   RIBA Housing Group *Community layouts in private housing* London, National House-Builders' Registration Council, 1970

75   Joint RIBA/FRHB Working Group *The house-builder and his architect* London, RIBA & Federation of Registered House Builders, 1970

76   RIBA Housing Working Group 'Housing: should national and local policies be radically revised?' *RIBA Journal* Vol 77 1970 Jul pp325—327

77   'Housing: is the RIBA working group radical enough?' *RIBA Journal* Vol 77 1970 Aug pp376—378

78   Gundrey, Walter 'Architects in the community' *RIBA Journal* Vol 78 1971 Jan pp21—25. Article on what the RIBA regions and branches were doing in the cause of amenity.

79   RIBA Intelligence Unit 'Architects and the environmental crisis' *RIBA Journal* Vol 78 1971 Oct pp429—430

80   RIBA Intelligence Unit 'The human habitat'. Typescript in RIBA Library, 1972

81   Gordon, Alex 'The President introduces his Long Life/Loose Fit/Low Energy study' *RIBA Journal* Vol 79 1972 Sep pp374—375

82   'Architectural advisory panels' *RIBA Journal* Vol 80 1973 Aug p391. Council paper on RIBA financial support for the Central Committee for Architectural Advisory Panels.

83   'RIBA/RTPI report: development control goes out of control' *RIBA Journal* Vol 80 1973 Aug p394

84   Tyler, Paul 'From donkeys to lions' *RIBA Journal* Vol 81 1974 Jan pp1—2. Reminiscences of his work at the RIBA as Admin. Asst. for Housing and Town Planning and then as Director, Public Affairs Department.

85   Gordon, Alex 'Architects and resource conservation' *RIBA Journal* Vol 81 1974 Jan pp9—12. Article on the Long Life/Loose Fit/Low Energy study.

86   RIBA Secretariat (Patrick Harrison) 'Our national housing crisis' *RIBA Journal* Vol 82 1975 Feb pp14—20

I I
Public relations and promotion of architecture

In this chapter are gathered together the records of various committees, groups and departments concerned with the public image of the Institute; its involvement in public affairs; the education of the public in the appreciation of architecture; promotion of the employment of architects; the regulation and promotion of architectural competitions; the administration of architectural awards and honours; the provision of architectural exhibitions and films; the production of the Institute's publications and the organization of the RIBA sessional programmes of lectures, annual conferences and other events.

Section 1 General, including public relations, press relations and publications

In 1905 the Council decided that the time had come 'to make some attempt to educate the public in the fundamental principles and elementary axioms of architecture' and appointed a special committee which recommended the publication of a pamphlet on architecture and a series of popular lectures illustrated with lantern slides. No further initiative was taken until 1926 when the Executive Committee appointed a special Publicity Committee to consider ways of achieving greater publicity for architecture and for the work of the RIBA. Following this, a standing Public Relations Committee was constituted in 1933 and Eric Bird was appointed as the first Public Relations Secretary. This committee, which stood until 1967, was mainly concerned with press relations, the promotion of lectures, films, sound broadcasts and television programmes on architecture, the publication of publicity pamphlets and the organization of exhibitions and conferences. It was also concerned with housing standards, 'jerry building', slum clearance, the problems of high density housing, the RIBA House Designs Scheme, the control of design by local authorities and the work of the joint RIBA, CPRE and IOB advisory panels.

In 1959 an Information Services Department was set up and Malcolm MacEwen was appointed Chief Information Officer. In 1960 the department changed its name to the Information and Liaison Services Department and became responsible for relations with the Allied Societies and overseas relations in addition to press relations, public relations and publications. In 1965 the department reverted to being the Information Services Department and liaison with the Allied Societies and the administration of awards and competitions became the responsibility of the Central Services Department. Also in 1965, a Press Officer was appointed and Malcolm MacEwen took over the editorship of the *RIBA Journal*. In 1967 a Membership and Public Affairs Department was set up which once again drew together membership relations, overseas relations, press relations, public affairs, competitions and awards. In 1971 membership relations were again separated from public affairs and overseas relations. In 1975 membership relations and public affairs were reunited in a new Membership and Public Affairs Department until, in 1983, a separate Promotions Department was set up which has responsibility for events, awards, competitions, press relations and the Clients Advisory Service.

RIBA publications

The *RIBA Journal* is the main source book of RIBA history and the main organ of publicity for RIBA activities. It started life as *RIBA Transactions*, in which the papers read at General Meetings were published, and a companion series of printed notices and leaflets on RIBA activities which gradually developed into *RIBA Proceedings* .

In the early years, these publications were compiled by the Honorary Secretaries, assisted by the Librarian. In 1885 new and improved series of *Transactions* and *Proceedings* were started, which in 1894 merged to become the *RIBA Journal*. In 1890 direct editorial responsibility had been passed from the Honorary Secretary to the RIBA Secretary, with the Librarian as Assistant Editor. In 1907 George Northover's title was changed from Librarian and Assistant Editor to Librarian and Editor and these functions continued to be combined until 1956. From 1973 the *RIBA Journal* was the responsibility of RIBA Services Ltd until 1981 when a new company, RIBA Magazines Ltd, was set up which now publishes the *RIBA Journal* and a new series of *Transactions* .

Another important source book of RIBA history is the *RIBA Kalendar*, now succeeded by the *RIBA Directory of Members* and the *RIBA Directory of Practices*. The *RIBA Kalendar* was produced annually by the General Office and subsequently the Central Services Department from 1886—1966. It contains lists of members of Council, members of the Allied Societies Conference, members of committees and boards, and staff officials; lists of RIBA members grouped in classes, with dates of their election and serial numbers from 1897 onwards; lists of Allied Societies and their members; lists of past-Presidents, Royal Gold Medallists, RIBA prizewinners and Architecture Bronze Medal winners. It also contains copies of the charters and by-laws and important Institute publications, regulations and codes of practice and conduct; details of examinations with, from 1920, lists of schools of architecture recognized for exemption from RIBA examinations; lists of RIBA publications and, up to 1939, almanacs of RIBA sessional events.

RIBA publications other than the *Journal* and the *Kalendar* were traditionally the responsibility either of the Secretary, the Deputy Secretary, the Chief Clerk of the General Office, or the particular department, board or committee concerned. In 1958 the Public Relations Committee set up a Typography Group which made recommendations concerning the design and stationery of RIBA publications. Since 1969 most Institute publications have been produced by the commercial companies, RIBA Services Ltd, RIBA Publications Ltd, National Building Specification Ltd, and RIBA Magazines Ltd.

11.1.1   RIBA PUBLICATIONS, 1834—1969

Official publications of the Institute before the establishment of the commercial companies RIBA Publications Ltd, National Building Specification Ltd, RIBA Services Ltd and RIBA Magazines Ltd, 1834—1969. They include the following series:

RIBA Proceedings (1st Series), 1834—1884
RIBA Transactions (1st Series), 1835—1884
RIBA Proceedings (New Series), 1885—1893
RIBA Transactions (New Series), 1885—1892
RIBA Kalendar, 1886—1966
RIBA Journal (Third Series) 1894—   (an amalgamation of Transactions & Proceedings)
RIBA Directory, 1966—1972 (successor to the *Kalendar*, now in three parts — *RIBA Directory of Members* , *RIBA Directory of Practices* and *RIBA International Directory of Practices*)

They also include the following: Pamphlets on RIBA examinations and qualifications for membership: RIBA examination question papers: pamphlets on RIBA prizes and studentships: RIBA charters and by-laws: annual reports of the Council: reports of many committees and working groups: lectures and conference speeches (offprints from the *RIBA Journal*): Annual Conference handbooks: RIBA exhibitions catalogues: RIBA Library catalogues: standard forms of articles of pupilage: standard forms of agreement and schedule of conditions for building contracts: fee scales and conditions of engagement: codes of practice and professional conduct: the centenary history *The growth and work of the Royal Institute of British Architects* ed. J. A. Gotch, 1934: the *Handbook of Architectural Practice and Management*, 1st ed. 1965:

publicity pamphlets: guidance pamphlets and leaflets. The first of these guidance pamphlets was *Questions upon various subjects connected with architecture suggested for the direction of correspondents and travellers and for the purpose of eliciting uniformity of observation and intelligence in their communications to the Institute*, 1st ed. 1835, by Thomas Leverton Donaldson, Hon. Secretary. This was followed by *Professional practice and charges of architects, being those now usually and properly made*, 1st ed. 1862; *Conservation of ancient buildings: general advice to promoters of restorations* and *Hints to workmen engaged on the repairs and restoration of ancient buildings*, 1st ed. 1865; and *Suggestions for the conduct of architectural competitions*, 1st ed. 1872.

(RIBA publications have customarily been individually classified and catalogued in the Library's main card catalogue and there is no comprehensive list of them. However, publications were listed in the annual *Kalendar* from 1886 onwards. The collection is not complete. Many of them are cited in the bibliography sections of this guide)

11.1.2   PUBLICITY COMMITTEE MINUTES, 1926—1930   1 vol
Signed minutes of meetings from Jul 1926—May 1930.
Subjects : Methods of obtaining more publicity for the profession and for the work of the RIBA: proposed appointment of a Publicity Secretary and a standing committee.

11.1.3   PRESS   CUTTINGS   COLLECTION,   1926—1961,   1965—
(1982)   7 vols & 38 boxes
Cuttings taken mainly from the national daily and weekly newspapers. Seven albums compiled by the General Office staff, 1926—1961, and 103 subject files compiled by the Press Office staff, from 1965. Some of these files were opened in 1965 but many were not opened until 1972—1973.
Subjects : Architects: architecture, including various building types: the architectural profession: the RIBA: housing: building industry: property development schemes: planning: environment: energy: transport: preservation of historic buildings: registration of architects: UIA Conference 1961: the Royal Gold Medal awards.

11.1.4   RIBA   JOURNAL   EDITOR'S   PAPERS,   1931—1935,   1968—
1970   8 boxes
Correspondence files of E. J. 'Bobby' Carter, 1931 and 1935, and Malcolm MacEwen, 1968—1970: includes copies of the minutes and report of the subcommittee appointed by the Literature Standing Committee to consider changes in the *Journal*, 1931.
Subjects : Contents and form of the *Journal* : contracts with printers and stationers: correspondence with authors.

11.1   General, including public relations, press relations and publications

See also Librarian's Papers Series for correspondence files of E. J. Carter, Librarian and Editor, 1930—1946

11.1.5   PUBLIC   RELATIONS   COMMITTEE   MINUTES,   1933—
1967   7 vols & 4 binders
Signed minutes of meetings, from Jun 1933—Jan 1967, with memoranda and reports.
Subjects : Competitions for slum clearance schemes and designs of speculative housing: 'jerry-building' and housing standards: RIBA centenary celebrations: CPRE, RIBA and IOB Advisory Panels: control of design by local authorities: films, lectures, sound broadcasts and television programmes on architecture: proportion of building work executed by architects: preparation of publicity pamphlets and handbooks: publicity for RIBA exhibitions and conferences: organization of RIBA exhibitions, sessional papers, and events programme (from 1946): the Architect in Industry Conference: the Festival of Britain: public relations in the Allied Societies' areas: formation of a collection of photographs of contemporary architects' work: the RIBA House Designs Scheme ('type plans' for small houses): problems of high density housing: architects' signboards: position of RIBA Probationers and Students: design of RIBA diplomas: education of the public in the built environment.

(The work of this committee was continued by the Membership and Public Affairs Board.)

11.1.6   LECTURES   SUBCOMMITTEE   MINUTES,   1938,   1943—
1948   2 vols
Signed minutes of meetings, Jan —Feb 1938 and Jul 1943—Nov 1948.
Subjects : Promotion of a national system of lectures on architecture for schools and adult audiences: 'Rebuilding Britain' exhibition lectures: proposed travelling exhibitions of photographs: Christmas holiday lectures for children.

(Re-started after the war as a subcommittee of the Public Relations Group of the Reconstruction Committee. The Teaching of Architectural Appreciation in Schools Committee combined with it in 1944 and in 1945 it became a subcommittee of the Public Relations Committee.)

11.1.7   FILMS   SUBCOMMITTEE   MINUTES   &   PAPERS,   1944—
1961   2 vols & 4 boxes
Signed minutes of meetings of the Films, Broadcasting and Television Subcommittee, Nov 1944—Apr 1945, and the Films Subcommittee Nov 1947—Jan 1961, and correspondence with RIBA members, film associations, film distributors, schools and colleges.

Subjects : Publicity for the profession by means of the broadcasting media: promotion of films on architecture and related subjects: setting up the RIBA Film Advisory Panel for the appraisal and grading of films: films for schools: films for architectural students: technical films: public relations films.

(Appointed by the Public Relations Committee in 1944 as the Films, Broadcasting and Television Subcommittee and reconvened in 1947 as two committees, the Films Subcommittee and the Sound Broadcasting and Television Subcommittee.)

11.1.8   SOUND BROADCASTING AND TELEVISION SUBCOM-MITTEE MINUTES & PAPERS, 1947—1961   1 vol & 2 boxes
Signed minutes of meetings from Mar 1955—Mar 1961, with correspondence files, 1947—1958, and record of broadcasts and contacts with the BBC, 1952—1958.
Subject : Publicity for architecture by means of the broadcasting media.

(A subcommittee of the Public Relations Committee. The business of this subcommittee had previously been dealt with by the Films, Broadcasting and Television Subcommittee which became the Films Subcommittee in 1947. The minutes from 1947—1954 are missing.)

11.1.9   PRESS SUBCOMMITTEE MINUTES, 1953—1956   1 vol
Signed minutes of meetings from Feb 1953—Jun 1956.
Subjects : Press relations: RIBA publications: press-cuttings: articles in newspapers & journals, including the *RIBA Journal* .

(Appointed by the Public Relations Committee in 1946. Its minutes from 1946—1952 are missing.)

11.1.10   ALLIED SOCIETIES PUBLIC RELATIONS OFFICERS & RIBA PUBLIC RELATIONS COMMITTEE JOINT MEETINGS MIN-UTES, 1954—1962   1 vol
Signed minutes of meetings, Nov 1954—Nov 1962.
Subjects : Publicizing the profession: travelling and local exhibitions: designing of houses by unqualified persons: the architectural advisory panel system: increased use of architects' services: popularizing architecture in schools: education of the public in the built environment.

11.1.11   RIBA PUBLIC RELATIONS OFFICER'S PAPERS, 1954—1963, 1967—1971   3 binders & 1 box
Typescript news sheets giving details of the Public Relations Committee's activities with guidance notes to the Public Relations Officers of the Allied Societies and copies of minutes of the joint meetings between Allied Societies Public Relations Officers and the Public Relations

Committee and, later, between the regional and branch Public Relations Officers and the Membership and Public Affairs Board, Dec 1954—Jul 1963, Feb 1969—Apr 1971. Also a correspondence file kept by David Crawford, RIBA Public Relations Officer, relating to factory building and the promotion of industrial architecture, 1967—1970.

11.1.12   PUBLIC RELATIONS WITHIN THE PROFESSION SUBCOM-
MITTEE MINUTES, 1956   1 vol
Signed minutes of meetings, Mar —Nov 1956.
Subjects : Proposed changes to the *RIBA Journal* : design and contents of the *Journal* .

(A subcommittee of the Executive Committee)

11.1.13   TYPOGRAPHY GROUP PAPERS, 1958—1965   1 box
Minutes of meetings from Jun 1961—Nov 1965, with correspondence, copies of reports, and memoranda, from 1958—1965.
Subject : Design of RIBA publications and stationery.

(A group of the Public Relations Committee)

11.1.14   JOURNAL COMMITTEE PAPERS, 1959—1965   1 box
Minutes of meetings from Mar 1959—Mar 1965, with correspondence, copies of memoranda and reports, and summary of journal costs, 1947—1964.
Subjects : Role, style and content of the *Journal* : editorial policy: change of editor: financing, administration, printing, etc.: proposed centralisation of all RIBA publications.

CHIEF INFORMATION OFFICER'S PAPERS
see 11.1.15 Information & Liaison Services Department Files, 11.1.4 RIBA Journal Editor's Papers and 12.1.9 Membership Relations Secretary's Papers

11.1.15   INFORMATION AND LIAISON SERVICES DEPARTMENT
FILES, 1960—1967   3 boxes
Correspondence files kept by Malcolm MacEwen, Chief Information Officer: Monica Bromley, Assistant Secretary Information & Liaison: Jill Thomson, Typography & Publications Group: and David Crawford, Assistant Press Officer.
Subjects: RIBA publicity, publications, and meetings.

(This department was also responsible for the preparation of the *RIBA Journal* and for relations with the Allied Societies and with overseas organisations *see* 11.1.4 RIBA Journal Editor's Papers, 12.1.9 Membership Relations Secretary's Papers and 12.2.6 Overseas Relations Secretary's Papers.)

11.1.16   PRESS RELEASES, 1962—1963, 1965—(1977)   4 boxes & 10 binders
Press releases and information sheets issued by the Public Relations Department, 1962—1963, and the Press Office, 1965—(1977).
Subjects : Topical matters relating to architecture, planning, housing, the architectural profession, RIBA affairs, architectural awards.

(Press releases from 1978 onwards can be consulted in the Press Office)

11.1.17   ALLIED SOCIETIES PUBLIC RELATIONS WORKING GROUP PAPERS, 1963—1965   1 box
Correspondence, memoranda, public relations questionnaire returns, copies of minutes of meetings, 1963 — 1965.
Subjects : Functions of Allied Societies' Public Relations Officers and preparation of a handbook to guide them.

(A working group of the Public Relations Committee.)

11.1.18   PUBLIC AFFAIRS DIRECTOR'S PAPERS, 1967—1975   18 boxes
Correspondence files kept by the directors and deputy directors of the Public Affairs Department.
Subjects : Public Affairs Department administration: parliamentary bills: government relations: Prices & Incomes Board and Monopolies Commission: public relations: press relations: salaried architects: local government reorganization: National Health Service reorganization: introduction of VAT on architects' services: environmental issues: town planning and housing issues: airports conferences: European Architectural Heritage Year 1975.

11.1.19   MEMBERSHIP AND PUBLIC AFFAIRS BOARD MINUTES & PAPERS, 1967—1971   4 binders
Signed minutes of meetings, Jul 1967—May 1971, with memoranda and reports.
Subjects : Membership relations: overseas relations: public relations: competitions: awards: nomination service: RIBA conferences and sessional programmes.

(Set up as part of a new structure for the RIBA administration in which the Institute's work was controlled by four departmental boards. In 1971, membership relations were separated from public affairs and overseas relations.)

11.1.20   HOUSING WORKING GROUP PAPERS, 1967—1968   1 box

File kept by the Public Relations Officer, containing copies of minutes of meetings, Jul—Dec 1968, with correspondence, presscuttings, drafts of talks and reports, 1967—1968.
Subjects : A publicity campaign to improve the standard of housing developments: housing cost yardstick: layout and management of housing estates.

(A working group of the Membership and Public Affairs Board.)

11.1.21   MEMBERSHIP AND PUBLIC AFFAIRS BOARD STEERING GROUP PAPERS, 1969—1971   1 box
Copies of minutes of meetings, from Dec 1970—Apr 1971, with reports of working groups for 1969, memoranda and draft of report of the Board to the Council, 1971.
Subjects : Policy and administration of the Board.

11.1.22   PUBLIC AFFAIRS BOARD MINUTES & PAPERS, 1971—1975   3 binders
Signed minutes of meetings, from Sep 1971—May 1975, with memoranda and reports from Sep 1971—May 1973.
Subjects : Overseas relations: awards: competitions: RIBA conferences and sessional programmes: press relations: relations with central and local government: RIBA Clients Advisory Service: salaried architects: radio & television programmes on architecture: concept of an Architecture Centre: control of development: conservation of buildings: environmental education of the public: European Architectural Heritage Year.

See also in 2.1 Early Committees Minutes Series:
Publication of Papers Read Subcommittee, 1862
and in 2.2 Special Committees Minutes Series:
Education of the Public Committee, 1905
Journal and Kalendar Subcommittee, 1912, 1914—1915
Information for Members on RIBA Activities Ad Hoc Committee, 1944—1946

Bibliography

1   White, William H. 'On "The hope of English architecture"' *RIBA Proceedings* 1st Series 1874/75 pp53—77
2   Clarke, T. Chatfield 'Popular criticism as applied to the architectural profession' *RIBA Transactions* 1st Series Vol 28 1877/78 pp240—246
3   Macartney, Mervyn 'The protection of the public', in Shaw, R. N. & Jackson, T. G. (eds) *Architecture: a profession or an art* London, J. Murray, 1892
4   'The education of the public in architecture' Papers and discussion, in *VIIth International Congress of Architects. Summary of proceedings.* Published as

special supplement to *RIBA Journal* Vol 13 1906 Aug 25

5   Locke, William J. Foreword to Cornford, Leslie Cope *The designers of our buildings* London, RIBA, 1921

6   Reilly, C. H. 'Propaganda and publicity' *RIBA Journal* Vol 28 1921 Aug 27 pp547—549

7   RIBA *The architect and his work* London, RIBA, 1924 (Revised edition issued, 1953)

8   RIBA *Architecture in public and secondary schools* London, RIBA [1929]

9   'Architecture in the newspapers' *RIBA Journal* Vol 41 1933 Nov 11 p43

10 Carter, Edward J. 'The RIBA Journal', in Gotch, J. A. (ed) *The growth and work of the Royal Institute of British Architects* London, RIBA, 1934

11 'Architecture and its mirror. The RIBA and the *Builder* ', *Builder* Vol 147 1934 Nov 2 pp767—768

12 Bird, Eric L. 'Architecture in the newspapers' *RIBA Journal* Vol 44 1937 May 22 pp734—736

13 RIBA Reconstruction Committee Teaching of Architectural Appreciation in Schools Committee 'A plea for the teaching of architectural appreciation in schools'. Typescript in RIBA Library, 1942

14 RIBA 'Report of a conference on the teaching of architectural appreciation in schools, January 6th 1944'. Typescript in RIBA Library.

15 'Future Journal policy' *RIBA Journal* Vol 53 1946 Feb pp117—120. Discussion of the future nature of the *RIBA Journal* .

16 Bradbury, Ronald 'The architect and the community' *RIBA Journal* Vol 56 1949 Jun pp366—368

17 'RIBA representation on other bodies' *RIBA Journal* Vol 65 1958 Sep pp383—385

18 'Appointment of Chief Information Officer, RIBA' *RIBA Journal* Vol 67 1960 Mar p150

19 Gordon, Alex 'The Public Relations Committee of the RIBA' *South Wales Institute of Architects Journal* 1961 Jan pp8—10

20 'Evidence by the RIBA to the Committee on the Future of Sound Broadcasting and Television' *RIBA Journal* Vol 68 1961 Feb pp139—140

21 RIBA Public Relations Department 'RIBA public relations' *RIBA Journal* Vol 68 1961 Nov pp511—513

22 RIBA *Choosing an architect* London, RIBA, 1963

23 RIBA *Working with your architect* London, RIBA, 1963 (Revised edition issued in Sep 1964)

24 Donat, John *Architecture in television and broadcasting* London, RIBA, 1964. Report of a research project commissioned by the Broadcasting and Television Subcommittee of the RIBA Public Relations Committee.

25 MacEwen, Malcolm 'From me to you, or some thoughts on the *RIBA Journal* and its readers' *RIBA Journal* Vol 71 1964 Nov pp458—459

26 RIBA Films Group *Films on architecture and environment* London, RIBA, 1965. Summaries and appraisals of films.

27 RIBA *The services of an architect* London, RIBA, 1965 (Revised edition issued 1971)

28 Musgrave, Noel 'Eric Bird, a memoir' *RIBA Journal* Vol 73 1966 Jan p38. Article on Eric Bird who was RIBA Public Relations Officer, 1933—1937 and RIBA Editor 1946—1956.

29 'Advertisement or publicity?' *RIBA Journal* Vol 73 1966 Mar p98

30 RIBA *Notes for Allied Societies' Public Relations Officers* London, RIBA, 1966

31 'The Department of Membership and Public Affairs' and 'Roger Walters. John Carter interviews the chairman of the Membership and Public Affairs Board' *RIBA Journal* Vol 74 1969 Oct pp436—440 and 441—442. Part of a feature article 'Inside the RIBA.'

32 'RIBA Publications Ltd and the RIBA Journal' *RIBA Journal* Vol 74 1969 Oct pp449—451. Part of a feature article 'Inside the RIBA'.

33 RIBA Membership and Public Affairs Department 'The work of the MPA Department' *RIBA Journal* Vol 77 1970 Jul p324

34 RIBA Management Advisory Service *Architects and public relations* London, RIBA, 1971

35 RIBA Membership and Public Affairs Board 'How to advance architecture' *RIBA Journal* Vol 78 1971 Aug pp362—363. Summary of a report to Council advocating radical change in the RIBA's character and a reorganization of the MPA Board and Department.

36 RIBA Public Affairs Department *Information officers' handbook* London, RIBA, 1973

37 Tyler, Paul 'From donkeys to lions' *RIBA Journal* Vol 81 1974 Jan pp1—2. Reminiscences of his work at the RIBA as Admin. Asst. for Housing and Town Planning and then as Director of Public Affairs.

38 Murray, Peter 'Nick Jones: Director of Public Affairs, RIBA' *Building Design* no 202 1974 May 24 p6

39 Saint, Andrew *The image of the architect* Newhaven & London, Yale University Press, 1983

Section 2 Exhibitions

In 1867, 1878 and 1914 the Institute played a leading part in the committees organizing the British section of the architecture exhibitions at the international exhibitions held at Paris. In 1906 the RIBA arranged an exhibition of British architecture at the VIIth International Congress of Architects held in London and another one at the International Exhibition of Architecture and the Decorative Arts in 1909. The Institute did not become seriously interested in mounting regular exhibitions for the public until 1921, when the Exhibitions Joint Committee was appointed. From then on exhibitions were mounted in most years, first at No. 9 Conduit Street and from 1934 at No. 66 Portland Place. The work of this original committee was continued by exhibition sub-committees of the Art Standing Committee and, later, of the Public Relations Committee. In 1931 G. E. Marfell was appointed Exhibitions Secretary and from 1946—1971 John Lander was Exhibitions Officer.

By 1930 a fully-fledged exhibition policy had been worked out and the RIBA started a system of touring exhibitions. Exhibitions were normally first shown at RIBA headquarters in London and afterwards in various centres throughout the country. Much use was made of photographs from the RIBA Permanent Collection, which consisted of standard size mounted photographs of their work presented to the Institute by its members. This later became the Loan Collection of Exhibition Photographs.

From 1946—1961 the Exhibitions Subcommittee of the Public Relations Committee dealt with all exhibitions. It ceased to exist in 1961 when it was decided that future RIBA exhibitions were to be organized by ad hoc working groups. From 1961 the Loan Collection of Exhibition Photographs became the responsibility of the Public Relations Information Group and, sometime in the 1970s, this collection was transferred to the RIBA Library where it formed the basis of the present Photographs Collection. By the late 1960s enthusiasm for RIBA exhibitions and the budgets provided for them had markedly diminished, though large exhibitions mounted by other organizations were often staged at RIBA headquarters. From 1971 when John Lander retired, the RIBA no longer had an Exhibitions Officer. Since 1972, when the RIBA Drawings Collections moved to No. 21 Portman Square, regular exhibitions have been mounted in the Heinz Gallery by the Drawings Collection staff and by others. The letting of exhibition space at No. 66 Portland Place is organized by the Events Office.

See also Appendix 5. Archive of the Architectural Union Company, 1857—1914.

11.2.1   PARIS EXHIBITION (1867) ARCHITECTURAL COMMITTEE
PAPERS, 1867   1 item
Printed catalogue of the architectural designs and models, photographs and 'artistic manufactures' exhibited at the Paris Exhibition, 1867.

(A committee composed of members of the RIBA, the Ecclesiological Society, the Architectural Association, the Architectural Museum and several provincial architectural societies, and chaired by A. J. Beresford Hope, PRIBA.)

11.2.2   EXHIBITIONS JOINT COMMITTEE MINUTES & PAPERS,
1921—1927   1 vol & 1 box
Signed minutes of meetings, from Jun 1821—Mar 1927, with correspondence, May 1921—Apr 1925.
Subjects : RIBA Exhibition of Contemporary British Architecture, 1922:
British Empire Exhibition (1924), exhibition of architecture: RIBA
Exhibition of Dominion and Colonial Architecture, 1926: RIBA Exhibition of Modern Architecture, 1927: travelling exhibitions of British
architectural work in Australia: proposed RIBA exhibition of Indian
and Burmese architecture.

(A joint committee of three delegates from each of the four departmental
standing committees, Art, Literature, Practice and Science, and three
Council members. Its work was taken over by the Exhibition Subcommittee of the Art Standing Committee.)

11.2.3   EXHIBITIONS RECORD FILES, 1921—1972   24 boxes
Record of over 200 exhibitions, including RIBA exhibitions at RIBA
headquarters and elsewhere, exhibitions to which the RIBA made a
contribution, and non-RIBA exhibitions held at RIBA headquarters.
Things to be found in these files include catalogues, photographs of
exhibits, layout plans, posters, official invitations, press releases, press-
cuttings, correspondence, copies of minutes of meetings of exhibition
working groups. Some files contain most of these things, but many have
only one or two items.

11.2.4   EXHIBITIONS OFFICER'S PAPERS, 1931—1971   4 boxes
An Exhibition Record Book, 1931—1934 and 1946—1971, and corre-
spondence files concerning exhibitions policy, administration of exhibi-
tions and production of posters, 1932—1971, kept in the early years by
G. E. Marfell, Secretary to the Exhibition Subcommittee, and then by
John Lander, Exhibitions Officer.

11.2.5   EXHIBITIONS SUBCOMMITTEE OF THE ART STANDING
COMMITTEE PAPERS, 1935—1939   1 box
A file relating to the RIBA annual exhibitions, kept by G.E. Marfell,
Secretary to the committee, containing correspondence, memoranda,
reports, copies of minutes of meetings.

(At this time two exhibitions were organized each year, a small one in
the autumn and a large one in the spring. After being shown at the
Institute headquarters they went on tour in the provinces, being shown
at museums and art galleries. For minutes of this committee and its
various sections *see* 10.4 Art Standing Committee Minutes Series.)

11.2.6   EXHIBITIONS EXPENSES JOURNAL, 1937—1946   1 vol
Record of all expenses incurred in connection with RIBA exhibitions,
Feb 1937—Jun 1946

11.2.7   EXHIBITIONS   SUBCOMMITTEE   OF   THE   PUBLIC
RELATIONS COMMITTEE MINUTES, 1943—1961   2 vols &
1 binder
Signed minutes of meetings, Oct 1943—May 1950 and Aug 1956—Apr
1961.
Subjects : RIBA exhibitions policy: RIBA travelling exhibitions: RIBA
participation in outside exhibitions: Building Now Exhibition, 1940:
Schools Exhibition, 1947: Industrial Architecture Exhibition, 1948:
Italian Architecture, 1949: Danish Architecture Exhibition, 1950: preparation for the Festival of Britain, 1951: Subtopia Travelling Exhibition,
1957

(Originally appointed by the War Executive Committee, it became a
subcommittee of the Public Relations Committee in 1945. In 1950 it was
decided that the Exhibitions Subcommittee was overloaded with work
and that RIBA exhibitions were to be organized by separate working
groups. The subcommittee was re-appointed in 1956 and ceased to exist
in 1961 when it was decided that in future exhibitions were to be
organized by ad hoc working groups. The work of this committee on the
RIBA Photographs Collection was continued by the Public Relations
Information Group.)

11.2.8   EXHIBITIONS ATTENDANCE BOOKS, 1946—1970   5 vols
Signatures of those attending RIBA exhibitions, Sep 1946—Nov 1947
and Feb 1955—Sep 1970, with titles and dates of exhibitions.

11.2.9   PUBLIC RELATIONS INFORMATION GROUP MINUTES,
1961—1968   1 binder
Minutes of meetings, Oct 1961—Apr 1968.
Subjects : RIBA photograph collections: RIBA Loan Collection of
Exhibition Photographs: exhibition of photographs of RIBA Architecture
Awards.

See also in 2.2 Special Committees Minutes Series:
Architectural Gallery at the Royal Academy Committee, 1869
Paris Exhibition Committee, 1877—1878
Hulot Drawings Committee, 1908
International Exhibition of Architecture and the Decorative Arts Committee,
    1908—1909
Royal Academy Exhibition Committee, 1909
Paris Exhibition (1914) Joint Committee, 1914—1915

and 10.4 Art Standing Committee Minutes Series, 1886—1939: 11.1.5 Public Relations Committee Minutes Series, 1933—1967: 11.1.10 Allied Societies Public Relations Officers & RIBA Public Relations Committee Joint Meetings Minutes, 1954—1962

Bibliography

1   RIBA 'Paris Exhibition Architectural Committee. Report to the Council' *RIBA Proceedings* 1st Series 1867/68, 17 Feb 1868
2   'Public Education in architecture. The exhibition policy of the RIBA' *RIBA Journal* Vol 42 1935 Oct 12 pp1145—1147

[Catalogues of most RIBA exhibitions are available in the Library]

Section 3 Awards and honours

The Royal Gold Medal awards, the Architecture Bronze Medal awards and the RIBA Distinction in Town Planning were administered by separate committees, serviced by the staff of the General Office, until the institution of an Awards Committee and the appointment of an Awards Secretary as part of the Information and Liaison Services Department in 1962. This Awards Committee also took over from the Secretary and the General Office staff the function of advising on the Ministry of Housing and Local Government Housing Medal awards, the Civic Trust Amenity Awards and the administration of RIBA Honorary Membership awards. In 1965 administration of awards was transferred to the Central Services Department, the successor to the General Office, and in 1967 to the new Membership and Public Affairs Department. The Awards Committee then became known as the Awards Group. In 1978 the Awards Office was moved to Birmingham where it shares the RIBA West Midlands Regional Office.

The Royal Gold Medal for architecture

At the Ordinary General Meeting on 20 April 1846 the President announced that Queen Victoria was to provide a gold medal each year to promote 'the useful purposes of the Society'. The Council decided to hold a design competition for the junior members, the winner of which would be given not only the medal but also a period of study in Rome. A competition was held in 1847 but none of the competitors complied exactly with the conditions and the medal was not awarded.

22 Obverse and reverse of the Royal Gold Medal for architecture (diameter 56 mm) awarded in 1851 to T. L. Donaldson. The medal is an annual award by the monarch to a person recommended by the RIBA and was first awarded in 1848. William Wyon RA was commissioned by the Keeper of the Privy Purse to execute the medal and he designed the obverse, showing the reigning monarch's head, to which Prince Albert added the inscription. The reverse was designed by Ambrose Poynter, with some modification by Wyon. The design of the medal has since remained substantially the same, with the necessary modifications on the accession of a new monarch. The name of the Royal Gold Medallist and the year is engraved on the rim. It is struck by the Royal Mint and presented with a royal blue ribbon (British Architectural Library Medals Collection)

At the OGM on 26 April 1847 it was announced that the Queen had agreed that the royal medal should be awarded to 'such distinguished architect or man of science of any country as may have designed or executed any building of high merit or produced a work tending to promote or facilitate the knowledge of architecture or the various branches of science connected therewith'. The General Meeting decided in February 1848 to award the first Royal Gold Medal to Charles Robert Cockerell and William Wyon was commissioned by the Keeper of the Privy Purse to execute the medal. He designed the obverse, showing the monarch's head, to which Prince Albert added the inscription 'Victoria Regina cudi iussit' and the reverse was designed by Ambrose Poynter, with some subsequent modification by Wyon. The design of the medal has since remained substantially the same, with the minimum of necessary modification on the accession of a new monarch.

It became the custom to award the medal to British subjects for two consecutive years and to a foreigner every third year. In 1883 a special committee of the Council reported on the history and procedure of the Royal Gold Medal awards. It pointed out that of the 35 medal winners, 33 had been RIBA members, 23 were British and 12 foreign, 21 were architects and 14 were either writers on architecture or archaeologists. This special Committee recommended the setting up of a standing Royal Gold Medal Committee of the Council and outlined the procedure this committee should follow. As both William Butterfield and John Ruskin had declined to accept the medal, it also recommended that it should first be ascertained that the nominee of the Council was willing to accept the honour before the nomination was announced.

The custom of awarding this medal has been continued by successive monarchs and in 1940 the following addition was made to the qualifying clause 'or whose life work has promoted or facilitated the knowledge of architecture or the various branches of science connected therewith'. In 1966 it was decided to broaden the terms of the award to enable it to be given to a group and not just to an individual. In 1970 some procedural changes were made: the Royal Gold Medal Committee was to be replaced by a Royal Gold Medal Jury nominated by the President and re-appointed each year, and nominations for the award of the medal were to be invited from the entire corporate membership of the Institute and not just from members of the Council as previously.

(For a list of Royal Gold Medal winners *see RIBA Directory of Members*)

Architecture Bronze Medal

The idea of bestowing awards for street architecture, to encourage excellence of design and increase public interest in architecture, started before the First World War with the London Society's Prize and was then discussed by the (RIBA) Street Architecture Committee in 1920. In 1922 a jury was appointed by the Council to draw up conditions for the award of medals for street architecture in London and to select an artist to design the medal and the plaque which was to be fixed to premiated buildings. The architect of an award-winning building received a bronze medal and a diploma and the building owner received a plaque and a replica of the medal. The medal was designed by Langford Jones and the preparation of a design for the plaque was delegated to the Art Standing Committee. London was at first defined as the area within a radius of four miles from Charing Cross but was later extended to include the counties of London and Middlesex. The award was for a street facade, later extended to include the whole building, as opposed to churches or other prominent public buildings. Any RIBA member could nominate a building which had been built during the previous year, later extended to three years, for consideration by the jury and from 1933 lists of buildings eligible for consideration were also prepared by the Library staff. Early juries consisted of three architects, a Royal Academician and an Honorary Fellow of the RIBA and were expanded in 1926 by the addition of a member of the LCC, a representative of the City of London and a representative of the London boroughs. Architects who were awarded the medal were asked to contribute a photograph of the award-winning building to the RIBA Collection of Exhibition Photographs.

The scheme for the award of bronze medals in the areas of the Allied Societies in the United Kingdom and overseas was instituted in 1923, the first award by an Allied Society being made in 1927 by the Royal Institution of Architects in Scotland. The medals, diplomas and plaques were provided by the RIBA and one RIBA representative, who normally acted as chairman, was appointed to serve on each jury. The award was not made in any one area more often than once in three years and was given to one building only per area. Certain changes in procedure were made in 1962 when it was decided to combine the London and provincial schemes, reduce the number of awards and allocate them in regions rather than in areas of individual Allied Societies. It was also decided that a building did not have to front on to a street or road or be accessible to the public to be eligible for an award and that the award could be made for a group of buildings not just for individual buildings. Overseas schemes for the RIBA bronze medal terminated in 1965 and in 1966 the United Kingdom bronze medal award scheme was replaced by the RIBA Architecture Awards.

(For a list of Architecture Bronze Medal winners *see RIBA Directory of Members* 1965)

RIBA Architecture Awards

Since 1966 these have been awarded annually to a building or group of buildings judged best of those completed in the previous two years in each of eleven regions of the United Kingdom. The award takes the form of a plaque to be attached to the winning building together with diplomas presented to the architects, the building owner and the contractor. The plaque was designed by Robert Welch and the diploma by Michael Stribbling. A member of the RIBA may nominate one or more buildings, including his own, and all nominations are sent to the Regional Awards Secretary in whose region the buildings are situated. Architects of nominated buildings must be registered architects and RIBA members and if a firm is

23   Obverse and reverse of the RIBA Street Architecture Medal (diameter 63mm), subsequently known as the Architecture Bronze Medal, awarded 1922 — 1964. The medal was designed by Langford Jones and the reverse shows stonemasons at work with St. Paul's Cathedral in the background. The architect of an award-winning building received the medal and a diploma and the building owner received a plaque and a replica of the medal. The award was intended to encourage excellence of design and increase public interest in architecture. It was replaced in 1966 by the RIBA Architecture Awards. (British Architectural Library Medals Collection)

nominated at least one of the partners must be a registered architect and a RIBA member. A first-stage jury of RIBA members is appointed in each award region and makes a short list of at least three and not more than five buildings. A second-stage jury is then appointed to consider the short-listed buildings, visit them and recommend for an award the building they consider to be the best. The chairmen of all the second-stage juries then meet with the Awards Group to review the recommendations before making the final proposals to the RIBA Council. The RIBA mounts annual exhibitions of the winning buildings and their names are published in the *RIBA Directory* .

RIBA Honorary Membership

Originally there were two classes of honorary members, Honorary Fellows and Honorary Members. Honorary Fellows were noblemen or gentlemen who were expected to contribute twenty-five guineas to the Institute's funds. Honorary Members were persons, other than British architects, eminent for their architectural works. They were not expected to make a financial contribution and, if they lived abroad, were called Honorary & Corresponding Members (*see* 1.2.3 Letters to Council Series, 1835—1907, for many letters written by Honorary and Corresponding Members *and* Chapter 5, Section 4 for the record series containing honorary members' nomination papers.)

In 1877 the Institute, having decided that from 1882 all RIBA Associates must have passed a professional examination before election, introduced a class of Honorary Associates who were to be persons engaged in the study but not the practice of civil architecture who could contribute to the advancement of professional knowledge. Under the 1971 Charter, the class of Honorary Associates ceased and all surviving members of that class became Honorary Fellows.

In 1978 the class of Honorary & Corresponding Members was closed and foreign architects formerly eligible for that class became eligible for election to the class of Honorary Fellows. The administration of RIBA Honorary Membership has successively been the concern of the Honorary Secretaries, the Secretary, the Art Standing Committee, the Foreign Relations Committee, the Overseas Relations Secretary, the Awards Secretary and the Awards Office.

(Honorary Members are listed in *RIBA Transactions*, 1835—1849, *RIBA Proceedings*, 1849—1885, the *RIBA Kalendar*, 1886—1965, and the *RIBA Directory*, from 1966)

RIBA Distinction in Town Planning

The RIBA Distinction in Town Planning was set up in 1945 in response to a demand from some members for a qualification in town planning more prestigious than the RIBA Diploma in Town Planning, awarded by the RIBA and Town Planning Institute's Joint Examination Board, and more suited to established architects with existing attainments in this field. In the early years it was possible to apply for it, write a thesis and take an oral examination but later on candidates had to be nominated by at least three sponsors who were RIBA members and who had to submit details of their candidate's qualifications and experience and evidence of their planning work.

(Holders of the RIBA Distinction in Town Planning are listed in the *RIBA Directory of Members* 1965).

11.3.1 LONDON ARCHITECTURE BRONZE MEDAL JURY MINUTES, 1922—1962   1 vol
Signed minutes of meetings of the juries, Feb 1922 — Apr 1962, with lists of nominated buildings and names of the architects.
Subjects : Conditions of the award: design of the medal, plaque and diploma: extension of the scheme to the provinces: consideration of nominated buildings: award of the New Zealand Institute of Architects' Gold medal from 1927—1940.

(*See also* the administrative files of the Chief Clerk, in 5.1.1 General Office' Papers Series. The New Zealand Institute of Architects Gold Medal was a similar type of award, the winners of which received a medal from the New Zealand Institute of Architects and a diploma signed by the RIBA jury. The Bronze Medal awards scheme was suspended during the Second World War. Award winners are listed in the *RIBA Kalendar*. The work of the Bronze Medal Jury was continued by the Awards Committee.)

11.3.2 * ROYAL GOLD MEDAL COMMITTEE MINUTES & PAPERS, 1927—1962   1 vol & 4 boxes
Signed minutes of meetings, Jan 1927 — Nov 1961, with lists of nominated architects and names of nominators. Also, files kept by the Secretary, RIBA, who was Secretary to this committee, from Oct 1940— May 1962, containing correspondence and nominations by Council members.

(The work of this committee was taken over by the Awards Committee. For the minutes of Royal Gold Medal Committees of Council, 1882— 1888 and 1914—1926 *see* 2.2 Special Committees Minutes Series. For particulars of Royal Gold Medal awards before 1882 *see* 1.2.2 Council Minutes Series *and* 1.2.1 General Meetings Minutes (Early Series). For elections of Royal Gold Medal winners up to 1930 *see* 1.2.7 Annual & Special General Meetings Minutes Series *and* 1.2.6 Ordinary General Meetings Minutes Series for 1895—1897 & 1906. For other correspondence concerning Royal Gold Medal awards *see* 4.1.3 Secretary's Correspondence: 11.3.8 Awards Secretary's Papers and 4.2.2 President's Correspondence Series. Royal Gold Medal winners are listed in the *RIBA Kalendar* and the *RIBA Directory* .)

* Access at the discretion of the Archivist

England: and under these circumstances, I cannot but feel that it is no time for us to play at adjudging medals to each other; and must, for my own poor part, very solemnly decline concurrence in such complimentary formalities, whether as they regard others or myself. For we have none of us, it seems to me, any right remaining either to bestow or to receive honours; and least of all those which proceed from the Grace, and involve the Dignity, of the British Throne.

May I beg Sir, that in communicating my reply to the Members of the Institute you will convey to them at the same time the assurance of my personal respect; and of the profound regret with which I find myself compelled to decline their intended kindness & courtesy. I have the honour to be,
Sir
Your obedient servant,
John Ruskin.

24   Part of a letter by John Ruskin, 20 May 1874, to Sir George Gilbert Scott, President RIBA, declining to accept the Royal Gold Medal. The main reason he gave for this action, which came as a tremendous shock to the Institute, was his distress at the widespread neglect, destruction and bad restoration of historic buildings. In a second letter he said 'The public, as a body, scarcely know the difference between good architecture and bad. On which — I must ask further — as a body, does the Institute? If it does, why has it not taught the public? If it does not, shall I take the medal implying the recognition of its authority?' (RIBA Archive:1.2.3   Letters to Council Series)

WESTERN UNION
(THE WESTERN UNION TELEGRAPH COMPANY)
CABLEGRAM

ANGLO-AMERICAN TELEGRAPH Co., LD.   CANADIAN NATIONAL TELEGRAPHS.

RECEIVED AT 151, WARDOUR STREET, LONDON, W.1. (Tel. No. Gerrard, 1257.)

FORM No. 6B.

PHOENIXARIZ 36 17

NLT MACALISTER

66 PORTLAND PLACE LONDON=

=YOU PROPOSE A GREAT HONOR I ACCEPT GRATIFIED THAT DURING

THIS TERRIFIC WAR ENGLAND CAN THINK OF HONORING AN ARCHITECT

A CULTURE LIKE THAT CAN NEVER LOSE=

=FRANK LLOYD WRIGHT....

Please send your Reply Via Western Union   *You may telephone us for a messenger*

25   Cablegram to the RIBA Secretary from Frank Lloyd Wright, 18 December 1940, accepting the offer of the Royal Gold Medal award for 1941. (RIBA Archive:11.3.2   Royal Gold Medal Committee Papers Series)

NEW ZEALAND INSTITUTE OF ARCHITECTS GOLD
MEDAL AWARDS 1927—1940
see 11.3.1

11.3.3 RIBA DISTINCTION IN TOWN PLANNING PRESIDENT'S
SUBCOMMITTEE MINUTES, 1945   1 vol
Signed minutes of meetings, Apr —Jun 1945.
Subject : Method of award of a diploma in town planning.

11.3.4 *RIBA DISTINCTION IN TOWN PLANNING EXAMINERS
MINUTES, 1945—1950   1 vol
Signed minutes of the panel of examiners, Jul 1945—Feb 1950.
Subjects : Applications from candidates to be examined: subjects of their
theses: arrangements for oral examinations: results, i.e. approved or not.

* Access at the discretion of the Archivist

11.3.5 *RIBA DISTINCTION IN TOWN PLANNING COMMITTEE
PAPERS, 1948—1963   2 boxes
Correspondence, copies of minutes, Jan 1948—Jun 1963: duplicates of
certificates, 1957—1961: candidates' files, 1954—1960.
Subject : Award of the RIBA Distinction in Town Planning.

(For minutes of this committee, 1947—1962 *see* 7.1.2 Board of Architectural Education Committees Minutes Series. This committee became a
subcommittee of the Awards Committee in 1962. Names of those awarded
this distinction, 1947—1964, are listed in the *RIBA Directory*, 1965.)

* Access at the discretion of the Archivist

11.3.6 BRONZE MEDAL AWARDS SUBCOMMITTEE PAPERS,
1961—1964   2 boxes
Correspondence, reports, copies of minutes of meetings, 1961—1964.
Subject : Revision of the Bronze Medal awards for architecture, schemes
for London and the areas of the Allied Societies.

(This subcommittee started as a subcommittee of the Design and Planning
Committee and became a subcommittee of the Awards Committee in
1964.)

11.3.7 AWARDS COMMITTEE MINUTES, 1962—1967   2 vols
Signed minutes of meetings of the committee, from Nov 1962—May
1967, and of the following subcommittees:
RIBA Distinction in Town Planning Committee, Apr 1962—Jun 1963.

London Architecture Bronze Medal Committee, Mar 1963—Jun 1964
Royal Gold Medal Committee, Nov 1963—Feb 1964
Bronze Medal Awards Subcommittee, 23 Sep 1964
Subjects : Awards of the Royal Gold Medal, the RIBA Distinction in Town Planning, and the Bronze Medals for Architecture: re-organization of the bronze medal award scheme: RIBA Architecture Awards: system of awards for young architects: RIBA Honorary Membership.

(The work of this committee was continued by the Awards Group)

11.3.8   * AWARDS SECRETARY'S PAPERS, 1962—1974   17 boxes
Files kept by the Awards Secretary, containing correspondence, copies of minutes of meetings of the Awards Committee, memoranda and reports, nominations for awards, particulars of candidates, arrangements for presentations, etc., 1962—1974.
Subjects : the Royal Gold Medal: the RIBA Distinction in Town Planning: RIBA Honorary Membership: the London Architecture Bronze Medals: the RIBA Architecture Awards: housing awards: Civic Trust awards, and many other awards with which the RIBA is concerned.

(Correspondence files continuing this series may, at the discretion of the Awards Secretary, be seen by prior appointment at the Awards Office at Birmingham, where there is also a series of press releases and brochures concerning awards from 1967 onwards.)

* Access at the discretion of the Archivist

11.3.9   * AWARDS GROUP MINUTES, 1968—   8 binders
Signed minutes of meetings, from Mar 1968 onwards, with memoranda and reports from the regions. Included are minutes of meetings of the Awards Group with the Chairman of Second Stage Juries for the RIBA Architecture Awards.
Subjects : RIBA awards and honours, e.g. RIBA Honorary Fellowship, RIBA Distinction in Town Planning, RIBA Architecture Awards: awards and honours in which the RIBA participates either by donating money, advising, or appointing assessors, e.g. the Royal Gold Medal, government housing design awards, Civic Trust awards, Financial Times Industrial Architecture awards, Concrete Society awards, Structural Steel Design awards, Rome Scholarship in Architecture, etc.: information on international prizes and awards.

(A group of the Membership and Public Affairs Board, it continued the work of the Awards Committee.)

* Access at the discretion of the Awards Secretary, by prior appointment with the Awards Office, Birmingham

11 Public relations and promotion of architecture

See also in 2.2 Special Committees Minutes Series:
Classes of Membership Committee (Hon. Associateship), 1920
Honorary Members Committee, 1910 & 1915
London Society's Prize Subcommittee, 1913—1914
Royal Gold Medal Committee, 1883—1888, 1909, 1914—1926
Street Architecture Committee, 1920
and 11.1.3 Press Cuttings Collection, 11.1.16 Press Releases, 11.1.19 Membership
and Public Affairs Board Minutes and 11.1.22 Public Affairs Board Minutes

Bibliography

1 RIBA 'Report of the Council on the subject of the award of the Royal Gold
  Medal' *RIBA Proceedings* 1st Series 1866/67, 28 Jan 1867
2 RIBA *The Royal Gold Medal. Notes prepared for the use of the special
  committee of the Council appointed to consider the question of the Royal Gold
  Medal, to report the past history thereof and to submit their recommendations
  for the future proceedings of the Council in relation to its appropriation.* Printed
  for circulation to Council members, 15 Jan 1883
3 Harris, John 'The Ruskin Gold Medal controversy' *RIBA Journal* Vol 70
  1963 Apr pp165—167
4 'New RIBA Architectural Awards system starts' *RIBA Journal* Vol 72 1965
  Nov pp527—528
5 *RIBA Architectural Awards* London, RIBA, annual publication 1966—   .
6 Barnard, Roger 'Improving the awards system' *RIBA Journal* Vol 77 1970
  Jan pp34—35
7 Strong, Judith 'Tenth anniversary for the awards scheme' *RIBA Journal* Vol
  82 1975 Jul/Aug pp6—8
8 *Awards for architects, building and the environment* London, RIBA, 1976
9 Games, Stephen 'The awards system — its successes and failures' *RIBA
  Journal* Vol 87 1980 Aug pp36—37
10 Osley, Julian 'Royal Gold Medallists 1848—1984' *RIBA Journal* Vol 91 1984
  May pp73—143

Section 4 RIBA sessional programmes, conferences and events

Sessional programmes of lectures and other events

It has been the custom from the beginning for learned papers to be read at General
Meetings of the Institute and, in addition to these, regular features of RIBA sessions
include the Inaugural Address of the President, the Annual Discourse and the

Royal Gold Medal presentation. The RIBA session now runs from September to July but in earlier years it ran from November to June. During the first 35 years the papers read at meetings were organized by the Honorary Secretaries with the help of the Librarian and, from 1862, of the Assistant Secretary. With the exception of the periods 1842—1849 and 1965—1981, most sessional papers were printed in either *RIBA Transactions* , *RIBA Proceedings*, the *RIBA Journal,* or *Transactions* .

From 1873—1884 the sessional programmes were organized by a Sessional Papers Committee; from 1886—1907, by the Literature Standing Committee; from 1908—1945 by a separate Sessional Papers Committee; from 1946—1964 by the Public Relations Committee; and from 1964—1967 by the Conference and Sessional Programme Committee. In 1967 four departmental boards were set up, one of which was the Membership and Public Affairs Board which took over the responsibility for organizing the sessional programmes, and since 1971 they have been the responsibility of the Public Affairs Department. Since the appointment of a permanent Events Secretary and support staff in 1971, to organize both the sessional programmes and the annual conferences, the sessional programmes have become fuller and more varied and are once again, as in the nineteenth century, providing a lively forum of debate on architecture, the architectural profession, architectural education and architectural history.

Conferences

The General Conference of Architects, in which the RIBA played a leading role, held meetings in London in 1871 and 1872 and then every two or three years during the 1870s and 1880s. In 1900 a General Congress of Architects was held under the auspices of the RIBA and in 1906 the RIBA was host to the International Congress of Architects in London. In 1920 the RIBA Council decided that henceforward an annual conference of British architects was to be held. These were to take place not in London but in provincial centres and the first was held in Liverpool in 1921. In 1962 it ceased to be called the British Architects Conference and became known as the RIBA Annual Conference. In recent years it has sometimes been organized in conjunction with other bodies.

11.4.1   PAPERS READ AT GENERAL MEETINGS, 1835—1858   13
vols
A series of volumes in which the manuscripts of papers read at General Meetings were bound together in a rather haphazard manner. Also included are obituaries of members: discussions following papers: documents referred to in papers, and letters read at the meetings (many of them from foreign architects and translated by T.L. Donaldson, the Hon. Secretary for Foreign Correspondence. These letters, if they had not been read out at meetings, would have been filed in the Letters to Council series.)

Subjects : Architectural aesthetics: archaeological remains: ancient Greek and Roman architecture: methods of construction: building materials: fire prevention techniques: use of colour: architectural ornament, including sculpture, mural paintings, decorative tiles and mosaics: descriptions of individual buildings: studies of building types: topographical studies: biographies of architects: preservation and restoration techniques: ventilation, heating and plumbing techniques: geology.

(Most of the material for the sessions 1835/6—1840/41 was printed in the *RIBA Transactions*, 1st Series, Vol 1 (2nd ed) and Vol 2: the 1849/50 session papers were printed in *RIBA Proceedings*, 1st Series, Vol 2: sessional papers from 1850/51 onwards were printed in *RIBA Transactions*, 1st Series, Vol 3 onwards: the papers read at General Meetings for the sessions 1841/42-1848/49 were not printed. A list of the papers appearing in these volumes is available for consultation in the RIBA Library.)

11.4.2   GENERAL CONFERENCE OF ARCHITECTS PROCEEDINGS, 1871, 1872, 1878, 1881 & 1887   2 vols
Printed proceedings at meetings, with reports of the various committees and texts of the papers delivered at the conferences, 1871, 1872, 1878 and 1881: manuscript verbatim transcript made from shorthand notes, of proceedings at the 1887 conference (bound into RIBA Pamphlets Series, Vol Q18).
Subjects : Professional practice and charges: architectural education and examinations: regulation of architectural competitions: bills of quantities: employment of surveyors to take out quantities: alliance between the RIBA and the provincial societies of architects: prevention of fire: destruction of buildings by fire during the Communist rising in Paris, 1871: use of iron and concrete in building: mural painting and coloured decoration of buildings: contemporary Scottish ecclesiastical architecture: ancient and classical architecture: model building by-laws.

11.4.3   ANNUAL CONFERENCES RECORD, 1921—1925, 1927—1964, 1966—   21 boxes
Annual files containing specimens of programmes, invitations, tickets, seating plans for banquets, menu cards, badges, local guide books and, occasionally, lists of members attending, statements of account and administrative correspondence. From 1964 onwards, the texts of papers read at conferences are usually included.
Subjects of the papers read include : Most matters of interest to the profession, including architectural history and aesthetics: architectural education and registration: architects and the public: town planning:

preservation and restoration of buildings: official architecture: improvement in design of specific building types, including housing: building contracts: building materials, techniques and economics: efficiency, productivity and management in architectural practice.

(The Annual Conference was not held in 1926, 1940—1946, 1961 (when it was replaced by the UIA Congress in London) and 1965. Texts or summaries of many papers read at the annual conferences were published in the *RIBA Journal*, and from 1982 in the new series *Transactions*. A chronological list of titles and authors of papers read at annual conferences from 1921—1964 is available for consultation in the RIBA Library.)

11.4.4   WREN BICENTENARY COMMITTEES MINUTES & PAPERS, 1922—1923   1 vol & 1 box
Signed minutes of meetings of the Wren Commemoration Joint Committee (members of the RIBA Art & Literature Standing Committees), May—Nov 1922: the Wren Bicentenary Grand Committee (representative of over 30 bodies), Nov 1922—Feb 1923, and the Wren Bicentenary Executive Committee, Feb —Apr 1923: with prospectus of the Wren Society and correspondence relating to the Wren Bicentenary Exhibition.
Subjects : Arrangements for commemorating the bicentenary of Sir Christopher Wren's death: formation of the Wren Society.

11.4.5   BRITISH ARCHITECTS CONFERENCE (1926) COMMITTEE MINUTES, 1925—1927   1 vol
Signed minutes of meetings of the committee and its subcommittees, Dec 1925—May 1927.
Subject : Arrangements for the British Architects Conference, 1926 (not held, due to the General Strike).

11.4.6   SESSIONAL   PAPERS   COMMITTEE   MINUTES,   1927—1945   1 vol
Signed minutes of meetings, Feb 1927—Jan 1945.
Subjects : Administration of the annual programmes of papers read at General Meetings: lists of suggestions and draft programmes: Architectural Science Board lectures.

(The work of this committee was continued by the Public Relations Committee.)

11.4.7   CENTENARY COMMITTEE MINUTES & PAPERS, 1933—1934   1 vol & 13 boxes
Signed minutes of meetings of the committee and its subcommittees, Jun 1933—Nov 1934, with correspondence and administrative files kept by

the Secretary RIBA, Jan —Dec 1934, and 66 addresses of congratulation from British and foreign architectural societies, professional institutions and building trade organizations.

Subjects : Royal opening of the new RIBA building on 8 Nov 1934, and RIBA centenary celebrations held in London from 21—24 Nov 1934, including a conference, a reception, a banquet, lectures, visits and tours.

11.4.8 CHRISTMAS HOLIDAY LECTURES, 1946/7—(1965/6) 3 boxes

Texts of illustrated talks for children by prominent architects and town planners, with some administrative correspondence, 1946—1966.

Subjects : Architectural history, aesthetics, techniques: urban development and planning: houses: street architecture: nature of the work of an architect: the South Bank exhibition, 1951: the new Coventry Cathedral: St. Paul's Cathedral: the Royal Festival Hall.

(*See also* 11.4.10 Sessional Programmes Record)

11.4.9 ANNUAL CONFERENCE COMMITTEE MINUTES & PAPERS, 1954—1964 2 vols & 1 box

Signed minutes of meetings of the British Architects Conferences Committee, Jul 1954—May 1962, and the Annual Conference Committee, Jul 1962—Jun 1964, with reports, memoranda, correspondence and accounts journal of payments received for conferences, 1957—1959.

(The work of this committee was continued by the Conference and Sessional Programme Committee.)

11.4.10 SESSIONAL PROGRAMMES RECORD, 1959/60— 22 boxes

Files containing programmes, posters, press releases, press cuttings, lists of guests and speakers and, for most years, texts of lectures and speeches given during the session. The events include the President's Inaugural Address, the Annual Discourse, the Royal Gold Medal presentation, evening lectures, Christmas holiday lectures, conferences held at the RIBA.

(This record is incomplete. However, many talks were published in *RIBA Transactions*, then the *RIBA Journal*, and, since 1982, in *Transactions*. Tapes of many talks given since 1975 can be listened to in the Library and a list of them is available.)

11.4.11 CONFERENCE AND SESSIONAL PROGRAMME COMMITTEE MINUTES, 1964—1967 3 binders

Minutes of meetings of the committee and its working groups, Dec 1964—Mar 1967, with reports and memoranda.
Subjects : Organization of the RIBA annual conferences and sessional programmes of meetings.

(This committee continued the work of the Annual Conference Committee and took over responsibility for the sessional programme from the Public Relations Committee. Its work was continued by the (Sessional) Programme Group and the Conference Working Groups of the Membership and Public Affairs Board.)

11.4.12   (SESSIONAL) PROGRAMME GROUP MINUTES & PAPERS, 1968—1971   3 binders
Minutes of meetings, Feb 1968—Apr 1970, with reports, memoranda, and a collection of posters, 1965—1971, and programmes, 1947—1971.

(A group of the Membership and Public Affairs Board. It continued the work of the Conference and Sessional Programme Committee in conjunction with the individual conference working groups.)

11.4.13   CONFERENCE   WORKING   GROUPS   MINUTES,   1969—1971   3 binders
Minutes of meetings of the York Conference Group, 1969: the Birmingham Conference Group, 1970: the Bristol Conference Group, 1971.
Subject : Organization of the annual conferences.

See also in 2.1 Early Committees Minutes Series:
Publication of Papers Read Subcommittee, 1862
 and in 2.2 Special Committees Minutes Series:
Proposed Annual Conference of Architects Committee, 1871
General Conference of Architects committees, 1872, 1874, 1876, 1878, 1881, 1884, 1887
Sessional Papers Committee, 1873—1884, 1908—1926
Improvement Committee, 1880 (improvement of Ordinary Meetings and papers read at them)
General Architectural Congress Committee, 1900
Informal Conferences Committee, 1916
Sessional Papers and Informal Conferences Committee, 1917—1918
Organisation of Future British Architects Conferences Ad Hoc Committee, 1953
 and 1.2.5 Reporter's Notes of General Meetings, 1850—1858: 1.2.8 General Meetings Transcripts, 1961, 1965—1971, 1973—1982: 6.7 Literature Standing Committee Minutes: 11.1.5 Public Relations Committee Minutes: 11.1.19 Membership and Public Affairs Board Minutes: 11.1.22 Public Affairs Board Minutes.

Bibliography

1   RIBA 'Statement of the regulations and practice respecting the publications of the Institute of British Architects from the foundation until the period previous to the recent regulations of the present session' *RIBA Proceedings* 1st Series 1862/63 19 Jan 1863
2   RIBA 'Report of sub-committee on the publication of papers read' (at Ordinary General Meetings) *RIBA Proceedings* 1st Series 1862/63 2 Feb 1863
3   'A new kind of conference' *RIBA Journal* Vol 69 1962 May p162. Article on the remodelling of the Annual Conference.
4   RIBA Annual Conference Committee 'Future of the RIBA Conference' *RIBA Journal* Vol 71 1964 Sep pp382—384
5   Jacques, Robin 'The Conference: soapbox or soporific?' *RIBA Journal* Vol 78 1971 Jul pp301—302. Article on the future of the RIBA Annual Conference.

Section 5 Competitions

In the 1830s architectural competitions for public buildings were usually conducted in an unfair and incompetent manner and there was considerable dissatisfaction with a completely unregulated system. More often than not building committees were unable to read plans or understand the designs; were unduly influenced by pretty coloured perspective views; failed to produce adequate preliminary instructions or, if they did, failed to reject those designs not in strict conformity with those instructions; failed to ascertain that the designs could be executed for the estimated sums and failed to appoint the architect of the winning design to execute the work. Opportunities for corruption of officials and exploitation of architects' plans were plentiful and often used to advantage by the unscrupulous. So unsatisfactory was the situation that many of the best architects refused ever to compete.

At the suggestion of Ambrose Poynter the Council in 1838 appointed a special committee to investigate the competition system. This committee did not produce a code of regulations but strongly recommended that competition drawings should always be made to one scale and limited to one style of finishing; that the perspective drawings should be restricted to specified points of view and that competition designs should always be exhibited to the public. It also urged architects to refuse to enter any competition which did not offer a sufficient guarantee that it would be conducted with intelligence and justice.

In 1850 a Competitions Committee appointed by the Architectural Association in 1849 published a report that contained a code of regulations for the conduct of competitions, which formed the basis of future codes. In 1856 the Office of Works invited architects to compete for the new Government Offices in Whitehall, but did not employ the successful competitor. The Institute memorialized the First Commissioner objecting to the appointment of Sir James Pennethorne, who was not a competitor, and to the stipulation that the premiated designs became the property of the government. After the General Conference of Architects in 1871 the RIBA appointed a special committee to draw up some model rules, which were approved at the General Conference in 1872 and published by the RIBA as *General regulations for the conduct of architectural competitions* .

In 1880 Cole Adams organized a memorial to the RIBA Council signed by 1,340 architects requesting the Institute to devise a scheme whereby architects could agree not to take part in any public competition unless a professional adjudicator of established reputation had been appointed. As a result, the Council appointed a special committee which recommended among other things that the promoters of competitions should appoint one or more Fellows of the RIBA as professional assessors. In 1883 the RIBA issued a revised and elaborated version of the 1872 regulations and set up a standing Competitions Committee to monitor competition conditions and deal with complaints sent in by members on the conduct of competions. In 1902 Alfred Cross and H.V. Lanchester formed the Competition Reform Society, the members of which all agreed not to take part in any open competition disapproved of by the Society's committee (*see* Appendix 8. Competition Reform Society Minutes, 1902—1906). The Society pressurized assessors appointed by the RIBA to refuse to act in any competition on its blacklist. Subsequently, the RIBA started to publish notices of unacceptable competitions in the *RIBA Journal* and in 1908 a special RIBA committee recommended that competitions should always be judged by a jury of at least three professional assessors.

In 1911 the RIBA finally began to put some teeth into its procedures by passing a Council resolution that any member who took part in any competition which the Council had declared by a resolution published in the *RIBA Journal* to be unapproved, because its conditions did not accord with the RIBA regulations for competitions, would be deemed guilty of unprofessional conduct. This was strengthened in 1921 by adding that any member who acted as architect or joint architect for a work resulting from a competition in which he had acted as an assessor became liable to reprimand, suspension of membership or expulsion from the Institute. An administrative procedure was set up in which the senior clerks of the General Office ordered two sets of conditions for all open competitions, checked them against the RIBA model forms, reported any differences to the Secretary and passed one copy to the Competitions Committee Secretary and one to the Library. This work was continued by the new Central Services Department and revised regulations were issued in 1962.

In 1967 responsibility for the work on competitions was passed to the new Membership and Public Affairs Board, which set up a Competitions Working Group and decided not just to monitor competitions but actively to promote them. From January 1969 a regular newssheet, 'Architectural Competition News', was compiled and distributed to members and the press. Also in 1969 new regulations were issued and in 1971 a permanent Competitions Officer was appointed.

Jurisdiction over international competitions in architecture and town planning is exercised by the Union Internationale des Architectes (UIA) of which the RIBA is a constituent body. Before the Second World War, this function was carried out by the Comité Permanent International des Architectes (CPIA) which issued its first regulations for international competitions in 1908 (*see* Chapter 13, Overseas Relations). From 1957—1970 RIBA work concerning international competitions was carried out by the Overseas Relations Secretary and from 1971 by the Competitions Officer.

11.5.1   PUBLIC COMPETITIONS FOR ARCHITECTURAL DESIGNS COMMITTEE PAPERS, 1838   1 box
Manuscript draft of the committee's report, 1838.
Subjects : Unsatisfactory conduct of public architectural competitions: ways of improving the competition system.

(A printed copy of this report is in the Architectural Competitions Committee Papers Series.)

11.5.2   ARCHITECTURAL COMPETITIONS COMMITTEE PAPERS, 1871—1872   1 vol
Transcripts of replies by members to the committee's questionnaire sent to them in Nov 1871, with summary by Alfred Strong of the opinions expressed, Jan 1872, and various memoranda by members. Copy of printed pamphlet *Remarks on proposed rules for the regulation of architectural competitions* by John Honeyman, 1862, and copy of the printed report of the Public Competitions for Architectual Designs Committee, 24 Jan 1839.
Subjects : Investigation of the architectural competition system: drafting a code of regulations for the conduct of competitions.

(This committee included representatives of the Architectural Alliance and the Architectural Association in London)

11.5.3   ARCHITECTURAL COMPETITIONS MEMORIAL, 1880   2 vols
Signed statements by 1340 architects, including Fellows and Associates of the RIBA and non-members, asking the RIBA Council to devise a remedy for the unsatisfactory state of public architectural competitions in the form of a scheme whereby all members of the profession could agree not to take part in any public competition unless a professional adjudicator of established reputation was appointed. The architects often give their full address, sometimes only the name of the town.

(This memorial was organized by Cole A. Adams, Hon. Secretary of the Memorial Committee and presented to the RIBA Council in May 1882. Following this, the Council set up the Competitions Committee *see* 2.2 Special Committees Minutes Series)

11.5.4 COMPETITIONS COMMITTEE MINUTES, 1920—1967   4 vols & 3 binders

Signed minutes of meetings, Aug 1920—May 1967, with memoranda, reports, transcripts of letters received and signed minutes of the following subcommittees:

Scale of Fees for Assessors in Town Planning and Improvement Scheme Competitions Subcommittee, Nov 1929

Competitions for Town Planning and Improvement Schemes Subcommittee, Jul 1930

Practice Standing Committee & Competitions Committee Joint Meetings, Jan —Mar 1931

Competition System Subcommittee, Feb —Apr 1933

Competitions for Town Planning and Improvement Schemes Joint Subcommittee (with Town Planning Institute), Mar 1933

Officers of the Competitions Committee Meetings, Oct 1939—May 1940

Subjects : Conditions and conduct of architectural competitions all over the world: details of hundreds of competitions, particularly in Britain: premiums for competitions: housing schemes competitions: RIBA approval or veto of competitions: limited competitions: assessors' fees and duties: RIBA Competition Regulations, Model Form of Conditions, and Directions to Assessors: town planning and improvement schemes competitions: appointments under seal: rules for international competitions: industrial design competitions.

(The work of this committee was continued by the Competitions Working Group. For Competitions Committee Minutes, 1883—1920 *see* 2.2 Special Committees Minutes Series.)

11.5.5 COMPETITIONS SECRETARY'S PAPERS, 1920—(1982)   124 boxes

Files kept by the Hon. Secretaries of the Competitions Committee, the RIBA Secretary and, later, the Competitions Secretary. There are files of correspondence with members: files on competition regulations and model conditions: files on preliminary enquiries from competition promoters: and case files on over one thousand individual competitions of all types, including abandoned competitions, from 1921 to the present. These files frequently contain draft and final conditions and competitors' questions and answers and occasionally contain information about appointment of assessors, copies of assessors' reports, details of results and sometimes protests and complaints.

(An alphabetical list of the individual competition files in this series is available for consultation in the Library. For international competitions from 1957—1970 *see* 12.2.6 Overseas Relations Secretary's Papers Series.)

11.5.6   COMPETITIONS   SUBCOMMITTEES   MINUTES,   1922—
1923   1 vol
Signed minutes of meetings of the Revision of the Regulations for Architectural Competitions Joint Subcommittee (with the Society of Architects), Mar 1922—Jun 1923, and the Town Planning and Layout Competitions Joint Committee (with the Town Planning Institute, Dec 1923.

11.5.7   MASONIC MEMORIAL COMMITTEE MINUTES, 1922—
1923   1 vol
Signed minutes of meetings, Apr 1922—Mar 1923.
Subject : Proposed deputation to the Grand Lodge of Freemasons urging the holding of a public competition for the design of the Masonic Memorial Building.

11.5.8   COMPLAINTS (COMPETITIONS) SUBCOMMITTEE MIN-
UTES, 1926—1928   1 vol
Signed minutes of meetings, Nov 1926—Jun 1928.
Subject : Complaints concerning the organization of various architectural competitions, including the Liverpool Cenotaph Competition and the Birkdale Elementary School Competition.

(A small committee of senior members of the Council who were neither in active competition practice nor members of the Competitions Committee. In 1928 this committee was absorbed by the Professional Conduct Committee.)

11.5.9   COMPETITIONS   WORKING   GROUP   MINUTES,   1967—
(1980)   3 binders
 Signed and unsigned minutes, with reports and drafts of RIBA regulations and model forms, of meetings of the following groups:
Ad Hoc Working Group on Competition Regulations, Sep 1967—May 1970
Panel of Supervisors, Sep 1970
Competitions Steering Group, Dec 1970—Mar 1971
Competitions Working Group, Aug 1971—Nov 1980
Regional Competitions Officers' Meetings, Nov 1972—May 1974

Subjects : Similar to Competitions Committee Minutes & Papers (q.v.) plus promotion of competitions: Preliminary Project competitions: Regional Special Category competitions: Design-Build competitions: Promoter Choice competitions.

11.5.10   ARCHITECTURAL COMPETITIONS NEWS, 1969—1974   3
binders
A series of monthly bulletins, Feb 1969—Dec 1974, issued by the RIBA Competitions Office, giving news of RIBA and international competitions. It provided particulars of preliminary announcements, competitions in progress, abandoned competitions, competition results and exhibitions of competition drawings.

See also in 2.2 Special Committees Minutes Series:
New Government Offices Competition Committee, 1883
Competitions Committee, 1883—1920
Assessorships Committee, 1902
Special Competitions Committee, 1908—1910
Barnet Competition Committee (Municipal Offices), 1914
Baden Competition Committee (RIBA Industrial Housing Competition sponsored
  by Bertram Baden), 1940
  and 6.8 Competition Conditions Collection 1884—: 11.1.5 Public Relations Committee Minutes, 1933—1967: 11.1.19 Membership and Public Affairs Board Minutes, 1967—1971: 11.1.22 Public Affairs Board Minutes, 1971—1975

For the RIBA Building competition 1932 *see* 5.3.5 New Premises Committee Minutes, 1930—1931, and 5.3.7 New Building Committee Minutes and Papers, 1932—1937

Bibliography

1   Institute of British Architects *Report of the committee appointed to consider the subject of public competitions for architectural designs* London, IBA, 1839

2   Austin, Henry *Thoughts on the abuses of the present system of competition in architecture: with an outline of a plan for their remedy. In a letter to Earl de Grey, President of the Royal Institute of British Architects* London, John Weale, 1841

3   Architectural Association Competition Committee *Report on architectural competitions* London, 1850

4   Morgan, George 'On public competitions for architectural designs' *RIBA Transactions* 1st Series Vol 8 1857/58 pp155—166

5   Manchester Society of Architects *Suggestions on the management of competitions* Manchester, 1867

6   Kerr, Robert 'Hints on the commercial aspect of architectural competitions',

in *General Conference of Architects 1871. Report of proceedings* London, RIBA, 1871

7 RIBA *General regulations for the conduct of architectural competitions* London, RIBA, 1872

8 Porter, Thomas 'Architectural competitions' *RIBA Transactions* 1st Series Vol 30 1879/80 pp65—84

9 RIBA *Report of the committee of the Royal Institute of British Architects on architectural competitions* London, RIBA, [1881]

10 Hodges, Robert F. *On architectural competitions in general with some reference to one in particular. An appeal to the Royal Institute of British Architects* London, 1887

11 RIBA *Suggestions for the conduct of architectural competitions* London, RIBA, 1888 (Revised editions issued in 1892, 1902, 1905)

12 Anderson, J. Macvicar 'Competitions' *RIBA Proceedings* New Series Vol 7 1891 Apr 9 pp247—249

13 RIBA *Suggestions for assessors in architectural competitions* London, RIBA, 1902

14 'The conduct of international architectural competitions' Papers and discussion, in *VIIth International Congress of Architects. Summary of proceedings* Published by the RIBA as a special supplement to *RIBA Journal* Vol 13 1906 Aug 25

15 'Regulations for international architectural competitions. Settled at Paris, November 1908 by the International Competitions Committee appointed by the VIIth International Congress of Architects' *RIBA Kalendar* 1909/10

16 RIBA *Regulations governing the promotion and conduct of architectural competitions as approved by the Royal Institute of British Architects and by its Allied Societies* London, RIBA, 1910 (Revised editions issued in 1915, 1921, 1924, 1926, 1928, 1931, 1933, 1934, 1936, 1937)

17 Lanchester, H. V. 'The evolution of the architectural competition' *RIBA Journal* Vol 22 1915 Jun 12 pp377—388

18 RIBA *Directions for assessors in architectural competitions* London, RIBA, 1915 (Revised editions issued in 1924, 1931, 1933)

19 Lanchester, H. V. & Thomas, Percy E. 'Competitions: past and present' *RIBA Journal* Vol 40 1933 May 13 pp525—537

20 Lanchester, H. V. 'Architectural competitions', in Gotch, J. A. (ed) *The growth and work of the Royal Institute of British Architects* London, RIBA, 1934

21 Macalister, Ian *An explanatory memorandum on the system of architectural competitions* London, RIBA, 1937

22 'The work of RIBA committees. No. 2 The Competitions Committee' *RIBA Journal* Vol 61 1953 Dec p56

23 RIBA Council 'Competition by tender' *RIBA Journal* Vol 67 1960 Sep pp409—410

24 RIBA *Architectural competitions* London, RIBA, 1963

25 RIBA Competitions Committee 'Notes on the revised regulations governing

architectural competitions' *RIBA Journal* Vol 70 1963 Aug pp307—308

26 Harper, Roger 'A sordid inheritance' *RIBA Journal* Vol 90 1983 Mar pp21—23

27 Harper, Roger H. *Victorian architectural competitions. An index to British and Irish architectural competitions in the 'Builder' 1843—1900* London, Mansell Publishing Ltd, 1983. Introduction, pp xi—xxvi

28 RIBA *The RIBA handbook for architectural competitions. Regulations for the promotion and conduct of competitions* London, RIBA, 1984

Section 6 Architects' employment

In this section are gathered together the records of various committees, groups and services specifically concerned with promoting and assisting the employment of architects; with schemes to provide additional employment for architects in times of crisis and with architectural patronage in general. (There is inevitably some overlap in this subject area with other chapters, *see* Chapter 8 for **RIBA** work campaigning against the employment of engineers and surveyors as architects by local authorities and other cases of architectural practice by unqualified persons; *see* Chapters 4 and 8 for **RIBA** work in relation to Government building programmes and as part of joint construction industry pressure groups; *see* Chapter 4 for **RIBA** regulation of professional advertisement by architects and for the collection of data and the production of statistics on the employment of architects).

In 1837 the Institute started a register of architects' assistants, improvers, clerks of works and others looking for employment. This register was maintained by the Librarian and in 1893 a companion register of architects requiring assistance was opened. These registers have not survived but the service continued and led eventually to the establishment of an Appointments Department in the 1950s, which continues today as part of RIBA Services Ltd. Another service was provided by the Chief Clerk who acted as an agent for members seeking partnerships.

The outbreak of war in 1914 caused sudden unemployment and distress for several hundred architects and the existing funds at the disposal of the Architects Benevolent Society were insufficient to cope with such an emergency. The RIBA was instrumental in setting up the joint Architects' War Committee which was broadly representative of the whole profession in the United Kingdom and one of its first tasks was to set up the Architects' War Relief Fund. It also prepared a scheme for a series of civic surveys on which professional people including architects could be employed. These surveys collected data on local government, industrial and residential conditions, recreation facilities, health, traffic conditions, climate, geology, schools, libraries, power supplies, drainage systems etc. and provided temporary employment for many architects. The Architects' War Committee was also responsible for finding architects suitable positions in the armed forces and in government departments and for helping to re-establish architects in practice after demobilization.

Unemployment amongst architects reached crisis proportions again in 1931 when the RIBA, in conjunction with the Association of Architects, Surveyors and Technical Assistants (AASTA) and the Architects Benevolent Society set up an Architects Unemployment Committee and an Architects Unemployment Fund (for minutes of the Architects Unemployment Committee *see* Appendix 4. Archive of the Architects Benevolent Society). By 1933 the funds collected were being used to employ 90 architects on survey schemes organized by the London Society, the London Survey Committee and the RIBA Allied Societies and to promote the work of the Architectural Graphic Records Committee (*see* Appendix 10).

The Second World War caused another unemployment crisis for architects. In 1938 the RIBA set up a National Emergency Panel and started to compile a national register of architects to try to ensure the efficient use of architects by the government in time of war and in 1939 the Institute conducted a survey to discover the extent of unemployment amongst architects caused by the sudden cessation of private building projects. The RIBA War Executive Committee, which ran the Institute on behalf of the Council from 1939—1945, managed to arrange many government appointments for architects particularly in the field of structural air raid precautions and repair of war-damaged buildings. It also influenced the terms on which architects and architectural students served in the armed forces, secured their early demobilization and helped to re-establish them in practice or continue their professional education after the war. In addition, the RIBA Refugees Committee helped many architect refugees from Nazi-occupied Europe to obtain professional employment in the United Kingdom.

Since the nineteenth century, the Institute has often been asked by intending clients to nominate suitable architects for specific jobs, both private and official. This task was traditionally the prerogative of the President who, by the 1930s, was nominating architects for two or three hundred jobs each year. By then an established nomination procedure had been developed whereby multiple nominations were made, in the case of the larger jobs in the London area or overseas, by the PRIBA advised by a small panel of counsellors and, for the smaller jobs, by the Secretary RIBA. For the larger jobs outside the London area names were put forward by the president of the local Allied Society to the PRIBA who could add nominations of his own and, for the smaller jobs, nominations were made by the local president or chapter chairman alone.

Experiencing a lack of adequate information about the work of practices, the Secretary RIBA began in 1958 to compile an index of practices designed to provide information on their achievements and particular expertise and began to keep a register recording particulars of the nominations made. In 1964 a Practices Index

Secretary was appointed who sent out regular questionnaires to practices and took over from the Secretary RIBA the responsibility of nominating suitable architects for the smaller jobs in the London area. At the same time, dissatisfaction with the working of the nomination service and difficulties caused by the uneven distribution and sudden fluctuations of workload being experienced by many practices, together with increasing competition for architectural work within the building industry and from other professions, caused the Institute to commission a research study by John Carter into the whole field of architectural patronage, distribution of work and corporate promotion of jobs for members. This study led to the report *The architect and his client* which in turn led to the development in 1971 of the Clients Bureau, renamed the Clients Advisory Service in 1972, and the further development of the Practices Index and the *RIBA Directory of Practices*. Indirectly, it has caused a reassessment of the thorny question of professional advertising by individual architects, which still continues to-day.

ARCHITECTS WAR COMMITTEE MINUTES, 1914—1917 (A joint committee of all the architectural societies)
see 2.2 Special Committees Minutes Series

11.6.1   PROFESSIONAL EMPLOYMENT COMMITTEE MINUTES, 1914—1919   1 vol
Signed minutes of meetings, Sep 1914—Jun 1919, with memoranda, reports and the committee's accounts.
Subjects : Provision of temporary professional employment for architects unemployed because of the war, who were ineligible for service in the armed forces: unemployment register organized by the Architectural Association: Belgian relief funds: civic surveys carried out by unemployed architects, especially a survey of London in co-operation with the London Society: refugee architects: co-operation with the Professional Classes War Relief Council and the Town Planning Institute: application for a grant from the Government Committee on the Prevention and Relief of Distress: the Architects' Loan Fund.

(A subcommittee of the Architects War Committee, it was a joint committee with members of the Architects Benevolent Society, the Society of Architects, the Architectural Association and the Architects and Surveyors Approved Society. It had the following subcommittees: Funds Subcommittee, Scheme Subcommittee, Applications and Immediate Works Subcommittee, Civic Survey Salaries Subcommittee, Architects Offices Subcommittee, Demobilisation Committee, and Architects Reorganisation Committee. This committee was at first called the Benevolent Subcommittee.)

11.6.2   *APPLICATIONS AND IMMEDIATE WORKS SUBCOM-
MITTEE MINUTES, 1914—1919   2 vols
Signed minutes of meetings, Dec 1914—Oct 1919, with transcripts of
letters received and reports.
Subjects : Schemes to provide temporary work for architects unemployed
because of the war: dealing with applicants, many of whom were given
jobs on the Civic Survey.

(A subcommittee of the Professional Employment Committee)

* Access at the discretion of the Archivist

11.6.3   CIVIC SURVEY JOINT COMMITTEE MINUTES, 1915—
1921   1 vol
Signed minutes of meetings, Jul 1915—Jan 1921, with statements of
expenditure and reports of surveys.
Subjects : Civic Survey of Greater London, including rainfall, vital
statistics, sewage disposal, refuse collection and communications: civic
surveys of South Lancashire, South Yorkshire, Devon and Exeter:
independent surveys organized by the Architects War Committee.

(A subcommittee of the Professional Employment Committee)

11.6.4   CIVIC SURVEY OF GREATER LONDON REPORTS, 1915   2
vols
Reports on London divisions of the Metropolitan Police area, on Poor
Law Unions, traffic, refuse collection, sewage disposal, water supply and
other topics for the Greater London area. One volume labelled 'Essex'
contains abstracts of information on Barking, Buckhurst Hill, Chigwell,
Chingford, Dagenham, East Ham, Ilford, Leyton, Waltham Cross,
Walthamstow, Wanstead, West Ham and Woodford.

ARCHITECTS REORGANISATION COMMITTEE MINUTES,
1917—1919
(A joint committee of all the architectural societies, which met at the
Society of Architects)
see Appendix 7. Archive of the Society of Architects

11.6.5   CIVIC SURVEY EXHIBITION JOINT COMMITTEE MIN-
UTES, 1920   1 vol
Signed minutes of two meetings, 13 Aug and 27 Oct 1920.
Subject : Organization of an exhibition and conference on the work of
the Civic Survey staff.

ARCHITECTS UNEMPLOYMENT COMMITTEE MINUTES,
1931—1935

(A joint committee of the ABS, the RIBA & the AASTA)
see Appendix 4. Archive of the Architects Benevolent Society

NATIONAL EMERGENCY PANEL MINUTES, 1938—1939
see 3.1.3

11.6.6   STOPPAGE OF WORK BY WAR SURVEY, 1939—1940   2 boxes
Returns by the Allied Societies of the RIBA and by London area practices
to a questionnaire on the number of building projects postponed or
abandoned due to outbreak of war, and on staff reductions and closures
of architects' offices, Nov 1939—Jan 1940

REFUGEES COMMITTEE MINUTES & PAPERS, 1939—1941
see 12.2.3

PRESENT AND FUTURE OF PRIVATE ARCHITECTURAL
PRACTICE COMMITTEE MINUTES, 1948 — 1950
See 8.3.11

FUTURE OF PRIVATE ARCHITECTURAL PRACTICE COM-
MITTEE MINUTES, 1950 — 1951
See 8.3.12

PRIAVTE ARCHITECTURAL PRACTICE BY UNQUALIFIED
PERSONS AD HOC COMMITTEE MINUTES, 1953
See 8.3.13

11.6.7   * PRESIDENT'S NOMINATIONS REGISTER, 1958—(1983)   4
vols
Record of nominations of architects for projects, from Jan 1958 onwards,
giving date, name of client, name of project, nominations submitted and,
from 1970, name of architect appointed. Also includes a record of the
appointment of competition assessors, Jul 1957—Dec 1959.

* Access at the discretion of the Clients Advisory Service director

11.6.8   ARCHITECTURAL PATRONAGE STUDY PAPERS, 1964—
1965   2 boxes
Correspondence, notes of discussions, memoranda, drafts of his report,
by John Carter who carried out the research project.
Subjects : Distribution of work in the private sector: fluctuations of work
flow to architects' offices: the private client: the public authority client: the
President's Nomination Service: proposed RIBA Directory of Practices:
promotion of overseas work.

11.6.9   * CLIENTS ADVISORY SERVICE PRACTICES RECORD, 1964—
(1983)   *c* .4000 files

Files on approximately 4000 private architectural practices in the United Kingdom and N. Ireland, which have a RIBA Corporate Member as a principal, partner or director, compiled to provide an information service to clients wishing to select architects for specific work. They contain completed Practice Index forms giving information on the nature, staff and expertise of each practice, with select lists of descriptions of completed jobs. They also frequently contain photographs of the firm's work, brochures and press-cuttings. Sometimes they contain RIBA Census of Private Architectural Practices completed forms from 1964—1972 and correspondence.

* This is a working record rather than an archive, but researchers may consult individual files at the discretion of the CAS staff.

11.6.10   PRACTICES INDEX SECRETARY'S PAPERS, 1965—1971   23 boxes

Correspondence files concerning the administration of the President's Nomination Service and the Practices Index, (forerunners of the Clients Bureau and the Clients Advisory Service). Includes 'The architect and his client', a study by John Carter, 1969—1970.

11.6.11   PATRONAGE WORKING GROUP PAPERS, 1966—1967   1 box

Copies of minutes of meetings, Mar 1966 — Nov 1967, with memoranda, reports and some correspondence.

Subject : Organization and financing of the Practices Section of the RIBA Directory.

(A working group of the Policy Committee. Its work was continued by the Patronage Subcommittee.)

11.6.12   PATRONAGE SUBCOMMITTEE PAPERS, 1968—1970   1 box

Copies of minutes of meetings, Jan 1968 — May 1970, with memoranda, reports, notes and correspondence.

Subjects : Architectural patronage: the RIBA Directory of Practices: the nomination service: collective promotion of the services of architects.

(A subcommittee of the Policy and Finance Committee. Its work was continued by the Clients Bureau Working Group.)

11.6.13   PUBLIC RELATIONS CAMPAIGN GROUP PAPERS, 1968— 1970   1 box

Copies of minutes of meetings, Oct 1968 — Jul 1969, with memoranda, reports and correspondence.

Subject : A publicity campaign to promote the role of the architect and advertise the nomination service.

(A group of the Membership and Public Affairs Board)

11.6.14   CLIENTS BUREAU WORKING GROUP MINUTES & PAPERS,
1970—1972   1 vol & 1 box
Minutes of meetings, Dec 1970—Dec 1972, with memoranda, reports,
correspondence, and consultant's report 'RIBA Clients Bureau' by L. A.
Dalglish, Jun 1971.
Subjects : Transformation of the nomination service and Practices Index
into a Clients Bureau (Advisory Service) and the appointment of a
director for it: form and functions of such a service.

(A group of the Policy and Finance Committee)

11.6.15   CLIENTS BUREAU DIRECTOR'S PAPERS, 1971   1 box
Administrative files kept by Larry Dalglish, Consultant/Director of the
bureau and Joyce Farrant, Assistant Secretary.
Subjects : Development and budget of the bureau: architect/developer
competitions.

(1971 was the Clients Bureau's first operational year. In 1972 Chris
Lakin became director and it was renamed the Clients Advisory Service.
In 1976 Gordon Mattey took over as director and he was succeeded
by Peter Sandy who was appointed director of the new Promotions
Department in 1983.)

See also in 2.2 Special Committees Minutes Series:
Architects War Committee, 1914, 1917
Civic Survey Conference, 1915
Civic Survey Subcommittee, 1915
Deputation Subcommittee (deputation to the Prime Minister on employment of
architects), 1917
Building after the War Conference, 1918
Exemption of Service Candidates (from the RIBA Final Examination) Conference,
1920
Stoppage of Building Committee, 1920
Overcrowding of the Architectural Profession Joint Committee, 1924—1925
Propaganda Joint Subcommittee (of the Deputation on Unemployment in the
Building Industry), 1932
Unemployment in the Building Industry Conference, 1932
War Office Advisory Appointments Committee, 1940—1941
Deferment of Military Service Committee, 1940—1944
Housing Production Ad Hoc Committee, 1945
Facilities for Young Architects to set up in Practice Ad Hoc Committee, 1946
Export Group of the Constructional Industries & the RIBA Joint Meeting, 1946
see also Appendix 4. Archive of the Architects Benevolent Society: War Loan
Fund & War Relief Fund Committees Minutes, 1915—1924
and 11.1.22 Public Affairs Board Minutes & Papers, 1971—1975

Bibliography

1   Lanchester, H. V. 'The civic development survey as a war measure' *RIBA Journal* Vol 22 1915 Jan 9 pp107—110

2   Townsend, C. Harrison 'The civic survey' *RIBA Journal* Vol 23 1916 Apr 1 pp177—180

3   Joint Committee of the RIBA & the AASTA on Overcrowding of the Architectural Profession. Report to the RIBA Council, in *RIBA Journal* Vol 32 1925 Aug 15 pp590—591

4   Unwin, Raymond 'The architectural profession and unemployment. An appeal by the President' *RIBA Journal* Vol 39 1931 Dec 19 p138

5   'The work of the RIBA Unemployment Committee' *RIBA Journal* Vol 41 1934 Jun 23 pp781—805

6   'Architecture and the next slump' *RIBA Journal* Vol 45 1938 Feb 7 pp347—348

7   RIBA Refugees Committee. Report *RIBA Journal* Vol 46 1939 Jun 26 pp826—831

8   RIBA Public Relations Committee 'The proportion of building work executed by architects' *RIBA Journal* Vol 46 1939 Jul 17 pp898—899

9   'The state of the profession' *RIBA Journal* Vol 48 1940 Nov 18 pp2-3. Extracts from a report on the results of a RIBA questionnaire sent to the Allied Societies on the state of the profession in their districts, particularly concerning the amount of unemployment.

10   RIBA Committee on Private Architectural Practice by Unqualified Persons. Report *RIBA Journal* Vol 61 1953 Dec pp65—67

11   Carter, John 'Stop-go in private practice?' *RIBA Journal* Vol 72 1965 Feb pp94—95

12   Carter, John 'Commissions: new RIBA services' *RIBA Journal* Vol 72 1965 Jul pp329—330. Summary of RIBA Council's decision to develop new services to assist clients in selecting architects and to maintain the flow of work to architectural offices.

13   Carter, John *The architect and his client* London, RIBA, 1970

14   Luder, Owen 'How many architects?' *RIBA Journal* Vol 77 1970 Jan pp23—24

15   RIBA Professional Services Board 'How much work for architects?' *RIBA Journal* Vol 77 1970 Jul pp328—329

16   Carter, John 'The Nomination Service: a study of the architect and his client' *RIBA Journal* Vol 77 1970 Aug pp373—375

17   Lakin, Chris 'Looking for work? The CAS can help your practice' *RIBA Journal* Vol 82 1975 Jan p26. Article on the RIBA Clients Advisory Service.

18   Melvin, Peter 'Clients Advisory Service' *RIBA Journal* Vol 83 1976 Mar p87

I 2
Membership relations and overseas affairs

Section 1 Membership relations

Before 1887 the Institute had no formal relationship with any other body except the Architectural Association of London which had for many years been represented on the RIBA Council. In the provinces there were independent architectural societies which had no connection with the RIBA except in so far as many of their members were also members of the RIBA. Many of these societies came into existence shortly after the formation of the RIBA, which at first had been almost entirely a London body. In 1887 a new charter gave the RIBA Council the capability of arranging formal alliances with these societies. An alliance would be created by both the RIBA Council and the council of the society concerned passing a resolution in its favour and could be terminated by three months' notice on either side. The RIBA would pay to the Allied Society a rebate not exceeding one quarter of the subscription paid to the RIBA by any member who was a member of both bodies. Nine seats on the RIBA Council were allotted to representatives of the Allied Societies and the first nine alliances were arranged in 1889.

It was not until after the First World War that there was a national network of Allied Societies, those closest to London being the latest to be founded. By 1939 there were 48 Allied Societies with 55 branches or chapters, and approximately half of their members were also members of the RIBA. There was, in addition, a Commonwealth network of Allied Societies. These overseas societies were entirely autonomous but their constitution and rules had first to be approved by the RIBA, except for the Royal Architectural Institute of Canada, the Royal Australian Institute of Architects, the Institute of South African Architects and the New Zealand Institute of Architects.

Affairs of the Institute 1874

At the third Meeting of the Committee on the Affairs of the Institute held on Wednesday the 4th of november 1874

Present

Professor Donaldson, Past President in the Chair

Messrs T. Chatfield Clarke   R. P. Spiers

F. P. Cockerell   T. H. Watson

E. B. Ferrey

T. H. Lewis   C. L. Eastlake Secy.

The Minutes of the last Meeting of the Committee were read & confirmed.

The Secretary reported that in accordance with the instructions which he had received at the last Meeting of the Committee he had written to the Secretaries of all the principal architectural Societies in the United Kingdom & requested them to supply this Committee with copies of their Rules. The request had been complied with in nearly every instance & the Rules of the Societies referred to were now open to the inspection of this Committee.

A letter dated May 22d 1874 was read from Mr Robert T. Hodges of Manchester, Associate offering certain suggestions with a view to secure "the more extended recognition of the R.I.B.A. as the head quarter of the Architectural profession" The Secretary explained that this letter had been intended for the General Conference of 1874 but was received for the consideration of this Committee.

A letter dated 11 Nov. 1874 was read from Mr Thomas Drew, Fellow, late President of the Royal Institute of Architects of Ireland proposing under certain conditions a union of that Institute with the Royal Institute of British Architects

26   Extract from the minutes of a meeting of the Affairs of the Institute Committee, 4 November 1874, when the first significant steps to be taken in the very long process of achieving the union of the RIBA and all the principal societies of architects in the United Kingdom were discussed. This process was not completed until the 1960s, when the RIBA became a regional as well as a national body. (RIBA Archive:2.2   Special Committees Minutes Series)

Although most of the Allied Societies were entitled to appoint a representative to serve on the RIBA Council, an additional body developed called the Allied Societies Conference. At a meeting of presidents of Allied Societies in January 1921 it was decided that the presidents or other representatives of the Allied Societies should meet in London three times a year on the days on which the RIBA Council meetings were also held. The main object of the Conference was to inform the Council of the views of the Allied Societies but by 1935 there was a danger of it becoming a sort of alternative RIBA Council and its functions were redefined as being a consultative body without executive powers. Matters discussed by the Conference, which should be 'limited to those concerning the Allied Societies', were to be remitted to the Council by means of a report through the RIBA Executive Committee. From 1945, however, annual joint meetings of the Conference and the Council were held, when matters of general policy could be raised with the chairmen of the main RIBA committees, who were present to answer questions. The Allied Societies Conference was composed of one representative of the governing body of each Allied Society and one representative of each branch or chapter in the United Kingdom. In the early 1960s it met twice a year, the Allied Societies Presidents Committee met four times a year and the Allied Societies Public Relations Officers met once a year.

By this time the RIBA Council were taking liaison with the Allied Societies very seriously. In the 1950s it had appointed a RIBA Public Relations Officer to liaise with the PROs of the Allied Societies and in 1963 the first RIBA Membership Relations Secretary was appointed. The report of the Allied Societies Presidents' Committee Working Group in 1964 took the first concrete step towards a regional structure for the RIBA by recommending the establishment of regional offices and urging societies to set up regional liaison committees. The Council set up a special committee under the chairmanship of Lord Esher, which in 1965 submitted the report 'Communications within the profession' which recommended regional constituencies for RIBA Council elections; the establishment of regional councils and a three-tier structure — RIBA, governed by the RIBA Council; region, governed by a Regional Council and branch, governed by a Branch Committee. All RIBA members would become members of the branch within whose area their electoral address was. The Constitution Committee was appointed in 1966 and its work led to the grant of a new charter in 1971 which formally recognized a regional structure for the RIBA. The first regional office, the Eastern Region Office, was opened in Cambridge in 1966, which was followed by the West Midlands Region Office in Birmingham and by 1971 nine regional offices had been established. Unfortunately it has not been possible to include the archives of the regions in this survey.

Membership relations were originally the responsibility of the Secretary RIBA and then of the General Office, the Deputy Secretary and the RIBA Public Relations Officer. In 1959 the Chief Information Officer, who was head of the new Information Services Department, took over this responsibility. In 1963 a Membership Relations Secretary was appointed, as part of the new Central Services

Department which succeeded the General Office. In 1967 a new Membership and Public Affairs Department was set up which took over the work of liaison with the new RIBA regions. In 1971 Membership Relations work was transferred to the Central Services Department which in 1973 changed its name to Membership Services. In 1975 Membership Relations was again combined with Public Affairs and in 1983 was again separated.

12.1.1   ASSOCIATES MEMORIAL, 1884   1 vol
Forms of petition signed by hundreds of RIBA Associates, bound together in alphabetical order and addressed to the President, Council and Fellows of the RIBA. Provides each Associate's signature and address.
Subject : Demand for Associates to have the right of voting on all matters relating to the affairs of the Institute, plus postal vote for provincial Associates.

(Resistance by the Fellows to the Associates' demands led to the formation of the Society of Architects *see* Appendix 7. Under the RIBA supplemental charter of 1887 and its ensuing by-laws Associates gained four places on the RIBA Council plus at least six places on each of the four departmental standing committees set up in 1886 and extended, but still limited, voting rights at General Meetings.)

ASSOCIATES COMMITTEE MINUTES, 1921 — 1922
See 3.2.2

12.1.2   ALLIED SOCIETIES CONFERENCE MINUTES & PAPERS, 1921—1964   7 vols, 1 binder & 4 boxes
Signed minutes of meetings, Jan 1921—May 1964, with copies of minutes of joint meetings of the Conference and the RIBA Council, 1945—1953 and 1956—1958: administrative correspondence, 1948—1950 and 1957—1964, memoranda and reports.
Subjects : Increased involvement of provincial architects in RIBA affairs and their increased representation on the RIBA Council and committees: federal grouping of Allied Societies: relations of Allied Societies with their branches: payment of RIBA contributions to the Allied Societies: views of Allied Societies on statutory registration of architects: absorption of the Society of Architects into the RIBA: architectural prizes, studentships and maintenance scholarships: minimum salaries for architectural assistants: professional practice and official architecture: the RIBA Development Scheme: the Institute of Registered Architects: representation of provincial associations on ARCUK: superannuation scheme for assistants in private practice.

12.1.3   * LICENTIATESHIP COMMITTEE MINUTES, 1930—1956   4 vols

Signed minutes of meetings, Oct 1930—May 1956, with lists of candidates' names, plus age, town (up to 1947) and name of approving Allied Society.

Subjects : Consideration of the qualifications, drawings, etc. of candidates for Licentiate membership: recommendations to Council.

(Entry to the Licentiate Class was closed on 31 Dec 1955)

* Access at the discretion of the Archivist

12.1.4 WOMEN MEMBERS COMMITTEE PAPERS, 1931—1942   1 box

Correspondence by the Hon. Secretaries to the committee with members of the committee and other women architects and with the Women's Advisory Housing Council (on the Executive Committee of which the RIBA Women Members Committee was represented), Nov 1931—Feb 1942, and copies of minutes of meetings, Jan 1932—Jul 1938: with lists of names of women members, 1931, 1932 and 1936.

Subjects : Slum clearance: housing standards: rural workers' housing: town planning: presence of women on the housing committees of local authorities: lower salaries of women architects: use of the services of women architects in war: social meetings of women architects: the Progress of Women Exhibition, 1936.

(The first woman member of the RIBA was Ethel Mary Charles who was elected an Associate on 5 Dec 1898. Her sister, Bessie Charles, was elected an Associate on 5 Mar 1900. On 13 Mar 1911 Florence Fulton Holson was elected a Licentiate. The first woman to become a Fellow was Mrs. Edith Gillian Harrison who was elected on 9 Mar 1931. Gertrude Leverkus was Hon. Secretary of this committee until Mar 1938 when Evelyn Drury took over.)

12.1.5 JUNIOR   MEMBERS   COMMITTEE   MINUTES,   1935—1939   2 vols

Signed minutes of meetings, Jul 1935—Jul 1939.

Subjects : Arrangement of the Informal General Meetings: liaison with other RIBA committees: participation in exhibitions: architectural education: right of assistants to have copies of drawings prepared by them: procedure in party wall cases: the RIBA constitution: the Northern Architectural Students Association: RIBA prizes and studentships juries: junior members and Allied Societies: conditions of employment of salaried assistants.

12.1.6 COORDINATION   COMMITTEE   MINUTES   &   PAPERS, 1939   1 vol & 1 box

Signed minutes of meetings, Feb —May 1939, with correspondence, memoranda and reports including background material back to 1933, and replies from Allied Societies to a questionnaire, Jan —Mar 1939.
Subjects : Whether the Allied Societies should become branches of the RIBA: whether all members of the Allied Societies should be members of the RIBA: the financial relationship of the RIBA with the Allied Societies.

12.1.7   INSTITUTE AFFAIRS COMMITTEE MINUTES, 1944   1 vol
Signed minutes of meetings, Jun —Nov 1944.
Subjects : Interests of junior members and salaried members: services offered by the RIBA: stronger action suggested with regard to matters of public interest and association with other bodies concerned with building.

ALLIED SOCIETIES PUBLIC RELATIONS OFFICERS & RIBA PUBLIC RELATIONS COMMITTEE JOINT MEETINGS MINUTES, 1954—1962
see 11.1.10

RIBA PUBLIC RELATIONS OFFICER'S PAPERS, 1954—1963, 1967—1971
see 11.1.11

12.1.8   ALLIED SOCIETIES SECRETARIES CONFERENCE MINUTES, 1955—1956   1 vol
Signed minutes of two meetings, 10 Oct 1955 and 8 Oct 1956.
Subjects : Liaison between RIBA Council, Allied Societies' Councils, branches and chapter executives: RIBA rebates to Allied Societies: Allied Societies' rules and bye-laws: regional and local joint committees of architects, quantity surveyors and builders: Ministry of Housing and Local Government housing medals.

12.1.9   MEMBERSHIP RELATIONS SECRETARY'S PAPERS, 1960— 1968   18 boxes
Correspondence files kept by Malcolm MacEwen, Chief Information Officer who acted as secretary for membership relations, 1959—1963; Chris Lakin, Membership Relations Secretary, 1963—1967, and Gordon Mattey, 1967—1968.
Subjects : Affairs and finances of the Allied Societies in Britain and Ireland and their liaison with the RIBA: RIBA regional meetings, 1962—1965: Allied Societies Spring Congresses, 1965—1966.

(Correspondence with U.K. Allied Societies up to 1960 and with overseas

Allied Societies up to 1964 was dealt with by the Deputy Secretary,
RIBA *see* 5.1.1 'General Office' Papers Series

12.1.10 ALLIED SOCIETIES PRESIDENTS COMMITTEE MINUTES
& PAPERS, 1960—1967   1 binder & 4 boxes
Signed minutes of meetings, Oct 1960—Mar 1967, with correspondence,
memoranda and reports.
Subjects : All matters of concern to the Allied Societies as a whole:
liaison with the RIBA Council: new regional structure for the RIBA.

12.1.11 ALLIED SOCIETIES PRESIDENTS COMMITTEE WORKING
GROUP ON FUNCTIONS AND ORGANISATION OF ALLIED
SOCIETIES PAPERS, 1962—1965   1 box
Correspondence, memoranda and reports, copies of minutes of meetings,
Nov 1962—Feb 1965.
Subjects : Functions of Allied Societies: Allied Society finance: proposed
Allied Society for London: reorganization of the Allied Societies Confer-
ence: proposed regional organization for the RIBA.

ALLIED SOCIETIES PUBLIC RELATIONS WORKING GROUP
PAPERS, 1963—1965
See 11.1.17

12.1.12 MEMBERSHIP (SPECIAL) COMMITTEE MINUTES &
PAPERS, 1963—1965   1 vol & 1 box
Signed minutes of meetings, Mar 1963—Mar 1965, with correspondence
and reports.
Subjects : Discussion of the Fellowship, Associateship, Licentiateship,
Studentship, Probationership, Honorary Membership, Retired Member-
ship: examination for the Fellowship: direct election to the Fellowship.

12.1.13 MEMBERSHIP STEERING GROUP PAPERS, 1965—1966   1
box
Minutes of meeting on 23 Sep 1965, with correspondence, and reports,
Apr 1965—Jul 1966.
Subject : A new RIBA membership structure.

(A group of the Policy Committee)

12.1.14 ESHER COMMITTEE MINUTES & PAPERS, 1965—1966   1
binder & 2 boxes
Minutes of meetings, Mar 1965—Mar 1966, with correspondence,
memoranda and reports, including background material back to 1964.
Subjects : A regional structure for the RIBA: constitution of regions and
branches: proposed regional offices.

12.1.15   RIBA SPRING CONGRESS REPORTS, 1965—1969
Reports of proceedings of annual meetings of representatives of the RIBA regions, branches and societies (Bound in with the Allied Societies Conference Minutes Series.)
Subjects : Regionalization: regional affairs: RIBA affairs in general

12.1.16   MEMBERSHIP WORKING GROUP PAPERS, 1967   1 box
Minutes of meetings, correspondence, memoranda and reports, Apr — Nov 1967.
Subject : Proposed revision of RIBA membership classes.

(A working group of the Board of Architectural Education)

CONSTITUTION COMMITTEE MINUTES & PAPERS, 1967
see 1.1.11

12.1.17   MEMBERSHIP AND PUBLIC AFFAIRS BOARD MINUTES, 1967—1971   1 binder
Signed minutes of meetings, from Jul 1967—May 1971.
Subjects : Public relations: overseas relations: membership relations: competitions: awards: nomination service: RIBA conferences and sessional programmes.

12.1.18   MEMBERSHIP AND PUBLIC AFFAIRS BOARD STEERING GROUP PAPERS, 1969—1971   1 box
Minutes of meetings, Dec 1970—Apr 1971, with reports of working groups, 1969, and draft of report of the Board to the Council, 1971.
Subjects : Policy and administration of the Board.

See also in 2.2 Special Committees Minutes Series:
Architectural Alliance Subcommittee, 1871
Position and Privileges of Country Members Committee, 1877—1878
Privileges of Non-Metropolitan Fellows Committee, 1882
Admission of Fellows Committee, 1884
Federation Committee, 1886
Fellows Committee, 1896—1897
Licentiates Admission Subcommittee, 1910
Honorary Members Committee, 1910, 1915
Licentiates and the Fellowship Committee, 1912
Provinces of the Allied Societies Committee, 1913—1914
Irish Societies Committee, 1916
Allied Societies & the RIBA Joint Committee, 1917—1918
Allied Societies Resolutions Committee, 1918
Classes of Membership Committee, 1920
Official Architects and the Fellowship Committee, 1921

Conditions of Membership Subcommittee, 1921
Junior Organisation Committee, 1947—1949
See also Chapter 1, Section 1: Chapter 3, Section 2: Chapter 8, Section 3 and
  Appendix 7, Archive of the Society of Architects. For the Deputy Secretary's
  correspondence with the Allied Societies *see* 5.1.1 'General Office' Papers.

Bibliography

1   'Federation of local societies and the Institute' *RIBA Proceedings* New Series
    Vol 2 1886 Jan 14 pp93—100
2   Caws, Frank 'The Fellowship question: a plea for sweet reasonableness' *RIBA
    Journal* Vol 4 1896 Dec 31 pp129—130
3   'The admission of lady Associates' *RIBA Journal* Vol 6 1898 Dec 10 pp77—
    78 & 1899 Mar 11 pp278—281
4   'Questions connected with the position of Associates' *RIBA Journal* Vol 7 1900
    Jan 13 pp89—93
5   'Representation of Associates on the Council' *RIBA Journal* Vol 19 1912 Mar
    9 pp346—350
6   'Unity of the profession' *RIBA Journal* Vol 25 1918 Jan pp49—58
7   'Report of a conference of representatives of the Allied Societies and the RIBA'
    RIBA Journal Vol 26 1918 Nov pp14—17
8   RIBA *Membership of the RIBA. Particulars of qualifications* London, RIBA,
    1923 (Revised editions issued frequently, 1926—1955)
9   'Proposals for the adoption of an academic dress for members and Licentiates
    of the Royal Institute of British Architects' *RIBA Journal* Vol 30 1923
    May 12 pp426—428, Vol 31 1923 Dec 22 p123 & 1924 Mar 22 pp315—
    317
10 Kirby, E. Bertram 'The Allied Societies', in Gotch, J. A. (ed) *The growth and
    work of the Royal Institute of British Architects* London, RIBA, 1934
11 'Members' subscription rates and rebate to Allied Societies' *RIBA Journal* Vol
    53 1946 Jun p315
12 Roberts, A. Leonard 'The work of an Allied Society' *RIBA Journal* Vol 57
    1950 Feb pp149—151
13 'The Allied Societies' liaison with the RIBA' *RIBA Journal* Vol 68 1961 Jan
    p93
14 RIBA Finance and House Committee 'Finance of Allied Societies in the United
    Kingdom' *RIBA Journal* Vol 68 1961 Feb pp126—127
15 'London architectural societies' *RIBA Journal* Vol 71 1964 Sep pp398—399
16 'The Allied Societies: three views on their future' *RIBA Journal* Vol 72 1965
    Feb pp66—68. Articles by Peter Sawyer, Vernon Royle & Anthony R.
    Laing.
17 'New RIBA membership structure' *RIBA Journal* Vol 72 1965 May p216
18 RIBA Council 'Regional organisation. The Esher Report' *RIBA Journal* Vol

72 1965 Aug p378. Includes a shortened version of the report of the Esher Committee.

19 Lakin, Christopher 'Finance for regions, branches and societies' *RIBA Journal* Vol 73 1966 Jan p9

20 'Regionalisation' *RIBA Journal* Vol 73 1966 Sep pp397—398

21 RIBA Charter Steering Group 'The case for the charter and bye-laws' *RIBA Journal* Vol 75 1968 Sep pp400—401. A statement on the proposed changes in RIBA membership classes.

22 'A single class of membership' *RIBA Journal* Vol 76 1969 Mar pp89—90

23 'The Department of Membership and Public Affairs' and 'Roger Walters. John Carter interviews the chairman of the Membership and Public Affairs Board' *RIBA Journal* Vol 74 1969 Oct pp436—440 & 441—442. Part of a feature article 'Inside the RIBA'

24 MacEwen, Malcolm 'Regionalisation takes command. A look at the new RIBA branches and regions' *RIBA Journal* Vol 76 1969 Dec pp520—530

25 RIBA Membership and Public Affairs Department 'The work of the MPA Department' *RIBA Journal* Vol 77 1970 Jul p324

26 Adams, Bernard 'Membership participation' *RIBA Journal* Vol 79 1972 Jun pp227—228. Article on the working of the regional structure of the RIBA.

27 'Constitution and organisation of branches and regions of the RIBA' *RIBA Journal* Vol 79 1972 Sep pp406—407

28 Stanley-Morgan, R. 'Architectural library facilities in the provinces' *RIBA Journal* Vol 70 1973 Jan pp24—29. A report drawn up at the request of the Allied Societies' Presidents' Committee.

29 Oldham, George 'RIBA Fellowships: for merit or for money?' *RIBA Journal* Vol 81 1974 Oct p2

30 Macintosh, Kate 'A matter of class' *Architects' Journal* Vol 160 1974 Nov 6 p1087. Article on the proposed revival of the RIBA Fellowship class.

31 Groves, Alan, Chairman of the Membership Relations Board 'A long term strategy for RIBA subscriptions' *RIBA Journal* Vol 81 1974 Nov pp21—22

32 Jones, Nicholas 'Are there better uses for the Institute's building?' *RIBA Journal* Vol 82 1975 Jan p19. Discussion of Malcolm MacEwen's proposal to turn the RIBA Building into an Architecture Centre open to the public, with a modified membership structure that would include clients, users and members of allied professions.

33 RIBA Membership Working Group 'An RIBA membership structure' *RIBA Journal* Vol 89 1982 Oct pp97—99

Section 2 Overseas affairs

Relations with foreign architects were assiduously cultivated on behalf of the Institute by Thomas Leverton Donaldson, one of the two original Honorary Secretaries. Eminent foreign architects were nominated for election as Honorary and Corresponding Members and were encouraged by Donaldson, who acted as Honorary Secretary for Foreign Correspondence from 1839—1858, to send news of architectural affairs in their countries and to donate examples of their own work. Many of their letters can be seen in the Letters to Council Series (*see* 1.2.3) and the books, pamphlets, manuscripts, engravings, drawings and photographs that they gave to the Institute's Library form an important part of its collections (*see* the introduction to Chapter 6).

At this time it was still frequently part of a young British architect's education to travel extensively for a period of two to five years, particularly in Western Europe and the East Mediterranean and the first official publication by the Institute was a pamphlet by Donaldson *Questions upon various subjects connected with architecture suggested for the direction of correspondents and travellers and for the purpose of eliciting uniformity of observation and intelligence in their communications to the Institute*, 1835. Donaldson also initiated reciprocal arrangements for hospitality to be afforded to British architects travelling abroad and foreign architects visiting Britain. By the 1880s members and students could apply to the Council for a travelling card or credential bearing the seal of the Institute to facilitate sketching and measurement of foreign buildings and monuments, while Soane Medallists and holders of other travelling bursaries were provided with letters of introduction to the Institute's Honorary and Corresponding Members.

The Institute continued to have an Honorary Secretary for Foreign Correspondence until 1878, when this function was continued by the (paid) Secretary of the RIBA. Both William White, Secretary from 1878—1896, and his successor William John Locke, Secretary from 1897—1907, being fluent in French and well-travelled were well-qualified to carry on this work. Locke acted as Secretary to the VIIth International Congress of Architects which was held in London under the auspices of the RIBA in 1906. From 1907—1939 the British Section of the Comité Permanent International des Architectes (CPIA) met at the Institute and RIBA members played a leading part both in this organization and in the British Section of the Franco-British Union of Architects (FBUA) from 1922—1939.

In 1936 the RIBA set up a Foreign Relations Committee to act as a link between the profession and the recently-established British Council. It included

Bruxelles le 30 Xbre 1864.

Monsieur et honoré Confrère.

En réponse à votre estimable lettre du 10 9bre dernier, j'ai l'honneur de vous informer qu'il m'a été impossible de satisfaire immédiatement à votre demande de renseignements.

L'architecture n'est pas dans une situation favorable en Belgique.

Le Gouvernement ne peut disposer de grandes sommes que pour les chemins de fer, les routes, les canaux, les fortifications et l'armée tout s'engouffre dans ces articles, il reste bien peu pour les arts.

Il nous faudra avoir contenté chaque représentant de nos Chambres; tant qu'un chemin restera à paver, ou une église à faire dans nos villages, le Gouvernement ne pourra pas encourager l'architecture.

Il manque, en Belgique, une école supérieure d'architecture, où l'élève puisse faire son éducation théorique et pratique. Aujourd'hui nous possédons une quantité d'Académies où l'on enseigne le dessin, la sculpture, et l'architecture pendant deux heures le soir. Ces écoles élémentaires se trouvent dans chacune des villes de la Belgique et ne peuvent servir qu'à inculquer les 1ers éléments de l'art.

Malheureusement, il arrive presque toujours que les jeunes gens qui ont passé quelques années dans ces académies, se croyent des aigles dans leur art, se déclarent architectes lorsqu'ils ont obtenu le 1er prix et se figurent réellement en avoir les capacités, qu'ils peuvent acquérir en trois ou quatre ans, en suivant pendant six

27 Part of a long letter to Charles Charnock Nelson, RIBA Secretary for Foreign Correspondence, by the architect Jean Pierre Cluysenaar, an Honorary and Corresponding Member of the Institute, 30 October 1864, reporting on the current state of architecture and architectural education in Belgium. (RIBA Archive:1.2.3 Letters to Council Series)

representatives of the Architectural Association, the FBUA, the CPIA, the MARS Group and the International Reunion of Architects. Due to the international interests of E.J. 'Bobby' Carter, RIBA Librarian and Editor, who acted as Secretary to this committee and to the Refugees Committee, RIBA responsibility for work on overseas relations and affairs (apart from the correspondence with the Overseas Allied Societies, which was conducted by the Deputy Secretary, RIBA *see* 5.1.1 'General Office' Papers Series) was transferred from the Secretary RIBA to the RIBA Librarian between 1936 and 1949. From 1949—1960, overseas relations work was continued under the aegis of the General Office by William Ellis, Deputy Secretary, then by C.G. Nears and David Taylor, Assistant Secretaries.

In 1948 the Union Internationale des Architectes (UIA) was formed by the fusion of the CPIA and the International Reunion of Architects. Its U.K. Committee met under the auspices of the RIBA and in 1961 the UIA Congress was held at the RIBA's London headquarters. In 1959 the RIBA set up a committee to prepare for a conference of the Overseas Allied Societies of the RIBA to discuss forming a new federation and to consider ways in which the standard of qualification as an architect might be unified throughout the Commonwealth. The conference was held in 1963 and resulted in the formation of the Commonwealth Association of Architects (CAA) which set up a Commonwealth Board of Architectural Education and took over the RIBA's role as a regulatory body. The RIBA then appointed a Commonwealth Relations Committee to liaise with the CAA and from 1966—1973 this work was continued by the Overseas Relations Committee; from 1973—75 by the Commonwealth and International Relations Board; from 1975—1979 by the Foreign Affairs Committee and, since 1979, by the CAA Subcommittee of the Overseas Affairs Committee.

In 1960 the RIBA had set up a new Information and Liaison Services Department which took over from the General Office the administration of RIBA staff work on overseas affairs and from 1962—1971 Kathleen Hall served as Overseas Relations Secretary. From 1967—1971 the overseas relations section formed part of the Membership and Public Affairs Department and, from 1971—1974, of the Intelligence Unit under the direction of Elizabeth Layton. In 1970 the RIBA and ARCUK set up a joint committee to discuss matters relating to the European Economic Community affecting the architectural profession and this was followed from 1973—1975, by a joint European Affairs Board. On the disbanding of the RIBA Intelligence Unit responsibility for RIBA overseas affairs work was split into two, with matters relating to the Liaison Committee of Architects of the Common Market (LCACM) going with Elizabeth Layton to the Education and Practice Department and being overseen by the European Affairs Committee and matters relating to the UIA and the CAA being dealt with by the Membership and Public Affairs Department, with Gillian Adams as Foreign Affairs Secretary, and overseen by the Foreign Affairs Committee. From 1979 Margaret Hallett has served as Overseas Affairs Secretary and all overseas affairs work, whether it relates to the Common Market, to the Commonwealth or to the UIA and foreign affairs in general, has been overseen by the Overseas Affairs Committee and carried out by the Overseas Affairs Section of the Membership and Public Affairs Department which in 1983 became the Membership and Overseas Affairs Department.

HONORARY SECRETARY FOR FOREIGN CORRESPONDENCE'S PAPERS
see 1.2.3 Letters to Council Series

12.2.1 COMITÉ PERMANENT INTERNATIONAL DES ARCHITECTES (BRITISH SECTION) MINUTES, 1908—1939   1 vol
Signed minutes of meetings, Oct 1908—Feb 1939.
Subjects : International factors concerning architects and architecture, especially international competitions: arrangements for international congresses: the protection of artistic and historic monuments and buildings in time of war.

12.2.2 FOREIGN RELATIONS COMMITTEE MINUTES, 1936—1948   2 vols
Signed minutes of meetings, Feb 1936—May 1948.
Subjects : Relations with the British Council for Relations with Other Countries (BCROC): RIBA Honorary Corresponding Members: exchange of architectural students, post-graduates and teachers: travel abroad by British architects: international exhibitions and conferences: entertainment of distinguished foreign visitors: employment of foreign architects in this country: examination of applications by foreign architects for naturalization: relations with foreign architectural societies: despatch of journals, etc. abroad: relations with UNESCO: creation of the Union Internationale des Architectes (UIA).

(The work of this committee was continued by the UIA: UK Committee)

12.2.3 *REFUGEES COMMITTEE MINUTES & PAPERS, 1939—1941   1 vol & 6 boxes
Signed minutes of meetings, Jan —Jul 1939, with committee correspondence to 1941, memoranda and case files going back to 1936 on individual refugee architects which contain letters from applicants, curricula vitae, photographs of their work and copies of journals illustrating their work.
Subjects : Application for emergency powers: statistical enquiry: problem of unemployment among British architects: co-operation between the RIBA and the Home Office on issue of labour permits to foreign architects.

(Before 1939 there were comparatively few architect refugees to Britain and these had been easily absorbed into the profession. The Home Office had made acceptance of the RIBA Code of Practice a condition of entry. Cases were occasionally referred to the RIBA for an opinion and, prior to the setting up of this committee, had been dealt with by the Practice Standing Committee. There were two stages in admission, first a residential permit and second a labour permit which allowed practice. By 1939 the trickle had become a steady stream of architects, mainly from Germany, Czechoslovakia, Austria and Hungary, and the RIBA Council appointed this committee which was composed of representatives of the RIBA Foreign Relations Committee and Practice Committee and the AASTA. It was concerned with supporting, or not supporting, applications by foreign architects for the issue by the Home Office of labour permits. Labour permits were issued only to those under 60 who had a guarantor and a definite promise of an approved job or to those with capital who were prepared to employ British assistants. ARCUK had set up a committee to consider terms on which foreign architects were to be permitted to practice in Britain. In Feb 1939 the situation was that all persons, British or foreign, who could prove that on 29 Jul 1938 they had been practising as an architect could be admitted to the register. After that, people must pass an examination of the standard of the RIBA Special Final before admission to the register.

This committee considered applications from foreign architects from a purely professional point of view. It did not deal with applications for visas, but passed these on to the Architects Refugee Committee, 9 Gower Street, WC1, which dealt with these matters.)

* Access at the discretion of the Archivist

12.2.4   * NATURALISATION   SUBCOMMITTEE   PAPERS,   1946—
1947   1 box
File kept by R. E. Enthoven, RIBA Librarian and Secretary to the Foreign Relations Committee, on applications by foreign architects for naturalization.

(A subcommittee of the Foreign Relations Committee. Its task was to rate applicants' capacity to render a substantial contribution to the national interest according to six grades from 'Outstanding' to 'Unsatisfactory'.

* No access

12.2.5   UNION INTERNATIONAL DES ARCHITECTES (UIA): UK COMMITTEE MINUTES & PAPERS, 1949—1961   3 vols & 1 box
Signed minutes of meetings, Mar 1949—Jan 1961, with memoranda and correspondence by C. G. Nears, Secretary to the committee in 1957 and David Taylor, Secretary to the committee, 1957—1961.

Subjects : As in Foreign Relations Committee Minutes plus membership of UIA committees: UIA assemblies and congresses: regulations for international competitions: UIA working commissions on professional practice, town planning, housing, school buildings, public health and architectural education.

(This committee continued the work of the British Section of the CPIA and the RIBA Foreign Relations Committee. Its work was continued by the UIA and Foreign Relations Committee.)

12.2.6   OVERSEAS RELATIONS SECRETARY'S PAPERS, 1949— 1976   43 boxes
Correspondence files, including memoranda and reports, kept by D. C. Taylor, Kathleen Hall and Elizabeth Layton.
Subjects : Affairs of the UIA and the Commonwealth Association of Architects: international competitions, 1957—1970: UIA working commissions: UIA congresses and assemblies, 1953—1972: overseas work for British architects: RIBA Honorary Corresponding Membership, 1955—1976.

12.2.7   UIA 1961 CONGRESS COMMITTEE MINUTES & PAPERS, 1957—1961   2 vols & 13 boxes
Signed minutes of meetings, Mar 1957—Jul 1961, correspondence by the Secretary and Chairman of the committee, 1959—1961, with memoranda, reports and copies of papers delivered at the congress.
Subjects : Choice of theme: draft of programme: appointment of committees and working groups: administration and financing of the congress: finances of the 1955 Congress at the Hague: temporary buildings for the congress exhibitions on the South Bank festival site.

(Originally called the UIA 1959 Congress Committee since that was the date originally proposed. The congress was held in London in 1961 and its theme was 'New techniques and materials — their impact on architecture'.)

12.2.8   COMMONWEALTH CONFERENCE COMMITTEE MINUTES & PAPERS, 1959—1963   1 vol & 5 boxes
Signed minutes of meetings, Jul 1959—Jul 1963, with correspondence, memoranda, reports, meetings files and working groups' files.
Subjects : Proposed Commonwealth organization of architects: educational standards and professional qualifications of architects in Commonwealth countries: freedom to practice throughout the Commonwealth: architects' registration: preparations for the Commonwealth Conference, 1963.

(Appointed following the report of the Overseas Examination Panel of the RIBA Board of Architectural Education. The conference led to the formation of the Commonwealth Association of Architects (CAA).)

12.2.9   UIA AND FOREIGN RELATIONS COMMITTEE MINUTES & PAPERS, 1962—1966   1 vol & 1 box
Signed minutes of meetings, Feb 1962—Jun 1966, with memoranda, reports and some correspondence.
Subjects : UIA affairs: implications of the EEC (Common Market): international conferences and exhibitions: international competitions: emergency technical aid to countries suffering disasters: RIBA Honorary Corresponding Membership.

(This committee took over from the UIA UK Committee and was superseded by the Overseas Relations Committee.)

12.2.10   COMMONWEALTH   RELATIONS   COMMITTEE   PAPERS, 1964—1967   1 box
Meetings files and correspondence, 1964—1967.
Subject : Relations with the Commonwealth Allied Societies and, from 1965, with the Commonwealth Association of Architects.

(The work of this committee was continued by the Overseas Relations Committee.)

12.2.11   OVERSEAS   RELATIONS   COMMITTEE   PAPERS,   1966— 1973   2 boxes
Copies of minutes of meetings, memoranda and reports, with some correspondence and budget details, Oct 1966—Jun 1973.
Subjects : Relations with the RIBA's overseas Allied Societies, the Commonwealth Association of Architects and the UIA.

(Took over the work of the UIA and Foreign Relations Committee and the Commonwealth Relations Committee. Its work was continued by the Commonwealth and International Relations Board.)

12.2.12   FUNCTIONING OF THE UIA WORKING GROUP PAPERS, 1967—1969   8 boxes
Correspondence with the UIA Secretariat, replies to a questionnaire, papers prepared for group meetings, drafts of preliminary and final reports, copies of minutes of meetings of the group, Oct 1967 — Aug 1968, which was based in London at the RIBA.
Subject : Review of the organization and methods of the UIA.

12.2.13   ARCUK/RIBA COMMON MARKET COMMITTEE PAPERS, 1970—1972   1 box

Copies of minutes of meetings, Dec 1970 — Dec 1971, with memoranda and reports, 1970—1972, with background material back to 1967.
Subjects : Matters relating to the European Economic Community which affected the British architectural profession.

12.2.14   UIA WORKING GROUP ON EDUCATIONAL SPACES: UK REP-RESENTATIVE'S PAPERS, 1970—1982   9 boxes
Reports of meetings of the Group and seminars held between 1970 and 1982, with correspondence and working papers of Geoffrey Hamlyn, the UK representative.
Subjects: Design, use and adaptability of school buildings and community centres.

See also in 2.2 Special Committees Minutes Series:
VIIth International Congress of Architects Executive Committee, 1904—1906
Permanent International Congress (British Section) Committee, 1907—1908
For the Deputy Secretary's correspondence with overseas Allied Societies *see* 5.1.1
  'General Office' Papers

Bibliography

1   Donaldson, T. L. *Questions upon various subjects connected with architecture, suggested for the direction of correspondents and travellers and for the purpose of eliciting uniformity of observation and intelligence in their communications to the Institute* London, IBA, 1835
2   *VIIth International Congress of Architects. Summary of proceedings* Published by the RIBA as a special supplement to the *RIBA Journal* Vol 13 1906 Aug 25
3   RIBA Refugees Committee. Report. *RIBA Journal* Vol 46 1939 Jun 26 pp826—831
4   Spragg, C. D. 'Diary of an overseas tour of the President and Secretary, RIBA' *RIBA Journal* Vol 64 1957 May pp265—267, Jun pp313—314, Jul pp374—376, Aug pp425—426 & Sep pp451—453
5   'Commonwealth architects' conference at the RIBA' *RIBA Journal* Vol 68 1960 Nov pp7—8
6   Pierce, S. Rowland 'Some early RIBA travellers, 1835—1845' *RIBA Journal* Vol 69 1962 Nov pp410—413
7   *Commonwealth and Overseas Allied Societies Conference 21—25 July 1963* London, RIBA, 1963. Final report and conference papers
8   'Alliance or association?' *RIBA Journal* Vol 70 1963 Jul p262. Concerning the relationship of overseas and Commonwealth Allied Societies.
9   'Conference of Commonwealth and Overseas Allied Societies' *RIBA Journal* Vol 70 1963 Sep pp344—354
10   Colchester, T. C. 'The Commonwealth Association of Architects' *RIBA Journal*

Vol 71 1964 Dec pp518—519

11 'The Commonwealth board' *RIBA Journal* Vol 72 1965 Aug p374. Article on the new Commonwealth Board of Architectural Education

12 *Architects in Britain*, London, RIBA, 1966. A handbook for foreign visiting architects.

13 Colchester, T.C. 'Overseas architects and the U.K.: the professional balance of trade' *RIBA Journal* Vol 76 1969 Nov p492. Concerning the proposed removal of nationality requirements for RIBA membership.

14 Hall, Kathleen *Architectural practice in Europe* 1. France 2. Federal Republic of Germany 3. Italy 4. Benelux. Published in London for the RIBA & the ARCUK by RIBA Publications Ltd, 1975

15 Austin-Smith, Michael 'Involvement overseas. Activities and competitions' *RIBA Journal* Vol 84 1977 May p198

16 Hamlyn, Geoffrey 'What's the use of the UIA?' *RIBA Journal* Vol 87 1980 Dec pp49—50

Appendixes

Appendix 1
Architects' Club Papers, 1791 —1797

The club was founded in 1791, its original members being Robert Adam, Robert Brettingham, Sir William Chambers, Samuel Pepys Cockerell, George Dance, Thomas Hardwick, Henry Holland, Richard Jupp, James Lewis, Robert Mylne, Richard Norris, James Paine Junior, Nicholas Revett, Thomas Sandby, John Soane, James Wyatt and John Yenn. Membership was in future to be restricted to Academicians or Associates of either the Royal Academy or the Rome, Parma, Bologna, Florence or Paris academies, or to those who had received the Royal Academy's gold medal for composition in architecture. It was essentially a prestigious dining club but in the early years it also functioned, with limited effect, as an association of professional architects concerned with questions of professional ethics, qualifications, charges and research. One of its first acts was to appoint a committee to foster and publicize research into methods of fire-preventive construction and subsequently, in 1795, it appointed a committee to consider architects' fees. The club sometimes referred to itself as 'The Associated Architects in London' or 'The Society of Architects in London'. Its history after the 1790s is obscure but it survived into the second half of the 1830s.

The papers described here form part of the British Architectural Library Manuscripts & Archives Collection's Henry Holland Papers.

Section 1 General

1.1   Note of proceedings at a dinner attended by Henry Holland, George Dance, James Wyatt and Samuel Pepys Cockerell at which it was decided to establish an architects' club, 1791 Sep 23.   HoH/1/1/1

1.2   Minutes of proceedings at a meeting at the Thatched House Tavern, St. James's Street, Westminster, which established the Architects' Club, 1791 Oct 20.   HoH/1/1/2—3

1.3   Draft of a proposed resolution concerning disciplinary measures to be taken in the event of one member of the club offending another. No date.   HoH/2/6/1

1.4   Memorandum on the rates of commission to be charged for architectural work, surveying and valuation. No date.   HoH/2/3/1

1.5   Copy of minutes of proceedings at a meeting of the club on 1796 Oct 6. Contains a draft of a resolution by Robert Mylne that any architect who interfered with another's commission would be acting in a manner 'derogatory   to   the   honour   of   the   profession   of   an architect'.   HoH/2/4/1

1.6   Letters to Henry Holland by club members Robert Mylne, S.P. Cockerell and Richard Jupp concerning disputes and club affairs, 1791 — 1795. 9 items.   HoH/2/7 & 2/10

Section 2 Papers of the Fire Prevention Committee of the Architects' Club

2.1   Minutebook of the committee appointed by the club to investigate the causes of the large number of recent fires and the best means of preventing them in the future, 1792 Mar 8 — 1797 Apr 6.   HoH/1/2

(Henry Holland was chairman of this committee which, as well as collecting evidence, conducted its own experiments in methods of fire-preventive construction in two houses in Hans Place, London SW1)

2.2   Notebook containing notes on fires, including cases of arson, occurring in private houses, farms and industrial premises mainly in England and Scotland but also in Ireland and Paris, France, between 1 Jan 1791 & 28 Dec 1792.   HoH/1/3

2.3   Correspondence and other papers of the Fire Prevention Committee, 1792 — 1797. 28 items, including:

2.3.1   Correspondence with Charles, 3rd Earl Stanhope, concerning his fire-preventive invention, 1792, and a fire at Chevening Place, Kent, 1797. 4 items   HoH/1/4 & 2/5

2.3.2   Memoranda re experiments at Nos. 5 & 10 Hans Place, SW1, 1792 — 1793. 4 items   HoH/1/5

2.3.3   Correspondence concerning the use of iron fireplates for preventing the spread of fire with David Hartley, the inventor, and John Hanson, Robert Brettingham and J. Lodge Batley, 1792 — 1793. 9 items   HoH/2/8/1—6, 2/10/3 & 9, 2/11/1

2.3.4   Papers re the report of the committee, which was published as *Resolution of the Associated Architects, with a report of a committee by them appointed to consider the causes of the frequent fires and the best means of preventing the like in future* in 1793, including a letter from Sir William Chambers agreeing to present a copy of it to the king and letters from S.P. Cockerell, John Bonnar Junior and James Gandon, 1793. 10 items   HoH/2/1/1—3, 2/2/1, 2/9/1—3, 2/10/8, 10 & 11

Bibliography

1   T. J. Mulvany (ed) *Life of James Gandon Esq.* Dublin, 1846. Appendix pp295—297. Includes details on the rules of the club.
2   Sirr, Harry 'The Architects' Club (1791) and the Architectural Society (1806)' *RIBA Journal* Vol 18 1911 Jan 7 pp183—184
3   Barrington Kaye 'Early architectural societies and the foundation of the RIBA' *RIBA Journal* Vol 62 1955 Oct pp497—499
4   Colvin, Howard 'The architectural profession' Introduction to his *Biographical dictionary of British architects 1600—1840* London, John Murray, 1978 pp34—35

Appendix 2
Architectural Students' Society Papers, 1817

The Architectural Students' Society was founded by Thomas Leverton Donaldson, subsequently a prime mover in the foundation of the RIBA, while he was a student at the Royal Academy. Its members met to make designs or sketches on a given subject or to discuss a paper by a member.

1   Papers relating to a petition to the President & Council of the Royal Academy by the Society requesting the Academy to form a School of Architecture and allow architectural students more opportunity to use the Academy library, in order to place the study of architecture on the same footing as that of painting and sculpture (Bound in Vol Q11 of RIBA pamphlets):

1.1   Printed resolution of the Society that a petition be made: followed by a list of the architectural students of the Royal Academy, 1817 Feb 25.

1.2   Printed circular letter by Thomas Lee, Secretary of the Society, 1817 Feb 28, giving details of a meeting to be held on Mar 7.

1.3   Ms. draft of the Society's petition to the President & Council of the Royal Academy. No date (1817, between Mar & Jul).

1.4   Printed circular letter by Charles Harriott Smith, Secretary of the Society, 1817 Dec 1, giving the text of a letter to the Society by Henry Howard, Secretary of the RA, 1817 Jul 19, saying that the petition had been presented to the Council who 'will give it such attention as the general circumstances of the establishment will allow'. (The only result of the petition was that they agreed to open the library twice a week in term-time instead of only once).

Appendix 3
Architectural Society Lectures, 1833 — 1840

Founded in 1831, the aim of the Architectural Society was to form 'a British School of Architecture, affording the advantages of a library, museum, professorships and periodical exhibitions'. It met at 35 Lincolns Inn Fields, London WC2, and was open to engineers and surveyors as well as architects. Its first president was W.B. Clarke and its members included David Brandon, G.E. Street, Ewan Christian and Sir William Tite, who was president of the society from 1838 to 1842 when it was amalgamated with the Institute of British Architects.

Manuscripts of nine papers read to the society between 1833 and 1840:

1   Thomas Henry Wyatt. An essay on the advantages likely to result from the establishment of the society, prefaced by 'a glance at the course of architecture from the building of St. Peter's', 1833 (19p.)   AS/1/1

2   Thomas L. Walker 'Essay on the study of gothic architecture', read on 31 Dec 1833 (52p.)   AS/1/2

3   Edward Henry Browne 'A sketch of the life, and observations on the work of, Sir John Vanburgh', read on 24 Feb 1834 (29p.)   AS/1/3

4   Martin John Stutely. An essay on the gothic and classical styles of architecture, May 1834 (23p.) AS/1/4

5   John Blore 'Remarks on the ancient architecture of England, its progress and applicability to modern purposes', Nov 1834 (29p.)   AS/1/5

6   George Moore 'On perspective', read on 13 Jan 1835 (28p.)   AS/1/6

7   John Burges Watson. An essay on 'the noble art of architecture', being a review of the history of architecture, read on 5 May 1835 (30p.)   AS/1/7

8   Robert Addams 'On the strength of beams to resist pressure and impact', no date (18p.)   AS/1/8

9   E. W. Brayley, Junior 'On the stone to be used in the construction of the new Houses of Parliament'. Part 1 (21p.), read on 25 Feb 1840. Part 2 (13p.), read on 24 Mar 1840   AS/1/8

see also RIBA Archives, Fellows Nomination Papers Series, Vol 1, and Associates Nomination Papers Series, Vol 1, for the declarations of the members of the Architectural Society who became Associates or Fellows of the Institute in 1842.

Bibliography

Laws and regulations of the Architectural Society, 35 Lincolns Inn Fields London, Architectural Society, 1835

Appendix 4
Archive of the Architects Benevolent Society, 1845 — 1965

* Access to this archive is at the discretion of the Society

The formation of the Architects' Benevolent Fund was proposed by John Turner on 31 October 1845 at the annual meeting of the former members and friends of the late Architectural Society, which had merged with the RIBA in 1842. The others present at the meeting, which was held at the Freemasons Tavern, Lincoln's Inn, were George James John Mair, nominated Honorary Secretary *pro tem* of the Fund, John Henry Hakewill, Edward Charles Hakewill, George Ostell Leicester, Edward Henry Browne and William Grellier. This committee met ten times over the next four years, seeking advice from William Tite, former president of the Architectural Society, the RIBA and others, in working out detailed proposals for the Fund. By July 1849 matters were sufficiently advanced for Sydney Smirke to be elected the first President and the following month the name was changed to the Architects Benevolent Society.

The Society was officially founded at the first General Meeting held at the Freemasons Tavern on 27 November 1850, with Smirke as President, Tite as Honorary Treasurer and John Turner as Hon. Secretary. Smirke remained President until 1877 when he was succeeded by Thomas Henry Wyatt who was in turn succeeded by John Whichcord in 1880. On his death in 1885 it was decided that in future the President of the RIBA should be *ex officio* the President of the ABS. John Turner was succeeded as Honorary Secretary by his son, John Goldicutt Turner, in 1876 and he was succeeded in 1880 by William H. White who held the post until 1893. After this date the Honorary Secretary had an assistant, which post gradually became a full-time salaried position. Subsequent Honorary Secretaries were Percival Currey, 1893—1918, Sir Charles Nicholson, 1918—1949, Charles Woodward, 1949—1953, and Howard Lobb, assisted by Rudolf Dircks, 1893—1921, Miss E.H. Mann, 1921—1937, Miss B.N. Solly, 1937—1958, and Miss I.M. O'Sullivan. The Society met mainly at the Freemason's Tavern until May 1851 and after that at the RIBA's premises.

For a long time the Society was concerned only with making grants for the relief of distressed architects and their dependents. Its activities expanded considerably during and after the First World War, when it administered the War Relief Fund to assist architects who had suffered hardship as a direct result of the war. Between 1931 and 1935 the Society was the principal component of the joint Architects

Unemployment Committee, which helped to relieve some of the worst effects of the slump upon the architectural profession at a time when private and public building came virtually to a standstill.

A significant long-term development was the introduction of an insurance scheme for architects, proposed by Maurice E. Webb in 1922 and developed over the next decade. This service is now one of the principal sources of income for what remains the fundamental role of the Society — as a charity for the profession — and, as well as providing grants and pensions, the Society owns and runs an estate of sheltered housing at East Horsley in Surrey, opened in 1958.

The ABS has always been an independent body but since 1849, when the Institute decided that it was constitutionally prevented from being directly connected with a benevolent fund but offered all the moral support and encouragement it could give, it has always had particularly close links with the RIBA.

Section 1 **Minutes**

1.1   COUNCIL MINUTES, 1845—1964   7 vols   ABS/1/1/1—7
        Signed minutes of meetings of the Council, Oct 1845 — Mar 1964, of
        the Insurance Committee, Oct 1922 — Oct 1931, and of various ad hoc
        subcommittees, with annual reports, the Treasurer's reports and accounts,
        subcommittees' reports and letters received.
        Subjects : Applications for grants and pensions; donations, subscriptions
        and investments; administration of war relief funds; establishment of
        homes for indigent architects and their dependents; fund-raising activities.

1.2   GENERAL   MEETINGS   MINUTES,   1850—1965   2
        vols   ABS/1/2/1—2
        Signed minutes of annual and special general meetings, Nov 1850 —
        May 1965, with annual reports, statements of account and balance sheets
        from 1878.
        Subjects : Approval of regulations, annual reports and accounts; election
        of officers and the committee; revisions of by-laws.

        PROFESSIONAL EMPLOYMENT COMMITTEE MINUTES,
        1914 —1919
        (A joint committee with the RIBA, the Society of Architects, the Architec-
        tural Association & the Architects and Surveyors Approved Society)
        see 11.6.1, 11.6.2, 11.6.3

1.3   WAR LOAN FUND & WAR RELIEF FUND COMMITTEES
        MINUTES, 1915 — 1916, 1919—1924   1 vol   ABS/1/3
        Signed minutes of the War Loan Fund Committee, Nov 1915 — May
        1916, and the Architects War Relief Fund Committee, Nov 1919 — Sep
        1924.

Subjects : Loans and grants to architects; subsidized employment of architects and draughtsmen on the London Society's Map of Central London from 1921 and the London County Council's Civic Survey of Greater London from 1922.

(These war relief funds were administered on behalf of the joint Architects War Committee)

1.4 ARCHITECTS UNEMPLOYMENT COMMITTEE MINUTES, 1931—1935   1 vol   ABS/1/4
Signed minutes of meetings, Dec 1931 — Oct 1935, with reports, applications for work, unemployment statistics and record of payments made.
Subjects : Provision of temporary work for unemployed architects, principally on the London Society's Survey of London and Central London Plan and on indexing the location of architectural records for the Architectural Graphic Records Society.

(A joint committee comprising representatives of the ABS, the RIBA Executive Committee and the Association of Architects, Surveyors and Technical Assistants)

1.5 ATTENDANCE BOOK, 1935—1959   1 vol   ABS/1/9
Signatures of those attending meetings of the Council, committees and subcommittees of the ABS.

Section 2 Accounts

2.1 CASH BOOK, 1938—1961   2 vols   ABS/2/1/1—2
Cash and bank accounts, Oct 1938 — Feb 1961, balanced annually with analyses.

2.2 LEDGER, 1942—1954   1 vol   ABS/2/2
Ledger, Jan 1946 — Jan 1961, sectionally divided according to nature of payment or receipt and balanced annually.

2.3 JOURNAL, 1946—1961   1 vol   ABS/2/3
Journal, Jan 1946 — Jan 1961, divided similarly to the ledger but in greater detail, and balanced annually.

2.4 ARCHITECTS UNEMPLOYMENT COMMITTEE'S CASH BOOK, 1932—1935   1 vol   ABS/2/4
Chronological record of income and expenditure of the Architects Unemployment Fund, Jan 1932 — Nov 1935, balanced annually.

Bibliography

1 'The Architects' Benevolent Society' in *Architect's, Engineer's and Building-Trades' Directory* London, Wyman & Sons, 1868 p75
2 Architects Benevolent Society *Scheme of insurance* London, RIBA 1924
3 Architects Benevolent Society *Group pension scheme for architects.* Under the auspices of the RIBA and the AASTA. London, 1931
4 Mann, Elizabeth H. 'The Architects' Benevolent Society', in Gotch, J. A. (ed) *The growth and work of the Royal Institute of British Architects* London, RIBA 1934
5 Double, Bob 'Architects Benevolent Society' *Portico* Vol 81 no 6 1977 Summer p33

Appendix 5
Archive of the Architectural Union Company, 1857 — 1914

The Company was formed in 1857 by members of the RIBA and the Architectural Exhibition to provide accommodation for themselves and other architectural societies. There had been dissatisfaction for some years with the inadequate facilities for exhibiting architectural drawings and with the small number of such drawings chosen for showing at the Royal Academy. The Company proposed to provide galleries and rooms which would be taken primarily by architectural societies. The original shareholders were almost all architects and the board of directors was chosen from those holding at least ten shares. Sir Charles Barry was the first chairman (1857—1859). Thereafter the succession was: Sir William Tite, 1859—1873; James Edmeston, 1873—1896; Arthur Cates, 1896—1901; Cecil F.J. Jennings, 1901—1910; E. Guy Dawber, 1910—1911; Reginald Blomfield, 1911—1912; Ernest Newton, 1912.

No. 9 Conduit Street was purchased from the Earl of Macclesfield in 1858. This house, designed in 1779 by James Wyatt, was remodelled inside by Charles Gray and James Edmeston in 1858—1859. There was a large space at the rear with access to Maddox Street and this area was filled in with exhibition galleries. The main societies which occupied rooms were: RIBA (1859—1934); Architectural Association (1859—1896); Architectural Exhibition Society (1859—1870); Architectural Publications Society (1859—1895); Biblical Archaeology Society (1870—1893); Builders Society (1863—1890); District Surveyors Association (1864—after 1906); Exhibition of Materials (1859—1866); Royal Academy Students Club

(1892—1897); Society for the Encouragement of Fine Arts (1860—1896). Many smaller societies, fine art dealers and individuals used the company's premises, especially in the period up to 1896. In 1867 a total of twenty-four tenants rented space. From 1897 the RIBA occupied most of the premises, the remaining galleries being taken by Knight, Frank & Rutley (Estate Agents) in 1898. They moved out and transferred their lease to the RIBA in 1908.

In 1910 the RIBA offered to buy all the shares in the Company which it did not own. This was accepted and on 6 Dec 1911 the decision was made to wind up the Company. At the final meeting of the liquidator (Harold Saffery) on 23 Nov 1914 the Company's property, books and papers were transferred to the RIBA. No. 9 Conduit Street continued to be the headquarters of the RIBA until 1934, when the present premises in Portland Place were completed.

1   ARTICLES OF ASSOCIATION, 1857   1 booklet   AUC/1/1
         Printed booklet containing the articles of association of the Company, registered on 5 Sep 1857.

2   BOARD OF DIRECTORS & GENERAL MEETINGS MINUTES, 1857—1914   4 vols   AUC/2/1/1—4
         Signed minutes of meetings, Jul 1857—Jul 1914, with reports and balance sheets.
         Subjects : Foundation of the company and raising of funds: purchase and alteration of No. 9 Conduit Street: hire of rooms: election of officers: acquisition of company by the RIBA and its liquidation.

3   SHAREHOLDERS   REGISTER,   1857—1912   2   vols AUC/3/2/1—2
         Register of shares Nos 1—1500; names, addresses and occupations of holders: date of entry as shareholders: notes of transfers: annual summaries, 1858—1912: with total numbers of shares held by each subscriber.

4   GENERAL CASH BOOK, 1857—1912   2 vols   AUC/4/1/1—2
         Concurrent accounts, income and expenditure.

5   LEDGER, 1857—1912   2 vols   AUC/4/2/1—2
         Income and expenditure, by subject.

6   LIST OF SHAREHOLDERS, 1858—1860   1 vol   AUC/3/1/1
         Names, addresses and occupations of original shareholders with numbers of shares and total holdings. Notes of subsequent transfers of shares, up to 1878.

7   DEEDS AND AGREEMENTS, 1858—1908   1 box AUC/5/1—
     22
     Copy agreements for purchase, lease of rooms, maintenance, alteration,
     mortgage and sale of No. 9 Conduit Street premises.

8   RENT BOOK, 1859—1906   1 vol   AUC/4/3/1
     Record of organizations renting rooms at No. 9 Conduit Street.

9   COMMITTEES   MINUTES,   1860—1861,   1865   1   vol
     AUC/2/2/1
     Mostly blank, containing three meetings of the Finance Committee,
     1860—1861, and three meetings of judges to award a medal for architec-
     tural drawings, 1865.

10   DIVIDEND LEDGER, 1861—1912   1 vol   AUC/3/3/1
     Record of amounts of dividend received by shareholders.

11   SHAREHOLDERS   CAPITAL   LEDGER,   1906—1912   1
     vol   AUC/3/4/1
     Record of transfer of shares.

Bibliography

1   Architectural Union Company *Memorandum and articles of association of
     the Architectural Union Company Limited. Registered September 5th 1857*
     London, AUC, [1857]
2   'Architectural Union Company' *Builder* Vol 18 1858 May 22 p353 & Dec 4
     p823 & Vol 19 1859 Dec 10 pp812—813
3   Several views of the exterior and interior of No. 9 Conduit Street are found
     in J.A. Gotch (ed.) *The growth and work of the Royal Institute of British
     Architects* London, RIBA, 1934

Appendix 6
Architectural Alliance Papers, 1863 — 1870

This was an alliance of several regional architectural societies which was formed
in 1862, at the instigation of the Northern Architectural Association, to promote

united action in professional matters among 'otherwise isolated' architectural societies. It comprised the Architectural Association (London), the Architectural Institute of Scotland, the Birmingham Architectural Society, the Glasgow Architectural Society, the Liverpool Architectural and Archaeological Society, the Manchester Architectural Association, the Northern Architectural Association and the Nottingham Architectural Association. Its first meeting was held in London on 2 Jul 1862. Most of the societies represented by the Alliance became allied societies of the RIBA in 1889, after the enabling supplemental royal charter of 1887.

1   Printed minutes of annual meetings:

1.1   Minutes of the second annual meeting, held on 1 Jul 1863, including a proposed scale of architects' charges.   AAl/1/1/1

1.2   Minutes of the fourth annual meeting, held on 5 Jul 1865, including a competition circular to be forwarded to all promoters of architectural competitions in the respective localities.   AAl/1/1/2—3

1.3   Minutes of the fifth annual meeting, held on 3 Jul 1866, including a proposed standard form of contract for architects.   AAl/1/1/4

2   Printed circular letter by J. Douglass Mathews, Hon. Sec. of the Alliance, to the Hon. Secs. of the member societies, concerning the holding of architectural examinations in the provinces; proposed exhibition of architectural drawings at the International Exhibition of 1871 and the question of a proposed amalgamation of the Alliance with the RIBA, 29 Dec 1970.   AAl/1/1/5

Appendix 7
Archive of the Society of Architects, 1884 — 1926

In 1884 a campaign by Associates of the RIBA to be allowed to vote on the Institute's affairs was resisted by the Fellows and resulted in the formation of the Society of Architects. The first meeting of those interested in forming the society met on 8 May 1884 under the chairmanship of E. J. Kibblewhite. On 23 June 1884 the first General Meeting was held, when Colonel Ellison was elected President, H. Roumieu Gough, Vice-President, and G. A. T. Middleton, Secretary.

Charles McArthur Butler became Secretary in 1898 and remained so until the Society amalgamated with the RIBA in 1925. The first headquarters were at No. 5 Gt. James Street, Bedford Row, moving in 1887 to St. James Hall, Piccadilly; in 1902 to Staple Inn Buildings, Holborn; in 1910 to No. 28 Bedford Square, where it remained until 1925 when the RIBA took over the lease of No. 28.

Soon after its incorporation in 1893 the Society decided to institute an entrance examination for membership and began to offer scholarships and awards for architectural design, measured drawings, essays and examination work. In 1913 the Society's Beaux Arts Committee set up the first atelier of architecture in London, at Wells Mews, Oxford Street, to promote a form of architectural training similar to that which existed at the Ecole des Beaux Arts in Paris (*see* para. 1.10). This atelier closed in 1923 having encouraged and assisted in forming similar ateliers in London and the provinces, which had been grouped together and associated with the Royal Academy. The Society also instituted a correspondence design course which was so successful that it was taken over by the Architectural Association Schools in 1925.

The Society had a Practice Committee and a professional defence organisation and worked in conjunction with the RIBA to promote reforms in matters relating to building regulations, architectural competitions, conditions of engagement, professional charges, housing fees, building contracts, architectural copyright, ownership of drawings, and codes of conduct. The Society published a form of building contract which was widely used and its Arbitration Committee was an effective organ for settling disputes.

At the beginning of the First World War the Society co-operated in the formation of the Architects' War Committee and initiated the Professional Employment Subcommittee, which was housed at the Society's premises until, for lack of adequate space, it moved to the RIBA premises. The Society was also very active in the war-time Architects' Advisory Council and the Demobilisation & Reorganisation Committees.

One of the main interests of the Society was its campaign for the statutory registration of architects. In 1886 an independent committee was formed, which promoted a bill for the registration of architects, engineers and surveyors. The chief bodies representing engineers and surveyors petitioned against it so the committee then drafted a new Architects' Registration Bill in 1889, which was strongly supported by the Society but not by the RIBA. In 1903, the Architects' Registration Bill Committee was absorbed by the Society, which continued active campaigning for a registration act. By 1905 it was evident that the profession as a whole was in favour of registration and the RIBA at last decided in principle that the satisfactory training of architects could only be obtained by statutory powers. In 1911 an amalgamation and registration scheme was agreed by the councils of the RIBA and the Society but before it could be accomplished it was necessary for the RIBA to apply for a supplemental charter. Another difficulty was that the general body of the Institute failed to support the scheme at that time. The First World War caused yet more delay and it was not until 1924 that the amalgamation was ratified by the general bodies of both organizations and carried out in 1925 after the RIBA had obtained a supplemental charter. McArthur Butler was then appointed secretary of the RIBA Registration Committee which successfully promoted the Architects' (Registration) Acts of 1931 and 1938.

On amalgamation the property of the Society of Architects was transferred to the RIBA and most of the members transferred their membership. Honorary Members of the Society could become Honorary Associates of the RIBA; Retired Members could have the privileges of Retired Fellows of the RIBA; Members could become Licentiates of the RIBA; those Members who had passed the Society's examination and who proceeded to pass the Special Examination in Design set by the RIBA could become Associates of the RIBA; Licentiates of the Society could become Students, RIBA; and Students of the Society could become Probationers, RIBA (all Fellows, Associates and Licentiates of the RIBA were now full corporate members of the Institute, with full voting powers on all matters).

The transfer of the Society's members and property to the RIBA was completed on 14 Jan 1926. In spite of a resolution passed at the final General Meeting of the Society on the same day, that the books and documents of the Society be retained by the liquidator (McArthur Butler) for a period of five years and then be destroyed, many of the records did survive, although there is, for example, no correspondence and nothing which fully complies with clause 8 of the amalgamation agreement between the Society and the RIBA which stipulated that all books and records relating to the qualifications, character and history of members be handed over to the RIBA.

Section 1 Minutes

1.1   GENERAL   MEETINGS   MINUTES,   1884—1926   3
        vols   SA/1/1/1—3
        Signed minutes of ordinary, annual and special meetings, Jun 1884—
        Jan 1926.
        Subjects : Drafting of and subsequent alterations to the articles of
        association: incorporation: election of members, Council members and
        officers: classes of membership: examination for membership: notes of
        papers read to the Society: approval of annual reports and accounts:
        statutory registration of architects: amalgamation with the RIBA:
        winding up of the Society.

1.2   COUNCIL & COMMITTEES MINUTES, 1884—1920   11
        vols   SA/1/2/1—11
        Signed minutes of meetings of the Council, Jun 1884—Oct 1920.
        Subjects : Activities, organization, management, finances of the Society:
        professional practice and ethics: architectural education and ateliers of

architecture: promotion of registration bills: building legislation: arbitration of contract disputes: regulation of competitions: relations with the RIBA.

Includes the signed minutes of the following committees:
Acoustics Subcommittee, Sep 1919
Advertising and Journal Subcommittee (of the Art and Literature Committee), Mar —Apr 1907.
Appointment of Honorary Solicitor Subcommittee, Apr 1907, Jun 1913
Arbitration Committee Rules Committee, Sep 1919
Arrears of Subscriptions Subcommittee (of the Finance Committee), Oct 1908—Oct 1916
Art and Literature Committee, May 1888—Sep 1920
Attendances on Subcontractors Subcommittee, Aug 1914
Board of Professional Defence, Jun 1915—Jun 1918
Building Bill Subcommittee, Feb 1892—Apr 1894
Building Contract Subcommittee, May 1918—May 1920
Burridge Bequest Committee, May 1891
Competitions Subcommittee, Oct 1912—Dec 1917
Cost of Buildings Subcommittee, Mar —May 1914
Defence Subcommittee (of the Practice Committee) *see* Board of Professional Defence.
Deputation to the Building Materials Supply Committee of the Ministry of Reconstruction, Jul 1918
Dilapidations Subcommittee (of the Practice Committee), Sep 1919
Dinner Committee, Oct 1892—Apr 1907
Dinner Subcommittee (of the Art and Literature Committee), Apr 1909
Education Committee, Oct —Dec 1912
Emden Prize Committee, Feb —Apr 1889
Entertainment Committee, Sep —Nov. 1891
Examination Committee, Apr 1894—Sep 1920
Examination Committee Subcommittee, May 1920
Excursion Committee, May 1891—Jun 1895
Farman Testimonial Committee, Nov 1893
Finance Committee, Feb 1885—Oct 1920
Formation of Practice Committee, Mar 1889
General Purposes Committee, Dec 1908—Sep 1920
Grading of Members Subcommittee (of the General Purposes Committee), Jan 1911
Heating and Ventilation Subcommittee, Jun 1917—Jan 1920
Incorporation Committee, Apr —May 1891
Joint Literature and Finance Committee, Oct 1908
Joint Registration Bill Committee *see* Registration Committee
Literary Committee *see* Art and Literature Committee

Literature Committee *see* Art and Literature Committee
London Building Act Committee, Feb 1905—Feb 1906
Members Examination Subcommittee, Dec 1893
Membership Subcommittee, Apr —May 1905
Membership Subcommittee (of the Practice Committee), Dec 1912—Oct 1920
Membership Certificate Subcommittee, Jun 1920
Membership Development Subcommittee (of the Practice Committee), Jul 1914
Membership Examination Committee *see* Examination Committee
New Premises Subcommittee (of the General Purposes Committee), Feb — Jul 1909
Nomination of Candidates for Council Subcommittee, Apr 1918—May 1920
Postgraduateship Subcommittee (of the Examination Committee), May 1917
Post-war Committee of the American Institute of Architects Subcommittee (of the Practice Committee), Jan 1920
Practice Committee, Jan 1890—Oct 1920
Practice Subcommittee on Code of Ethics and the Ecclesiastical Commissioners and Parsonage Houses, Mar 1911
Recognition of the Services of the Retiring President [Edwin J. Sadgrove] Subcommittee, Jun 1920
Registration Committee, Mar 1894—Jun 1908
Registration Subcommittee, Mar 1907
Research Subcommittee, May 1918—Sep 1919
Research on Supply of Cheaper Building Materials Subcommittee, Jan 1916
Student Classes Subcommittee (of the Examination Committee), Feb 1907
Submission of Names for Officers and Council Committee, Feb 1892
Subscription Subcommittee (of the Finance Committee), Mar 1920
Testing (of materials) Committee, Oct 1898—Jul 1899
Town Planning Special Subcommittee, May 1914
Vacancy in the Office of Secretary Committee, Dec 1892
Ventilation Subcommittee *see* Heating and Ventilation Subcommittee
War Risks Subcommittee, Sep 1918

1.3 COUNCIL MINUTES, 1920—1925   1 vol   SA/1/3
Signed minutes of meetings, Nov 1920—Jun 1925.
Subjects : Registration of architects: amalgamation with the **RIBA**: reports of subcommittees: election, resignation and expulsion of members: award of scholarships and prizes: relations with government and other professional bodies.

1.4 SUBCOMMITTEES OF COUNCIL MINUTES, 1920—1924 1
vol SA/1/4
Signed and unsigned minutes of meetings of the following subcommittees:
Diary Subcommittee, Nov 1920—Feb 1921
Dinner Subcommittee, Jan 1922
Higher Buildings Subcommittee, May 1922
Nominations Subcommittee, May 1922
Resolutions of the Assistants' Welfare Committee Subcommittee, Nov
1920
Scholarships and Journal Subcommittee, Jun 1924

1.5 FINANCE COMMITTEE MINUTES, 1920—1925 1
vol SA/1/5
Signed minutes of meetings, Nov 1920—Jun 1925.
Subjects : Members' subscriptions: investments and prize funds: the
Professional Defence Fund: annual accounts.

(For Finance Committee Minutes, 1885—1920 *see* 1.2 Council &
Committees Minutes, 1884—1920.)

1.6 GENERAL PURPOSES COMMITTEE MINUTES, 1921—
1925 1 vol SA/1/6
Signed minutes of meetings, Mar 1921—Apr 1925.
Subjects : Changes to the articles of association and by-laws: staff
appointments and vacancies on Council: dinners and other social
functions: maintenance of premises: starting the journal *Architecture*:
proposed royal patronage: proposed academic dress for members:
registration of architects: amalgamation with the RIBA: dissolution of
the Society.

(For General Purposes Committee Minutes, 1908—1920 *see* 1.2 Council
& Committees Minutes, 1884—1920.)

1.7 ART AND LITERATURE COMMITTEE MINUTES, 1920—
1923 1 vol SA/1/7
Signed minutes of meetings, Dec 1920—Feb 1923.
Subjects : The Society's journal and yearbook: the reading of sessional
papers: the library catalogue: new accessions for the library.

(For Art and Literature Committee Minutes, 1888—1920 *see* 1.2 Council
& Committees Minutes, 1884—1920.)

1.8 EDUCATION AND EXAMINATION COMMITTEE MINUTES,
1920—1925 1 vol SA/1/8
Signed minutes of meetings, Dec 1920—Feb 1925.

Subjects : Award of prizes and scholarships: administration of membership examinations: the Society's design correspondence course: applications for membership: changes in membership: disciplinary matters.

(For Examination Committee Minutes, 1894—1920 *see* 1.2 Council & Committees Minutes, 1884—1920.)

1.9 PRACTICE COMMITTEE & MEMBERSHIP SUBCOM-MITTEE MINUTES, 1920—1925   1 vol   SA/1/9
Signed minutes of meetings, Nov 1920—Feb 1925.
Subjects : Applications for membership: professional etiquette: fee scales and other charges: scrutiny of competitions.

(For Practice Committee Minutes, 1890—1920, and Membership Subcommittee Minutes, 1912—1920 *see* 1.2 Council & Committees Minutes, 1884—1920.)

1.10 BEAUX ARTS COMMITTEE MINUTES, 1913—1925   2 vols   SA/1/10/1—2
Signed minutes of meetings, Jan 1913—Jan 1925.
Subjects : Setting up and administering the First Atelier of Architecture: award of prizes and administration of prize funds: proposed second atelier: Royal Academy scheme for a national school of architecture, involving the amalgamation of the various London ateliers: proposed affiliation of the First Atelier with the Ecole des Beaux Arts, Paris, and separation from the RA Group of Ateliers.

(The First Atelier, opened at Wells Mews, Oxford Street in 1913 continued for ten years and led to the foundation of others in London and the provinces, including those of the Architectural Association and London University, which were grouped together as the Royal Academy Group of Ateliers.)

PROFESSIONAL EMPLOYMENT COMMITTEE MINUTES, 1914—1919
(A joint committee with the RIBA, the Architects Benevolent Society, the Architectural Association and the Architects and Surveyors Approved Society)
see RIBA Archive, 11.6.1, 11.6.2, 11.6.3

1.11 ARCHITECTS' REORGANISATION COMMITTEE MINUTES, 1917—1919   1 vol   SA/1/11
Signed minutes of meetings, Feb 1917—Jun 1919.
Subjects : Question of giving architects priority in demobilization: employment of demobilized architects: appointment of architects to

government departments and public offices: training of disabled servicemen: exemption of servicemen from examinations: setting up of cooperative architectural offices: proposed Architects General Council to regulate the profession: post-war growth in the rate of new building, especially housing, and the availability of materials.

(Appointed by the Architects' War Committee; an independent body composed of the architectural societies and financed by the RIBA. This was a joint committee of the Professional Employment Committee of the Architects' War Committee and the Council of the Architectural Association and included the presidents of all the Allied Societies of the RIBA. It met at the Society of Architects' premises and its Hon. Secretary was C. McArthur Butler.)

Section 2 Accounts

2.1   ACCOUNT BOOKS (Early), 1884—1893   2 vols   SA/2/1/1—2
Secretary's Cash Account Book, May 1884—Dec 1893, and the Treasurer's Account Book, Jun 1884—Sep 1893. Chronological records of receipts and payments, balanced annually.

2.2   MEMBERSHIP SUBSCRIPTIONS ACCOUNT BOOKS & LEDGERS, 1884—1924   10 vols   SA/3/1/1—10
Members' subscription accounts, 1884—1893: Associates' subscription accounts, 1886—1892: Members ledger, 1893—1924: Fellows and Licentiates ledger, 1912—1924: Students ledger, 1912—1924. Usually give full name, address and details of subscriptions paid.

2.3   LEDGERS, 1893—1925   5 vols   SA/2/2/1—5
Ledgers, Jul 1893—Dec 1925, sectionally divided according to the nature of the payment or to name of payee and balanced annually. Vols 1—3 also contain the advertising accounts of the yearbook and journal, later kept in a separate book.

2.4   CASH BOOKS, 1893—1926   8 vols   SA/2/3/1—8
Record of cash and bank accounts, balanced monthly.

2.5   JOURNALS, 1893—1925   3 vols   SA/2/4/1—3
Daily record of financial transactions.

2.6   ADVERTISEMENTS ORDER BOOK, 1908—1925   1 vol   SA/2/5

Annual and alphabetical summary, Nov 1908—Apr 1925, of payments received for advertisements placed in the yearbook and journal of the Society.

2.7   ADVERTISEMENTS LEDGER, 1912—1925   1 vol   SA/2/6
Ledger, divided alphabetically by name of advertiser, of accounts for advertisements placed in the Society's yearbook and journal, Nov 1912—May 1925, balanced annually.

2.8   LEDGER OF THE FIRST ATELIER, 1915—1923   1 vol   SA/2/7
Ledger, Jan 1915—Dec 1923, of the atelier which was supported by subscriptions, atelier fees and donations.

2.9   FIRST ATELIER FEES BOOK, 1913—1914   1 vol   SA/2/8
List of members for the sessions 1913 & 1914, giving name and address of student with details of entrance fees and subscriptions paid.

Section 3 Membership Records

3.1   ROLL OF MEMBERS, 1884—1923   1 vol   SA/3/2
Chronological list of members giving name, date of election, town of registered address (from 1901), serial number, details of termination of membership (where appropriate) and, occasionally, signature of member.

3.2   ROLL OF ASSOCIATES, 1886—1899   1 vol   SA/3/3
Chronological list of Associates (17 only) giving name, year or date of election, details of termination of membership (where appropriate) and sometimes signature of Associate.

3.3   EXAMINATION FOR MEMBERSHIP REGISTER, 1898—1924   1 vol   SA/3/4
Register of membership examinations, Dec 1898—Aug 1924, including examinations held at Johannesburg, 1907—1910, and a Special War Examination held at Cologne, 1919. Gives candidates' name and address and details of fees paid: from 1908, details of marks awarded and results: from 1921, subjects of theses, with separate marks for oral examination.

(Examinations for membership were first held in 1897. The examination was compulsory for all applicants who were not over 28 years old and who had not been principals for 7 years or assistants for 10 years.)

Bibliography

1   *Society of Architects. Proceedings* 1888—1893, Monthly journal of the Society.
2   *Journal of the Society of Architects* 1893—1900 and 1907—1922
3   *The Architects Magazine* Journal of the Society of Architects, 1900—1907
4   *Architecture* The journal of the Society of Architects, 1922—1925
5   'The Institute and the Society of Architects' *RIBA Journal* Vol 19 1912 Feb 24 pp306—320
6   Goulburn Lovell, R. 'The Society of Architects' scheme for ateliers' *Architects' and Builders' Journal* Vol 37 1913 Jan 8 p35
7   Blomfield, Reginald 'Architectural training: the atelier' *RIBA Journal* Vol 20 1913 May 10 p493
8   'The First Atelier of Architecture' in *Who's Who in Architecture* London, Technical Journals Ltd, 1914
9   Butler, C. McArthur *The Society of Architects* London, Society of Architects, 1926. Includes a complete list of the officers of the Society.

Appendix 8
Competition Reform Society Minutes, 1902 — 1906

A meeting for the constitution of this society was held at the premises of the RIBA at No. 9 Conduit Street on 12 May 1902. Alfred W. S. Cross was elected Chairman; H. V. Lanchester, Vice-Chairman; H. W. Wills, Hon. Sec. and C. E. Hutchinson, Asst. Hon. Sec. Its main aim was to reform the methods used for the conduct of architectural competitions. Its members had to undertake not to participate in any open competition the conditions of which had been disapproved by the committee of the Society. This committee drew up a model set of competition conditions and pressurized assessore appointed by the RIBA to refuse to act in any competition the conditions of which were considered unsatisfactory. Partly as a result of the efforts of this society, the RIBA tightened up its competition-monitoring procedures.

1   Volume (ms. 356p.) of signed minutes of meetings of the Society's committee, 1902 May — 1906 Mar   CRS/1
         Includes opinions of the committee on over a hundred competitions mainly in England, Scotland, Wales and Ireland for town halls, hospitals, workhouses, orphanages, libraries, schools, artisans' dwellings, churches,

chapels and the Liverpool Anglican Cathedral. (Notices of disapproved competitions were sent out by the committee to members of the Society).

Appendix 9
Archive of the Architects', Engineers' and Surveyors' Defence Union Ltd, 1927 — 1929

A RIBA Board of Professional Defence was active from 1904—1914. It sometimes gave grants to support individual architects involved in legal cases if it considered such action to be in the interest of the profession as a whole. The idea of a defence union was revived in 1921 but, due to lack of support, remained in abeyance until 1925 when a scheme for the formation of a defence union distinct from the RIBA or any other professional body was formulated by the RIBA Practice Standing Committee and approved by the RIBA Council. The scheme was adopted at an open meeting of architects and surveyors on 18 Oct 1926 and subsequently enlarged to include engineers. Terms and conditions of an indemnity insurance policy were agreed with Alex Howden & Co, insurance brokers and the Cornhill Insurance Co Ltd. The union was registered as a company and the scheme came into operation in Jul 1927. Benefits to members included defence in actions for professional negligence, slander or libel, ownership of copyright and recovery of fees and litigation expenses. Due to insufficient support the company was wound up in Mar 1929.

1   SECRETARY'S PAPERS, 1927—1929   2 boxes   AESDU/1—2
           Files kept by the Secretary of the Union, G. McArthur Butler, between Apr 1927 and Mar 1929, including register of members, copies of minutes of meetings, reports of Council, copies of the articles of association, statements of accounts, printed circulars, blank proforma for membership, proposals for insurance, copies of the Cornhill Indemnity Policy and general correspondence.

           See also in RIBA Archives:
           Board of Professional Defence Minutes, 1904—1914, in 2.2 Special
               Committee's Series.

Professional Defence Union Subcommittee Minutes, 1925—1927, and
Architects Indemnity Insurance Subcommittee, 1936, in 8.1.2 Practice
Standing Committee Minutes Series.

Bibliography

1   'Proposed Architects' Defence Union' *RIBA Journal* Vol 34 1926 Nov 20
pp69—72. Report of a meeting of architects and surveyors at the RIBA on 18
Oct 1926.

Appendix 10
Architectural Graphic Records Committee Minutes, 1931 — 1939

This committee was set up in 1931 by a group of people interested in the accurate
restoration of buildings, the immediate catalyst being the delay and expense caused
by the problem of locating measured drawings of Chingford Old Church which
had fallen into a state of severe disrepair. The first meeting was held on 21
Jan 1931, when Walter Godfrey was elected Chairman and Herbert Mansford,
Secretary. Members were drawn from the RIBA, the Society for the Protection of
Ancient Buildings, the Royal Archaeological Society, the London Society and other
interested bodies. The aim was to compile a card-index, to be housed at the
RIBA Library, recording the location of architects' drawings, measured drawings,
contemporary topographical drawings and prints of buildings in Britain over a 100
years old. Indexers were funded by the Architects Unemployment Fund and
unemployed architects were also used to make new measured drawings where none
existed. By 1941 the index contained *c* .35,000 cards. A combined effort by John
Betjeman; E. J. 'Bobby' Carter, RIBA Librarian; W. H. Ansell, RIBA President;
Walter Godfrey; John E. M. McGregor, Secretary of SPAB, and Sir Kenneth
Clark led to the establishment by the Ministry of Works and Buildings in 1941 of
the National Buildings Record, forerunner of the National Monuments Record,
which took over both the AGRC card index, the RIBA collection of measured
drawings and the Conway Library of photographs from the Courtauld Institute of
Art. Walter Godfrey was appointed the first director and John Summerson, deputy
director.

Appendixes

1   Volume (ms. 35p.) of signed minutes of meetings of the Committee, 1931
           Jan 21 — 1939 Jun 6   AGRC/1
           Interleaved material includes accounts and annual reports.

see also RIBA Archive: 6.7 Literature Standing Committee Minutes Series; minutes
of the Architectural Graphic Records Committee Subcommittee, Mar 1931.

Bibliography

1   RIBA editorial *RIBA Journal* Vol 39 1932 Apr 30 pp499—500
2   'National Buildings Record' *RIBA Journal* Vol 48 1941 May pp115—117

Index to RIBA Record Series Titles

see also Reception Subcommittee Minutes, 1954

Annual Reports of Council, 1836—(1984)   1.2.4

Appeals Committee Papers, 1969—   7.2.24

Application of Major Morant to be a Fellow Committee of Council, 1884   2.2

Application of Science to Building Construction Subcommittee Minutes, 1927   9.3

Applications and Immediate Works Subcommittee Minutes, 1914—1919   11.6.2

Applications for Admission to the Examination for the RIBA Diploma in Town Planning Special Committee Minutes, 1934   7.1.2

Applications for Deferment of Military Service Committee *see* Deferment of Military Service Committee Minutes, 1941—1944

Appointment of a Paid Secretary Committee Minutes, 1866   2.1

Appointment of Architects as Chief Officers to Local Authorities Subcommittee Minutes, 1957—1958   8.3.10

Appointments with Building Materials Manufacturers Subcommittee Minutes, 1934   8.1.2

Arbitration Cases Register, 1965—   4.4.4

Arbitrators Fees Subcommittee Minutes, 1939   8.1.3

Arbitrators Register, 1960—   4.4.2

Archibald Dawnay Scholarship essays and reports: *see* Prizes and Scholarships: Essays and Reports

Archibald Dawnay Scholarships Jury Minutes, 1923—1950   7.1.2

Architects and Builders Consultation Board Minutes, 1925—1929   8.2.8

Architects and Builders Joint Consultative Committee Minutes, 1944—1953   8.2.13

Architects and Operatives Consultation Board Minutes, 1926—1933   8.2.9

Architects and Quantity Surveyors Joint Committee Minutes, 1932—1935   8.1.2

Architects and Quantity Surveyors Joint Committee Minutes, 1939—1947   8.1.3

Architects and Quantity Surveyors Joint Committee Minutes, 1950—1953   8.2.17

Architects and Surveyors Assistants Professional Union & the RIBA Joint Conference Minutes, 1924   2.2

Architects and the Organisation of the Building Industry Subcommittee Minutes, 1942   2.2

Architects Benevolent Fund Committee Minutes, 1847—1848   2.1

Architects Central Technical Service (ACTS) Working Group Papers, 1967—1970   9.40

Architects Fees for Speculative Housing Work Conference Minutes, 1922—1923   8.1.2

Architects Fees in Law Cases Subcommittee Minutes, 1937   8.1.2

Architects Indemnity Insurance Subcommittee Minutes, 1936   8.1.2
see also Board of Professional Defence Minutes, 1904—1914 *and* Professional Defence Union Subcommittee Minutes, 1925—1927

Architects Registration Council of the United Kingdom *see* ARCUK

Architects, Registration of *see under* Registration

Architects Reorganisation Committee Minutes, 1917—1919   App. 7

Architectural Graphic Records Committee Subcommittee Minutes, 1931   6.7
Architectural Libraries Conference Papers, 1950—1970   6.15
Architectural Patronage Study Papers, 1964—1965   11.6.8
Architectural profession, Overcrowding of *see* Overcrowding of the Architectural Profession Joint Committee Minutes, 1924—1925
Architectural profession, Structure of *see* Representation of Members in Salaried Employment & Review of the Structure of the Profession Ad Hoc Committee Minutes & Papers, 1955—1959
Architectural schools *see under* Schools
Architectural science *see also under* Science
Architectural Science Board Minutes, 1950   9.10
Architectural Use of Building Materials Committee Minutes, 1942—1944   10.20
Architectural work by municipal officials *see* Municipal Officials and Architectural Work Committee Minutes, 1904
Architectural work by unqualified persons *see* Private Architectural Practice by Unqualified Persons Ad Hoc Committee Minutes, 1953
Architectural Work carried out by Auctioneers and Estate Agents, Concrete Engineers etc. Subcommittee Minutes, 1936   8.1.2
Architecture, Future of *see* Future of Architecture Committee & Subcommittee Minutes, 1918—1919
Architecture in Public and Secondary Schools Special Committee Minutes, 1930   7.1.2
    see also Methods of Interesting Boys and Girls in Schools of Architecture and Kindred Subjects Subcommittee Minutes, 1928 *and* Prizes for Public and Secondary Schools Jury Minutes, 1929—1930
Architecture schools *see under* Schools
ARCUK Professional Purposes Committee, RIBA Practice & Public Relations Committees Joint Meeting Minutes, 1955   8.1.3
ARCUK/RIBA Common Market Committee Papers, 1970—1972   12.2.13
Art, Science, Literature & Practice Standing Committees & the Town Planning and Housing Committee Joint Meeting on the Royal Commission on Greater London Minutes, 1922   2.2
Art Standing Committee Minutes & Papers, 1886—1939   10.4
Arterial Roads Subcommittee Minutes, 1923   10.5
Arthur Cates Prize essays and reports *see* Prizes and Scholarships: Essays and Reports
Arthur Cates Prize Subcommittee Minutes, 1926   7.1.2
Artistic Architectural Education Committee Minutes, 1864—1868   2.1
Artistic Copyright Committee Minutes, 1860—1861   2.1
Assessors *see* Scale of Fees for Assessors in Town Planning and Improvement Scheme Competitions Subcommittee Minutes, 1929
Assessorships Committee Minutes, 1902   2.2
Assistants, Minimum wage for *see* Minimum Wage for Architectural Assistants Subcommittee Minutes, 1924—1925

British Standards steering group *see* Metric Change, British Standards, Standardisation Steering Group Minutes & Papers, 1967—1969

Britton Memorial Committee Minutes, 1857   2.1

Broadcasting *see* Films, Broadcasting and Television Subcommittee Minutes & Papers, 1944—1945 *and* Sound Broadcasting and Television Subcommittee Minutes & Papers, 1947—1961

Bronze Medal awards *see also* Street Architecture Committee Minutes, 1920 *and* London Architecture Bronze Medal Jury Minutes, 1922—1962

Bronze Medal Awards Subcommittee Minutes, 1964   11.3.7

Bronze Medal Awards Subcommittee Papers, 1961—1964   11.3.6

Budget and Income Subcommittee Minutes, 1963   5.2.7

Buchanan Report Standing Joint Committee Papers, 1963—1965   10.33

Builders, Relations with *see* Architects and Builders Consultation Board Minutes, 1925—1929; Architects and Builders Joint Consultative Committee Minutes, 1944—1953; Architects and Operatives Consultation Board Minutes, 1926—1933; National Federation of Building Trades Employers & RIBA Joint Conferences Minutes, 1923—1925; National Federation of Building Trades Employers & Practice Standing Committee Joint Meetings Minutes, 1929—1930; London Architects and Builders Joint Committee Minutes, 1948—1953; London Architects, Quantity Surveyors and Builders Joint Committee Minutes, 1955—1957 *see also under* Building Industries; Building Industry

Building after the War Conference Minutes, 1918   2.2

Building Centre, Exhibition at *see* Exhibition at the Building Centre Subcommittee Minutes, 1960

Building Code Joint Committee Minutes, 1922   8.4.4

Building Committee of Council Minutes, 1879   2.2

Building contracts *see under* Contract *and* Contracts

Building Control Panel Papers, 1962—1972   8.4.6

Building costs *see* Cost of Building during and after the War Committee Minutes, 1915; Economies in Building Practice Subcommittee Minutes, 1927; Building Economics Study Group Minutes, 1950; Cost Research Committee Papers, 1956—1959

Building Economics Study Group Minutes, 1950   9.10

Building, Industrialised *see* Industrialisation of Building Panel Papers, 1962—1965

Building Industries Consultative Board Minutes, 1919—1921   2.2

Building Industries National Council: RIBA Representatives Committee Minutes, 1944   8.2.14

Building Industry, Advisory Council of *see* Advisory Council of the Building Industry Minutes, 1931

Building industry, Architects and the organisation of *see* Architects and the Organisation of the Building Industry Subcommittee Minutes, 1942

Building Industry Committee Minutes & Papers, 1962—1967   9.24

Building Industry Communications Research Project Papers, 1963—1969   9.26

see also SfB Building Communications Committee: RIBA Representative's Papers, 1964—1967

Building Industry Section Files, 1962—1969   9.25

Building industry, Unemployment in *see* Unemployment in the Building Industry Conference Minutes, 1932

Building Industry Working Party & Anglo-American Productivity Team Committee Minutes & Papers, 1950—1951   8.2.16

Building Legislation Joint Committee *see* Joint Committee on Building Legislation Papers, 1965—

Building materials, Architectural use of *see* Architectural Use of Building Materials Committee Minutes, 1942—1944

Building materials, Experiments with *see* Experiments and Professional Investigations Committee Minutes, 1854 *and* Materials and Construction Committee Minutes, 1876. *see also under* Science

Building materials, Grading of *see* Grading of Buildings and Building Materials Subcommittee Minutes, 1934

Building materials manufacturers, Appointments with *see* Appointments with Building Materials Manufacturers Subcommittee Minutes, 1934

Building materials, Standardisation of *see* Standardisation of Building Materials Subcommittee Minutes, 1942

Building methods *see* Rationalisation of Traditional Building Panel Minutes & Papers, 1962—1963

Building Needs Study Group Minutes, 1950   9.10

Building practice, Economies in *see* Economies in Building Practice Subcommittee Minutes, 1927

Building regulations, By-laws and *see* By-laws and Building Regulations Committee Minutes, 1959

Building Regulations for the United Kingdom Committee *see* General Building Regulations Committee Minutes, 1876

Building science *see* Application of Science to Building Construction Subcommittee Minutes, 1927. *see also under* Science

Building Science Laboratories Subcommittee Minutes, 1927   9.3

Building Stones Photographs Album, 1911   9.4

Building stoppage *see* Stoppage of Building Committee Minutes, 1920 *and* Stoppage of Work by War Survey Papers, 1939—1940

Building surveyors examination *see* RIBA Examination for Candidates for the Office of Building Surveyor under Local Authorities: Recommendations for Certificates, 1856—1905

Building surveyors examination results *see* Statutory Examination for Building Surveyors Results, 1927—1932

Building Surveyor Examiners *see* RIBA Examiners for the Examination for the Office of Building Surveyor under Local Authorities Minutes, 1855—1984

Building, Traditional *see* Rationalisation of Traditional Building Panel Minutes & Papers, 1962—1963

Examiners, Board of *see* Board of Examiners

Examiners Committees Minutes, 1913—1977   7.2.10

Examiners, Fellowship *see under* Fellowship

Examiners for the examination of building surveyors *see under* RIBA Examiners for the Examination for Candidates for the Office of Building Surveyor under Local Authorities

Examiners for the examination of Licentiates wishing to become Fellows *see under* Fellowship Examination for Licentiates Examiners

Examiners (Intermediate, Final & Special Examinations) Minutes, 1913—1925   7.2.10

Examiners, Payment of *see* Payment of Examiners Committee Minutes, 1911—1914

Executive and General Purposes Committee of the Architects War Committee Minutes, 1914—1920   2.2

Executive Committee & Official Architects Committee Joint Meeting Minutes, 1937   3.1.2

Executive Committee Minutes, 1925—1959   3.1.2

Executive Committee, Public Relations Committee & Central Advisory Planning Committee Joint Meeting Minutes, 1948   3.1.2

Exemption of Service Candidates (from the RIBA Final Examination) Conference Minutes, 1920   2.2

Exemptions Committees Minutes, 1913, 1920—1922   7.1.2

Exhibition at the Building Centre Subcommittee Minutes, 1960   7.1.3

Exhibition buildings at South Kensington *see* Proposed Purchase of the International Exhibition Buildings at South Kensington Committee Minutes, 1863

Exhibition Joint Committee Minutes & Papers, 1921—1927   11.2.2

Exhibition of Architecture and Complementary Arts Subcommittee Minutes, 1923   10.4

Exhibition of Architecture Paris 1914 Joint Organising Committee *see* Paris Exhibition 1914 Joint Committee Minutes, 1914

Exhibition of Architecture Subcommittee Minutes, 1921   10.4

Exhibition of Black and White and Colour Work by Members Subcommittee Minutes, 1928   10.4

Exhibition photographs *see* Permanent Collection Section of the Exhibition Subcommittee Minutes, 1937—1938

Exhibition Subcommittee, Aerodromes Subcommittee & Organisers of the Permanent Collection General Meeting Minutes, 1936   10.4

Exhibition Subcommittee Minutes, 1929—1939   10.4
see also Organising Section of the Exhibition Subcommittee Minutes, 1936—1939

Exhibitions *see also* City Churches Exhibition Subcommittee Minutes, 1925; Civic Survey Exhibition Joint Committee Minutes, 1920; Congress Exhibition

Fine Arts Copyright Consolidation and Amendment Bill Committee Minutes, 1869   2.2
  see also under Copyright
Fire insurance claims, Fees for *see* Fees in connection with Fire Insurance Claims Subcommittee Minutes, 1945
Fire prevention *see also* Prevention of Fire Joint Subcommittee Minutes, 1929
Fire Prevention Circular Committee Minutes, 1911   2.2
  see also Prevention of Fire Joint Subcommittee Minutes, 1929
Florence Bursary *see under* Henry Florence Bursary
Foreign correspondence, Papers of Honorary Secretaries for *see* Letters to Council, 1835—1907
Foreign relations *see also under* Overseas *and* UIA
Foreign Relations Committee Minutes, 1936—1948   12.2.2
Foundation (of the Institute) Papers, 1834—1848   1.1.1
Freehold Premises at 20 Hanover Square Subcommittee of Council Minutes, 1883   2.2
Functioning of the UIA Working Group Papers, 1967—1969   12.2.12
Funds *see under* Trust Funds; Ordinary Funds; Premises Funds
Future Constitution of the Board of Architectural Education Subcommittee Minutes, 1920   7.1.2
Future of Architecture Committee & Subcommittee Minutes, 1918—1919   2.2
  see also 3.2.1
Future of Private Architectural Practice Committee Minutes, 1950—1951   8.3.12
Future Shape of Practice Working Group Papers, 1967—1969   8.1.13

Garage Competition Jury Minutes, 1928   7.1.2
Garden Drawings Exhibition Subcommittee Minutes, 1926   10.4
General Architectual Congress Committee Minutes, 1900   2.2
General Building Regulations Committee Minutes, 1876   2.2
General Conference of Architects *see also under* Conference
General Conference of Architects Committee Minutes, 1871—1878   2.2
General Conference of Architects Proceedings, 1871, 1872, 1878, 1881, 1887   11.4.2
'General Office' Papers, 1896—1964   5.1.1
General Meetings Minutes (Early series), 1834—1885   1.2.1
General Meetings Minutes, 1885— *see* Annual and Special General Meetings Minutes, 1885—1968 *and* Ordinary General Meetings Minutes, 1885—1962
General Meetings, Papers read at *see* Papers Read at General Meetings, 1835—1858
  see also Reporter's Notes of General Meetings, 1850—1858
General Meetings Transcripts, 1961, 1965—1971, 1973—(1982)   1.2.8
General purposes committees *see under* Selection and General Purposes
Godwin Bursary Committee Minutes, 1883   7.4.2
Godwin Bursary essays and reports *see* Prizes and Scholarships: Essays and Reports

Goss Implementation Committee Papers, 1964—1967   10.35
Goss Report Steering Committee Papers, 1963—1965   10.34
Grading of Buildings and Building Materials Subcommittee Minutes, 1934   8.4.3
Grading of Buildings and Means of Escape in case of Fire Subcommittee Minutes, 1932   8.4.3
Greater London *see also under* London; LCC
Greater London, Civic survey of *see under* Civic Survey
Greater London, Royal Commission on *see* Royal Commission on Greater London Committee Minutes, 1922
Greater London Town Planning Joint Conference Minutes, 1913   2.2
Grey Books Index, 1920—1974   6.10
Grissell Prize Subcommittee, 1921   7.1.2
Group Practice and Consortia Research Study Papers, 1963—1965   4.5.4

Hackney Baths Competition Subcommittee Minutes, 1937   3.1.2
Harpenden Hall Competition Subcommittee Minutes, 1936   3.1.2
Health and Sport Exhibition Section Minutes, 1937   10.4
Health Conference Committee Minutes, 1884   2.2
Henry Florence Bursary essays and reports *see* Prizes and Scholarships: Essays and Reports
Henry Jarvis Bequest Committee *see* Jarvis Bequest Committee Minutes, 1911—1912
Henry Saxon Snell Prize essays and reports *see* Prizes and Scholarships: essays and reports
Henry Saxon Snell Prize Joint Committee Minutes, 1927   7.1.2
Henry Saxon Snell Prize Jury Minutes, 1928   7.1.2
Herbert Baker Scholarship Committee Minutes, 1912—1920   7.1.2
Historic buildings, Preservation of *see* Conservation of Ancient Monuments and Remains Committee Minutes, 1864—1886; Art Standing Committee Minutes & Papers, 1886—1939; Preservation of Historic or Architecturally Interesting Buildings, Villages etc Subcommittee Minutes, 1937—1938; Houses of National Importance Committee Minutes, 1949
Home Counties Area Committee for the RIBA Maintenance Scholarships Minutes, 1922—1924   7.1.2
Home Counties Province Subcommittee of the Maintenance Scholarships Committee Minutes, 1930—1931   7.1.2
Honorary and Corresponding Members' correspondence *see* Letters to Council, 1835—1907
Honorary and Corresponding Members' nomination papers *see* Fellows Nomination Papers, 1834—1882 *and* Honorary Fellows & Honorary and Corresponding Members Nomination Papers, 1882—1980
Honorary and Corresponding Members Register, 1835—1892 *see* Membership Register (Early Series)
Honorary Associates Nomination Papers, 1877—1966   5.4.5

Metropolis Management and Building Acts Amendment Bill 1878 Committee Minutes, 1878—1879   2.2

Metropolitan Board of Works By-laws Committee Minutes, 1886   2.2

Metropolitan Buildings and Management Bill Committee Minutes, 1868—1874   2.2

Metropolitan Buildings Bill 1855 Committee Minutes, 1855   2.1

Metropolitan Improvements Committee Minutes, 1864   2.1

Metropolitan Water Board Lead Services Subcommittee Minutes, 1924   2.2

Metropolitan Water Board Regulations Subcommittee Minutes, 1923   8.1.2

Military Service, Deferment of *see* Deferment of Military Service Committee Minutes, 1941—1944

Minimum Wage for Architectural Assistants Subcommittee Minutes, 1924—1925   8.1.2

Ministry of Health & the RIBA Joint Meeting Minutes, 1922   2.2
   see also Housing Committee, Ministry of Health & Practice Committee Joint Meeting Minutes, 1944

Ministry of Town and Country Planning Ad Hoc Committee *see* Town and Country Planning Bill Ad Hoc Committee Minutes, 1944

Model Building By-laws Joint Subcommittee Minutes, 1938   9.3

Model By-laws Joint Subcommittee Minutes, 1939   9.8

Moderators, Board of *see under* Board of Moderators

Moderators Committee & the Examiners for the Intermediate, Final and Special Final Examinations Joint Meeting Minutes, 1946   7.1.2

Moderators Committee & the Final Examiners Joint Meetings Minutes, 1947—1949   7.1.2

Moderators Committee Minutes, 1945—1954   7.1.2

Monitoring Group Papers, 1971   5.2.16

Monopolies and Mergers Commission *see under* Monopolies Commission

Monopolies Commission *see* National Board for Prices and Incomes and Monopolies Commission Steering Group Minutes & Papers, 1967—1970

Monuments, Ancient *see* Historic buildings, Preservation of

Mr Peek's Prizes Committee Minutes, 1872   7.4.2

Municipal Officials and Architectural Work Committee Minutes, 1904   2.2

Municipal Officials and Architectural Work Committee Papers, 1904   8.3.1

Municipal Officials and Public Works Committee *see* Municipal Officials and Architectural Work Committee

Museums and Galleries Subcommittee Minutes, 1928   6.7

Music Group *see* Social Committee Minutes, 1932—1939

National Board for Prices and Incomes and Monopolies Commission Steering Group Minutes & Papers, 1967—1970   8.2.25

National Book Council Subcommittee Minutes, 1927 & 1929   6.7

National Consultative Council of the Building and Civil Engineering Industries (NCC): RIBA Secretary's Papers, 1948—1979   4.1.4

Premises of the Institute, Alterations to *see* Building Committee of Council Minutes, 1879

Prentice Bequest essays and reports *see* Prizes and Scholarships: Essays and Reports

Present and Future of Private Architectural Practice Committee Minutes, 1948— 1950   8.3.11

Preservation of Historic or Architecturally Interesting Buildings, Villages etc. Subcommittee Minutes, 1937—1938   10.5
  see also under Historic buildings, Preservation of

Preservation of Whitgift Hospital Croydon Joint Conference Minutes, 1922— 1923   10.4

Preserving the Open Space adjoining St. Paul's Churchyard Committee Minutes, 1854—1858   2.1

President, Vice-Presidents & Honorary Secretary Special Meeting Minutes, 1930   3.1.2

President, Vice-Presidents & Officers of the Institute Meeting (re war-time arrangements) Minutes, 1939   3.1.2

Presidential Portraits and Busts Collection, *c* .1850—   6.3
  see also Cockerell Portrait Committee Minutes, 1861; Tite Portrait Committee Minutes, 1868

Presidents' Addresses, 1859—(1983)   4.2.1

President's Correspondence, 1953—(1980)   4.2.2

Presidents' Inaugural Addresses *see* Presidents' Addresses

President's Nominations Register, 1958—   11.6.7

Presidents of Allied Societies Committee *see* Provinces of Allied Societies Committee

Presidents of Professional Bodies Meetings: RIBA Presidents' Papers, 1969— 1976   4.2.3

President's War Emergency Committee Minutes, 1939   3.1.2
  see also National Emergency Panel Minutes, 1938 — 1939

Press Cuttings Collection, 1926—1961, 1965—(1982)   11.1.3

Press Releases, 1962—1963, 1965—(1977)   11.1.16

Press Subcommittee Minutes, 1953—1956   11.1.9

Prevention of Fire Joint Subcommittee Minutes, 1929   9.3
  see also Fire Prevention Circular Committee Minutes, 1911

Prices and Incomes Board *see* National Board for Prices and Incomes and Monopolies Commission Steering Group Minutes & Papers, 1967—1970

Private Architectural Practice by Unqualified Persons Ad Hoc Committee Minutes, 1953   8.3.13

Private Practitioners and Official Architects Subcommittee Minutes, 1943— 1945   2.2

Privileges of Non-Metropolitan Fellows Committee of Council Minutes, 1882   2.2

Privy Council Certificates, 1889—(1981)   1.1.4

Prize essays and reports *see* Prizes and Scholarships: Essays and Reports, 1839— 1963

Prizes and Medals, Deeds of Award of *see* Ordinary General Meetings Minutes

Revision of the RIBA Code of Professional Conduct Subcommittee Minutes, 1961   8.1.3

Revision of the RIBA Code of Professional Conduct Subcommittee Papers, 1961—1962   8.1.7

Rheumatic Heart Disease in Children Subcommittee *see* Damp Houses Subcommittee

RIBA affix *see* Illegal Use of (RIBA) Affix Case Files, 1924—1954

RIBA & the Allied Societies Joint Committee *see* Allied Societies & the RIBA Joint Committee

RIBA Booklist, 1969—   6.20

RIBA Building *see* New Building Committee Minutes & Papers, 1932—1937 *see also under* House; New premises; Premises

RIBA centenary *see* Centenary Committee Minutes & Papers, 1933—1934

RIBA conference *see under* Annual Conference *and* Conference

RIBA, Development of the *see* Development of the RIBA Subcommittee Minutes, 1928

RIBA dinners *see under* Annual Dinner; Dinner; Institute Dinner; Conversazione

RIBA Diploma in Town Planning Examination, Applications for admission *see* Applications for Admission to the Examination for the RIBA Diploma in Town Planning Special Committee Minutes, 1934

RIBA Diploma in Town Planning Examination Results, 1927—1931   7.2.13

RIBA Diploma in Town Planning Examiners Minutes, 1924, 1927—1930   7.1.2

RIBA Diploma in Town Planning Examiners Minutes, 1924—1927   7.2.10

RIBA Distinction in Town Planning Ad Hoc Committee Minutes, 1953   7.1.2

RIBA Distinction in Town Planning Committee Minutes, 1947—1962   7.1.2

RIBA Distinction in Town Planning Committee Minutes, 1962—1963   11.3.7

RIBA Distinction in Town Planning Committee Papers, 1948—1963   11.3.5

RIBA Distinction in Town Planning Examiners Minutes, 1945—1950   11.3.4

RIBA Distinction in Town Planning President's Subcommittee Minutes, 1945   11.3.3

RIBA Emergency Panel *see* National Emergency Panel

RIBA Examination for Candidates for the Office of Building Surveyor under Local Authorities: Recommendations for Certificates, 1856—1905   7.3.2

RIBA Examination in Architecture *see also under* Examination *and* Examinations

RIBA Examination in Architecture Implementation Committee Papers, 1968—1969   7.2.23

RIBA Examiners for the Examination for Candidates for the Office of Building Surveyor under Local Authorities Minutes, 1855—1965, 1977—1984   7.3.1

RIBA Examiners for the Examination for Candidates for the Office of Building Surveyor under Local Authorities Minutes, 1966—1977   7.2.10

RIBA Finances Subcommittee Minutes, 1957   5.2.7

RIBA foundation *see* Foundation Papers, 1834—1848

RIBA Journal *see also under* Journal

RIBA Journal Editor's Papers, 1931—1935, 1968—1970   11.1.4

Town Planning Exhibition for Sweden Subcommittee Minutes, 1945—1946   10.23

Town Planning Group Papers, 1966—1967   10.37

Town Planning, Housing and Slum Clearance Committee Minutes & Papers, 1936—1939   10.5

Town planning in Greater London *see* Greater London Town Planning Joint Conference Minutes, 1913

Town Planning Section Files, 1962—1971   10.32

Town planning work, Fees for *see* Fees for Town Planning Work Joint Committee Minutes, 1945

Towns, New *see* New Towns Subcommittee Minutes, 1946

Traffic roundabouts, Design of *see* Design of Traffic Roundabouts Special Committee Minutes, 1936

Training and Organisation of a Second Category Subcommittee *see* Second Category Subcommittee Minutes, 1958—1959

Training of Architects in Town Planning Committee Minutes, 1942—1944   7.1.2

Training of Technicians and Technologists and Classes of Membership Committee *see* Training of Technicians Committee

Training of Technicians Committee Minutes, 1959—1962   7.1.2

Travelling Libraries (Allied Societies) Subcommittee Minutes, 1928   6.7

Travelling Studentships Special Committee Minutes, 1886   7.4.2

Trust Funds Cash Books, 1932—1973   5.2.8

Trust Funds Deeds, Bequests & Deeds of Covenant, 1864—(1981)   5.2.4

Trust Funds Ledger, 1942—1952   5.2.11

Typography Group Papers, 1958—1965   11.1.13

UIA and Foreign Relations Committee Minutes & Papers, 1962—1966   12.2.9

UIA, Functioning of the *see* Functioning of the UIA Working Group Papers, 1967—1969

UIA 1961 Congress Committee Minutes & Papers, 1957—1961   12.2.7

UIA: UK Committee Minutes & Papers, 1949—1961   12.2.5

UIA Working Group on Educational Spaces: UK Representative's Papers, 1970—1982   12.2.14

Ulster Alliance Subcommittee Minutes, 1908—1909   2.2

Ulster Subcommittee *see* Ulster Alliance Subcommittee

Unemployment in the Building Industry Conference Minutes, 1932   2.2

Unification and Registration Committee Minutes & Papers, 1920—1922   3.2.1

Union International des Architectes *see under* UIA

Units of design, Standardisation of *see* Standardisation of Units of Design Joint Subcommittee Minutes, 1933

Urban Design Diploma *see under* RIBA Urban Design Diploma

Valuation of Books for Fire Insurance Subcommittee Minutes, 1912   6.7

Vauxhall Bridge Committee of Council Minutes, 1899   2.2

Ventilation of the Meeting Room Committee Minutes, 1876 2.2
Victoria Embankment Approach Act *see* Charing Cross and Victoria Embankment Approach Act (Clause 30) Committee Minutes, 1877
Victory Scholarship essays and reports *see* Prizes and Scholarships: Essays and Reports
Victory Scholarship Jury Minutes, 1926—1928 7.1.2
Victory Scholarship Medal Subcommittee Minutes, 1926 7.1.2
Visiting Board Minutes, 1925—1938, 1951—1962 7.1.2
  see also Officers of the Board of Architectural Education & the Visiting Board Joint Meeting Minutes, 1927
Visiting Board Papers, 1961—(1976) 7.1.6
Visiting Board Special Meeting Minutes, 1935 7.2.10
Voluntary Architectural Examination Committee Minutes, 1860—1868 2.1
Voluntary Architectural Examination Committee Minutes, 1869—1873 2.2
Voluntary Architectural Examination Lectures, 1865 7.2.2
Voluntary Architectural Examination Question Papers, 1863—1881 7.2.1
Voluntary Architectural Examiners & Moderators Meetings Minutes, 1870 2.2

War Committee, Architects *see* Architects War Committee
War Damage Commission Scale of Fees Joint Committee Minutes, 1944—1945 8.1.3
War Emergency Committee *see* President's War Emergency Committee Minutes, 1939
War Executive Committee Minutes, 1939—1945 3.1.2
War Executive Committee & Architectural Science Board Joint Meeting Minutes, 1942 3.1.2
War Executive Committee & Housing Committee Joint Meeting Minutes, 1944 3.1.2
War exemption from examinations *see* Special War Exemption Candidates Subcommittee Minutes, 1920
War Memorial Committee Papers, 1946—1948 5.3.9
War Memorial Subcommittee Minutes, 1946 2.2
War Office Advisory Appointments Committee Minutes, 1940—1941 2.2
War Record Committee Minutes, 1915 2.2
Warehouses Subcommittee Minutes, 1943 10.19
Waterloo Bridge Conference Minutes, 1926 2.2
Waterloo Bridge Conference Committee Minutes, 1925—1926 2.2
Waterloo Bridge Conference Drafting Committee *see* Waterloo Bridge Conference Committee
Waterloo Bridge Memorial Papers, 1932 10.14
Wellington Arch *see* Proposed Alterations to Hyde Park Corner and the Removal of the Wellington Arch Committee Minutes, 1882
Westminster Abbey Committee (protection from war damage) Minutes, 1915 2.2

Whitgift Hospital, Croydon *see* Preservation of Whitgift Hospital Croydon Joint Conference Minutes, 1922—1923

William Woodward Presentation Committee Minutes, 1926   2.2

Women Members Committee Papers, 1931—1942   12.1.4

Woodward, William *see* William Woodward Presentation Committee Minutes, 1926

Working of the RIBA Scale of Charges Committee *see* Scale of Charges Committee

World Refugee Year British Architects Appeal Committee Minutes & Papers, 1959—1960   5.3.10

Wren Bicentenary Committees Minutes & Papers, 1922—1923   11.4.4

Xanthian Marbles Committee Papers, 1843   9.2